AF505830

CULTURAL GENOCIDE AND ASIAN STATE PERIPHERIES

CULTURAL GENOCIDE AND ASIAN STATE PERIPHERIES

Edited by

Barry Sautman

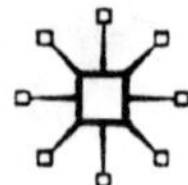

First published in 2006 by
PALGRAVE MACMILLAN™
175 Fifth Avenue, New York, N.Y. 10010 and
Houndmills, Basingstoke, Hampshire, England RG21 6XS
Companies and representatives throughout the world.

PALGRAVE MACMILLAN is the global academic imprint of the Palgrave Macmillan division of St. Martin's Press, LLC and of Palgrave Macmillan Ltd. Macmillan® is a registered trademark in the United States, United Kingdom and other countries. Palgrave is a registered trademark in the European Union and other countries.

ISBN-13: 978–1–4039–7574–4
ISBN-10: 1–4039–7574–4

Library of Congress Cataloging-in-Publication Data is available from the Library of Congress.

A catalogue record for this book is available from the British Library.

Design by Newgen Imaging Systems (P) Ltd., Chennai, India.

First edition: November 2006

10 9 8 7 6 5 4 3 2 1

Printed in the United States of America.

CONTENTS

CHAPTER 1

CULTURAL GENOCIDE IN INTERNATIONAL CONTEXT

Barry Sautman

Introduction

As human rights concerns have become central to discourses of indigeneity and ethnicity in Asian states, indigenous and minority activists have borrowed from international law the concept of cultural genocide. The origin of the concept in a universalistic discourse and its deployment in ethnic politics on every continent allow representations of cultural genocide to be used both to mobilize the putatively affected peoples and to enlist the support of international elites and activists. Whether found in international agencies, national parliaments, human rights Nongovernmental Organizations (NGOs), or solidarity groups, global elites and activists are perceived as key bases of potential sustenance for political formations among aggrieved indigenous and ethnic minority communities.

Political actors have found the charge of cultural genocide to have particular resonance among global elites because cultural genocide is a largely unexamined concept that allows for individualized imaginings. It is also a product of processes familiar to Westerners and the Western-trained, especially the continuous efforts in Europe to construct culturally homogenous nation-states, often through forced assimilation or ethnic cleansing.[1] Westerners aware of their own countries' genocide of ethnic minorities and indigenous peoples at home and in colonial empires, may intuit that any majority people will do the same.[2]

Activists often use "cultural genocide" metaphorically to denote any undesired, exogenous change in the culture of a subaltern ethnic group. The concept of cultural genocide does however have a known origin and a more-or-less accepted definition, derived from its tenuous, but long-standing link to international law. We will first examine the evolution of the concept of cultural genocide in international law and its relation to cognate notions, especially ethnocide. The current state of the "law" of cultural genocide, such as it is, indicates that it is properly conceived as an adjunct of physical and biological genocide. Only intentional and systematic state actions qualify as cultural genocide, not the unintended deleterious by-products of benign policies or even malign policies not purposed on the destruction of an ethnic or religious group.

We then review five recent scholarly studies of peoples inhabiting peripheries of Asian states in which the concept of cultural genocide has been applied or implied: Michael Rudolph of the University of Heidelberg, Germany, on aborigines in Taiwan; Katarina Sjoberg of Lund University, Sweden on the Ainu of Japan; John Otto Ondawame of the University of Sydney, Australia, on West Papuans in Indonesia; Dolly Kikon of Stanford University on Nagas in India; and Barry Sautman of the Hong Kong University of Science and Technology on Tibetans in the People's Republic of China. These cases all involve long-term conflicts between states and indigenous or minority peoples; in three cases, secessionist forces have been active for decades, while in the other two cases indigenous people have not sought to secede, but have had to engage in a long struggle for cultural autonomy. Conflict has involved not only issues of political status, but also questions about the repression, subordination, or erosion of central elements of culture—especially language and religion—and of state and majority group misrepresentations of indigenous and minority peoples.

While there is an explicable sense of grievance about ways in which states have treated these indigenous and minority cultures, is a discourse of cultural genocide intellectually rewarding, either as an application of a legal concept or as a political metaphor? Evidence may be lacking that the state intends to destroy a culture: discourses and practices designed to foster "modernization," "development," "nation-building," and so on, may negatively affect indigenous and minority sensibilities and interests without being demonstrably intended to actualize ethnic animus by extirpating a culture. Alternatively, the state may have once had that intention, but has since been forced to abandon it; the state may now (for its own political purposes) even celebrate indigenous or minority cultures.

In the conclusion to the chapter, we will consider the effects of misplaced contentions concerning cultural genocide. It will be argued that where a discourse of cultural genocide is not apt, it also is not fruitful in resolving conflicts between states and indigenous or minority groups over cultural policies. The levelling of a charge of cultural genocide may be an effective mobilizatory device, especially among external actors, but it may also harden state actors against compromise, including those state officials drawn from indigenous or minority peoples, who often adamantly reject the idea that they are furthering the destruction of their own culture. In cases where a charge of cultural genocide is inapt, it may also be counter-productive to the general advancement of minority and indigenous rights by diminishing the analytical utility of what is, in proper circumstances, a useful concept and by reducing the forcefulness of condemnation that the concept can bring to appropriate cases.

The Genocide Convention and Cultural Genocide

Referring to the ongoing Nazi genocide in 1944, Winston Churchill stated that "There is no doubt that this is . . . the greatest and most horrible single crime ever committed in the whole history of the world."[3] In that year, a Polish-born lawyer in the United States first used the term "genocide," in a study of German atrocities. Rafael Lemkin, *animateur* of the Convention on Genocide,[4] created the neologism "genocide" from *genos*, Greek for "race" or "nation," and *caedere*, the Latin verb "to kill." He defined it as "a coordinated plan of different actions aiming at the destruction of essential foundations of the life of national groups, with the aim of annihilating the groups them-selves."[5] As means for this annihilation he included mass murder, "the preven-tion of life (abortions, sterilizations) and also devices considerably endangering life and health (artificial infections, working to death in special camps, deliber-ate separation of families for depopulation purposes and so forth)."[6]

In the years since then, scholars and activists have argued over how geno-cide should be defined, with "definitions of genocide often revolv[ing] around particular political agendas of inclusion and condemnation."[7] Differences in definition have naturally led to debates among scholars about which modern cases should be denominated as genocide, with the number ranging from one (the Jewish Holocaust)[8] to scores.[9] Some scholars and activists have attempted to broaden the definition beyond the one found in the Convention, but as a recent study argues

> [R]egardless of how many varying and conflicting academic opinions there may be on the "best" definition of genocide, there is only one universally accepted *legal* definition of genocide upon which effective international prevention, sup-pression, and punishment can be authoritatively based . . .[T]he definition

> found in the Convention is [also] the only *practical, workable* definition of
> genocide, if the international community is ever to have any hope of cooperat-
> ing in halting genocide. International law offers the one authoritative source for
> legitimate collective action, as it represents the highest level of political unity
> among nation-states on a difficult issue . . . Any attempt at broadening the def-
> inition, without first demonstrating a willingness to enforce the present definition,
> would make multilateral action to stop genocide *less* likely rather than more.[10]

The same concerns have been evident in the first judicial decisions on
genocide, which were only handed down a half-century after the promulgation of the Genocide Convention. In the late 1990s, international criminal tribunals for the former Yugoslavia and Rwanda have sought to "avoid
trivializing the genocide concept and . . . to reserve genocide to the most
egregious and widespread atrocities."[11]

When in 1946 the UN General Assembly first discussed genocide, it was
noted that among its incidents are "great losses to humanity in the form of
cultural and other contributions."[12] A Secretary-General's commentary on
the draft convention proposed that an article prohibit cultural genocide,
including proscriptions of national languages and the systematic destruction
of monuments or other historical, artistic or religious objects.[13] A UN Ad
Hoc Genocide Committee produced an initial draft convention, Article III
of which proposed to ban

> any deliberate act committed with the intent to destroy the language, religion
> or culture of a national, racial or religious group on grounds of national or
> racial origin or religious belief such as:
>
> 1. prohibiting the use of the language of the group in daily intercourse or
>   in schools, or the printing and circulation of publications in the lan-
>   guage of the group;
> 2. destroying, or preventing the use of, libraries, museums, schools, his-
>   torical monuments, places of worship or other cultural institutions and
>   objects of the group.[14]

Another example was soon added:

> 3. subjecting members of a group to such conditions as would cause them
>   to renounce their language, religion or culture.[15]

The rationale for including Article III in the draft treaty was articulated
by one of its proponents on the Ad Hoc Committee:

> [T]he cultural bond was one of the most important factors among those
> which united a national group and that was so true that it was possible to wipe

out a human group, as such, by destroying its cultural heritage, while allowing the individual members of the group to survive. The physical destruction of individuals was not the only possible form of genocide; it was not the indispensable condition of that crime.[16]

There was also a proposal that "cultural genocide" be covered in the Universal Declaration of Human Rights (UDHR),[17] which the Third Committee was drafting while the Ad Hoc Committee worked on the Genocide Convention. Several European states proposed that a UDHR article guarantee minorities a right to have their own schools and cultural or religious institutions and to use their languages in the press and public assemblies and before courts and other state authorities. The United States, through its delegate Eleanor Roosevelt, asserted that it had no minorities and insisted that minority rights be excluded from the UDHR because there were no minority problems anywhere in the Western Hemisphere. It then misrepresented the degree of support for the article by other states in order to defeat it in a committee maneuver. Communist states had supported the clause and proposed that it be expanded to provide that minorities be entitled to public funds for use in preserving their cultures.[18]

In the Ad Hoc Committee that drafted the Genocide Convention, the United States was the only member to oppose inclusion of a ban on cultural genocide. It argued that matters covered by the article should be dealt with elsewhere, in connection with protection of minority rights, while at the same time the United States opposed a UDHR minority rights provision. When the draft Convention reached the Sixth Committee, Britain also opposed Article III, arguing that the concept of cultural genocide was so indefinite that it would render meaningless the idea of genocide *tout court*. Communist and some Middle Eastern states argued for a cultural genocide provision, pointing out that physical and cultural genocide have been linked ways of destroying ethnic groups.[19]

Two of three experts consulted by the Secretary-General had opposed including a ban on cultural genocide in the treaty, on the ground that protection of culture would be an undue extension of the struggle against genocide, which is designed to protect the physical integrity of groups. It was contended that forced assimilation did not constitute the crime of genocide and could be dealt with through a system for the protection of minority rights.[20] Rafael Lemkin favored a cultural genocide clause because it would protect groups that could not continue to exist without the "spiritual and moral unity" provided by their culture. He added however that a ban on cultural genocide must not be directed against policies designed to assimilate a group into a larger society, but only against "drastic methods, used to aid in the rapid and complete disappearance of the cultural, moral, and religious life of a group of human beings."[21]

The Sixth Committee rejected Article III in the face of arguments that physical genocide was so much more serious a crime than cultural genocide that the two should not be placed on the same level, that a ban might be interpreted so as to inhibit ethnic assimilation and hence cause states to not ratify the Convention,[22] that an article barring cultural genocide would lead to spurious claims that detract from the Convention's main concern in preventing the extermination of protected groups,[23] and that cultural genocide claims would prove problematic because of the Convention's intent requirement.[24] Delegates from several countries, including Sweden and Canada, were also nervous about potential claims from indigenous groups.[25] In rejecting "cultural genocide," the UN limited genocide to "essentially physical acts."[26]

The UN of the 1940s in which the major Western powers prevailed against the concept of cultural genocide, was an exclusive organization, but there is no indication that in the expanded postcolonial UN most states would favor a ban on cultural genocide, as the actions of many states may give rise to charges against them. Leaders from the United States, for example, feared that their actions during the Vietnam War might subject them to a claim of cultural genocide.[27] A review of the Convention by the UN Sub-Commission on Prevention of Discrimination and Protection of Minorities [the "Sub-Commission"] in 1984 recommended consideration of a cultural genocide provision, perhaps through an optional protocol.[28] No change has taken place however and "Recent United Nations activity in this area suggests that ratification of [a contemporary equivalent of] Article III . . . would take a long time and might find only a few signatories."[29] While some scholars complain that cultural genocide is not criminalized under the Convention,[30] international lawmakers have shown no interest in doing so. The Rome Statute of the International Criminal Court, for example, brings genocide, but not cultural genocide, within its ambit.[31] Critics of a ban on cultural genocide remain wary that it may impede assimilationist policies. Arguing in favor of a prohibition of cultural genocide, a leading scholar nevertheless recognizes that it can be realized only if framed as an adjunct of physical genocide:

[T]here is a distinction between [assimilationist] programs and "the deliberate destruction and desecration of icons, libraries, monuments," and coercive religious conversion. The latter violent acts might be prohibited when undertaken in conjunction with acts of physical genocide. In such cases there is little doubt that there is an intent to both physically exterminate the group and eliminate all remnants of its existence.[32]

This was precisely the conclusion reached by analysts about the wars of the1990s in the former Yugoslavia, where ethnic-based organized mass murders and expulsions were accompanied by a systematic destruction of hundreds of mosques, churches, museums, libraries, archives, and ancient houses.[33]

It has been observed that "What was left out of the Convention is as important as what was included."[34] That proposals were made in the 1940s for a ban on cultural genocide and were not adopted in a binding legal instrument has implications for how malign state actions affecting culture should be characterized. Proposals to the UN more than a half-century ago do provide parameters of the concept—the essential link of cultural genocide to physical and biological genocide and a requirement of intent. Their rejection by the UN mandates that no implication be made that a crime of cultural genocide exists[35] and that the concept be strictly construed. Thus the foremost specialist of the law of genocide argues that although the defrocking of Buddhist monks and nuns and repression against Muslim Chams in Khmer Rouge-ruled Cambodia (1975–1979) may be crimes against humanity, as "persecutions on political, racial, or religious grounds" during wartime,[36] and may also violate the International Covenant on Civil and Political Rights (ICCPR),[37] these actions would not amount to genocide, which under Article II of the Convention

> means any of the following acts committed with intent to destroy, in whole or in part, a national, ethnical, racial or religious group, as such:
>
> a. Killing members of the group;
> b. Causing serious bodily or mental harm to members of the group;
> c. deliberately inflicting on the group conditions of life calculated to bring about its physical destruction in whole or in part;
> d. imposing measures intended to prevent births within the group;
> e. forcibly transferring children of the group to another group.

The Genocide Convention requires "a very specific intent . . . not only the intent to kill or destroy people but to kill or destroy them because they form a group such as referred to in Article II."[38] Genocide is a "premeditated, calculated, systematic, malicious crime, authorized by a state's political leaders"[39] and is distinguishable as such from atrocities such as ethnic cleansing, which may be intended to drive a people from a territory, but not to exterminate them. Studies of late twentieth century civil wars and ethnic conflicts include only two instances of genocide (Rwanda and Bosnia) among scores of cases.[40] The International Law Commission has pointed out that in genocide "the destruction in question is the material destruction of a group either by physical or biological means . . . ."[41] As two leading scholars of genocide point out, "[t]he suppression of a culture, a language, a religion, and so on is a phenomenon that is analytically different from the physical extermination of a group."[42]

The Khmer Rouge intended not to destroy Buddhists as such, but to eliminate Buddhist cultural institutions in order to diminish popular adherence to religion. It sought not to wipe out the Chams as such, but to force their assimilation into the Khmer majority. The Khmer Rouge killed people to accomplish these goals, but there was no "cultural genocide" as the original proponents of the concept conceived it, because the actions were not an adjunct to physical destruction of protected ethnic or religious groups *as such*. As William Schabas has put it, "in light of the *travaux preparatoires* of the Genocide Convention, it seems impossible to consider acts of cultural genocide as punishable crimes if they are unrelated to physical or biological genocide."[43] The effort to attach a label of "genocide" to these actions is, under a reasonably strict construction of the Convention, merely "an attempt to stigmatise behavior [with] a word loaded with such terrible connotations."[44]

Despite the idiosyncratic preferences of some scholars,[45] the acts originally contemplated as cultural genocide would not have been crimes under international law unless they were part of a pattern of exterminating a protected group as such, and were demonstrably intentional.[46] In genocide, physical or cultural, "organizers and planners must have a racist or discriminatory motive, that is, a genocidal motive, taken as whole. Where this is lacking, the crime cannot be genocide."[47] The International Criminal Tribunal for Rwanda (ICTR) has said of the mass murders of 1994–1995 in that country that "many facts show that the intention of the perpetrators of these killings was to cause the complete disappearance of the Tutsi people."[48] International Covenant on Civil and Political Rights (ICCPR) Article 27, which states that group members cannot be denied the right to enjoy their own culture, differs from the proposed ban on cultural genocide under the Genocide Convention precisely because the latter "expressly prohibited acts intended to destroy culture on grounds of racial origin or religious belief," while Article 27 does not require a showing of *scienter* or knowledge of the circumstances of the act.[49] *A fortiori*, there can be no unintentional or unconscious cultural genocide.

Acts destructive of minority cultures are chargeable under the ICCPR against states that have ratified it, but neither it nor any other treaty denominates a violation as "cultural genocide." To do so would be to require that the acts be deemed violative only if they are genocidal, that is, part of an intended program of mass killings of a protected group. Such an implication would raise the bar on the protection of minority cultural rights that should be guarded by law even where the violation of a culture is not part of a concerted extermination of an ethnic or religious group.

That there is no binding international law of cultural genocide reflects UN and state reluctance to mandate protection of minority rights: the 1992 UN Declaration on the Rights of Persons Belonging to National or Ethnic, Religious or Linguistic Minorities is not binding and has no enforcement mechanism.[50] The same is true of a draft UN instrument on indigenous peoples' rights that speaks of cultural genocide.

Indigenous Peoples, Cultural Genocide, and Ethnocide

Although not inscribed in binding international instruments or customary law,[51] the concept of cultural genocide has been introduced into proposed protections of the rights of indigenous peoples. The latter are defined not by treaty, but in a variety of ways by international organizations and diplomats.[52] The most commonly relied-upon definitions suggest "indigenous peoples" include only those who were affected by classic modern colonialism. A somewhat more encompassing definition appeared in a draft "International Covenant on the Rights of Indigenous Peoples," prepared for the World Council of Indigenous People. It stated that an indigenous people is one

a. who lived in a territory before the entry of a colonizing population, which colonizing population has created a new state or states or extended the jurisdiction of an existing state or states to include the territory, and
b. who continue to live in the territory and who do not control the national government of the state or states within which they live.[53]

That definition however was dropped from the final text. The only definition that fully dispenses with a link between indigenous peoples and colonialism is that of the World Bank, but it counter-intuitively and counterfactually eliminates the criterion of historical continuity and the implied notion of historical priority, by terming as indigenous all "groups with a social and cultural identity distinct from the dominant society that makes them vulnerable to being disadvantaged."[54] This over-inclusive definition erases any distinction between indigenous and ethnic minority peoples, while a UN Special Rapporteur has adjured that indigenous peoples is a category that "should not be confused with ethnic, religious or linguistic minorities."[55]

The most widely-cited definition of indigenous peoples and one that to some extent has guided UN practice,[56] is that of UN Special Rapporteur Jose Martinez Cabo:

> Indigenous communities, peoples, and nations are those which, having a historical continuity with pre-invasion and pre-colonial societies that developed on their territories, consider themselves distinct from other sectors of the societies now prevailing in those territories, or parts of them. They form at present non-dominant sectors of society and are determined to preserve, develop and transmit to future generations their ancestral territories, and their ethnic identity, as the basis of their continued existence as peoples, in accordance with their own cultural patterns, social institutions and legal systems.[57]

Martinez Cabo's definition likely influenced the definition in International Labour Organization Convention No. 169, which refers to indigenous peoples as descended from inhabitants of a country "at the time of conquest or colonisation."[58] Mobilizations among the 300 million *indigenes* led to the 1981 formation of a UN Working Group on Indigenous Populations and to a series of UNESCO regional meetings on "ethnocide" in the early 1980s.[59] A Latin American meeting produced the Declaration of San Jose, which states that "ethnocide, that is, cultural genocide, is a violation of international law equivalent to genocide, which was condemned by the United Nations Convention on the Prevention and Punishment of the Crime of Genocide."[60] The conferees erred in calling cultural genocide a violation equivalent to genocide: the latter is the most serious of crimes, while "the crime of cultural genocide" has only been an unsuccessful proposal. The Declaration drafters and others have also been mistaken in equating ethnocide and cultural genocide.[61]

Unlike cultural genocide, which is invariably connected to mass ethnic murder on a grand scale,[62] ethnocide as envisaged by proponents of the concept is not necessarily tied to killing.[63] An influential early work on ethnocide identified it exclusively with the Western capitalist state,[64] while cultural genocide has not been so circumscribed. Scholars have defined ethnocide in many ways. Alex Alvarez calls it "the assassination of a culture and of identity. It is the murder of the ties that bind a group of people together and make them unique."[65] Kazuo Sumi terms it "a dislocation of indigenous people from their homeland, destruction of their way of life, and denial of their culture and language."[66] For Maivan Clech Lam, ethnocide "is the destruction, or severe disruption, of the social and material bases necessary to a people to sustain its human relations, body of knowledge, and sense of existential purpose, such that an essentially 'de-knowledged' community now looks out at a world of chaos in which it may never again find its place."[67] The Declaration of San Jose, while not as lyrical as academic pronouncements, assigns the term to actions of unambiguous malignancy:

> Ethnocide means that an ethnic group is denied the right to enjoy, develop and transmit its own culture and its own language, whether collectively or individually. This involves an extreme form of massive violation of human rights and, in particular, the right of ethnic groups to respect for their cultural identity.[68]

"An extreme form of massive violation of human rights" presupposes intent, which can be inferred from the nature of the acts, not actions that are "unintentional" or "unconscious."[69] As one scholar has observed, "Usually the term ethnocide is applied to intentional acts resulting in culture death."[70] The intent that underlies ethnocide may not be identical to the intent that underlies cultural genocide because ethnocide is not tied to the physical or biological destruction of a group, and is thus typically aimed at forced assimilation, not population decimation. In any case, because "'ethnocide' does not exist in UN human rights instruments"[71] it is indeterminate, as everyone imagines what they will about it. Indeed, the term has been applied to scenarios where forced assimilation and other obviously intentional acts were carried out[72] and to situations where no intent to harm is apparent.[73]

The Draft Declaration on the Rights of Indigenous Peoples[74] speaks moreover of "cultural genocide *and* ethnocide," with use of the conjunctive indicating that the drafters held the two concepts to not be identical. In international law, the term "ethnocide" has only been applied to indigenous peoples and not colonized peoples or ethnic minorities. It is found only in the Draft Declaration and not other UN documents.[75] The experiences of many minority and colonized peoples nevertheless resemble ethnocide.[76] For example, in Japan's Taiwan colony from 1895 to 1945 school curricula were purged of anything that might remind students that they were Chinese and students who spoke Chinese in schools were penalized or even assaulted.[77] In its Korean colony from 1919 onwards, Japan enforced

> a policy of "cultural control" or "material assimilation." This entailed the enforcement of Emperor worship and prohibition both of the teaching of Korean history and of the use of the Korean language in public places. Koreans were obliged to learn Japanese and to adopt Japanese names.[78]

In Turkey from the 1920s, the secular republican regime attempted to suppress Kurdish identity. A then-Minister of Justice stated "Those who are not of pure Turkish stock can have only one right in this country, the right to be servants and slaves." The Kurdish language was outlawed, Kurdish organizations banned and Kurdish land expropriated for settlement by Turks. Kurds, a fifth of Turkey's people, were deported across the country to force their assimilation and guarantee that no area was more than five percent Kurdish. Kurdish dress was banned, Kurds designated as "mountain Turks," and the term "Kurd" officially promoted as an insult. Kurdistan was termed the "East" of Turkey.[79] It was only in 2001 that it became legal in Turkey to publish or broadcast in Kurdish; the language is still banned from schools.[80]

Cultural repression against colonized peoples and minorities has been more than matched by like actions against indigenous peoples. Well-known examples that included arguable forms of cultural genocide involved Native Americans, Canadian First Nations, and Australian aborigines. Genocide Convention Article II (e) bans the forcible transfer of children of a protected group to another group, a process indigenous activists term cultural geno-cide, although the Convention framers rejected the concept and the Convention specifies that forcible transfer is genocide per se, if committed with the intent to destroy, in whole or part, a protected group. The International Law Commission treats Article II (e) as a type of "biological genocide."[81] It was framed because Nazi Germanization policy in Poland and other occupied states included mass kidnapping and transfer of children to German families or orphanages, to be raised as Germans who would disdain their former Slavic ethnic group.[82] The transfer program in Poland accom-panied a slaughter of several million Poles and a plan to murder Poles not deemed of "good blood," Germanize part of the remainder, and reduce the rest to serfs.[83] Attending the slaughter of Serbs by Croatian fascists, thousands of Serbian Orthodox children were forcibly transferred to Croatian Catholic orphanages and homes.[84] Forcible transfer was thus an adjunct to physical genocide, as were, in varying degrees, transfers of indigenous children in the United States.

After two centuries of warfare intended to destroy Native Americans in whole or in part, including their cultures,[85] by the mid-nineteenth century US "public sentiment overwhelmingly favored destruction by civiliza-tion rather than by killing."[86] Ninety boarding schools for Native American children were established between 1878 and 1902. Richard Pratt, an "Indian fighter" who founded the first school, stated that "the sooner all tribal relations are broken up; the sooner the Indian loses all his Indian ways, even his language, the better it will be for him and for the government."[87]

In contrast, European immigrants to the United States were allowed to have mother tongue schools.[88] The Native American boarding schools existed until the mid-twentieth century and "attempted to break the cultural continuity of tribal peoples by radically altering the cultural and social identities of Indian children," who were expected to become laborers or servants alienated from Native America.[89] Claims of cultural genocide of Native Americans have been made long after the end of physical genocide.[90]

There has been an upsurge in the past decade of research on the colonial and postcolonial assault on Australia's Aborigines.[91] Some recent works argue that there was a physical genocide[92] and others contend that cultural genocide was implicated in the use from 1910–1970 of the Aborigine Protection Act to remove from their parents and place some 100,000 Aborigine children in white foster homes or state orphanages, where they were mainly raised to be domestics.[93] This process, dramatically illustrated in the film "Rabbit Proof Fence," was connected to what was arguably cultural and biological genocides in which part of the Aboriginal population was to be forced to abandon native languages and customs and permitted to marry only whites.

The Canadian government generally did not wage a war of extermination against the First Nations, although some were annihilated, and did not practice biological genocide by forced transfers to white homes. It is nevertheless charged that

> Canada's Native people have survived an intentional, sustained, well financed, and cleverly executed program of cultural genocide perpetrated by the government of Canada [waged by] stealing their past through eradicating their culture, by stealing their future through kidnapping their children, and by stealing their present by attacking their pride.[94]

The Canadian government aimed to absorb into the general population the First Nations through a scheme to use treaties to acquire their lands without promised payments and through forced inclusion of native children in residential schools that trained them as laborers, punished them for any use of native languages, and taught them to despise native culture. While most residential schools were phased out by the 1950s, the forcible transfer of thousands of native children to distant foster homes began, so that by the end of the 1960s, First Nations members, who constituted four percent of Canada's population, were 40 percent of children in "protective custody."[95] The Canadian case is thus more akin to ethnocide, while U.S. and Australian cases implicate cultural genocide.

Despite a misapprehension of the concepts of ethnocide and cultural genocide, the Declaration of San Jose did provide impetus to the composition, beginning in 1985, of the Draft Declaration on Indigenous Rights, which was presented in final form in 1994 to the Sub-Commission and adopted by it without change. Since then, debate on the Draft Declaration in the Commission on Human Rights continues, but only two of its forty-five articles had been adopted as of 2001.[96] The Draft Declaration provides that

> Indigenous peoples have the collective and individual right not to be subjected to ethnocide and cultural genocide, including prevention of and redress for:
>
> a. Any action which has the aim or effect of depriving them of their integrity as distinct peoples, or of their cultural values or ethnic identities;
> b. Any action which has the aim or effect of dispossessing them of their lands, territories or resources;
> c. Any form of population transfer which has the aim or effect of violating or undermining any of their rights;
> d. Any form of assimilation or integration by other cultures or ways of life imposed on them by legislative or other measures;
> e. Any form of propaganda against them.[97]

Under the Draft Declaration and in contrast to the evident intentionality prescribed in the Declaration of San Jose, either "aim or effect" may provide the basis for a claim of ethnocide. The Draft Declaration, however, "is not binding upon U.N. member states . . . does not currently comport with international accepted definitions of genocide and does not establish a recognized norm of customary international law."[98] It applies only to "indigenous peoples," not to ethnic minorities.[99] In contrast to the situation of colonies, whose status the UN Special Committee on Decolonization determines,[100] no international body judges whether a population is an indigenous people or an ethnic minority—not surprisingly, given the lack of generally accepted definitions of "indigenous peoples" and "minority" in the international community.[101] Because it is within the reserved sovereignty of states to make a designation, the Draft Declaration applies only to those groups that are recognized as indigenous peoples in their homelands.[102] While "the labels 'ethnic minority' and 'indigenous peoples' are . . . both highly political and subjective, reflecting competing efforts to define the social basis of nation-states,"[103] most Asian states reject the idea that there are indigenous peoples within their borders.[104] Some UN officials assert that Asia is home to most of the world's indigenous people,[105] but UN and state practice does not designate any indigenous peoples outside the Americas, Australasia and Oceania.[106] As an ILO official who formerly worked for the International Commission of

Jurists explains

> "Indigenous" implies historical precedence in a particular area, and this is
> sufficiently true in the Americas and in parts of Oceania to be a useful term.
> However, only some ten percent of the indigenous and tribal peoples in the
> world live in North and South America. In much of the rest of the world,
> those who are covered by the two ILO Conventions [No. 169 and No. 107]
> were probably not in the region before other groups that now form the dom-
> inant population.[107]

Some Western scholars argue, for example, that China has *indigenes*,[108]
but the Peoples Republic of China (PRC) has stated

> The indigenous issues are a product of special historical circumstances. By and
> large, they are the result of the colonialist policy carried out in modern history
> by European countries in other regions of the world, especially on the conti-
> nents of America and Oceania.[109]

The Chinese government contends that there are no indigenous peoples
or issues in China because "As in the majority of Asian countries, the various nationalities in China have all lived for aeons on Chinese territory."[110]
A PRC spokesman told a UN International Conference on Indigenous
People in 1993 that

> China's nationalities, including the Han nationality, have lived and multiplied
> in China for generations. Since no people of a particular nationality came
> from outside, differences between indigenous people and outsiders do not
> exist. The issue of indigenous people does not exist in China.[111]

While the idea of long-fixed Chinese borders is ahistorical, China is not
associated with the "invasion" and "colonizing" referents of definitions of
"indigenous people," namely colonial-era aggression and settlement that
involved several West European states, the United States and Japan. It is
thus not unreasonable for China to deny that peoples it designates as
minorities are indigenous people, despite their historical priority to Han
migrants in minority areas, the statelessness of these autochthonous peoples
at the time of their incorporation into China, and other popular indicia of
the indigenous. Whatever protections for indigenous peoples emerge will
thus not bind China.

Indeed, not every preexisting nationality in Asian states claims indigenous status. For example, Western elites sometimes refer to Tibetans as
"indigenous people,"[112] but the India-based Tibetan émigré administration

under the Dalai Lama does not use the term, while international law scholars sympathetic to the émigré cause find it uncertain that Tibetans come under its rubric.[113] The Draft Declaration on the Rights of Indigenous Peoples is occasionally cited in connection with the Tibet Question[114] and an émigré activist has proposed that Tibetans "take the indigenous route." Emigré leaders, however, see that as conflicting with their insistence that Tibet is an occupied state since, in popular conception, indigenous people were mainly stateless before the advent of the colonizers.[115] They may also be influenced by the social evolutionism still pervasive in India and China. One émigré scholar has said about most of China's ethnic minorities that "such pre-literate tribes cannot be compared with Tibetan people" and that "As far as the Tibetans are concerned, they are neither a tribe nor an ethnic group; they constitute a distinct civilizational category."[116] Because claims to indigenous status are eschewed,[117] the concept of ethnocide and a de-linking from intentionality are not relevant to Tibetan émigré discourse, which from the outset has been framed in terms of genocide[118] and, latterly, cultural genocide.

Cultural Genocide in Asian State Peripheries: Five Case Studies

Charges of cultural genocide should be examined for accuracy, but equally importantly is what such cases tell us about the ways in which political actors use representations of cultural genocide to affect the perceptions of parties to conflicts between states and indigenous or minority peoples. Such representations generally play a significant role in shaping the course that the conflicts take and in determining whether they will be mitigated or intensified. We begin our review of five case studies of possible cultural genocide with two that involve peoples now regarded by the relevant political authorities as indigenes, rather than ethnic minorities.

Taiwan's aboriginal people (*yuanzhumin*) are not overwhelmingly residents of a peripheral part of the island. Instead, Taiwan is itself peripheral to China, the country or cultural area of which it is a part. Taiwan's dozen or so Malayo-Polynesian groups comprise 1.6 percent of Taiwan's 23 million people and have since 1994 been constitutionally recognized as indigenous peoples.

During a half century of Japanese colonialism on Taiwan (1895–1945), aborigines lost a third of their numbers, due in part to the suppression of resistance to imperial efforts to acquire the resources of mountainous areas where about half the aboriginal population lived. In the subsequent four decades of harsh authoritarian rule by the Guomindang (KMT or

"Nationalists"), a party led almost exclusively by mainland Chinese who fled to Taiwan in the late 1940s, much of aboriginal land was seized by the government and sold off to Han entrepreneurs, forcing many aborigines to migrate to a hostile urban environment. Regarded by many Han as undisciplined simpletons, Taiwan's aborigines faced discrimination in employment and education. At the same time, the KMT denied that aborigines were ethnic minorities, let alone indigenous peoples, claiming that they, like the Han and virtually all those within China's borders are "descendants of the Yellow Emperor" (*yan huang zi sun*). At the same time, the KMT regime pursued a determined cultural and linguistic homogenization.

Beginning in the early 1980s, an aboriginal movement formed in alliance with the native Taiwanese political opposition, which chafed under the exclusionary rule of the mainlander-led KMT. After 1987, when martial law was lifted and Taiwan began to experience a gradual liberal democratization, the aboriginal movement launched demonstrations for land rights and against discrimination, raising charges of genocide, forced assimilation, and the intentional destruction of aboriginal culture. Aboriginal organizations began to participate in gatherings of the World Group of Indigenous Populations, which was concerned with questions of cultural genocide and ethnocide. The aboriginal movement was also strongly influenced by the Christian churches to which four-fifths of aborigines adhere, with liberation theology Presbyterian leaders emphasizing that the aborigines were an ethnie threatened with extinction.

In the 1990s, liberalization in Taiwan included the provision of rights to aborigines, such as increased reservation land and political representation, mother tongue education, and the establishment of cultural institutions. Aboriginal elites nevertheless continued to charge the KMT regime with genocide and ethnocide. Michael Rudolph explains that the use of such "rough and sometimes exaggerated language" was part of efforts by aboriginal elites to establish their own subjectivity and to gain attention for their cause, particularly from the local and international mass media. The continued levelling of such charges was also seen as helpful to the aboriginal leaders' allies in the political opposition, the Democratic Progressive Party, which won power in 2000. After that event, charges of genocide and the like have virtually disappeared, despite the still highly disadvantaged position of aboriginal peoples in Taiwan society. Rudolph contends that claims of cultural genocide, even where solely polemical and metaphorical, may be unavoidable given the fierce jockeying for media attention engaged in by many groups and, however false the charge may be, its levelling still might be acceptable "as a kind of 'warning signal,' " designed to alert the world to the precarious situation of an indigenous or minority peoples' culture.

In Japan, the Ainu population is also regarded as indigenous. This population is highly concentrated on the northern island of Hokkaido, with one survey showing that about 24,000 people there regard themselves as Ainu. Politicians in Japan have long contended that Japanese are an homogenous people, the Wajin, being the majority ethnic group of the country. In 1991, however, the state accorded the Ainu the status of a cultural and religious minority and Ainu leaders now assert that the state recognizes the Ainu as an "indigenous people." In any case, the Hokkaido Ainu have struggled in recent years to gain cultural autonomy, a difficult goal given the seriousness with which the myth of ethnic homogeneity continues to be cultivated by official Japan.

The Hokkaido Ainu were largely hunters and gatherers when, beginning in the eighth century, they came into contact with Wajin, with whom they traded game and fish in return for cereals, cloth, ornaments, liquor, and other products. Eventually, large-scale Wajin migration to Hokkaido caused conflicts that lasted until the mid-sixteenth century, when the Japanese state began a four-hundred-year process of incorporating Hokkaido. Over this period, repression and the spread of new diseases caused the Ainu population to decline by 79 percent and resources on Hokkaido were depleted by increased hunting, fishing, and prospecting. After the Meiji Restoration (1868), the annexation of Hokkaido was completed and forced assimilation was initiated, with Ainu prohibited from using their own language and performing their native religious rituals. Ainu lands were turned into government-managed farms and the Ainu themselves were represented as a feeble-minded, primitive, and dying people.

Part of the Ainu population did accept assimilation, reasoning that the gods of the better-off Wajin must be more powerful than their own. Most Ainu, however, continued to regard themselves as a distinct people, doing so in the face of official Japanese pronouncements that, as late as the 1980s, denied their existence. In the early 1980s, Ainu began to attend international conferences of indigenous peoples and hosted the Nibutani Forum, an international conference on indigenous affairs, in 1993. Four years later, the "Hokkaido Former Aborigines Protection Act" of 1899 was repealed in favor of a new "Law on Promotion of Ainu Culture and Facilitation of Ainu Tradition." In the same year, a court in Hokkaido recognized the Ainu there as an indigenous minority within the Japanese nation-state.

Although official recognition has been won, some 60 percent of Ainu must depend to one degree or another on social welfare payments for their survival and few are self-employed, even in agriculture. Ainu face discrimination in employment and social intercourse with Wajin. In 2001, a Japanese cabinet minister was met with protest from Ainu organizations and was forced to apologize after he reiterated the claim that Japan is a "racially homogenous country." The statement of a senior member of the ruling Liberal Democratic Party that the Ainu had been assimilated into Japan also met with strong objections. Meanwhile, the village of Nibutani, where the international forum took place in 1993, has become a gathering place for indigenous peoples from around the world, allowing Hokkaido Ainu to network with indigenes from abroad on such matters as resisting the exploitation of their natural resources and incorporating indigenous languages in national educational curricula.

In her essay, Katarina Sjoberg stresses how, as Hokkaido Ainu have become global actors, they have politicized the interest shown in their traditions and practices, debating interpretations of Ainu material culture, customs, and beliefs. By doing so and by placing themselves within the international indigenous peoples' movement, the Hokkaido Ainu challenge the ideas that their customs are backward and that the Japanese nation-state has the sole prerogative in shaping Ainu affairs.

West Papua (until recently known to Indonesians as Irian Jaya), occupies the western half of New Guinea and is mainly populated by Melansian peoples. In 1963, over the objections of native leaders, West Papua was transferred from Dutch colonial rule to Indonesian sovereignty. John Otto Ondawame argues that the Indonesian state turned West Papua into a colony and that genocide is a consequence of colonialism. He cites the large-scale West Papua copper and gold operations of Freeport Indonesia (FI), a subsidiary of the U.S. company Freeport McMoRan Mining, which were closely connected to the authoritarian Suharto regime (1965–1999), as an example of colonial exploitation. Apart from severe Indonesian military suppression of pro-independence expressions and a quotidian lack of civil liberties, Suharto criminalized West Papuan self-identity. Repression continues in the post-Suharto era and has included murder by a military death-squad of a prominent West Papuan nationalist leader in 2001.

Dr. Ondawame also contends that the Suharto regime's transmigration program, which brought to West Papua settlers from such densely populated islands as Java and Sumatra, was part of a program that envisaged the long-run disappearance of ethnic differences in Indonesia and that the post-Suharto regime continues to encourage spontaneous migration. Transmigration and FI's operations are alleged to forcibly displace tens of thousands of West Papuans. He relates the state's poor record in providing health care and checking the spread of HIV/AIDS in West Papuan cities to the evisceration of traditional social structures and beliefs and connects rising pollution to increased mortality and falling birth rates among West Papuans. It is argued that "genocide" inheres in policies that permit the widespread availability of alcohol and drugs, that present obstacles to relief agency access to remote areas, and that discriminate against West Papuans in education and employment.

Ondawame finds discussions between the Indonesian government and West Papuan organizations on proposals for "special autonomy" for the region to be problematic because they do not devolve sufficient power to West Papuans to counter the ongoing "genocide." He concludes that only independence, achieved through peaceful dialog, will allow West Papuans to save themselves and their culture from extinction. Although he attempts to key his analysis of Indonesian policies in West Papua to specific parts of the Genocide Convention, Dr. Ondawame's evocation of cultural genocide is largely and almost classically metaphorical.

In her study of education policy in Nagaland, Dolly Kikon takes a tack that is both similar and different from that taken by John Otto Ondawame. She argues that the state's denial of the identity of the Nagas of northeast India amounts to a form of cultural genocide. This denial of identity is manifest in the use of educational institutions for "nation-building" among a people who do not want to be part of the nation in question. Because such resistance exists, there has also been a militarization of Naga society over the course of more than five decades of insurgency.

As with the Taiwan aborigines, Ainu and West Papuans, British colonial policy in Nagaland in the nineteenth century and first half of the twentieth century were premised on the representation of the native people in question as a "savage and primitive race." The Nagas resisted and, with their defeat at arms, there was widespread dispossession and mortality. Nagaland had strategic position to offer the British, which the colonialists maintained by isolating the Nagas from neighboring ethnies with whom they had long had profitable relationships. A cultural autonomy was proclaimed and exercised at the village level, but ultimate powers of administration were reserved to the Crown.

Christianity was spread through British missionaries and Naga preachers and, as elsewhere, important aspects of native culture were suppressed in this "civilizing" effort. The educational system, run by missionaries and the British administration prepared most recipients for nonexistent positions in government, but did however bring together a new group of educated Nagas, who developed a national consciousness and a resistance to the dichotomization of "advanced" colonialism and "barbaric" nativism. Naga exposure to global events in both world wars especially spurred the crystallization of nationalist politics and, at the time of Indian independence, gave birth first to the Naga National Council and then to a long-running struggle for political separation from mainland India. The Indian state rejects separation, refuses to consider the Nagas an indigenous people (on the ground that migration and mixing made it impossible to say that any people fits into this category), and divides the Naga population among four northeastern states.

Nagas are scarcely represented in school curricula in Nagaland. Where they are, it is in terms of such negative characteristics as backwardness, laziness, and dishonesty, leading students to alienation from their own culture and from social involvement. In speaking of "the right to equality" and other human rights concepts in the context of continuous military repression, the school texts and the education system as a whole seek to mediate, rather than clarify the conflict between Nagas and the Indian state. In fact, the education system is designed to fulfil the militarized "national security" goals of the state and not the needs of Naga civil society. Cultural genocide, Dolly Kikon argues, is thus a silent and insidious process, in which the Indian state recolonizes the minds of Nagas.

The Tibet case involves a sustained and explicit discourse of cultural genocide. Claims of physical genocide by China against the Tibetans were first made after the Dalai Lama fled Tibet in 1959 and are still made by the top leaders of the Tibetan émigré administration.[119] By the early 1980s, the émigrés were speaking also of cultural genocide; a concept then being promoted by the nascent indigenous peoples movement and their supporters. The discourse of cultural genocide became a mainstay of efforts to internationalize the Tibet Question. Ironically, it began at the same time that state pressures on Tibetan culture eased considerably after the suppressive Cultural Revolution.

Claims of cultural genocide in Tibet often focus on "demographic aggression": assertions that migration by non-Tibetans to Tibetan areas, plus state family planning restrictions on births among Tibetans, amount to cultural genocide. The essay by Barry Sautman argues that the state's role in migration to Tibetan areas, the number of migrants, and their degree of permanency have been vastly exaggerated. Most Tibetans moreover are rural and have little contact with the overwhelmingly urban Han. Just as there has been no program of "ethnic swamping" in Tibet, state restrictions on births are much more liberal for Tibetans than for Han. With increased education and urbanization among Tibetans, the desire for large families has diminished, but Tibetans in Tibet still have larger families than Tibetans in exile.

The exiles charge that surveillance and restrictions, including bars on the public propagation of the *dharma* and attempts to minimize popular allegiance to alternative, religious centers of influence are part of an attempt to root out Buddhism as the central element of Tibetan culture. The essay argues that because Tibet was formerly a theocracy and China is led by atheists who are also the inheritors of the imperial tradition of regulating religion for security reasons, religious influence over politics and society in Tibet has necessarily diminished. Chinese leaders do however recognize the staying power of religion and mainly restrict it in order to prevent the consolidation of separatist influences within and by the religious community (*sangha*). Tibet nevertheless remains the Buddhist land with the highest proportion of "clergy" in its population and most Tibetans engage in open religious practice.

It has also been charged that the Tibetan language is endangered by an education system that stresses the acquisition of Chinese language skills and by the dominance of Chinese in administrative and economic affairs in Tibet. The essay contends that education is mainly in Tibetan for primary students and most Tibetans do not go on to secondary education. For those who do, their education will be bilingual in most Tibetan areas or mainly in Chinese if they study in China proper. The few Tibetans who do not speak Tibetan live mainly at the edge of the Tibet plateau. Most Tibetans may not read or write the language, but that has always been the case. Less than 15 percent of ethnic Tibetans can manage in Chinese, which is dominant in state functions at the prefecture or regional level in Tibetan areas, but not generally at lower levels.

The Tibetan exiles decry "Chinese influences" in the arts that have altered their traditional (largely religious) content. They also charge that various popular "vices," including prostitution, drug use, karaoke, billiards, and so on, evidence cultural genocide. Scholars of Tibetan culture, including some sympathetic to the Tibetan exile cause, generally recognize, however, that there have been significant, state-supported efforts to preserve traditional Tibetan cultural inheritances and to generate new forms of cultural production, especially in literature and painting. Most "vices" in urban Tibet are widespread elsewhere, including in the émigré "capital" of Dharamsala, India. The Sautman essay concludes with a discussion of the use of the charge of cultural genocide to scuttle international involvement in a state sponsored migration across Qinghai province of tens of thousands of very poor, mainly ethnic minority, Chinese to a "Tibetan area" and argues that this deployment of the discourse may actually have injured the interests of local Tibetans and other minority peoples.

Conclusion

Genocide has been called the "crime of crimes" and "crime of the century."[120] A UN body terms it "the ultimate crime and the gravest violation of human rights it is possible to commit."[121] Martti Koskenniemi observes that

> To be branded as a genocidal State is to be classified as the worst kind of criminal, a pariah, an outlaw among States, to have been put beyond the pale of civilised humanity. The evocative strength or the symbolic value of genocide is formidable . . . Even to be accused of genocide affects a State's international standing, its political, diplomatic and commercial contacts with other States.[122]

Genocide scholars have deplored use of the term as a tactic to bring maximum opprobrium to opponents, rather than to characterize mass murder intended to destroy a protected group. One scholar states that "the notion of genocide is marked by conceptual confusion, often compounded by its rhetorical use on the part of those seeking to inflame and stigmatize social and political discourse."[123] Others have catalogued misuses of the term,[124] with one concluding that "when one needs a catch-all term to describe 'oppression' of one form or another, one often resorts to labelling it 'genocide.' The result is the debasement of the concept."[125]

Nationalists and regional interests commonly charge cultural genocide to oppugn lifestyle or economic changes. A Canadian First Nations leader has stated that animal rights activists who seek restrictions on trapping fur-bearing animals commit cultural genocide of the Inuit by taking away their means of subsistence[126] and Newfoundland politicians accuse Ottawa of cultural genocide for closing down cod fisheries.[127] Non-Christian Australian Aborigines criticize Christian Aborigines evangelists' "cultural genocide" in diminishing traditional tribal spirituality.[128] The Turkish media attacked as cultural genocide the Saudi demolition of Ecyad Castle in Mecca because it removed a reminder of former Ottoman rule.[129] Coca leaf farmers decry Bolivian anti-drug eradications of their crops as cultural genocide because Andeans use the plant for ritual and health purposes. These complainants may raise legitimate issues, but it is misleading to imply that their cultures are threatened with destruction from actions that are not based on that intent and cannot have that effect.

If those who have legitimate grievances can play that game, so too can oppressive forces that now claim that their cultures are threatened by resistance to oppression. Since the 1980s, neo-fascists such as Jean-Marie Le Pen in France and Gianfranco Fini in Italy have glommed onto "cultural genocide" in attacks against immigrants and foreigners who allegedly threaten European culture,[130] while the secessionist League of the South in the United States mines similar veins.[131] The Grand Orange Lodge, a cornerstone of the Northern Ireland Protestant ascendency, has denounced as cultural genocide police rerouting of a march through a Catholic community, on the ground that such marches are integral to "loyalist culture."[132] Politicians in South Carolina and Georgia argue that efforts to remove the official status of the Confederate "stars and bars" in those U.S. states is cultural genocide because the flag is integral to the South's heritage.[133] New Mexico stockmen charge cultural genocide when environmentalists seek to protect endangered species through measures that may adversely impact the cattle-raising that the stockmen argue is basic to Southwest U.S. culture.[134]

With many causes competing for attention, it may appear that the most extreme, not the most accurate, language best serves a cause. Koskenniemi has described the deleterious effects of such a course with regard to the concept of genocide:

> To accuse one's adversary of having committed genocide may have powerful ideological effects, whatever the substance for such claim. The doubt is inserted in the minds of outsiders ("but what if that is true . . . ?") and half the ideological battle may already have been won. An indiscriminate and proliferating use of the tag will lose its normative or evocative strength. The more accusations of genocide are routinely thrown by political and military adversaries against each other, or the more the notion is defensively used in order to direct attention away from one's own acts, the less power the notion is going to have . . . The concept of genocide will be associated in the popular mind with the kind of politics as usual that it so delights in cynically dismissing; as just another meaningless phrase concocted by politicians or ideologists to support whatever agendas they may have.[135]

A "sobering contrast" between the "rhetorical overuse of the concept of genocide" and "its practical impact in halting state-sponsored mass killing"[136] has been noted and may rest on a causal link: with so many claims made without connection to the Convention conception of genocide, it may be hard to recognize a serious instance when it is in progress. There are scholars, such as Adam Hochschild, who in a study of Belgian colonial depredations in the Congo that caused 10 million unnatural deaths, recognize that even huge brutality may not be genocide where it does not involve an intended pattern of extermination,[137] and then there are nationalists who are oblivious to the consequence for other peoples of making the most serious of charges without a solid evidentiary foundation. Loosely grounded attempts to associate state leaders with the level of criminality implied in a charge of genocide, even if "only" cultural,[138] moreover, hardens state leaders' distrust of those who make the charge and often evokes a ready counter-charge. Thus, after a U.S. Congressman invoked cultural genocide in Tibet, a PRC organ responded

> Remember, American troops slaughtered native Americans and drove them into small reservations. In the United States in the 18th century there were one million Indians on the new continent. But by the end of the 19th century, the number of Indians had slumped to 240,000. And what the remaining Indians faced was not the increasing economic prosperity other Americans enjoyed, but barren land, rising unemployment and disappearing languages. In the reservation areas, the Indians were left isolated from the outside world, living in poverty. This was how the Americans "preserved the Indians' cultural, religious, linguistic, and ethnic identity."[139]

One should also consider whether an exclusive focus on national responsibility for undesired cultural change serves to obviate the much-needed analysis of a more generalized imposition of cultural forms impelled by the globalization of capitalism. A philosopher who studies the politics of cultural difference argues that general structural transformations in state, markets, firms, and bureaucracies may determine what is sometimes experienced in local communities as ethnic oppression:

> What if groups systematically misread the effects of these social and economic transformations and ascribed to their minority position developments which in fact affected minority and majority cultures alike? What if late modernity posed a generalized cultural threat which all collectivities had to deal with as they tried to reformulate their traditional lifeways in a context of constant radical change?[140]

State responsibility for cultural genocide thus needs to be distinguished from the effects of asymmetrical, U.S.-centered, global transformations that impinge on the cultures of both majority and minority groups. A leading proponent of globalization observes, "Culturally speaking, globalization is largely the spread (for better or worse) of Americanization—from Big Macs and iMacs to Mickey Mouse."[141] Opponents of globalization assert that it brings "cultural genocide" even to developed countries.[142] "Cultural genocide" is thus often the cultural erosions resulting directly or indirectly from U.S.-led globalized commodification, with impoverished subaltern peoples more lacking in the resources needed for cultural preservation than those more favored by the privileging of certain regions, states, sectors, and classes.

The case studies discussed above raise questions about the parameters of cultural genocide and about the appropriateness of the concept as a concomitant of "strategic essentialization," that is, the casting by ethnies of their public images and identities to accord with dominant stereotypes, in order to secure recognition and rights.[143] Such stereotypes require not only a showing that a people in question eschew hybridity in favor of adherence to tradition and have a firm sense of ethnic boundedness, but also that indigenous and minority cultures are so weak that they cannot be preserved without protections from state "nation-building" projects and the attractions of "modern" cultures. Strategic essentialism is useful in securing rights in the short term, but perpetuates the power asymmetry between subaltern peoples and the agents of national and international political economic systems. To gain support from such elites, indigenous peoples and minorities must represent themselves as having much less variegated views and interests than they actually do and as being interested in "cultural survival," rather than social and political justice.[144] The long-run benefits of invoking cultural genocide as an adjunct of such strategic essentialism may prove elusive for the indigenous and minority peoples of Asian state peripheries.

Notes

1. Tony Judt, "Nineteen eighty-nine: the end of which European era?" *Daedalus*, Vol. 123, no. 3 (1994), pp. 1–19.
2. Robert Clinton, "The rights of indigenous peoples as collective group rights," *Arizona Law Review*, Vol. 32 (1990), pp. 739–746.
3. Quoted in Martin Gilbert, *Auschwitz and the Allies* (New York: Henry Holt, 1981), p. 341.
4. [Genocide Convention], 78 *U.N.T.S.* 277 (adopted December 9, 1948). For the three drafts of the Convention, those of the UN Secretariat, an Ad Hoc Committee, and the Final Draft, see William Schabas, *Genocide in international law* (Cambridge: Cambridge University Press, 2000), pp. 553–568.
5. Rafael Lemkin, *Axis rule in occupied Europe: laws of occupation, analysis of government, proposals for redress* (Washington, DC: Carnegie Endowment for International Peace, 1944), p. 79.
6. Raphael Lemkin, "Genocide as a crime under international law," *American Journal of International Law*, Vol. 41 (1947), pp. 145–151 (p. 147). The means discussed by Lemkin are sometimes labelled as "physical" and "biological."
7. Alex Alvarez, *Governments, citizens and genocide: a comparative and interdisciplinary approach* (Bloomington: Indiana University Press, 2001), p. 34.
8. Steven T. Katz, *The Holocaust in historical context* (New York: Oxford University Press, 1994).
9. Helen Fein, *Genocide watch* (New Haven, CT: Yale University, 1992).

10. Kenneth J. Campbell, *Genocide and the global village* (New York: Palgrave, 2001), pp. 22–23.

11. David Alonzo-Maizliish, "In whole or in part: group rights, the intent element of genocide, and the 'quantitative criterion,' " *New York University Law Review*, Vol. 77, no. 5 (2000), pp. 1369–1403 (p. 1375).

12. G.A. Res. 96 (I), U.N. GAOR, 1st Sess., pt. 2, U.N. Doc. A/64/Add. 1, at 189 (1946).

13. Draft Convention on the Crimes of Genocide, U.N. ESCOR, 5th Sess., at 6–7, U.N. Doc. E/447 (1947).

14. *Summary record of meetings* 175–225, U.N. ESCOR, 3rd Year, 7th Sess., Supp. No. 6, p. 6, U.N. Doc. E/3/SR.175–225 (1948).

15. U.N. ESCOR Ad Hoc Comm. On Genocide, 5th Sess, 14th mtg., U.N. Doc. E/AC.25/SR.14 (1948), p. 14.

16. U.N. ESCOR Ad Hoc Comm. On Genocide, 6th Sess, 5th mtg., at 2–3, U.N. Doc. E/AC.25/SR.5 (1948) (statement of Mr. Perez-Perozo, representative of Venezuela).

17. [UDHR], U.N. Doc. A/810 (1949) (adopted December 10, 1948, G.A. Res. 217A (III)).

18. Johannes Morsink, "Cultural genocide, the Universal Declaration, and minority rights," *Human Rights Quarterly* 21:4 (1999), pp. 1009–1060.

19. Morsink, 1999, pp. 1021–1055, William Schabas, "Le droits des minorities: une declaration inachevee," in Commission Nationale Consultative des Droits de l'Homme, *La declaration universelle des droits de l'homme 1984–1998, Avenir d'un ideal commun* (Paris: La Documentation Francaise, 1999), pp. 223–242.

20. *Draft Convention on the Crime of Genocide*, Commentary, U.N. Secretary-General, 23 U.N. Doc. E/447 (1947), pp. 24, 27.

21. Draft Convention, p. 27; Matthew Lippman, "Art and ideology in the Third Reich: the protection of cultural property and the humanitarian law of war," *Dickinson Journal of International Law* 17 (1998), pp. 1–96 (p. 60). Martin Krygier and Robert van Krieken, "The character of the nation," in Robert Manne (ed.), *Whitewash: on Keith Winschuttle's Fabrication of Aboriginal History* (Melbourne: Black Inc. 2003), 81–108, have noted that "The United Nations Genocide Convention was written at a time when just about every member state of the United Nations would have presumed that assimilation of indigenous populations was generally unproblematic and that it was desirable that 'primitive' cultures be modernised, making it very difficult to argue that the UNGC was intended to include the concept of non-physical, 'cultural' genocide."

22. Matthew Lippman, "The 1948 Convention on the Prevention and Punishment of the Crime of Genocide: forty-five years later," *Temple International and Comparative Law Journal,* Vol. 8 (1994), pp. 1–84 (p. 38).

23. Steven Ratner and Jason Abrams, *Accountability for human rights atrocities in international law: beyond the Nuremberg legacy* (Oxford: Clarendon Press, 1997), p. 29.

24. "Defining protected groups under the Genocide Convention," *Harvard Law Review* 114 (2001), pp. 2007–2024 (p. 2011).

25. William Schabas, "Were the atrocities in Cambodia and Kosovo genocide?," *New England Law Review* 35 (2001), pp. 287–302 (p. 292); Schabas, 2000, p. 184. In 1948, the influential African-American scholar WEB DuBois attempted to have the UN censure US racial discrimination, only to have his efforts blocked by the US delegation, which included Eleanor Roosevelt. Neil Smith, The Endgame of Globalization (New York: Routledge, 2005): 112. According to Macquarie University's Konrad Kwiet, Australia had not, as of 2001, incorporated the Genocide Convention into domestic law because it feared the Convention may be used against it by Aborigines. "Latvia claims right to try 'war criminal,' " *The Guardian* [London], May 28, 2001, p. 12.

26. Thomas W. Simon, "Defining genocide," *Wisconsin International Law Journal* 15 (1996), pp. 243–256 (p. 243).

27. Matthew Lippman, "The Convention on the Prevention and Punishment of the Crime of Genocide: fifty years later," *Arizona Journal of International and Comparative Law* 15 (1998), pp. 415–514 (476–478).

28. Benjamin Whitaker, Special Rapporteur, *Review of further developments in fields with which the Sub-Commission has been concerned: preliminary revised an updated report on the question of the prevention and punishment of the crime of genocide,* U.N. ESCOR, Human Rights Subcommission on the Prevention of Discrimination and Protection of Minorities, 38th Sess., 37, U.N. Doc. E/CN. 4/Sub.2/1985/6 (1985).

29. Morsink, 1999, p. 1055.

30. See Matthew Lippman, "The drafting of the 1948 Convention on the Prevention and Punishment of the Crime of Genocide," *Boston University International Law* Journal, Vol. 3 (1984), pp. 1–65.

31. "Rome Statute of the International Criminal Court," UN Doc. A/CONF.183/9, Article 5 (1998).

32. Lippman, 1994, p. 77.

33. Michael Sells, *The bridge betrayed: religion and genocide in Bosnia* (Berkeley: University of California, 1996); Aryeh Neier, *War crimes: brutality, genocide, terror, and the struggle for justice* (New York: Times Books, 1998); "Bricks and mortars," *Independent*, September 3, 2001, p. 10.

34. Diane Orentlicher, "Genocide," in Roy Gutman and David Rieff (eds.) *Crimes of war: what the public should know* (New York: WW Norton, 1999), pp. 153–157 (p. 154).

35. The émigré leaders have argued that the whole half-century of "Chinese rule" in Tibet amounts to "a crime of cultural genocide against the Tibetan people." "Prepared testimony of Lodi G. Gyari, President, International Campaign for Tibet before the House International Relations Committee hearing on religious persecution," *Federal News Service* [FNS], September 10, 1997.

36. See the definition of "crimes against humanity" in Agreement for the prosecution and punishment of the war criminals of the European Axis, August 8, 1945, art. 6[c] Charter of the International Military Tribunal [the Nuremberg trials], 59 Stat. 1544, 82 U.N.T.S. 279, 288.

37. ICCPR, December 19, 1966, 6 I.L.M. 268 (1967), Article 27 ("In those states in which ethnic, religious or linguistic minorities exist persons belonging to such minorities shall not be denied the right, in community with the other members of their group, to enjoy their own culture, to process and practise their own religion, or to use their own language").

38. Martti Koskenniemi, "Evil intention or vicious acts: what is prima facie evidence of genocide?" in Matti Tupamaki (ed.), *Liber amicorum Bengt Broms* (Helsinki: Finnish Branch of the International Law Association 1999), pp. 180–207 (p. 182).

39. Campbell, 2001, p. 34.

40. Ted Gurr and Barbara Harff, *Ethnic conflict in world politics* (Boulder, CT: Westview, 1994), pp. 160–166; Charles Kegley and Eugene Wittkopf, *World politics: trend and transformation*, 7th ed. (New York: St. Martin's Press, 1999), pp. 367–368.

41. *Report of the International Law Commission on the work of its forty-eighth session, May 6–July 26, 1996*, U.N. Doc. A/51/10, p. 102, para. 4.

42. Frank Chalk and Kurt Jonassohn, *The history and sociology of genocide: analyses and case studies* (New Haven, CT: Yale University Press, 1990), p. 23.

43. Schabas, 2000, p. 187.

44. Schabas, 2001, pp. 292, 301. See also Simon, 1996, p. 252. That label is much more supportable in the case of the Khmer Rouge anti-Vietnamese killings, which were intended and virtually succeeded in annihilating 400,000 Vietnamese Cambodians. Ben Kiernan, *The Pol Pot regime: race, power, and genocide in Cambodia under the Khmer Rouge* (New Haven, CT: Yale University Press, 1996).

45. George Tinker, *Missionary conquest: the Gospel and Native American cultural genocide* (Minneapolis MN: Forest Press, 1993), p. 6; Mark Michaels, "Indigenous ethics and alien laws: native traditions and the United States legal system," *Fordham Law Review*, Vol. 66 (1998), pp. 1565–1584. (U.S. law allowing Indian tribes to own casinos is cultural genocide); Julie Lythcott-Haims, "Where do mixed babies belong? Racial classification in America and its implications for transnational adoption," *Harvard C.R-C.L. Law Review*, Vol. 29 (1994), pp. 531–558 (interracial adoption termed cultural genocide).

46. George Andreopoulos, "Introduction: the calculus of genocide," in G. Andreopolous (ed.), *Genocide: conceptual and historical dimensions* (Philadelphia: University of Pennsylvania, 1994), pp. 1–27.

47. Schabas, 2001, p. 255.

48. ICTR, *Prosecutor v. Akayesu*, Summary of judgment delivered on September 2, 1998, 37 ILM 1998, p. 1403.

49. Richard Herz, "Litigating environmental abuses under the Alien Tort Claims Act: a practical assessment," *Virginia Journal of International Law*, Vol. 40 (2000), pp. 545–636 (p. 629). For a violation of Article 27 to be established, however, the action in question must have "effects as severe as might be expected in a cultural genocide claim . . ." Ibid., p. 631.

50. Declaration . . . adopted December 18, 1992, F.A. Res. 47/135, U.N. GAOR, 47th Sess, Annex, U.N. Doc. A/Rev/47/135/Annex (1992), in 32 I.L.M. 911.

51. See *Beanal v. Freeport-McMoRan, Inc.*, 969 F. Supp. 362, 373–373 (E.D. La. 1997), *aff'd*, 197 F.3d 161 (5th Cir. 1999); Whitaker, 1985, p. 17.

52. See Terri Leon, "The Draft Declaration on the Rights of Indigenous Peoples: three case studies," *New Engiand International and Comparative Law Annual* 6 (2000), pp. 47–61 (p. 58).

53. The former World Council of Indigenous Peoples (WCIP) definition found in the 1984 draft of the "International Covenant" and quoted in Benedict Kingsbury, "The applicability of the international legal concept of 'indigenous peoples' in Asia," in Joanne Bauer and Daniel Bell (eds.), *The East Asian challenge for human rights* (Cambridge: Cambridge University Press, 1999), pp. 336–377 (p. 348) is absent in the "Authorized version" of the "International Covenant" of 1994, found at www.cwis.org/icrin-94.html.

54. World Bank Operational Directive 4.20, in IWGIA, *Newsletter*, November/December 1991, p. 19.

55. Aurelie Cristescu, *Self-determination: historical and current development on the basis of United Nations instruments*, U.N. Doc. E/CN.4/Sub.2/404/Rev. 1 (1981).

56. Benedict Kingsbury, " 'Indigenous peoples' in international law: a constructivist approach to the Asian controversy," *American Journal of International Law* 92 (1998), pp. 414–457 (p. 419).

57. Jose Martinez Cabo, *Study of the problem of discrimination against indigenous populations*, U.N. Doc. E/CN.4/Dub.2/1986/7/Add.4, 1986), paras. 379–380.

58. Convention Concerning Indigenous and Tribal Peoples in Independent Countries [Article I(1)], June 27, 1989, 28 ILM 1382, 1384–1385 (1989). As of the end of 2001, only fourteen states had ratified this Convention, all of them, except Mexico, small and none of them Asian. See http://iloex.ilo.ch:1567/newratframeE.htm.

59. UNESCO, Meeting of Experts on Ethno-Development and Ethnocide in Latin America, *Final Report*, San Jose, Costa Rica (December 7–11, 1981); UNESCO Meeting of Experts on the Study of Ethno-Development and Ethnocide in Africa, *Final Report*, Ouagadougou, Upper Volta (January31– February 4, 1983); UNESCO, *UNESCO and resistance to ethnocide: conclusions of the Ouagadougou meeting* (February 1983); UNESCO, Meeting of experts on the study of ethnodevelopment and ethnocide in

Europe, *Final report and conclusions and suggestions*, Karasjok Norway (May 29–June 2, 1983).

60. UNESCO Latin-American Conference, *Declaration of San Jose*, December 11, 1981, UNESCO Doc. FS 82/WF.32 (1982).

61. See Dean Suagee, "Self-determination for indigenous peoples at the dawn of the solar age," *University of Michigan Journal of Law Reform* 26 (1992), pp. 671–749 (p. 685); Thomas R. Moore, "SIL and the 'new-found tribe': the Amarakaeri experience," *Dialectical Anthropology*, Vol. 4, no. 2 (1979), pp. 113–125. See also a definition of cultural genocide ("the destruction of the defining characteristic and qualities of a group [that] involves forced assimilation and suppression of their ethnic characteristics") that is also descriptive of ethnocide. Vahakn Dadrian, "A typology of genocide," *International Review of Modern Sociology*, Vol. 5 (1975), pp. 201–212 (p. 205).

62. See John Burton, "Development and cultural genocide in the Sudan," *Journal of Modern African Studies*, Vol. 29, no. 3 (1991), pp. 511–520; Sells, 1996; Robert van Krieken, "The barbarism of civilization: cultural genocide and the 'stolen generations,' " *British Journal of Sociology*, Vol. 50, no. 2 (1999), pp. 297–315; "Citizens tribunal indicts Modi for riots," *Economic Times*, November 22, 2002.

63. Alison Palmer, "Ethnocide," in Michael Dobkowski and Isidor Wallimann, *Genocide in our time: an annotated bibliography with analytical introductions* (Ann Arbor, MI: Pierian Press, 1992), pp. 1–6.

64. Pierre Clastres, *Archeology of violence* (New York: Semiotext(e), 1994 [1980]).

65. Alvarez, 2001, p. 51.

66. Quoted in David Weissbrodt, et al., "Prospects for U.S. ratification of the Convention Against Torture," *American Society of International Law Proceedings,* Vol. 83 (1983), pp. 529, 547.

67. Maivan Clech Lam, *At the Edge of the State:Indigenous Peoples and Self-Determination* (Ardsley, NY: Transnational Publishers, 2000), p. 31.

68. Declaration of San Jose, 1982, Preamble. See also, Herz, 2000, p. 633. ("Cultural genocide is an extreme form of discrimination in that it consists of an effort to obliterate an entire culture.)"

69. Chalk and Jonassohn, 1990, p. 23; *Discrimination against indigenous peoples: report of the Working Group on Indigenous Populations on its eighth session*, UN ESCOR, 8th Sess, UN Doc E/CN.4/Sub.2/1990/42 (1990) p. 47.

70. Dennis O'Neil, *Culture change: an introduction to the processes and consequences of culture change: glossary of terms*, http://anthro.palomar.edu/change/default.htm.

71. Kathryn Boyd, "Collective rights adjudication in U.S. courts: enforcing human rights at the corporate level," *Brigham Young University Law Review* 1999, pp. 1139–1213 (p. 1174).

72. David Maybury-Lewis, *Indigenous peoples, ethnic groups and the state* (Boston, MA: Allyn & Bacon 1997), pp. 15–39.

73. Joe Thomas, *Ethnocide: a cultural narrative of refugee detention in Hong Kong* (Aldershot: Ashgate 2000)(temporary detention of Vietnamese refugees), pp. 33–34. "Cultural genocide" is even more often applied to situations where there is no intent to harm an ethnic group. See, e.g., "My Italian TV hell," *Financial Times*, January 18, 2003, p. 1 (film director declares television is used to commit cultural genocide by diminishing creativity of Italians); "For the young Elvis, a brand new accompaniment," *New York Times*, August 11, 2002, p. 2:23 (music critic declares other critics guilty of cultural genocide for writing hostile biographies of Elvis Presley).

74. *Draft United Nations Declaration on the Rights of Indigenous Peoples, UN Subcommission on Prevention of Discrimination and Protection of Minorities,* (August 26, 1994), U.N. Doc. E/CN.4//1995/2/1994/56, reprinted in *I.L.M.* 34 (1995), pp. 541–552; For analyses of the Draft Declaration, see Robert Coulter, "The Draft Declaration on the Rights of Indigenous Peoples: what is it? what does it mean?" *Netherlands Quarterly of Human Rights* (1995), pp. 123–138; Julian Burger, "The United Nations Draft Declaration on the Rights of Indigenous Peoples," *St. Thomas Law Review* 9 (1996), pp. 209–229.

75. Julian Burger, "Indigenous peoples and the United Nations," in Cynthia Price Cohen (ed.), *The human rights of indigenous peoples* (Ardsley, NJ: Transnational Publishers, 1998), pp. 3–16 (p. 7).

76. See, e.g., Rene Lemarchand, *Burundi: ethnocide as discourse and practice* (Cambridge: Cambridge University Press, 1995).

77. Ping Chen, "Policy on the selection and implementation of a standard language as a source of conflict in Taiwan," in Nanette Gottlieb and Ping Chen (eds.), *Language planning and language policy: East Asian perspectives* (New York: Curzon, 2001), pp. 95–110 (p. 97).

78. Bruce Armstrong, "Racialisation and nationalist ideology: the Japanese case," *International Sociology*, Vol. 4, no. 3 (1989), pp. 329–343 (p. 339).

79. Jack David Eller, *From culture to ethnicity to conflict: an anthropological perspective on international ethnic conflict* (Ann Arbor: University of Michigan Press, 1999), pp. 171–173; Michael Gunter, *The Kurds and the future of Turkey* (New York: St. Martin's Press, 1997), pp. 5–10.

80. "22 held over Kurdish education campaign," *South China Morning Post* [*SCMP*], January 19, 2002, p. E5.

81. International Law Commission, *Report of the Commission to the General Assembly on the work of its forty-first session,* UN Doc. A/CN.4/SERA.A/ 1989/Add.1/(Part 2), p. 102, para. 4. Biological genocide has typically been an adjunct of physical genocide, but there has been biological genocide without physical genocide, for example the sterilization of the African-Germans by the Nazis. Susan Samples, "African Germans in the Third Reich," in Carol Aisha Blackshire-Belay (ed.), *The African-German experience* (Westport CT: Praeger, 1996), pp. 53–70.

82. Polish Government-in-Exile, *The quest for German blood: policy of Germanization of Poland* (London: Polish Ministry of Information, 1943);

International Military Tribunal [IMT], *USA trial briefs U: Germanization of occupied territories* (Washington: National Archives, 1976 [1946–1949]). SS leader Heinrich Himmler is quoted in *France, et al. v. Goering, et al., IMT* Vol. 23 (1946), p. 480, as stating "What happens to a Russian, a Czech, does not interest me in the slightest. What the nations can offer in the way of good blood of our type, we take. If necessary, by kidnapping their children and raising them here with us. Whether nations live in prosperity or starve to death interests me only in so far as we need them as slaves for our Kultur, otherwise it is of no interest to me."

83. Michael Burleigh, *The Third Reich: a New History* (New York: Hill & Wang, 2000), pp. 44–1457; R.J. Rummel, *Democide; Nazi genocide and mass murder* (New Brunswick, NJ: Transaction Publishers, 1992), pp. 31–42. The physical genocide of Poles and other Slavs was to be accompanied by a cultural genocide. See Christopher Browning, *Nazi policy, Jewish workers, German killers* (Cambridge: Cambridge University Press, 2000), pp. 14–24.

84. Menachem Shelah, "Genocide in satelite Croatia during the Second World War," in Michael Berenbaum, *A mosaic of victims: non-Jews persecuted and murdered by the Nazis* (New York: NYU Press, 1990), pp. 74–79.

85. Ward Churchill, *Indians are us? Culture and genocide in Native North America* (Monroe, ME: Common Courage Press, 1994).

86. Robert Utley, "Introduction," in Robert Utley (ed.), *Battlefield and classroom: four decades with the American Indian, 1867–1904* (Lincoln: University of Nebraska Press, 1964), p. 35.

87. Quoted in Debra Barker, "Kill the Indian, save the child: cultural genocide and the boarding school," in Dane Morrison (ed.), *American Indian studies: an interdisciplinary approach to contemporary issues* (New York: Peter Lang, 1997), pp. 47–68 (p. 52).

88. James Crawford, "Endangered native American languages: what is to be done and why?" in Thomas Ricento and Barbara Burnaby (eds.), *Language and politics in the United States and Canada* (Mahwah, NJ: Erlbaum, 1998), pp. 151–165.

89. Jeffrey Hamley, *Cultural genocide in the classroom: a history of the Federal Boarding School Movement in American Indian education: 1875–1920* (Cambridge: Unpublished Harvard University Ed.D. dissertation, 1994), p. 208; Barker, 1997, pp. 59–63.

90. See, e.g., Parker Nielson, *The dispossessed: cultural genocide of the mixed-blood Utes: an advocate's chronicle* (Norman: University of Oklahoma Press, 1998).

91. See, e.g., Bruce Elder, *Blood on the wattle: massacres and maltreatment of Australian aborigines since 1788* (Frenchs Forest, NSW: National Book Distributors, 1996); Russell McGregor, *Imagined destinies: Aboriginal Australians and the doomed race theory, 1880–1939* (Carlton, Vic.: Melbourne University Press, 1997); Rosalind Kidd, *The way we civilise: Aboriginal affairs, the untold story* (St. Lucia, Qld: University of Queensland Press, 1997). The assault had, in common with other colonial infringements, dispossession

facilitated by an assumption that Australia was *terra nullius* (no one's land), even though the land is the situs of Aboriginal spiritual life and culture. Genevieve Lloyd, "No one's land: Australia and the philosophical imagination," *Hypatia*, Vol. 15, no. 2 (2000), pp. 26–39.

92. Henry Reynolds, *An indelible stain? The question of genocide in Australia's history* (Ringwood, Vic.: Viking, 2001); Tony Barta, "Relations of genocide—land and lives in the colonization of Australia," in Wallimann and Dobkawski, 1987, pp. 237–253; Alison Palmer, *Colonial genocide* (Adelaide: Crawford House, 2000); Colin Tatz, *Genocide in Australia* (Canberra: Aboriginal Studies Press, 1999).

93. Ron Brunton, *Betraying the victims: the 'stolen generation' report* (Jolimont, Vic.: Institute of Public Affairs, 1998); *Stolen children: from removal to reconciliation* (Kensington, NSW: University of New South Wales Law Journal, 1997); Dolores Estrada, *Australia's aboriginal battle for self-determination and equal justice: a case study of the stolen generation* (Unpublished MA thesis, Georgetown University, 1998); R. Van Krieken, "The 'stolen generations' and cultural genocide" *Childhood: a Global Journal of Child Research*, Vol. 6, no. 3 (1999), pp. 297–311.

94. John Boyko, *Last steps to freedom: the evolution of Canadian racism* (Winnipeg: Watson & Dwyer, 1995), p. 176.

95. Ibid., pp. 180–197, Michael Downey, "Canada's genocide: thousands taken from their homes need help," *Maclean's*, April 26, 1999, p. 56; Kevin Annett, *Hidden from history: the Canadian Holocaust: the untold story of the genocide of Aboriginal peoples by church and state* (s.l. Truth Commission into Genocide in Canada, 2001); Ben Swankey, *National identity or cultural genocide? A reply to Ottawa's new Indian policy* (Toronto, ON: Progress Books, 1970).

96. Warren Allmand, "Canada needs to move on aboriginal rights declaration," *Gazette* (Montreal), June 20, 2001, p. B2.

97. Draft Declaration Article 7.

98. Martin Geer, "Foreigners in their own land: cultural land and transnational corporations—emergent international rights and wrongs," *Virginia Journal of International Law*, Vol. 38 (1998), pp. 331–398 (p. 396).

99. Leon, 2000, p. 57.

100. *Special Committee on Decolonization: what it is, what it does, how it works* (New York: United Nations, 1987).

101. Geer, 1998, p. 346, n. 50.

102. Leon, 2000, p. 57.

103. Gerard Clarke, "From ethnocide to ethnodevelopment? Ethnic minorities and indigenous peoples in Southeast Asia," *Third World Quarterly*, Vol. 22, no. 3 (2001), pp. 413–436 (p. 416).

104. Kingsbury, 1999, pp. 349–350.

105. "Press briefing on International Day of the World's Indigenous People," *M2 Presswire*, August 8, 1998; "Indigenous peoples: pressing for greater rights," *UN Chronicle*, Vol. 30, no. 1 (1993), pp. 95–96.

106. Richard Thompson, "Ethnic minorities and the case for collective rights," *American Anthropologist*, Vol. 99, no. 4 (1997), pp. 786–798.

107. Lee Swepston, "The ILO Indigenous and Tribal Peoples Convention (No. 169): Eight years after adoption," in Cynthia Price Cohen, *The human rights of indigenous peoples* (Ardsley, NY: Transnational Publishers, 1998), pp. 17–36 (p. 21).

108. Dru Gladney, "The question of minority identity and indigeneity in post-colonial China," *Cultural Survival Quarterly*, Vol. 21, no. 3 (1997), pp. 50–54; Alexander Woodside, "Territorial order and collective-identity tensions in Confucian Asia: China, Vietnam, Korea, Early modernities," *Daedalus*, Vol. 127 (1998), pp. 191–220.

109. "China concerned with protection of indigenous peoples' rights: Long," *Xinhua*, April 3, 1997.

110. *Considerations of a draft United Nations Declaration on the Rights of Indigenous People*, U.N. Doc. E/CN.4/WG.15/2, October 10, 1995.

111. "PRC representative claims no problem of indigenous people exists in China," *Xinhua*, September 17, 1993, in *British Broadcasting Corporation, Summary of World Broadcasts [BBC/SWB]*, September 30, 1997.

112. "Testimony of Rep. Christopher H. Smith, Chairman, House International Relations Committee, Sub-Committee on International Operations and Human Rights," *FNS*, December 8, 1999; "China's unsavoury resettlement plan," *Boston Globe [BG]*, June 22, 1999, p. A14 [editorial].

113. Hurst Hannum, "The limits of sovereignty and majority rule: minorities, indigenous peoples and the right to autonomy," in Ellen Lutz, et al. (eds.), *New directions in human rights* (Philadelphia: University of Pennsylvania Press, 1989), pp. 18–22.

114. Laura Ziemer, "Application to Tibet of the principles on human rights and the environment," *Harvard Human Rights Journal*, Vol. 14 (2001), pp. 233–275 (p. 242).

115. See Yodon Thonden, "The indigenous route to independence: arguments for a path not yet taken," *Tibet Review*, Vol. 30, no. 4 (1995), pp. 15–16; Eric Cleven and Chungdak Koren, "The correct route to independence: for Tibet, the indigenous route is, at best a detour," ibid., pp. 17–18. Ironically, some pro-Tibet independence Western scholars regard Tibet as having been stateless or "almost stateless." Gabriel Lafitte, "Tibetan futures: imagining collective destinies," *Futures*, Vol. 32, no. 2 (1999), pp. 155–169 (p. 164). See also Geoffrey Samuel, "Tibet as a stateless society and some Islamic parallels," *Journal of Asian Studies*, Vol. 41, no. 2 (1982), pp. 215–229.

116. Dawa Norbu, *China's Tibet Policy* (Richmond, UK: 2001), pp. 387, 381.

117. Self-identification as indigenous has been considered an important defining element for indigenous status. Independent Commission on International Humanitarian Issues, *Indigenous peoples: a global quest for justice* (London: Zed Press, 1987).

118. Rodney Gilbert (ed.), *Genocide in Tibet: a study in Communist aggression* (New York: American–Asian Educational Exchange, 1959).

119. "Dalai Lama to visit Toronto," *Gazette* (Montreal), July 9, 2002, p. A13 (Tibetan exile "prime minister" accuses China of physical and cultural genocide in Tibet).

120. "Report of the Working Group on a Draft Statute for an International Criminal Court," *Yearbook of the International Law Commission, 1994 (Geneva: ILC 1994)*, 2358th meeting, p. 208, para. 41 (remarks of Rapporteur James Crawford); Matthew Lippman, "Genocide: the crime of the century: The jurisprudence of death at the dawn of the new millennium," *Houston Journal of International Law*, Vol. 23 (2001), pp. 467–535.

121. *Revised and updated report on the question of the prevention and punishment of the crime of genocide*, E/CN.4/Sub.2/1985/6, p. 5, quoted in Malcolm Shaw, "Genocide and international law," in Yoram Dinstein (ed.), *International law at a time of perplexity: essays in honour of Shabtai Rosenne* (Dordrecht: M. Nijhoff, 1989), pp. 797–820.

122. Koskenniemi, 1999, p. 186.

123. Alvarez, 2001, p. 33.

124. See, e.g., Helen Fein, "Genocide, terror, life integrity and war crimes: the case for discrimination," in Andreopoulos, 1994, pp. 95–107 (p. 95); Walter Ezell, "Investigating genocide: a catalog of known and suspected causes and some categories for comparing them," in Yehuda Bauer, et al. (eds.), *Remembering the future: the impact of the Holocaust on Jews and Christians* (Oxford: Pergamon Press, 1989), Vol. 3, p. 2881.

125. Jack N. Porter, "Introduction: What is genocide? Notes toward a definition," in J.N. Porter (ed.), *Genocide and human rights: a global anthology* (Lanham: University Press of America, 1982), pp. 9–10.

126. "Inuit accuse fur activists of 'cultural genocide,' " *Toronto Star*, July 27, 1989, p. A22.

127. "Martin stumbles out of the gate," *Toronto Star*, April 29, 2003, p. D01.

128. "Indigenous group slams holy divide," *Townsville Bulletin* (New Zealand), October 29, 2001, p. 2.

129. "Strange defense by Saudis," *Turkish Daily News*, January 10, 2002.

130. M. Guerrin, "Front tries to seize cultural high ground," *Manchester Guardian*, February 23, 1992, p. 14; Allison Tarmann, "The flap over replacement migration," *Population Today*, Vol. 28, no. 4, pp. 1–2; "Europe's new political generation: ascendant right, groping left," *AP*, December 25,1994.

131. James Cobb, "Offering sweet deals to industry puts South in worldwide spotlight," *Atlanta Journal-Constitution*, July 7, 2002, p. 1F.

132. Kevin Meyers, "An Irishman's diary," *The Irish Times*, July 5, 2001, p. 17.

133. R. Taft, "Flying a flag of distrust and division," *The Scotsman*, February 19, 2000, p. 11; "Lessons learned in flag fracas," *Atlanta Constitution*, April 27, 2003, p. 6C.

134. Jeffrey St. Clair, "From Belgrade to Santa Fe?" *In These Times*, September 19, 1999, p. 6.

135. Koskenniemi, 1999, pp. 186–188.

136. John Torpey, " 'Making whole what has been smashed': reflections on reparations," *Journal of Modern History*, Vol. 73 (2001), pp. 33–358 (347).

137. Adam Hochschild, *King Leopold's ghost: a story of greed, terror and heroism in colonial Africa* (New York: 1998), p. 225.

138. See, e.g., "Prepared testimony of Lodi Gyari, Special Envoy of His Holiness the Dalai Lama and President, International Campaign for Tibet before the Senate Foreign Relations Committee," *Federal News Service*, May 13, 1997 (claim that "the history of Chinese rule of Tibet" since 1949–1950 has been "a crime of cultural genocide").

139. "Ignorant or just arrogant?" *China Daily*, May 14, 2001.

140. Walker, "Plural cultures, contested territories: a critique of Kymlicka," *Canadian Journal of Political Science*, Vol. 30, no. 2 (1997), pp. 211–234 (p. 222).

141. Thomas Friedman, "Dueling globalizations," *Foreign Policy*, no. 116 (1999), pp. 110–127.

142. Peter Newman, "Why I'll fight the FTAA," *MacLean's*, April 30, 2001, p. 20.

143. Dorothy Hodgson, "Introduction: comparative perspectives on the indigenous rights movement in Africa and the Americas," *American Anthropologist*, Vol. 104, no. 4 (2002), pp. 1037–1049.

144. Renee Sylvain, " 'Land, water and truth': San identity and global indigenism," ibid., pp. 1074–1085.

CHAPTER 2

REDEFINING THE PAST, TAKING CHARGE OF THE PRESENT, APPROPRIATING THE FUTURE; THE HOKKAIDO AINU CASE

Katarina Sjöberg

Introduction

In the early 1980s, the point in time my interest in the Hokkaido Ainu began, it was more or less generally accepted among social scientists that the Hokkaido Ainu constituted an extinct or shortly extinct group of people. This perception is a scientific construction based on ethnocentric views, portraying the Hokkaido Ainu as a primitive and backward people, freezing their life-style in an obscure past and placing their ethnic identity in the context of extinct races. This misconception of a people and their ways is nourished and supported in social and political rhetoric in Japan. Among other things, it aims at upholding the notion of Japan as inhabited by one homogenous group of people, namely the *Wajin*, the majority ethnic group in Japan.[1] Even though, this state of affairs fallouts in much hardship and suffering for the Hokkaido Ainu, it has discouraged them neither from challenging the hierarchical and holistic identity of the *Wajin* nor from practicing and taking part in activities belonging to their cultural tradition. In recent times, the Hokkaido Ainu have joined the global community of indigenous peoples.

By and large, this article emphasizes the Hokkaido Ainu ways of maneuvering in a larger sociocultural system cherishing ethnic and cultural homogeneity as a strong value orientation. My understanding builds on a view of the Hokkaido Ainu as active players in the world that surrounds them and of which they are a part. The main focus is their indigenous understanding and practicing of their material culture and lifestyle and their active involvement in the global community of indigenous peoples. To a large extent, scientists within the Ainu field, have adopted the state ideology that ranks rather than analyzes, holding on to a view of the Hokkaido Ainu as a backward and primitive group of people, arriving at conclusions that it is elements of this nature that are the ultimate causes of their present status as a group of individuals depending on social welfare for their survival.[2] Against this background, the first part of the article discusses scientific interpretations of the Ainu, particularly their origins. This research, more than any other, has contributed to a view of the Hokkaido Ainu as backward and primitive. However, to understand their situation, we have to look back. Hence, I start with a brief presentation of the Historic Hokkaido Ainu.

The main methods used in the article are within the field of qualitative research technique and the material comes from my fieldwork conducted during the years 1986–1988, a follow-up study in the year 1995, and from archival, historical, and contemporary sources as well as websites on the Internet.

The Historic Hokkaido Ainu

The Ainu are, traditionally described by anthropologists, in the general category of hunters and gatherers, primarily inhabiting the northern island of Hokkaido.[3] Their contact with values and norms belonging to people of *Wajin* descent dates back to the eighth century. These people are known to have immigrated to Hokkaido for an extended period of time. They came to Hokkaido as constant fighting over land between different *Uji*, domains in Honshu, the main island of the Japanese archipelago, made living in this island insecure and dangerous. The two groups of people shared and used the natural resources in Hokkaido in much the same way and intermarriage between members of the two groups is being reported as frequent. Apart from hunting and fishing activities, their activities also included agriculture, horticulture, and trade with Ainu people coming from the Sakhalin and the Kurile Islands, as well as people coming from Honshu. The Hokkaido Ainu traded fish, edible seaweed, hawks, and a number of rarities such as bear liver, seal skin, and eagle feathers. In return, the Hokkaido Ainu received, rice, sugar, sake, lacquer ornaments, and cotton cloths. This was a time when their lifestyle was enriched and "there arose chiefs of tremendous power among their people."[4]

Before long, immigration on a large scale resulted in conflicts between the two groups of people. At the beginning, the people of *Wajin* descent were defeated and driven out of their territories in Hokkaido. These people turned to Honshu for support, which was also given them. The support was insufficient. As a result, the conflicts went on for a considerable amount of time, until the middle of the sixteenth century. At that time, the authorities in Honshu changed their policy to one of reconciliation. With the reconciliation policy, the prelude to the annexation of Hokkaido to the Japanese Nation-State to be, began, comprising a period of more than four centuries, stretching from the sixteenth to the nineteenth century. During the reconciliation period their number declined by 79 percent. Distinctive causes were a depletion of resources caused by intensified hunting activities, the construction of fishing industries, and gold prospecting.[5] In Japanese records, the deterioration of life-style and the decrease in number are related to *Wajin* superiority of "race" and culture.

The first years of the *Meiji* era saw Hokkaido annexed to Japan, a colonization office was established in Sapporo and the process of assimilating the Hokkaido Ainu began.[6] The new era brought Japan into the world market, modernization and the development of capitalism were urgent, espousing slogans such as, *fukoku kyohei* and *shokusan kogyo* standing for enrichment of the country, strengthening the military, and industrialization, respectively.[7] The Hokkaido Ainu were registered as *Kyodojin* or *Dojin*, concepts standing for aborigines and natives to the Hokkaido Island. According to the official policy of assimilation, they were to be incorporated into the Japanese Nation-State on equal terms with the *Wajin*. This has not happened. Today the Hokkaido Ainu are a marginal minority on the outskirts of the larger society.[8]

Redefining the Past

In the year 1999, "The Arctic Center, National Museum of Natural History, Smithsonian Institution" in association with "The University of Washington Press," published a book titled *Ainu: Spirit of a Northern People*.[9] Apart from bringing together the works of scholars in the Ainu field, this book also incorporates Ainu writings. Considering the fact that researchers have been persistent in their view of the Ainu voices and experiences as irrelevant, this is a fresh and highly welcomed approach. In the introduction, an essay titled *Ainu Ethnicity: A History*, written by one of the editors,[10] the author approaches the Ainu as having living cultures that have exhibited much creativity, a theme taken up by other contributors to this volume. Although the book deals with some aspects of the Ainu living cultures, many of the texts stand as a testimony to researchers' fixation with the preservation of the customs of a "dying people" and to their analyses of the Ainu—particularly their ways and belief systems—as primitive and retarded. Such characterizations were legitimized by the use of the term "traditional."[11] Furthermore, these texts show no attempt to analyze or question the harm inflicted on account of the hierarchical and holistic identity of the *Wajin*, especially when it comes to research on the ethnic identity of the Ainu, which, by the way, has been extensive. Hence, the focus in this part of my article is on scientific studies on the Ainu origins and ways in which this research has supported the idea of Japan as inhabited by one homogenous group of people, namely the *Wajin*, smoothing the way for a view of the assimilation of the Hokkaido Ainu as successful.

Ainu Origins

The Ainu origins have been, and still are, a scholarly mystery as well as a source of speculation. Investigations into their origins are as complex as they are confusing. Even though the Ainu culture is not monolithic but rich in intercultural variations, representing the Sakhalin Ainu, the Kurile Ainu, and the Hokkaido Ainu with clearly distinguishable lifestyles, with the exception of Ohnuki-Tierney, the blanket term "Ainu" is commonly used.[12]

According to cultural anthropologist Kodama, researchers dealing with the identity of the Ainu represent five different positions. These are the Mongoloid theory, the Caucasoid theory, the Oceanic Race theory, the Palaeo-Asiatic Tribe theory, and the Rasseninsel theory. The Mongoloid, Caucasoid, and Oceanic Race theories are based on conformities in material culture, customs, weapons, ornaments, utensils, similarities in ritual and ceremonial performances, as well as correlation in word arrangements. The Palaeo-Asiatic Tribe theory and the Rasseninsel theory are based on conformities in the craniological, somatological, and cultural material gathered in the studies of the Hokkaido Ainu and Jomon, the people who lived in Japan in prehistoric time.[13]

Ainu Origins from the Standpoint of Their Relationship to the Aboriginal Population in Japan

The identity of the Ainu has been studied in several different ways. To solve the problem from the standpoint of their relationship to the aboriginal population in Japan is an approach attracting the interest of several researchers. According to the reports of some of the scholars within this field, the original inhabitants of Japan were not the Ainu but an ancient group known in Ainu legend as the *Koropok-un-guru*. It is believed that this population expanded to its greatest number about the year 3000 BC. A rival view claimed that the close resemblance of Japan's Neolithic populations and the Ainu must be seen as evidence that they were the aboriginal settlers of Japan. These views were challenged by a third, putting forth an argument that builds on the idea that the aborigines of Japan were the populations from which both recent Ainu and the historic Japanese population were derived. With this view, the Ainu were the result of a mixture of the aboriginal Japanese populations, of unknown origins, and the peoples who later migrated to the islands from the north-eastern parts of Siberia. This view was also challenged and this time by a theory building on the idea that the ancestors of the Ainu came from the north to Hokkaido, whereas the ancestors of the historic Japanese population came from the south of China to the Japanese island of Kyushu and then moved north to Honshu.

The theory in fashion, for the present time, is that the Ainu, as well as the *Ryukyuans*, inhabitants of the Okinawa Islands, represent more-or-less direct descendants from the Neolithic people of the Jomon culture, the prehistoric culture in Japan.[14]

The Ainu Origins from the Standpoint of Territorial Concepts

Another approach, closely linked to the one above and also attracting several researchers, has been to solve the identity of the Ainu from the standpoint of territorial concepts, particularly the names of territorial locations in Honshu in mythical and historic time. This is an extremely difficult task, partly due to the inconsistency in the reports of territorial locations in mythical and historic times, and partly due to contradiction in adjecto in the classification of the Ainu.[15] This puzzling situation has been the battlefield on which researchers within this field have fought each other. In retrospect, their texts are deceptive since issues related to the question of Ainu origins have been mixed up with the issue of establishing unanimity with respect to territorial names and locations in mythical and historic time.[16]

Suffice it to say in this context, there existed two main rivaling views, one in support of the existence of the Ainu in Honshu and another opposing this view. In the texts of both these categories, *the Emishi*[17] are in focus, and these people are reported as having a hierarchical lifestyle with a mixed economy. Yet, these texts do not elaborate on the question regarding the generally accepted definition of the Ainu as hunters and gatherers, preferring instead to neglect to discuss the possibility that the Ainu were, at one time, a hierarchical society with a mixed economy.[18] This neglect is political in essence, if such discussions had been incorporated into these texts, the Ainu status as hunter/gatherer could prove, either a scientific construction, freezing their lifestyle in an obscure past, or a consequence of a long and painful integration into the Japanese Nation-State to be.

The confusing picture—the legacy of investigations into the ethnic identity of the Ainu—and the resulting falsification of all the various theories are political in essence. The center of attention of these studies has not been to solve the question of their origins but to make it an issue of never-ending scientific debates in the sense that researchers have been concerned with falsifying each other's theories rather than solving the question of the origins of the Ainu.

The Image of a "Successful" Assimilation Policy

Parallel to such scientific constructions, the official policy of assimilation was well underway and in political and social rhetoric this policy was referred to as successful. This state of affairs is partly related to the fact that among the Hokkaido Ainu, at this particular time, there were those who welcomed the assimilation policy. This in turn, had to do with indigenous explanations to, or understandings of, their poor condition—in their minds this had to do with bad relations with their ancestors, gods, and supernatural beings who had deserted them because Ainu humans had not fulfilled their obligations toward them. As it turned out, their own disgrace and the favorable situation of the people of *Wajin* descent extended over a long period of time; some of the Hokkaido Ainu reasoned that the ancestors, gods, and supernatural beings of the *Wajin* must be more powerful than those whom they themselves worshipped.[19] Hence, at the time of the annexation of Hokkaido to Japan there were those who devoted much time and effort to become fully assimilated.[20]

The combination of a focus on those Hokkaido Ainu who willingly accepted the assimilation policy, the state of their condition at the time of the annexation and finally, Japanese records as well as scientific texts relating their poor condition to *Wajin* superiority of race and culture, has become a cardinal point in launching the idea of a successful assimilation.

Taking Charge of the Present

As a signatory to the International Covenant on Civil and Political Rights ratified in 1979, the Japanese government is required to report on the measures it has adopted to ensure protection of the rights contained in the covenant. In the first report in 1980, Japan denied the very existence of the Hokkaido Ainu. In 1986, Prime Minister Nakasone univocally stated, "Japan's success on the world market is due to its homogenous population." This statement has its root in another statement made in 1976. In the words of Prime Minister Miki "Japan should become a model country for the world with her high standard . . . and no problem of racial discrimination."

Considering the fact that research for a long period of time has been successful in incorporating the Hokkaido Ainu into an image of a dying, primitive, and backward group of people, I place my point of departure in an area of research where the Hokkaido Ainu are seen as active players in the world that surrounds them. By virtue of being of Ainu descent, they are the true exponents of their lifestyle and living condition. Naturally, not the entire Hokkaido Ainu population takes an interest in their Ainu descent or their customs and ways and there are Ainu who hide their Ainu identity. My concern is, of course, not people belonging to these groups.[21] My focus is those Ainu who view themselves as a distinct cultural and religious group and who acknowledge their Ainu identity. These people identify themselves as Ainu in a national context, whereas in a regional and local context they use the term *un-guru*. This is a concept expressing a sense of belonging— *Nibutani un-guru*, *Shiraoi un-guru*, and so on, namely people belonging to such and such a settlement, *kotan*—distinguishing people from different settlements. The Hokkaido Ainu identifying themselves in this way are using their identity for "clarification" purposes, implying a strictly horizontal use of the identity concept.[22] Tired of being victimized and defined as passive object with inferior lifestyles and customs, the contemporary Hokkaido Ainu are taking matters into their own hands.

Display of the Hokkaido Ainu Material Culture and Lifestyle

One way chosen by them is to put themselves and their culture on display. This approach includes inviting the larger public to buy Ainu made products, watching the Ainu manufacturing them, and allowing the public to experiment in manufacturing these products. Furthermore, during these events the larger public is also given opportunities to learn about Hokkaido Ainu mythology, ritual and history, to taste Ainu food and, to live in their homes. Moreover, they are also offered the opportunity to join excursions to settlements important to the Hokkaido Ainu, and are given information about the characteristics of the places.

In addition, the larger public is also invited to take part in important Hokkaido Ainu events and gatherings, such as the *Marimo*[23] ceremony, dedicated to a powerful lake god whom the Hokkaido Ainu used to fear because it was believed that this god fed on humans, the *Iyomante*[24] ceremony, a distribution ceremony including the killing of a bear, the *Shakushain* ceremony, celebrating a Hokkaido Ainu hero in the battle of *Shaushain* in 1669 and held in the honor of Ainu ancestors, and the *Chip Sanke ceremony* a ceremony held in honor of the river god when launching canoes in the Saru River, which reoccurs on a yearly basis.

Intervention with Research

Another approach is to intervene with scientific presentation of facts about these cultural events and gatherings by taking part in, discussing, and scrutinizing foreign as well as the *Wajin* interpretations. During my fieldwork among the Hokkaido Ainu, problems of incompatibility between their own interpretations and the picture emerging from the texts produced about them, were a recurring topic of debate, and many of my informants were unwilling to accept "scientific" interpretations of their lifestyle and ways.

To counteract a development where the voices and interpretations of foreign and *Wajin* scientists are given priority they organize *Ainu Itak*, Ainu native language, classes, supervised by Ainu *Ekashi*, Ainu elders, giving the Ainu opportunities to practice their own language, read about the deeds of their heroes, and learn their history. The curricula includes also discussing such things as correct terminology when referring to Hokkaido Ainu place names, analyzing the ways in which these names have been altered and how this has led to the loss of essential knowledge about the characteristics of the places. Hokkaido Ainu place-names give information not only about the general topography but also about other characteristics, such as the place where benevolent gods live, the river with an abundance of trout fish, the place where people may hunt but not settle down, and so forth. With the hope of replacing the standard picture of the "traditional" Hokkaido Ainu way of life with a picture of diversity, the participants are also informed about local and regional variants of their native language.[25] Recent and much debated concepts are those depicting the Saru River, a river of great importance to the Hokkaido Ainu, and the proper concept for addressing the salmon, the staple food among the Ainu. For example, the Hokkaido Ainu do not use the term *Saru Pet*,[26] the Japanese word for Saru River, but refer to the river as *Shi –shi- ri-muka* and when addressing the salmon, they use the Ainu concept *Shiepe*, where *shi* stands for real, *e* for eating and *pe* for things—real eating things. Such practices and interests have resulted in plans to write an Ainu-Japanese dictionary, the intension being to establish a link between their indigenous language and the inherent ideological substance or meaning of their activities and practices. Historically, the critique against *Wajin* and foreign attempts to translate their language has been strong among the Hokkaido Ainu. Linguists, ever since it has been studied have labeled the Ainu language a dying language.[27] To the contemporary Hokkaido Ainu, the Ainu *Itak*, especially the use of the proper Ainu words, is a matter of great concern.[28]

The initiative for the development described above, is largely through the work of Shigeru Kayano who is of Ainu descent. His interest in his Ainu origins, his concern for the situation of the Hokkaido Ainu and also his writings, depicting their traditional and contemporary lifestyle and belief system, have inspired many Hokkaido Ainu to follow his example.[29] Today we find Ainu all over Hokkaido who are creating a manifold picture of the Hokkaido Ainu customs and ways. At the present time, Shigeru Kayano is not only commonly accepted as a virtual authority on the culture of the Hokkaido Ainu, but he is, in a sense, the embodiment of their entire culture. This is an image created as much by his interest in and his work with Hokkaido Ainu matters as by his frequent appearances on television and radio where he acts as an official representative of the Hokkaido Ainu people.[30]

An Integrated Project

The two different approaches illustrated above are, in fact, not two distinct and separate approaches but an integrated project. The display of themselves and their material culture in combination with the teaching, learning, discussing, and debating of their cultural and religious heritage serve as a means, for the Hokkaido Ainu, to work with, recapture and/or learn skills and practices belonging to their sociocultural tradition. Such activities emanate from a concern with building knowledge of their Hokkaido Ainu heritage and material culture, lifestyle, and belief system. It is as much a way of understanding one's past and present, as it is a means to establish belonging, that is, identifying with people of Hokkaido Ainu descent and their ways. For the Hokkaido Ainu, the act of putting a face to their culture is an indispensable means of unequivocally defining their own position. This presentation of their otherness, in a Nation-State where cultural and ethnic homogeneity constitute the very foundation on which it is built, encompasses a larger authenticating project manifest via a commodity form of a profound constitutive process of cultural identity, one that must be manifested for others—and the majority ethnic group in particular—if it is to have any real existence. It is in defining themselves for the *Wajin*, their significant Other, that they establish their specificity.

Alternative Ways of Understanding the Present Development

In conclusion, and to nuance the above understanding, I like to insert a brief discussion reflecting my view when it comes to alternative ways of understanding their activities and in doing this I limit myself to two perspectives. The first one deals with a perspective where the activities of the Hokkaido Ainu are seen as folklore, that is, a mere display of their values and beliefs for tourists and the larger public. The second one deals with a perspective incorporating their activities and the understanding of these activities into a commercial model.

The folkloristic model is, in my view, a serious misinterpretation of those who fail to see the relationship between their beliefs and the activities behind the practicing of them. This misinterpretation, I link to an understanding of their activities as a means to creating themselves, experiencing their customs and belief system as parts that have been lost, namely, something external to themselves that they strive to regain. With this approach, a deeper understanding of how and why the Hokkaido Ainu explore their past and present is lost. In my opinion, such an approach tells more about the state ideology in Japan and its influence on mainstream research than the beliefs and practices behind the activities of the contemporary Hokkaido Ainu.

The latter model, the one dealing with commercial aspects of their activities, has some bearing in the sense that, of the Hokkaido Ainu 60 percent depend on social welfare to a greater or lesser extent. Undoubtedly, their activities provide them with means to support their families and themselves. Hence, I would not go so far as to deny commercial aspects of their activities. Yet, such aspects should not, in my opinion, overshadow the time and effort the Hokkaido Ainu devote to learn about their social and cultural heritage. Their involvement, as well as the skills required, must be ascribed their rightful value and viewed as a means to stimulate or activate traditionally based activities, incorporating them into their present conditions rather than satisfying purely material needs.

Appropriating the Future

Under this heading, I emphasize two different themes. One theme deals with the recent development occurring in the Nibutani village, especially the years following the recognition of the Hokkaido Ainu as a cultural and religious minority. The other theme deals with aspects related to their active involvement in the global community of indigenous peoples. When discussing the first theme, I place my point of departure in an area of research that explores the relationship of their customs and ways with reference to indigenous understandings of them, focusing especially on questions concerning the ideological content in relation to performance and display.

Ideological Content in Relation to Performance and Display

On my arrival in 1995, the activities in Nibutani seemed to adhere to the pattern revealed to me in 1985–1988. In the interviews, they spoke with enthusiasm about Hokkaido Ainu networking, about associating with and learning from each other about their joint participation in various Ainu related projects and religious activities. However, when discussing the *Iyomante* ceremony, they gave voice to uncertainties concerning possibilities to continue the practicing of this ceremony. They mentioned problems related to the length of time and efforts for its preparation. The bear cub has to be kept in human custody until it reaches fertility, which involves it being, looked after and fed by members of the "host family." They also mentioned the danger involved when catching the bear cub and when sending away the bear to its ancestors. This way of talking about the ceremony was new to me. In my previous interviews such practical obstacles were never an issue. At that time, they spoke with enthusiasm about Nibutani hosting the ceremony in 1989.

Another example was their discussion of the use of modern equipment when performing the *Chip Sanke* ceremony, the exclusion of the building of canoes for the ceremony and their transportation to the Saru River. In the views of my informants, the canoes cannot be used a second time, which was the case when performing the ceremony in 1995. The construction of canoes for the ceremony is an enterprise involving the selecting and cutting of appropriate trees and engaging the most skilled wood carvers in the Hokkaido area, who perform various rituals tied to the canoe-building process. In the year 1995, these rituals were not performed. Furthermore, instead of enrolling the participants for transporting the canoes to the Saru River, an enterprise aimed at instilling the participants with feelings of responsibility and belonging, big trucks equipped with hydraulic lifts were used.

A third example deals with the Nibutani Ainu Cultural Museum. This museum is built with funds from the prefecture government. It is located on a hill overlooking the Saru River, with a cluster of *Chise*,[31] at one of its sides. The demand to construct a Hokkaido Ainu museum in Nibutani village was a topic much discussed during my previous visits. At that time, it was wishful thinking, due both to economic costs and the fact that Nibutani already had one exhibition area, the *Shiryoka*.[32]

When presenting Ainu lifestyle, religious beliefs and myths, the museum uses videocassettes and taped recordings. With a push on a button, the visitors can either watch such things as Ainu "traditional" wedding ceremony, how to build an Ainu-style house, children's games, the *Iyomante* ceremony, or listen to such things as *Yukara*, *Kamuiyukara*, and *Uuepekere*, standing for epics, myths, and old tales, respectively. In the interviews, my informants gave voice to a certain degree of skepticism toward this way of presentation. Among other things, they mentioned feelings of alienation. In their opinion, the museum has no Ainu spirit and "smell," meaning that the museum lacks an Ainu atmosphere. They preferred the *Shiryoka*. With this development, questions concerning the ideological content in relation to performance and display are actualized. At that time, and with practical issues related to the *Chip Sanke-* and *Iyomante* ceremonies as well as the design and presentation of their material culture and lifestyle in the Nibutani Ainu Cultural Museum as points of references, performance and display have come to play the upper hand. The picture is, however, not complete. Using other aspects of the *Chip Sanke* ceremony such as the word arrangements in the ceremonial speeches and the Nibutani Ainu Cultural Museum arrangements when putting their handicrafts on display as points of reference, the picture becomes more complex.

An important ingredient in the *Chip Sanke* ceremony consists of the ceremonial speeches held by Ainu *Ekashi*. In the year 1995, the *Ekashi* spoke in their native tongue and with word arrangements that differed from *Wajin* translations of their language. This is a powerful statement, reflecting both their resistance to use *Wajin* translations of their Ainu *Itak* and the importance they attach to the linking of their native language to the inherent ideological substance or meaning of their practices and activities.

When referring to the museum's display of their handicrafts; in connection with the display of these items, photo images of the local crafts men/women were placed next to their products, a design very much appreciated by the Hokkaido Ainu craftsmen/women. In their opinion, this way of presentation instilled both feelings of craftsmanship pride and a sense of connectedness with craftsmen/women in fields related to the production and manufacture of Ainu material items. Together, these two aspects show the importance they attach to associating with and learning from each other, serving the purpose of creating a manifold picture of their heritage as well as a profound knowledge of Ainu craftsmanship.

Taking view of these developments as a whole, I interpret it as a way of linking past and present practices. It is a way of establishing continuity between the two. In this light, display and performance issues become a question of making their traditions "living, social and networking practices." This is a perspective counteracting, among other things, a view of their practices and activities as something external to themselves, or as something belonging in the past.

The Hokkaido Ainu as a Part of the Global Community of Indigenous Peoples

When discussing this theme, my focus is on a development where feelings of joint participation in a common tradition have come to include not only one's own group but also indigenous groups coming from all over the world. I start with the grassroot level enivsaged in the *Ichi Man Nen Sai* ceremony.

Authenticity vis-à-vis Uniting Aspects of the Living Cultural Traditions of Indigenous Peoples

In the case of the Nibutani Ainu, the *Ichi Man Nen Sai* ceremony has come to intensify questions concerning authenticity vis-à-vis uniting aspects of the living cultural traditions of indigenous peoples. This ceremony is a joint Ainu *Wajin* ceremony stretching over a period of five days, dating back to the year 1989. It is a camping arrangement held in the bush, one hour's drive from Nibutani village. In 1995, this event gathered some three hundred people coming from all over the world and with the sole purpose of paying indigenous peoples their respect. When interviewing participants of non-Ainu and non-*Wajin* descent they declared that they attended because they share indigenous peoples concern for Mother Nature, and that they support demonstrations against the exploitation of the natural resources. When interviewing participants of *Wajin* descent they declared that the Ainu are the aboriginal inhabitants in Japan and they view themselves as of Ainu descent.

The Nibutani Ainu did not like this mixture. They did not attend the ceremony but referred to it as a kind of hippie gathering. In the interviews, this negative attitude was traced to the strong leadership of Shigeru Kayano, directing the development occurring in Hokkaido Ainu matters with a firm grip. Tracing the negative response amongst the Nibutani Ainu to Shigeru Kayano's strong leadership is not un-reflected. There are those who have strong objections. There is a variation in language, custom, and lifestyle in the Hokkaido area and with Shigeru Kayano's strong leadership there is a risk that these will be understood as mere variations of the Nibutani variant—a way of monopolizing the existing dialects, customs, and lifestyles. In this light, local and regional variants run the risk of being ranked. This is a development pointing to the fact that the Nibutani Ainu, under Shigeru Kayano's leadership, have taken over the Japanese model of ranking cultures rather than analyzing them.

With this development, there exist three different views. One gives the Nibutani area a kind of exclusiveness when it comes to defining Hokkaido Ainu language, customs, and lifestyle, as well as the inherent ideological content to go with them. This is a view focusing on the necessity to isolate and separate the inherent ideological content of this specific understanding of the Hokkaido Ainu culture and tradition from other living indigenous cultures and traditions. It is an authenticating project within specific and defined borders. One emphasizes the manifoldness in Hokkaido Ainu language, lifestyle, and customs. It is an authenticating project, recognizing differences and variations within the Hokkaido area. Finally, there is the one emphasizing uniting aspects of the living cultural traditions of indigenous peoples, taking a view of the ideological content as something transparent and transforming, locating it in an ever changing reality.

However, in the Hokkaido Ainu case, these views can be understood as complementary in the sense that they serve as a focal point activating internal debates and discussions concerning what are and what are not, their Hokkaido Ainu cultural and social tradition. At the same time, they also function as a means to establish continuity with certain aspects of their past. In this way, the different views create an opening for the Hokkaido Ainu to elaborate and develop, both in their practices and performances, understandings of their customs and beliefs, linking these to their present activities and practices.

A Political Dimension

By joining the global community of indigenous peoples, the Hokkaido Ainu are given a means to fight subordination and discrimination on the international arena. For example, in response to the indifference of their own view of themselves as a distinct ethnic minority within the Japanese Nation-State, they dispute the idea that indigenous issues are the sole jurisdiction of the Japanese Nation-State. In the late 1970s, Hokkaido Ainu representatives traveled to China and Alaska to participate in meetings on indigenous affairs and in the early 1980s they attended international indigenous conferences in Greenland and Asia. Such actions made it difficult to deny their existence and in 1991, they received status as a cultural and religious minority. In 1993, The Nibutani Forum Organizing Committee arranged The Nibutani Forum, an international conference on indigenous affairs, a conference they hosted again in the year 2005. The main aim of the Nibutani Forum in 1993, was to share and discuss problems concerning steps to be taken in the future, consequences concerning the exploitation of their natural resources, political, social, and economic factors more generally, as well as educational preferences, especially, the necessity to incorporate the language of indigenous peoples in the curricula of the nations to which they belong. Above all, this conference gave the Hokkaido Ainu an opportunity to discuss and elaborate the premises governing their present condition with indigenous groups coming from all over the world.[33]

The initiative to arrange this forum indicates that the Hokkaido Ainu view the international arena of indigenous peoples as a resource in their discussions and negotiation with the Japanese Nation-State, using the situation and development of other indigenous peoples as a platform for future development and practices. It has paid off. In 1997, The New Ainu Law, *Ainu Shinpo* "Law on Promotion of Ainu Culture and Facilitation of Popular Understanding of Ainu Tradition," replaced the old law from 1899, "The Hokkaido Former Aborigines Protection Act." At this same time, that is in 1997, The Sapporo District Court recognized the Hokkaido Ainu as an indigenous minority within the Japanese Nation-State.[34]

Modern technique, in the form of the newly established ainunews website on the Internet increases and broadens the international arena of the Hokkaido Ainu. It reaches out to a variety of peoples and groups of people representing various intellectual and political schoolings and influences. The mailing list consists of, besides persons of Ainu descent—politically active persons as well as scholars—native peoples, persons with an interest in the lives of indigenous peoples, persons belonging to stigmatized and discriminated groups of peoples, human rights and environmental activists as well as *Wajin* and foreign scientists of various disciplines. The ainunews covers a great variety of topics, such as environmental and human rights issues, issues concerned with how to get access to and find reliable statistics on Hokkaido Ainu living in Japan and elsewhere, their socioeconomic situation, where to find literature about the Ainu lifestyle, tradition, language, belief-system, Japanese as well as foreign, and so forth. In addition, the ainunews informs about gatherings, and meetings, not only international gatherings of indigenous peoples, excursions and ceremonial gatherings, but also Ainu music- and dancing events. Without doubt, this composition of topics and persons constitutes an important asset both in a political sense and with respect to information and research. In the following, I place my point of departure in the ainunews of January 21, 23 and February 7, 2005, when the dam-building project in the Saru River and also the incorporation of the language of indigenous peoples in the curricula of the nations to which they belong, were on the agenda. These issues were debated and discussed during the Nibutani Forum in 1993. Before entering the issue of the exploitation of Saru River, I give a brief view of the discussions related to the building of the Nibutani Dam during my fieldwork. At that time, the construction of a dam in this area was lively debated and discussed and the Ainu saw it as a severe crime against Nature. Acres of their lands would be flooded and it would also affect the spawning of the salmon in the Saru River. The Hokkaido Ainu only catch the salmon after spawning, and with a dam, the spawning was jeopardized. In the discussions with the authorities, it was understood that individuals whose land would be covered with water would receive compensation in the form of cash money. Everybody agreed money does not compensate such damages.[35]

The Nibutani Dam project was taken up, Sunday, January 23, 2005, as a response to an e-mail sent Friday, January 21, 2005, to the moderator. The ainunews participants were informed about an article by Georgina Stevens on the Nibutani Dam project titled "More Than Paper: Protecting Ainu Culture and influencing Japanese Dam Development."[36] The article discusses the views expressed by the authorities of Biratori region, where the Nibutani village is located, and who, from the new cultural and ecological preservation perspective, view the Nibutani Dam initiative as an exceptional positive development for an indigenous population. In addition to this information, the participants were further informed that, under the title "The Ainu and Human Rights: Domestic and International Legal Protection," the article had been published in 2001 in "Japanese Studies."[37] The participants were recommended to read the article; "If you haven't read it yet, it's well worth it. It is very thought provoking and shows you what the situation is like. It's also encouraging to know that there are laws in place that could help protect Ainu culture, language and land."

At this same date, the participants were also informed about a day nursery, built in 1982, in Biratori town. This nursery was built for the purpose of nurturing Ainu children in the Ainu language and it was funded with money collected from Ainu people and donations by others. As it turned out, the Hokkaido Prefectural government and the Ministry of Health and Welfare, notified the nursery that no other language than the Japanese should be used in the nursery if it wished to receive operational subsidies from the government body. The reason for their decision was based on the monolingual requirements of Article 24 and 35 of the Children's Welfare Law and "the law concerning a proper execution of budgets concerning subsidies and others." As a result, the plans to nurture Ainu children in their own language at the day nursery was abandoned. The question asked by the person who raised the subject, was if anyone on the mailing list knows what has happened with respect to Article 24 and 35, since the new law, the Cultural Promotion Act for the Preservation and Dissemination of the Ainu Culture of 1997, replaced these two laws. Monday, February 7, 2005, the question was answered by an inserted copy of Georgia Stevens' article on "The Ainu and Human Rights," mentioned earlier giving detailed information concerning Articles 24 and 35, urging the participants on the mailing list to look further into the matter.

The above examples illustrate the ainunews as a platform for taking up and continuing debates and discussions of Hokkaido Ainu topics on the agenda of the international indigenous peoples group. In this regard, and on this level, the ainunews constitutes an important additional resource in the Hokkaido Ainu negotiations with the Japanese Nation-State. On another level and with the versified knowledge of the participants in mind, the ainunews puts the Hokkaido Ainu matters, historic as well as more recent affairs and conditions, under multifaceted lenses. In this regard, and with respect to research, the body of knowledge inherent in the ainunews functions as a means to work against scientific analyses of the Hokkaido Ainu as a primitive and backward group of people. In this light, the collective knowledge serves the Hokkaido Ainu in more than a political sense. It serves to instill them with a sense of pride and self-esteem, helping them restore their past and present. Looking at it from this angle, it may work to encourage those who hide their identity to come forward and acknowledge their Ainu identity, read about their history, learn Ainu skills, and so on. However, due to the fact that the ainunews profile is political more than anything else, the body of knowledge runs the risk of being reduced to a means of politicizing the development occurring among the Hokkaido Ainu. This has a positive as well as a negative side. On the positive side, this politicizing constitutes a forceful tool when it comes to support and backs up the Hokkaido Ainu rights to determine the future of their community. Considering the fact that the Hokkaido Ainu have suffered tremendous hardship in Japanese custody, being robbed of their territories, their customs, language and lifestyle as well as their means to support themselves and their families, this politicizing is not bad a thing. Rather, it is highly relevant. Yet, on the other hand, it easily disguises other aspects of the reality in which the Hokkaido Ainu live and operate. Hence, on the negative side, this politicizing threatens to downgrade the collective activities of the Hokkaido Ainu, the interest and engagement in their Ainu heritage, practices and ways, to issues of subordination and discrimination. Looking at it from this angle, it does not work to include those Hokkaido Ainu who have other interests than purely political ones, that is, those who hide their Ainu identity as well as those who place collective- and networking activities of the Hokkaido Ainu community at the center of interest and whose engagement is a way of identifying with the past and be proud of it.

Summary

In this article, I discuss the Hokkaido Ainu situation. It emphasizes the Hokkaido Ainu ways of maneuvering in a larger sociocultural system cherishing ethnic and cultural homogeneity as a strong value orientation. My understanding builds on a view of the Hokkaido Ainu as active players in the world that surrounds them. The article begins with a brief presentation of the Historic Hokkaido Ainu, followed by a discussion of scientific interpretations of them and their lifestyle, particularly research on their origins. In my opinion, this research, more than any other, has contributed to a view of the Hokkaido Ainu as backward and primitive. In my discussions, I point to a political dimension of this research, aimed at smoothing the way for a view of the assimilation policy as being successful.

This is followed by a discussion where my focus is on ways in which the Hokkaido Ainu take matters into their own hands, emphasizing two different themes. One theme deals with the display of their material culture and lifestyle and the other deals with their intervention with research, showing how these two together encompass a larger authenticating project, manifest via a commodity form of a constitutive process of cultural identity.

The final and most extensive part of the article, deals, on the one hand, with the relationship of Ainu customs and ways with reference to indigenous understandings of them. On the other hand, it deals with their entrance into the global community of indigenous peoples. The focus, in the first part, is on questions related to ideological content in relation to performance and display, showing how they interconnect, contributing to making the Hokkaido Ainu ways, living, social and networking practices, counteracting a view of their practices and activities as something external to themselves. The focus, in the second part, is on the international indigenous peoples group and the newly established ainunews website on the Internet. In my discussion, I show how these two resources intertwine. In different, yet complimentary ways, they function as important resources in the Hokkaido Ainu negotiations with the Japanese Nation-State.

Notes

1. "Wajin" is an ethnic concept, whereas "Japanese" is a national concept. For a lengthy discussion of these concepts, see Sjöberg 1993.
2. Government recognition of the Hokkaido Ainu beyond mere acknowledgement of their existence has been, and still is, a highly political issue. See Dietz 1999, Tsunemoto 1999.
3. See for instance, Munro 1962, Seligman 1962, Lèvi-Strauss 1969, Watanabe 1972, 1975, Lee and DeVore 1975. See also Kreiner 1993,

Fitzhugh and Dubreuil 1999, volumes bringing together research material on the studies of the Ainu religious beliefs, language, history, and material culture.

4. Takakura 1960: 23.

5. See Takakura 1960, Cornell 1964, Sjöberg 1993, Kayano 1994, Fitzhugh and Dubreuil 1999.

6. Meiji as a concept stands for "enlightened government." The Meiji era started in the year 1868.

7. Baba 1980: 63, Smith 1983.

8. See Cornell 1964, Utari Kyokai 1987, Sjöberg 1993. See also Howell 1999, Ohtsuka 1999, Siddle 1999.

9. Fitzhugh and Dubreuil 1999.

10. Fitzhugh 1999: 9–28.

11. See for instance, Batchelor 1932, 1971, Munro 1962, Seligman 1962, Hilger 1967, Kodama 1970, Watanabe 1972, 1975, Peng and Geiser 1977, Refsing 1980, Kreiner 1993, Fitzhugh and Dubreuil 1999.

12. See for instance, Levin 1958, Kodama 1970, Peng and Geiser 1977, Ohnuki-Tierney 1981, Arutiunov 1999, Yamaura 1999, Kikuchi 1999, Ishida 1999.

13. Kodama 1970.

14. Arutiunov 1999.

15. See Kojiki and Nihonshoki, ancient Japanese records and Munro 1911, Takakura 1960, Kodama 1970.

16. For a lengthy discussion see Sjöberg 1993.

17. Researchers are in disagreement concerning both the origins of the concept of *Emishi* and the territories they are supposed to have populated and at what point in time (see for example Takakura 1960, Kodama 1970, Sjöberg 1993).

18. For a lengthy discussion of the theories related to who the *Emishi* people are and their origin see for instance Takakura 1960, Kodama 1970.

19. See Sjöberg 1993.

20. See for instance, Cornell 1964, Hilger 1967, Peng and Geiser 1977, Refsing 1980.

21. Since registration as "Ainu" is an individual choice many Hokkaido Ainu do not come forward and this in turn has to do with discrimination against them. At the present time registered Ainu amounts to 24.000 individuals. See for instance Utari Kyokai 1987, Sjöberg 1993, Dietz, 1999, Siddle 1999, Tsunemoto 1999.

22. Sjöberg 1993.

23. This ceremony was "originally" performed on an individual basis, whereas today it is transformed into a collective ceremony.

24. According to most reports, the *Iyomante* ceremony is the most precious of all ritual performances practiced by the Hokkaido Ainu. It connects to the hunting activities of the men and it is included into the sacred realm. According to Batchelor, the *Iyomante* ceremony represented "the outward

expression of the greatest racial religious act of worship of the Ainu brotherhood" (1932: 37).

25. See Sjöberg 1993, 1997a, b, 1999.

26. During my fieldwork the proper Ainu name of this river was lively discussed and debated. Yet, at that time people seemed to have settled for the term "Saru pet," where "pet" stands for river in the Ainu language. In the Japanese language "pet" has been replaced by the term "betsu," due to the fact that the Japanese can neither pronounce the word "pet," nor depict it in writing (Sjöberg 1993).

27. See for instance, Batchelor 1938, Naert 1960, Tamura 1983, 1999, Refsing 1986, 1993, 1998.

28. "To us the Ainu Itak is so important that a person will feel that he must die early so that the proper words can be spoken for his requiem. When a person is born on earth, who would wish to die early? But my father and his friends wished to die early, because they wanted to have a proper Ainu requiem" (Gathering in Ainu Moshir, 1994).

29. Kayano 1974a, b, c, d, 1975, 1976, 1977a, b, c, 1978, 1979, 1980, 1985, 1987, 1988, 1994.

30. See Sjöberg 1993,1997a, b, 1999.

31. *Chise* are Ainu-style houses built of oak and linden pillars and with thatched roofs.

32. Today, the profile of the *Shiryoka* is somewhat changed, compared to my previous visits, aiming at displaying various cultural items belonging to indigenous groups all over the world.

33. Resulting in a report published in a book entitled *Gathering In Ainu Moshir, The Land of the Ainu: Messages from Indigenous Peoples in the World* (1994). The various indigenous groups, presenting reports are the following; USA: Chippewa, Chemehuevi, Abenaki, Tolova, Onondaga, Western Shoshoni; Canada: Kwagiulth, Nisgaa, Mamalilikala, Namgis, Haida, Heiltsuk, N'akwaxdaw, Sansei, Mohawk; Cree: Republic of South Africa; Phillipines; Cordelliera, Sweden; Sami, Japan; Ainu, Guatemala; Maya, Republic of Nicaragua.

34. See Utari Kyokai 1987, Sjöberg 1991, 1993, 1995, 1997a, b, 1999, Dietz, 1999, Siddle 1999, Tsunemoto 1999.

35. Sjöberg 1993, 2004.

36. Cultural Survival Quarterly (CSQ) Winter 2005, pp. 44–47.

37. Stevens, Georgia 2001, The Ainu And Human Rights: Domestic and International legal Protection, in *Japanese Studies* 21, 2: 121–198.

References

Arutiunov, S. A. 1999 Ainu Origin Theories, in *Ainu Spirit of a Northern People*, 29–31, edited by William W. Fitzhugh and Chisato O. Dubreuil, Smithsonian Institute: University of Washington Press.

Baba, Y. 1980 Study of Minority–Majority Relations: The Ainu and the Japanese in Hokkaido, in *The Japanese Interpreter*, 60–92.

Batchelor, J. 1932 *The Ainu Bear Festival*, Sapporo: The Transaction of the Asiatic Society of Japan.

———, 1938 *Ainu Eiwa Jiten*, Tokyo: Iwanami Shoten.

———, 1971 *The Ainu Life and Lor*, New York: Johnsson Reprint Corporation.

Burger, J. 1990 *The Gaia Atlas of First Peoples: A Future for the Indigenous World*, New York: Anchor Books Doubleday.

Cornell, J. 1964 Ainu Assimilation and Cultural Extinction. *Ethnology*, 3: 287–304.

Davis, G. 1987 Japan's Indigenous Indians: The Ainu. *Tokyo Journal*, October issue: 7–13, 18–19.

Dietz, Kelly L. 1999 Ainu in the International Arena, in *Ainu Spirit of a Northern People*, 359–365, edited by William W. Fitzhugh and Chisato O. Dubreuil, Smithsonian Institute: University of Washington Press.

Fagan, B. 1984 *Clash of Culture*, New York: E. F. Freeman & Co.

Fitzhugh William W. and Chisato O. Dubreuil. 1999 *Ainu Spirit of a Northern People*, National Museum of Natural History Smithsonian Institution: University of Washington Press.

Hilger, M. 1967 *Together with the Ainu: A Vanishing People*, Oklahoma: University of Oklahoma Press.

Howell, David L. 1999 The Ainu and The Early Modern Japanese State, in *Ainu Spirit of a Northern People*, 96–101, edited by William W. Fitzhugh and Chisato O. Dubreuil, Smithsonian Institute: University of Washington Press.

Ichida, H. 1999 Ancient People of the North Pacific Rim: Ainu Biological Relationship with Their Neighbors, in *Ainu Spirit of a Northern People*, 52–56, edited by William W. Fitzhugh and Chisato O. Dubreuil, Smithsonian Institute: University of Washington Press.

Kayano, S. 1974 *Kaze no Kamui to Okikurumi*, Tokyo: Komine Shoten.

———, 1974 *Kiboro no Okami*, Tokyo: Komine Shoten.

———, 1974 *Kitsune no Charanke*, Tokyo: Komine Shoten.

———, 1974 *Okikurumi no Bouken*, Tokyo: Komine Shoten.

———, 1975 *Ore no Nibutani*, Tokyo: Suzusawa Shoten.

———, 1976 *Chise Akara*, Tokyo: Miraisha.

———, 1977 *Honoo no Uma*, Tokyo: Suzusawa Shoten.

———, 1977 *Ainu no Min wa Shuu*, Sapporo: Hokuto Shoten.

———, 1977 *Ainu no Mingu*, Tokyo: Suzusawa Shoten.

———, 1978 *Mono to Kokoro*, Tokyo: Komine Shoten.

———, 1979 *Hitotubu no Satoro*, Tokyo: Heibonsha.

———, 1980 *Ainu no Ishibumi*, Tokyo: Asahi Shinbunsha.

———, 1985 *The Romance of the Bear God*, Tokyo: Taishukan.

———, 1987 *Nibutani ni Ikite*, Sapporo: Hokkaido Shinbunsha.

———, 1988 *Kamui Yukar to Mukashibanashi*, Tokyo: Sogakukan.

———, 1994 *Our Land was a Forest—An Ainu Memoir*, Oxford: Westview Press.

Kikuchi, T. 1999 Ainu Ties with Ancient Cultures of Northeast Asia, in *Ainu Spirit of a Northern People*, 47–51, edited by William W. Fitzhugh and Chisato O. Dubreuil, Smithsonian Institute: University of Washington Press.

Kodama, S. 1970 *Ainu Historical and Anthropological Studies*, Sapporo: Hokudai University Press.

Kreiner, J. 1993 *European Studies on Ainu Language and Culture*, edited by Kreiner, J. Muenchen: Iudicium-Verl.

Lee. R. B. and I. DeVore 1975 *Man the Hunter*, Chicago, IL: Aldine Publication Co.

Levin, M.G. 1958 Ethnic Origins of the People of Northeastern Asia, in *Arctic Institute of North America, Anthropology of the North 3*, edited by H. N. Michael, Toronto: University Press of Toronto.

Lévi-Strauss, C. 1969 *The Elementary Structure of Kinship*, Boston, MA: Beacon Press.

Munro, N. 1911 *Prehistoric Japan*, Tokyo: Daiichi Shobo.

———, 1962 *Ainu Creed and Cult*, London: Greenwood Press.

Naert, P. 1960 *Aiona: En Bok om Ainu—Det Vita Folket I Fjärran Östern*, Stockholm: Natur och Kultur.

Nibutani Forum Organizing Committee 1994 *Gathering in AinuMoshir The Land of the Ainu: Messages from Indigenous Peoples in the World*, Japan: Eikoh Educational and Cultural Institute/Yushisha Co, Ltd.

Ohnuki-Tierney, E.1981 *Illness and Healing among the Sachalin Ainu, A Symbolic Interpretation*, Cambridge: Cambridge University Press.

Ohtsuka, K. 1999 Tourism, Assimilation and Ainu Survival Today, in *Ainu Spirit of a NorthernPeople*, 92–95, edited by William W. Fitzhugh and Chisato O. Dubreuil, Smithsonian Institute: University of Washington Press.

Peng F. C. C. and P. Geiser 1977 *The Ainu: The Past in the Present*, Hiroshima: Bunka Hyoron Publishing Company.

Refsing, K. 1980 The Ainu People of Japan, *IWGIA Newsletter*, no. 24: 79–92. Copenhagen.

———, 1986 *The Ainu language: The Morphology and Syntax of the Shizunai Dialect*, Aarhus: Aarhus University Press.

———, 1993 The Ainu Concept of Time as Expressed Through Language, in *European Studies on Ainu Language and Culture*, 91–100, edited by Kreiner, J. Muenchen: Iudicium-Verl.

Reischauer, E. O. and Craig, A. M.1973 *Japan, Tradition and Transformation*, Cambridge: Cambridge University Press.

Saito, H. 1912 *Japan's Historia*, Stockholm: P. A. Nordstedt och Söner.

Seligman, B. Z. 1962 Social Organization, Postscript, in *Ainu Creed and Cult*, 141–158, edited by Munro, N. Cambridge University Press.

Siddle, R. 1999 From Assimilation to Indigenous Rights: Ainu Resistance Since 1869, in *Ainu Spirit of a Northern People*, 108–115, edited by William W. Fitzhugh and Chisato O. Dubreuil, Smithsonian Institute: University of Washington Press.

Sjöberg, K. 1991 Mr. Ainu: The Ainu Struggle for a Cultural Definition, in *Perspectives on Japan and Korea*, 122–142, edited by Kalland and Sörensen, NIAS/NAJAKS.

———, 1993 *The Return of the Ainu*, London: Harwood Academic Publichers.

———, 1995 Practicing Ethnicity in a Hierarchical Culture, in *Indigenous Peoples of Asia*, 373–389, edited by R. H. Barnes, Andrew Gray, and Benedict Kingsbury, Michigan: Ann Arbor, Michigan.

————— 1997a Ainufolkets religion i historiskt och antropologiskt perspektiv, i *Svensk religionshistorisk årsskrift*, 66–86, edited by Westerlund, D., Uppsala: Svensk religionshistorisk årsskrift.

————— 1997b Ainu och Naturen i *Att kräva livet åte,r* 122–134, edited by Dahre, U., Lund: Agora.

————— 1998 *The Methodological Looking-glass Principles in Practice, the Case of the Lubicon Cree Group*, Lund: Studentlitteratur.

————— 1999 En resa i identitet, tid och geografi—ainufolket på Hokkaido, i *Mer än Kalla Fakta*, 146–164, edited by Sjöberg, K., Lund: Studentlitteratur.

————— 2001 *Asian Folklore Studies 2001.*: 354–356, edited by Knecht, P., Nagoya: Nanzan Institute.

————— 2004 Rethinking Indiegenous Religious Traditions: The Case of the Ainu, in *Beyond Primitivism: Indigenous Religious Traditions and Modernity*, 224–244, edited by Jacob K. Olupona, New York: Routledge.

Smith, R. J. 1983 *Japanese Society: Traditional Self and the Social Order*, Cambridge: Cambridge University Press.

Stevens, G. 2001 The Ainu And Human Rights: Domestic and International Legal Protection, in *Japanese Studies*, 21, 2: 121–198.

————— 2005 More Than Paper: Protecting Ainu Culture and Influencing Japanese Dam Development, Cultural Survival Quarterly, Winter: 44–47.

Takakura, S. 1960 The Ainu of Northern Japan. *Transactions of the American Philosophical Society*, Philadelphia, 50: 1–92.

Tamura, S. 1983 *Ainu Itak*, Tokyo: Tokyo University Press.

————— 1999 Ainu Language: Features and Relationships, in *Ainu Spirit of a Northern People*, 57–66, edited by William W. Fitzhugh and Chisato O. Dubreuil, Smithsonian Institute: University of Washington Press.

Tsunemoto, T. 1999 The Ainu Shinpo, in *Ainu Spirit of a Northern People*, 366–368, edited by William W. Fitzhugh and Chisato O. Dubreuil, Smithsonian Institute: University of Washington Press.

Utari Kyokai 1987 *Statement Submitted to the Fifth Session of the Working Group on Indigenous Population*, Geneva, Switzerland.

Watanabe, H. 1972 *The Ainu Ecosystem*, Tokyo: Tokyo University Press.

————— 1975 Subsistence and Ecology of Northern Food Gatherers, with Special References to the Ainu, in *Man the Hunter*, 69–77, edited by Lee and DeVore, Chicago: Aldine Publication Co.

Yamaura, K. 1999 Prehistoric Hokkaido and Ainu Origins, in *Ainu Spirit of a Northern People*, 39–46, edited by William W. Fitzhugh and Chisato O. Dubreuil, Smithsonian Institute: University of Washington Press.

CHAPTER 3

FROM FORCED ASSIMILATION TO CULTURAL REVITALIZATION: TAIWAN'S ABORIGINES AND THEIR ROLE IN TAIWAN NATIVISM

Michael Rudolph

Introduction

Since the beginning of the nineties, Taiwan's society faced a situation of rapid political and cultural change. After four centuries of domination by foreign powers—the Spanish, the Dutch, the Chinese, the Japanese, and the "mainlanders" who had come from the mainland as refugees with Chiang Kai-shek after 1945—the first Taiwan-born president in Taiwan's history Li Denghui was officially confirmed in his office in 1990. Though Li belonged to the Chinese Nationalist Party (KMT) that had ruled Taiwan for over forty years, the change was enthusiastically welcomed by Taiwan's Han, since Li had his cultural and religious roots in Taiwan and was believed to work much more on behalf of Taiwan's population than the mainland-born presidents of the Jiang family before who had never relinquished the hope to return to China someday. Only in this moment the issue of identity search of "the Taiwanese" could become a theme of growing significance in the political arena, tolerated now as it did not collide with Li's endeavor to consolidate his power vis-à-vis the mainlanders who were still represented in the government and in the military. At the same time, there also occurred a re-evaluation of Taiwan's relationship to the communist mainland, that tried to hinder this development by more and more aggressive contests of its sovereignty and that once again emphasized its conviction of cultural and genetic homogeneity of Taiwan's and China's population.

The re-negotiation of cultural identities in Taiwan and the construction of a particular history and culture that differentiated Taiwan from China also had its impacts on Taiwan's indigenous population, that—though consisting of at least twelve Malayo-Polynesian groups—makes up no more than 1.6 percent of the population in Taiwan. For the first time in the history of interaction of Han and Non-Han, the languages, cultural traditions and value-systems of ethnic minorities now received growing attention—an attention that in its last consequence not only involved the official recognition of Taiwan's Aborigines as indigenous people in the constitution (1994), but that was also accompanied by the increase of reservation land (1990), the increase of the number of political representatives (1992), the right for rehabilitation of personal names (1995), the implementation of aboriginal mother-languages education (1996), as well as the implementation of specified cultural institutions like the Council of Indigenous Peoples (1996). Partly responsible for these political successes were the endeavors of the social movement of Taiwan's Aborigines (*Taiwan Yuanzhumin shehui yundong*),[1] a movement that in the years following its first blossoming in 1983 had developed rather slowly in its struggle against discrimination and social marginalization, but that after 1990 suddenly received growing respect.

However, if the uninformed reader looks at the manifests and pieces of documentary literature written and published by members of Taiwan's aboriginal elite in the course of the 1990s, he can easily get the impression that all endeavors of Taiwan's Han to create a democratic and multicultural Taiwan vis-à-vis the mainland's authoritarian rule were in vain: Charges of "internal colonialism" and "forced assimilation" of Taiwan's aboriginal people, "intentional destruction" of their cultures and languages by the Han-government, and even of "persecution" and "genocide"[2] were no rarity. The image suggested by this terminology hardly matches with the fact that any declarations connected to these charges could be openly discussed and published in Taiwan at that time, nor does it match with the long list of successes mentioned above.

This chapter will on the one hand discuss the political background that made these successes possible. The influence of Taiwan's political opposition, the Christian church, the anthropologists, but also the nativist tendencies within the ruling KMT government itself were important factors. On the other hand, the article tries to shed some light on the reasons for the harsh and drastic undertones in the voices of aboriginal elites. Besides the contention that several problems still need to be solved—like the nuclear waste problem on Orchid Island or the economical misery of Taiwan's Aborigines in general—and that competing aboriginal leaders often tended to put some stress on such deficiencies in order to appear more convincing in their activities, I also argue that the use of a rough and sometimes exaggerated language was "part of the play" in the Taiwan of the 1990s, where nativist aboriginal elites in a Fanonian sense tried to display an un-dominated aboriginal "subjectivity"[3] and where the main supporters of the aboriginal movement—that is, the oppositional Taiwanese Han elites—did not mind that the KMT regime was put under some additional pressure. After Chen Shuibian's election and the government take-over by the political opposition—the *Democratic Development Party* (DPP)—in May 2000, slogans like those just mentioned were hardly heard anymore.

Genocide, Assimilation, and Discrimination in the Past: Japanese Colonialism and the KMT's Assimilation Policy[4]

The Japanese Period

In order to give the reader a better understanding of the dramatic changes that took place in Taiwan in the beginning of the 1990s, I will first give a short description of the preceding periods, that is, Japanese colonialism and KMT-rule under martial law.

When the Japanese left Taiwan in 1945 after half a century of colonial rule, it soon became clear that Taiwan's aboriginal population had profited much less from the modernization policy of its rulers than their Chinese counterparts on the island. While the latter unexpectedly found themselves in a situation they would hardly have dreamt of in their most courageous dreams—over night they had inherited a large infrastructure that they were also able to run with the know-how that they had been trained in during the preceding decades. Furthermore, they could eventually practice their own culture again, after eight years of harsh Japanization policy (*huangminhua*) in the course of the Japanese endeavor to build up a Pacific empire—Taiwan's different aboriginal societies were left in a situation of complete helplessness and disorientation. Though liberated from such "bad habits" as head-hunting and tattooing, and though they spoke the language of their former oppressors much more fluently than their Han neighbors, the so-called highsand people (in Japanese: *takasagozoku*) found themselves bare of any means to survive economically or culturally in the new surrounding now dominated by the Han again: Neither did they have the education, the resources or the networks to make investments in the fast growing industry society, nor could they rely on their traditional ways of living anymore, as their social and religious institutions had been largely destroyed by the Japanese who had spent strong efforts to civilize the aboriginal headhunters. The main aim of this civilization project however had been to get hold of the resources in the mountain areas that were desperately needed to build up the Pacific Empire envisaged by the Japanese. Vast loss of human life—also on the Japanese side where large numbers of soldiers and policemen became victims of the aboriginal habit of head-hunting—was the result of the confrontations that evolved.[5] After a number of riots and uprisings, the colonial government in 1917 even agreed to build an airport in order to bomb the areas inhabited by the rebellious Aborigines. Besides of resettlement of the most ferocious tribes to areas near the plains, the Japanese also built electric fences as protection walls against the Aborigines. Nevertheless, the confrontation could not be stopped before 1930, when a last uprising of the Atayal of Wushe occurred. In this uprising, more than 100 Japanese and almost 1,000 Atayal lost their lives. German anthropologist Gudula Linck-Kesting (1978) estimates that aboriginal population was decimated by about one-third in the years from 1895 to 1945.[6]

Authoritarian KMT-rule

When the KMT took over the government in Taiwan after Japan's surrender, it adopted the system of reservation zones that had once been established by the Japanese colonial government for better control and more effective exploitation of the mountain areas. Many of these areas now received the additional status of military zones that were closed to the public and only accessible by the local residents. However, this land could only serve as a provisory shelter for about half of Taiwan's aboriginal population, as the other half of them who already lived together with Han in the plains were not given any rights on reservation land. While those who had stayed in the mountains and who from now on were called "mountain compatriots of the mountain areas" (*shandi shanbao*) enjoyed economical aid and privileges like tax exemplification and special quotas in medical and peda-gogical advancement, the so-called mountain compatriots of the flatland (*pingdi shanbao*) had almost totally to rely on themselves and lived in hard competition with their Han neighbors.[7] In the first years after Taiwan's "liberation" they could still make use of pieces of land registered as national land that had been customarily left to them during the Japanese period. But this land afterwards was step-by-step sold to private Han entrepreneurs and enterprises, so that more and more flatland mountain compatriots were forced to go to the big cities where they earned their living either in the construction sector or in the service sector.

Nevertheless, from today's viewpoint, it seems hard to say which of them was the luckier—the mountain compatriots of the mountain areas or the mountain compatriots of the flatland. While those confronted early with modern life—especially the Ami, the Puyuma, and parts of the Paiwan[8]—learnt to cooperate with the Han people, adapted somehow to modern life and were even able to preserve some of their traditions in the urban slums where they lived in groups after their arrival, those Aborigines who had continued to live isolated in the mountains—especially the Atayal, Taroko, Bunun, and Zhou—more and more suffered from their lack of competition ability. On one hand, aboriginal production methods with poor tools on poor land could in no way compete with Han agriculture. On the other hand, the reservation land was diminishing rapidly, as Han population increased steadily and land was getting more valuable every day: Though the reservation land belonged to the state, Han entrepreneurs succeeded in getting that land sold illegally to them, relying on the fact that the state—which confiscated mountain land itself whereever it needed it—would not intervene. Thus, the fate of the mountain compatriots of the mountain areas was even crueller than that of their compatriots in the flatland. When they had to change their life in their communities as per that in the big cities in the end of the sixties, they were not able to catch up with the island's industrialization process that by then had reached a high tide, nor were they able to adapt to a surrounding that was—partly because of their differing living styles, partly because of their looser working habits—extremely hostile to them.[9] Many of them returned frustrated to their crumbling communities. Alcohol, of course, played an important role in this tragedy. A study led by the Taiwan University Medical College in 1992 showed that alcohol abuse was regular in more than 45 percent of the Atayal and Taroko.[10] Though the percentage of alcohol abusers in Ami society was not much lower, they obviously had found better ways to deal with addiction, as there were hardly any violent clashes with Han society. As anthropologist Xu Muzhu from the *Academia Sinica* in Taibei has shown, there were also sociocultural factors that allowed the Ami to adapt more smoothly to Han society: the age-grade hierarchy of this ethnic group—the most salient characteristic of the social system of the Ami—had much more similarities with the social characteristics of Han society than the Atayal's system that formerly had been based on the reverence of the ancestors' souls and norms attached to it like head-hunting, but that was forcibly abolished in the first half of the twentieth century through pressure of the Japanese and Christian missionaries.[11]

However, apart from these historical factors and the sociocultural differences in adaptation behavior,[12] the main reason for the generally bad situation of Taiwan's Aborigines was a sociopolitical one. First, there must be named the inadequate minority policy of the KMT-government. As the KMT tried to hold up the myth that all people on Taiwan were Chinese and that the mainland that belonged to all Chinese would be recovered some day, it not only pursued a policy of severe cultural and lingual homogenization, but also denied to admit the true ethnic and lingual origin of Taiwan's Aborigines. Together with the speakers of the languages of the Sino-Tibetan language family as the Hoklo, the Hakka, and the "mainlanders" who are traditionally all defined as Han Chinese, these peoples whose languages belonged to the Austronesian language family were identified as "descendants of the Yellow Emperor" (*yanhuang zisun*).[13] This was also the reason for the upholding of the official term "mountain compatriots" instead of using terms like "Indigenes" or "Aborigines," terms that would have implied the ethnic minority status of these people including all the cultural and autonomy rights attached to this status guaranteed in the constitution of the Republic of China (ROC).[14] Especially in the field of education, such a classification that denied different cultural backgrounds and adaptation preconditions was not suitable to assist Aborigines in their struggle to cope with their new surrounding. Despite a bonus system that allowed Aborigines as "people of special regions" to have worse grades than average Han to advance in Taiwan's education system, Aborigines showed very bad results, and the percentage of those who proceeded to higher education—their only chance for social mobility—stayed extremely low.

Second, there was the attitude of Han toward ethnic minorities in general that made it hard for Taiwan's Aborigines to adapt to the main society. In the eyes of the Han, Aborigines had "simple brains and well-developed limbs," thus they were only employed in physical work. Known for their "bad working morals" ("work two days and rest three days"), it was very hard for them to find any work at all; once employed, they often faced severe exploitation. Likewise, aboriginal children were discriminated against in school. The Han children, many of whom were jealous because of the bonuses Aborigines enjoyed, teased them with expressions like "savages" and "tattooed people."[15] The superiority feeling expressed by the Han was still intensified by stories like the Wu Feng myth in the schoolbooks, a saga of a noble Confucian in the eighteenth century who tried to liberate the Aborigines from their bad habits and who was cruelly killed for this by the headhunters.

Gradual Changes for Taiwan's Aborigines in the 1980s

Alliance with the Political Opposition: The Formation of the ATA

First signs of change to the situation described above could be observed in the first half of the eighties, when international and domestic pressure on the KMT regime grew after the ROC's exclusion from the UN and social movements received room to develop in Taiwan.[16] One of the first social movements directly following the reorganization of the political opposition movement in the beginning of the 1980s was that of Taiwan's Aborigines. Its origins can be dated back to 1983, when a group of aboriginal intellectuals with strong feelings of cultural alienation and alarmed by the existential and social crisis of their people began to build up ties with the political opposition movement in Taipei. Similar to the latter, the main impetus of the aboriginal movement—after 1984 represented by the Alliance of Taiwanese Aborigines (ATA)—was directed against the continuing rule of the mainlander regime and its inadequate ethnic and cultural policy. Though the "mountain compatriots" had some representatives in Taiwan's parliament bodies—that is, in the Legislative Yuan and in the National Assembly—these were all nominated by the KMT. So they were loyal to the party and did not dare to become a hindrance to party politics. Criticizing these officials for their opportunistic behavior, the members of the ATA fought against the KMT's assimilation policy that they believed was drawing Taiwan's Aborigines close to extinction.[17] They also protested against further exploitation of aboriginal workers made possible by insufficient legislation, as well as against the continued discrimination of Aborigines, as it was expressed by the Wu Feng myth in Taiwanese schoolbooks. When in 1987 the local government of Nantou demolished and desecrated large numbers of aboriginal graves in the course of the opening up of aboriginal land in Dongpu in Northwest-Taiwan, this incident provoked the first major action of the ATA, as the incident was seen representative for the exploitation and discrimination Aborigines endured in Taiwan. On April 3, 1987, the ATA organized a demonstration to the Executive Yuan, where it presented a petition with the following remarks:

> To us aboriginal people, ancestral land is the same as life. Our distinctive culture, vital communities, and whether or not our ethnic consciousness (*zuqun yishi*) can be preserved all depend on land. In fact land is life, land is identity.

Further, four demands were raised:

1. Punish the officials responsible;
2. The Executive Yuan should take immediate steps to show its respect for aboriginal culture (including an aboriginal director of the Pingdong Aboriginal Culture Park, more money for aboriginal culture, and removing Wu Feng from textbooks);
3. Temporarily stop implementation of Mountain Reserve Land policies, have hearings and organize a national Mountain Reserve Land Rights Review Commission of respected aboriginal people to oversee Mountain Reserve Land Policy.
4. Aboriginal constitutional rights should be guaranteed by law passed by the Legislature.

The petition ended with the warning that

> If you do not accept our demands, apart from continued protest, we will present a formal charge to the Legislature, accusing the ROC Government of violating the constitution, and genocide, under the ILO Convention 107.[18]

The petition had not much impact at that time: except for a formal apology and some more welfare money from the side of the local government, nothing happened. However, from these remarks we can see that the ATA intellectuals linked the destruction of aboriginal culture through Taiwan's government directly to the extermination of the aboriginal people as a whole. To make this clear, they made use of internationally known concepts like "genocide." Furthermore, the remarks also show that aboriginal activists in Taiwan at this time were already very well aware of international organizations in other parts of the world that supported indigenous people. However, as pressure from the KMT regime was still strong at that time, it was not before 1991 that ATA members openly admitted their participation in the annual assemblies of the World Group of Indigenous Populations (WGIP) in Geneva.[19]

In all its actions, the ATA was strongly encouraged by the political opposition that realized this organization's engagement as an additional support in their own struggle against the mainlander regime and its exclusive ethnic politics. From their perspective, there were some striking similarities in the situation of Taiwan's Han vis-à-vis the mainlander-regime with that of Taiwan's Aborigines vis-à-vis the Han in general. This could be particularly well observed in the claim for correction of the ethnonym put forward by both groups: same as the members of the DPP who pleaded for a Nation's name "Taiwan" (instead of "Taiwan province") inhabited by "Taiwanese" (instead of "Chinese") who wanted to speak their own "languages" (the term "dialects" used by the KMT was rejected by the members of the political opposition), Aborigines according to the DPP had a good right to be recognized as a distinct ethnic group with a self-chosen name and own languages (and not dialects) that had to be protected.

As I stated above, the contact with oppositional circles also influenced the aboriginal movement's ideology: Its members knew very well that only an overthrow or a thorough reform of the mainlander's totalitarian regime would bring about some changes in Taiwan's aboriginal politics and a realization to their own aim to serve as legitimate representatives of their people. And they also knew very well that only an "upgrading" of their status from "compatriots" to "aborigines" would have some effects on the KMT's national politics, as the KMT would finally have to admit that Taiwan's population was by no means homogeneous Chinese and that the soil under their feet had not belonged to the Chinese since aeons. Nevertheless, despite these similarities with regard to ideology, the ATA's members also scrutinized the political opposition with some suspicion, because it mainly consisted of Hoklo who were believed to work mostly on their own behalves.[20]

However, the leaders of the aboriginal movement were by no means only ideologically influenced by the political opposition. As one can see at a closer look, there were also strong influences from the side of the Presbyterian Church of Taiwan (PCT) as well as from the side of Taiwan's anthropologists.[21]

The Christian Church

After Japan's surrender, Christian missionaries were finally allowed to re-enter the mountain areas and to spread the gospel. Though this work had been begun by English and Canadian Presbyterians as early as in the middle of the nineteenth century, the missionaries of that time had only reached the so-called "plain dwelling Aborigines" (*pingpu*) with their message.[22] When the Japanese rulers left the island, they also left a deep spiritual vacuum in aboriginal society. Quite differently from Taiwan's Han who had never really relinquished their folk religion.[23] in spite of compulsory Shintoism after 1938, the animist belief systems of the Aborigines had almost totally crumbled at that time, so that most of them happily converted to Christianity that seemed strong and prestigious enough to them to help them in times of uncertainty. Even the more doubtful among them could finally be convinced with food donations and other sorts of presents.

As a consequence, more than 80 percent of aboriginal society had become Christians by the 1980s, most of them Presbyterian or Roman Catholic, but other dominations were represented as well. Though the Roman Catholic Church always offered a helping hand to the socially weak, it generally tried—linked to Rome and with most of its members being mainlanders who had come to Taiwan with Chiang Kai-shek—to keep away from political issues. This formed a sharp contrast to the Presbyterian Church of Taiwan, that not only boasted itself to be an indigenized Christian Church consisting mostly of native Taiwanese—that is, Hoklo, Hakka, and Aborigines—but that also harbored strong elements of "liberation theology" or "homeland theology" (*xiangtu shenxue*) as it was called in Taiwan. Before the 1980s, the PCT was the only nongovernmental organization in Taiwan that dared to discuss the matter of "independence of the Taiwanese" in public. In its "Declaration on Human Rights" of 1977, the PCT called on the United States to guarantee the "security, independence and freedom of the people of Taiwan" and urged "our government to face reality and to take effective measures whereby Taiwan may become a new and independent country." And with respect to land, the PCT stated here:

> Our church confesses that Jesus Christ is the Lord of all mankind and believes that human rights and a homeland (*xiangtu*) are gifts bestowed from God.[24]

Several incidents of severe state suppression in the 70s—that is, the confiscation of bibles in aboriginal languages, the arrest of the director of the PCT's aboriginal college and the taxation of mountain church land by the government—led to a radicalization of the PCT's homeland theology in the 80s. In the conflict that followed, the church could not only rely on a strong infrastructure led by well educated Han-clergy, but also on large numbers of aboriginal clergy, most of them graduates from the PCT's own educational institutions.[25] Another important support came from the World Council of Churches (WCC) and from foreign missionaries. The Canadian missionary Michael Stainton, who came to Taiwan in 1980 and who assisted the aboriginal youth groups of the PCT in Taibei, can be named as an example. Many of the later leaders of the aboriginal movement took part in activities organized by him, like symposiums on anti-hegemonic struggle, land issues, and so on. He supported the organization of the "Return Our Land Movement" of the years 1988 and 1989—the most successful mobilizations of the aboriginal movement that were originally initiated as protests against the government's sudden taxation of Church land in the mountain areas, but that soon also attracted large numbers of

Aborigines who were just dissatisfied with their own land situation, as the plain mountain compatriots who had no reservation land at all.[26]

Other demonstrations initiated by the PCT on behalf of the Aborigines were the protests in 1987 and 1988 against aboriginal girls' prostitution in Taibei's brothel district Huaxijie.[27] All the demonstrations mentioned took place in the years directly following the lifting of martial law in 1987. The PCT expressed a clear standpoint in all these issues: as an indigenous church it was not going to tolerate a foreign regime to exert its tyranny over the people of Taiwan. According to the PCT, it was necessary to support and strengthen the indigenous elements in Taiwan. This policy of "indigenisation," that was originally begun in the sixties as a consequence to a decreasing percentage of followers after the rising influx of other churches, was not only strongly supported by an international community represented by the World Council of Churches, but also helped the PCT to strengthen its influence in Taiwan vis-à-vis other churches that were not spreading the gospel in the different Chinese dialects and aboriginal mother tongues. By the beginning of the 1980s, one-third of the PCT's 210,000 followers in Taiwan were Aborigines. Its influence was strongest among those who had been raised within the PCT's own educational institutions and many of whom later organized themselves in the ATA. They were fervent supporters of the PCT's indigenization policy, that was based on a contextualized bible exegesis that emphasized "the right on resistance," as it could help them to overcome their negative self-perception as members of an inferior Ethnie. Yet another reason that took them to activism was the fact that they had been raised in an educational system not compatible to the KMT-sanctioned system: therefore they hardly had any job-opportunities outside of the PCT's infrastructure.[28]

It was within this environment that the self-perception of an "Ethnie threatened by extinction" first began to take shape: As Michael Stainton shows in his account of the actions taking place in the preparation phase of the "Return our Land" movement from 1981 to 1987, aboriginal PCT-preachers tried to convince their followers in their sermons that Taiwan's Aborigines, who were not even officially recognized as Aborigines and who were heavily exploited by the Han people, were in a situation very similar to that of the Israelians in the story of "Exodus": if they wanted to escape elimination, they had to rely on the aboriginal preachers who like Moses had the role to lead them out of danger. Another analogism frequently used was "The People of God": Although Aborigines until recently lived in the darkness of head-hunting, they eventually decided—differently from Taiwan's Han who would have had the same chance—to convert to Christianity, a transformation that indicated that they were in fact "God's chosen people." A third theme often referred to was "The Promised Land": Aborigines had a responsibility for their land that was god-given; they had the duty to demand it back and return to that land.[29]

Similar to the attitude expressed toward ethnic identity and land were the attitudes toward aboriginal mother languages. As Atayal preacher Duo Ao, one of the leading activists of the "Return our land movement" stated in an article in the ATA's magazine *Aboriginal* where he criticized the prohibition of mother languages in schools and churches:

> The languages that god gave to every people are extremely valuable. What conspiracy do those have in mind who boast themselves to have the dragon's brain, but destroy our languages? . . . Is it a policy for faster elimination of our people?[30]

The same suspicion—that the destruction of the mother languages aimed at the elimination of the people as a whole—was expressed by Paiwan-preacher Jingruo Mashigeshige in another article of the same magazine.[31]

Altogether, we can see that many of the key metaphors and concepts of the aboriginal movement derived from the PCT. However, as the PCT wanted to avoid a further escalation of its conflict with the KMT regime, it tried to conceal its leading role behind this movement. The ATA, that was financially and logistically dependent on the PCT for all of its successful mobilizations, was a reliable tool through which the church was able to exert its influence.[32]

Taiwan's Anthropologists

As the only scholars who were encouraged to undertake research on issues that were connected to a particular Taiwanese culture in times of authoritarian rule, Taiwan's anthropologists were those Han who had the closest contact with Aborigines. Thus it is not astonishing that they were the earliest advocates and supporters of these people that by the greater public were believed to be no more than "slow-witted savages" and "drunkards." Among the founding members of the ATA there were also several anthropologists; the adoption of the pan-ethnic name "Taiwan's Aborigines" (*Taiwan Yuanzhumin*) must be attributed to their advice.[33] As early as in 1980, ethnologist Chen Qinan from the *Academia Sinica*, who in 1992 became vice president of the Council of Cultural Planning, uttered his doubts about the credibility of the Wu Feng saga printed in Taiwanese schoolbooks, and pointed to the negative impacts of it on Aborigines. At the same time, a growing number of anthropologists switched their research focus from traditional culture to social problems of Aborigines. Many of them now published articles in the newspapers where they criticized the government's attitude on questions concerning ethnic minorities. The most important work with the largest impact was the "Evaluation Report" on the social situation of Taiwan's Aborigines in 1983, an examination that was sponsored by the Executive Yuan and was guided by the head of the *Academia Sinica*, Li Yiyuan. The report's results point to the cultural and social decline of the different aboriginal ethnic groups in the last decades that was mainly caused, the report concludes, by the assimilation policy of the KMT government. If the government really wanted to increase the living standard of the different aboriginal ethnic groups, it should not only lead them to more autonomy as had been done by other governments in states with indigenous populations, but should also grant them special cultural rights, particularly in respect to language and religious traditions. Apart from a detailed description of the situation of indigenous peoples in other parts of the world, the report also contained a translation of the crucial parts of the "ILO Convention 107" of 1957. In many of their later writings on aboriginal rights and welfare, ATA activists relied on the information in this report.[34]

A second anthropological work with much impact was Xie Shizhong's book *Ethnic Contacts, Stigmatised Identity* and Pan-Taiwan Aboriginalism in 1987, where Xie not only describes the psychological effects of marginalization and discrimination on the Aborigines mentality in general, but where he also gives an account of the self-perceptions and convictions of the ATA activists. The information offered in the book was not only important for Aborigines themselves to learn about the actions of their intellectuals, but also for the greater Taiwanese public who at that time slowly began to take interest in the island's society and in Taiwan's local culture. In another article on the aboriginal movement published in the same year, Xie even suggested to look at the problem from the perspective of "internal colonialism", as the socio-political situation of Aborigines in Taiwan fulfilled all characteristics in this categorization. According to Xie, the movement principally aimed at a "re-adjustment of ethnic power constellations within Taiwan's society."[35]

In the following years, Xie—today professor at the Department of Anthropology of National Taiwan University—became an important advisor and mentor of the movement.[36] Together with several anthropologists from Qinghua University and the Academia Sinica, he was one of the main supporters of the name correction movement that stood up for the correction of the term "mountain compatriots" to "Aborigines," which in 1994 was finally successful after many years of fierce rejection by the mainlander wing within the KMT.[37]

Paradigm Change for Taiwan's Aborigines in the 1990s

Nativism and Multiculturalism

As I already stated in the introduction to this article, major changes took place in Taiwan since the beginning of the 1990s. With the official election of the Taiwanese Li Denghui as president, the power struggle within the KMT that had begun after the lifting of martial law in 1987 gradually came to an end. A constitutional reform with the aim to lead Taiwan to democracy was begun in 1991, in the same year that the claim to recover the mainland was officially given up. Though it was still the KMT that ruled Taiwan, the party now underwent a profound transformation in its interior. After the drain of those party members with mainlander origin into the CNP, most of the remaining KMT's members were native Taiwanese, that is, Hoklo and Hakka. The homogenization and amalgamation of Taiwanese society as it had previously been pursued by the KMT—embodied in slogans like "Children of the Yellow Emperor"—suddenly belonged to the past. With rising efforts of the Taiwanese to point out their differences first from the mainlanders (*waishengren*) and later also from mainland China in respect to culture, history, and consciousness, the former "question of provincial descent" developed into an "ethnic question."[38]

It was at this time that claims for recognition of the multiculturality of Taiwanese society and the implementation of multicultural politics became louder every day. After 1993, not only governmental institutions like the Council of Cultural Planning, but also politicians from the opposition party referred more and more often to Taiwan's society as a "multi-cultural society." Almost imperceptibly, the postulate of the mono-cultural, homogeneous society had been replaced by the "discourse of difference."

The new political climate also affected aboriginal politics. This seems particularly astonishing, as in the past all administration measures regarding Aborigines were handled as "temporary regulations" which would soon become unnecessary.[39] In 1993, the "International Year of Indigenous Peoples," a five year plan for "development and improvement of mountain compatriot's education" was put into force.[40] In that very year Guo Weifan, minister of education, and Wu Boxiong, minister of the interior, openly admitted mistakes in former education policies and promised the implementation of classes in vernacular languages and local knowledge by 1996. After the change of government in the year 2000, the Ministry of Education even determined that next to Mandarin one of Taiwan's other languages was to be included in the course curricula of the nine-year compulsory education (i.e., the primary and secondary school). The new language education policy became effective in September 2001.

But the "recognition of difference" was not limited to the field of education: Important concessions were also made in general policy, for instance, concerning the recognition of the self-chosen name of the Aborigines, "*Yuanzhumin,*" in 1994, the right for rehabilitation of traditional front- and family-names in 1995, and the establishment of "Committees for Indigenous Peoples" not only in the two metropoles Taibei and Gaoxiong, but by late 1996 also on the central level, with representatives of all ten different ethnic groups, including the Shao that in the past had been discarded from the list of groups because of their low population. After 1991 the government also gave increasing attention to aboriginal communities in the course of its efforts toward "community reconstruction." Every ethnic group was now encouraged to search for its own cultural particularities.[41]

The official change toward multiculturalism also caused a change of the government's attitude toward the nativist aboriginal elite[42] that meanwhile had generated new groups and wings next to the ATA, the most important of them being the "Tribalist Movement" (*buluo zhuyi yundong*) that concentrated on the living conditions and on the political mobilization of the people in the tribal areas.[43] In the course of the cultural reconstruction of aboriginal society, the members of the nativist elites—many of them artists, writers, scholars, or other kinds of "culture workers"—were increasingly integrated and engaged into projects initiated by central government institutions. The Ministry of Education and the Council of Cultural Planning now became frequent dispensers of jobs. Since 1992, the teachers college in Hualian organized regular classes for aboriginal teachers as well as for aboriginal students of teachers' colleges who were to teach in aboriginal schools, to improve their teaching-ability in themes related to aboriginal culture. Furthermore, teachers were encouraged to participate in the work of compiling aboriginal teaching materials in every aboriginal language, and a special committee for this work was founded under the Ministry of Education. The central government thereby joined the efforts of the opposition, who had started to engage nativist aboriginal elites in the education sector as early as 1990 (just about the time when the opposition also started to organize homeland and vernacular education).[44]

The development depicted here led to an increasing amalgamation of the two originally antagonistic and mutually despising wings of the aboriginal elites, the nativist and the KMT-loyal, political elite.[45] In the newly established Council of Indigenous Peoples, the two elites now began to work closely together. Before this important step could be accomplished, however, the dynamics of this initial stage of multicultural politics generated some tensions that in some cases also triggered the use of a rough and sometimes exaggerated terminology.

Temptations from the "Fourth World": Charges of Indigenous Human Rights Violations

In spite of the speed with which the development described above took place from today's point of view, the pace seemed still far too slow for many of the intellectual leaders of the aboriginal movement. Particularly in those issues that concerned claims like the self-chosen ethnic name, aboriginal land, and an un dominated autonomous existence; they often resorted to a harsh language and drastic manners when addressing governmental bodies. Especially the year 1993, that the UN had proclaimed as the "International Year of Indigenous Peoples," seemed to offer a good opportunity to accelerate the decision-making of the KMT government.

As early as in 1990, anthropologist Xie Shizhong had published an article on "The Establishment of the Fourth World: On the Opportunities and Crisis of the Indigenous World," a very theoretical work, but where he urges indigenous peoples in general not to put themselves into too much antagonism with the dominating regime. As an explanation, he points—on the one hand—to the general indifference of the UN to the problem of indigenes, the incapability of international law, and the powerlessness of international organizations. On the other hand, he does not conceal his conviction that the regime—in the case of any conflict—would probably be stronger.[46]

However, nativist aboriginal elites, who since 1991 regularly participated in the World Group of Indigenous Populations (WGIPs) meetings in Geneva, seemed to have their own convictions of international solidarity. The former ATA leader Liu Wenxiong in 1994 remembers that the contact with the WGIP enlarged their horizon in a significant way: They now felt even more convinced that Taiwan's Aborigines—once recognized— would be entitled to collective ethnic rights like indigenous peoples of other countries, that is, to cultural rights, intellectual property rights, land rights, and the right of self-determination.[47] On December 10, 1993 the International Day of Human Rights, the ATA and other aboriginal groups marched to the Ministry of Exterior "to initiate a dialogue between the Han-nation and Taiwan's aboriginal nation(s)." They handed in a petition entitled "Struggle of Taiwan's Aborigines against Intrusion, for Survival, and Return our Land." Referring to intrusion, they demanded a stop to the occupation of aboriginal reservation land by companies as well as by the state and to ensure Aborigines' intellectual property rights in order to limit the damages caused by the marketing of aboriginal culture; referring to the crisis of survival, they demanded for better surveillance of the physical and cultural development of aboriginal society and for better assistance in the field of economy;[48] and, referring to the return of land, they demanded that property rights on reservation land should be given to Aborigines[49] and that the remaining confiscated reservation land should be given back.[50] Generally it was demanded that the state should give legal status to Aborigines and the cultural and autonomy rights connected to this status.

At the end of the petition, it was stated:

> as long as the Han-government does not recognize and respect Taiwan's Aborigines' fundamental human rights and their status as a people, it has neither the right to condemn the PRCh for suppressing Taiwan's international right of existence, nor does it have the right to claim any international right of existence in front of the international community.

This of course was hard to bear for Taiwan's government that had just begun to apply internationally for Taiwan's return to the UN.[51] However, the KMT was wise enough not to intervene. At least the reformers within the party around Li Denghui knew very well that the recognition of aboriginal status and rights had been long time overdue and that Aborigines could not be any longer appeased with terms like "early inhabitants" or "earlier inhabitants" suggested by the KMT in the course of the constitutional reforms of 1991 and 1992: any further rejection of the issue would have strengthened the arguments of the political opposition that—because of the ideological reasons just mentioned—fully supported the nativist aboriginal elites. When the latter repeated their demands in a so-called Cultural-head-hunting-raid at the First Aboriginal Culture Congress in 1994 and gained even more public attention,[52] the KMT changed its former attitude and finally accepted the status reform in the third constitutional amendment of July 1994. Nevertheless, the government still hesitated to yield to the demand to implement governmental institutions for Aborigines on the central level, arguing that there already existed a central level institution for Mongolians and Tibetans. This was perceived as a serious affront, because nativist aboriginal elites had fought since 1991 for the removal of this institution (that represented about 700 Tibetans and Mongolians who had come to Taiwan after 1945 with the KMT) in favor of an aboriginal committee. When in 1995 two well-known leaders of the aboriginal movement were convicted for offending the demonstration law during the demonstration against the Committee for Mongolians and Tibetans of 1991 and had to serve a one-year sentence, the members of the ATA reacted furiously and organized several demonstrations together with other aboriginal groups, the largest one to the Taiwanese parliament—the Legislative Yuan—where they tore off the sign of the institution and protested "Against Judiciary Persecution—Return Aborigines' Human Rights" (*fan sifa pohai, huan Yuanzhumin renquan*). This and another incident shortly afterwards made the KMT realize once again that it could no longer hold things back anymore: Just before an important parliament vote in the beginning of 1996 at a time when the KMT was already close to losing its majority in the Legislative Yuan two aboriginal KMT legislators—until 1996, all aboriginal representatives belonged to the KMT—threatened to withhold their votes if the implementation of the committee was further postponed. The KMT finally agreed to implement the Council of Indigenous Peoples (CIP) until the end of 1996.[53] Since then, the formulation of indigenous policies has been placed in the hands of the CIP and all indigenous affairs are brought under the jurisdiction of this specific ministerial-level agency.[54]

Competing Elites: The Splitting Up of The Movement

Nativist aboriginal elites had avoided too close contact with the DPP in the 80s, but this phenomenon changed with the growing legitimacy of the opposition party and its goals in the 90s. The increasing involvement of the intellectuals in DPP party politics during the 90s also led to growing tension and antagonism between different wings of the pan-ethnic movement that had developed since 1990 in the course of Taiwan's nativization process. Although the DPP tried to attract aboriginal elites with very progressive minority programs, the number of offices it could offer to Aborigines was limited. An intense struggle evolved when the DPP in 1995 and 1996 was able to offer two seats for aboriginal parliament representatives. During the election campaigns, aboriginal candidates not only surpassed each other in vote-buying,[55] but also in mutual abuses and accusations. An example for the latter phenomenon is Atayal woman-activist Liyijing Youma, leader of the Union of Native Taiwanese Villages. In her book *Handing on the Tradition: Walking out to Denounce*, where she idealizes the brave commitment of Aborigines in the aboriginal movement as an extension of the noble traditions of the brave hunter in modern times, she dedicates a whole chapter to what she calls "The degeneration of the tradition," a reprint of an article that had already appeared in the weekly newspaper *Austronesian News* on December 22, 1995. Her key theme here is the so-called line-correction project (*daozheng zhuan'an*) pursued by the KMT and KMT-loyal aboriginal elites from 1987 to 1989, a secret project in which some of the ATA leaders were persuaded to offer internal information to the KMT as a compensation for regular salaries paid to them (here we see another reason why ATA-members avoided too close contact with the political opposition in these years). What Liyijing worries most about is that the same corrupt leaders who betrayed the movement in the 80s were still put forward as candidates for governmental offices in 1995/96, and she finds hard words to express her worries:

> Experiencing all sorts of genocidal methods [*miezu shouduan* here stands for the assimilation policy, as she explains before] and being forced to live in the cold and indifferent society of the chauvinistic Han, Aborigines should utter harsh protest. But if the young aboriginal intellectuals lack this deep experience and this sincere sense of mission, then they will not be able to produce enough impetus.[56]

She then goes on explaining the psychology that brings about such lack:

> If a people live for a long time under restriction let us say for 40, 50 years, then the economy of this people will be totally collapsed! And if the experience of restriction lasts more than a century, then the basic character of this people will undergo severe degeneration. The characteristics of the nature man will gradually transform, what remains are inferiority complexes, these in turn will produce arrogance, strong superiority feelings and exclusive manners. They will not be able to trust other people, they will look down on their compatriots, and they will trample on them just to bring up themselves.[57]

What eventually remains according to Liyijing are corrupt and selfish individuals who even do not shrink from "betraying their own compatriots."

> The fact that there was the "line-correction project" incident demonstrates that the eleven-year-old aboriginal rights movement has failed. The aboriginal movement has not only thoroughly failed; the incident also caused the young aboriginal intellectuals to split up.[58]

Uttered at a time when the Aborigines' situation had already changed dramatically and the successes of the movement—although reached with the help of others—were all too obvious, Liyijing's warnings sound exaggerated and grotesque. Among the texts I viewed, her book contains the fiercest accusations and strongest expressions, and though there were no incidences of physical or cultural genocide in Taiwan in the nineties, Liyijing uses these and very similar expressions at least a dozen times in her book. However, what is important to know is that Liyijing Youma published her book (or better the articles on the sensitive topics) just before parliament elections were taking place in Taiwan. During the election campaigns, she herself supported an Atayal candidate who had been less prominent in the initial phase of the movement and who had therefore not been involved in the line-correction project.[59]

The Limits of Multiculturalism

As it was to be expected, protests of aboriginal elites became very rare after the implementation of the CIP and almost ceased when the political opposition—the DPP—replaced the KMT in the central government in 2000. Had accusations like "racial suppression," "distortion of human rights," "persecution" and even "genocide" belonged to the standard vocabulary before 1996, Aborigines afterwards only used these expressions on very rare occasions.[60] Not only were they now over-represented in the parliament,[61] but they also controlled a quasi-ministerial institution with enough financial resources to employ approximately 120 members, not to mention the institutions for Aborigines' administration that existed on other levels like the Committees of Indigenous Peoples of Taibei and Gaoxiong.[62]

Of course, there still remained some issues where intellectuals expressed their strong discontent, arguing that Aborigines' minority rights and Aborigines' particularity were not respected in a sufficient way. Nevertheless, as all these issues also touched the well-being and the living conditions of the Han-majority, even the reform-orientated forces in Taiwan's government showed themselves reluctant or sometimes unable to fulfil the demands.

Nuclear Waste on Orchid Island

One of these issues is the deposal of nuclear waste on Orchid island (Lanyu), a little island southeast of Taiwan that is inhabited by the Yami people.[63] Without asking the Yami, the KMT government had built the waste dump in 1980 and since that time all nuclear waste of Taiwan had been deposited on Lanyu. After 1988, the problem became an important issue in the pan-ethnic aboriginal movement, especially after it was proved that several waste barrels already leaked. Since then, Yami intellectuals and ATA elites orga-nized protests almost every year, demanding that no more waste should be brought to Lanyu and that the already existing waste should be taken away. On many occasions, the PCT-trained Yami intellectuals pronounced very clearly that Taiwan's government should stop its "genocidal policy" toward the Yami.[64] Working closely together with Taiwan's environment protec-tion movement, the Lanyu antinuclear-waste movement was a pressure group that had to be taken seriously. Therefore, the KMT government in 1999 finally signed a treaty where it promised to abolish the dump until

2002. When the DPP government had to apologize openly in May 2002 for their incapability to find an alternative place for the waste, Lanyu activists took to action again. However, as the government claimed to be helpless, aboriginal legislators also were not able to offer much support.

Autonomous Zones

Another issue is the claim to establish autonomous zones. Until today, the land on which Aborigines live is state land that is administrated by the state. This annoys aboriginal politicians. They claim that there is an "aboriginal right" on self-governance and on autonomous zones, as the constitution prescribes that the state has to protect and foster the ethnic minorities' institutions for self-governance. For Han-politicians, however, this claim seems hard to fulfil, as Taiwan is a multicultural society consisting of at least fifteen different ethnic groups on an island as big as the Netherlands.[65] Besides, critics of such demands argue that aboriginal society should first solve its most urgent social problems before discussing autonomy. Today, the people in autonomous zones would be dependent on the state's support in every aspect. Despite all these doubts, the issue is developing steadily. Shortly before Chen Shuibian was elected president, he signed a paper were he promised to make Lanyu an autonomous zone as soon as possible. And in 2002, the Ministry of Interior and the CIP drafted a law according to which the reservation zones should be administrated by Aborigines themselves and not by the state anymore.[66] A concrete legal step in the direction indicated was finally taken on January 21, 2005, when the "Aboriginal Basic Law" (*Yuanzhuminzu jibenfa*) was passed by the legislature. This law, which had been over ten years in the making, guaranteed that government support and resources would be given to the development of a self-governing system for the nation's indigenous people. It stipulated that the government would create agencies for aboriginal language research and cultural promotion through media channels, and that it would give preference to aboriginal land names.[67]

Hunting and Gathering

Closely connected to the issue of aboriginal self-governance in the reservation zones is the issue of hunting. Prohibition to hunt protected animals as wild boar, deer, and the like, is handled particularly strictly in the seven National Parks that were established since 1985. As most of the latter were set up on aboriginal reservation land, Aborigines today feel strongly restricted in their cultural habits. Every year many of them have to face high fines after being caught in the act of hunting.[68] They claim that their social systems and inner-social solidarity depend on the exertion of hunting and the rituals connected to it. The state, however, is also under strong pressure from the side of the environmental protection movement. Its followers claim that wildlife in Taiwan is close to extinction and that indigenous people's interaction with nature is not as harmonious as is often believed or emphasized by aboriginal elites. In fact, it can hardly be said that Aborigines hunt in a sustainable way today, as they use traps and fish with the help of electricity. In many cases the prey is directly sold to Han who order the so-called mountain-meat.[69] A very similar problem is the illegal exploitation of other natural resources in the mountains like wood or marble.

Native Languages

Finally, there must be mentioned the issue of native languages. As stated before, the new government under Chen Shuibian in January 2000 announced the inclusion of "compulsory mother tongue" classes for primary and middle school students starting from 2001.[70] The government proclaimed that the main aim of this policy was to help Taiwan's different ethnic groups to regain their self-respect and help students to understand more about Taiwan.[71]

The planned education policy aroused an intense controversy in Taiwan. Being strongly opposed to the intended measures, the *Taipei Times Editorial* on January 10, 2000, contended that native language classes, being billed as compulsory courses, would inevitably increase students' class load. Furthermore, they argued that Taiwan's pluralism was not only one of Taiwan's greatest assets, but was also the source of Taiwan's pride as a "maritime culture" as opposed to the "continental culture" of mainland China. Putting too much emphasis on "nativeness," would hinder Taiwan's efforts to increase its internationalization. They therefore argued that native-language education should not be compulsory, instead, elective courses should be held on the basis of students' needs and the ability of schools to provide the courses.[72] Other critics pointed to the impracticability of these languages: The reason for the lack of success in the earlier efforts for promotion of mother-tongue education, in their opinion, was that many people did not regard these languages as useful. Different from English, they were not part of school entrance and civil service examinations, nor were they valuable in the employment market.[73]

For activists that fought for language-revitalization, such objections of course sounded very unsatisfactory. In their opinion, every single mother language was extremely precious, and the great variety of languages on the island was Taiwan's real asset that had to be protected and fostered. With respect to the usefulness of these languages, it was suggested that for national examinations, Aborigines who benefited from weighted grades based on their ethnic identity, should have to pass a language test in their "mother tongue." By implementing measures such as this, local languages would again be regarded as "useful" and students would be motivated to learn them.[74] The most furious outcries however came from Western observers. A Canadian activist even suspected genocidal intentions in the attitude of the *Taipei Times* "Editorial" cited above: Heavily criticising the Editorial's worry that too much emphasis on "Nativeness" might have negative impacts on Taiwan society's further integration, he reminds the reader of one of Raphael Lemkin's definitions of genocide where the latter holds that genocide also meant the

> co-ordinated plan of different actions aiming at the destruction of essential foundations of the life of national groups, with the aim of annihilating the groups themselves.[75]

And another advocate of compulsory mother-tongue education wrote:

> In truth, the fact that Hokkien [i.e., the language of the Hoklo] is increasingly not being transmitted to children, particularly in northern Taiwan, is an ominous sign that the "linguicidal" policies of the ROC education system are finally working as they were originally intended to. . . . Without a sweeping change in public-school policy, there is little realistic chance that Hokkien and other "mother tongues" will survive.[76]

Considering the fact that mother tongues were taught in Taiwan's schools—although not compulsory and without much success—on a nationwide scale since 1996, such criticism sounds highly exaggerated.[77] The main idea behind it was of course the conviction that people in Taiwan were already too much assimilated to the main hegemonic culture to be able to understand the benefits of cultural revitalization, therefore the government should promote its conviction of the necessity to retain these languages with much more emphasis. What the critics did not seem to realize however was that such intercession on behalf of the mentally colonized would just mean a new form of hegemony.

Although "compulsory mother tongue education" was finally implemented in fall 2001, the Taiwanese government wisely avoided such hegemony by allowing students to choose one out of the three alternatives, that is Hoklo, Hakka, and aboriginal languages that were taught no longer than 1–2 periods per week.[78]

Conclusion

In this chapter I discussed the impact of Taiwan's nativization process on Taiwan's Aborigines. Had there occurred situations of genocide in the time of Japanese Colonialism and cases of forced assimilation under authoritarian KMT rule, Aborigines experienced a dramatic change of status and prestige during the last two decades of the twentieth century. This change of course could not be reached without the massive support of powerful societal groups within Han-society. Main supporters were the political opposition and the Presbyterian Church of Taiwan that also shaped the ideological basis of the aboriginal movement in a decisive way. The nativist ideology of these two societal groups provided the crucial analytical framework that allowed Aborigines to perceive themselves as members of an exploited and threatened Ethnie that had to be protected. The support of Taiwan's anthropologists as advisers and advocates also played an important role in this awakening, as these scholars provided the knowledge about the situation of indigenous peoples elsewhere and about their status in international human rights conventions.

It was under the impact of these ideological influences that aboriginal activists in the 80s began to charge the ruling KMT regime for violations of indigenous human rights. In some occasions the government that at this time pursued a strict assimilation policy was even accused of "genocidal measures." Though this terminology was not correct in the original sense of the term where "genocide and cultural genocide are invariably connected to intended mass ethnic murder on a grand scale" (Sautman),[79] it must have corresponded to the self-perception of these intellectuals who on the one hand experienced open discrimination by the Han-people in the metropoles where they lived and on the other hand had no prospect to return to their own communities whose cultures and mother tongues they saw crumbling away. A strong feeling of loss of identity was the inevitable consequence, a feeling that was so severe that it was equated with the elimination of the people as a whole. A closer look at the administration policy before 1990 however shows that the KMT never intended the elimination of the mountain-compatriots, but rather envisaged a gradual cultural "integration" that would merge them into the Chinese people and would eventually also solve their social problems.[80]

In spite of the united efforts of Taiwanese and aboriginal intellectuals and in spite of the strong accusations directed against the KMT regime, all endeavors to bring about a change to Taiwan's Aborigines situation would probably have been in vain, had there not been the regime's change to nativism in the 90s that induced a paradigm change for Taiwan's different ethnic groups as a whole. Only the conviction of Taiwan's policy makers—in particular politicians of the KMT's mainstream faction and DPP politicians on the county-level—that "Aborigines" should be an integral part of the island's historical, cultural, and political identity, eventually pushed the development toward multiculturalism and a growing appreciation of Aborigines. Although this appreciation was soon felt by aboriginal intellectuals and although the fear of identity loss must thus have lost its former intensity, they not only proceeded with their struggle for constitutional recognition, but also continued to accuse the government of colonialization, suppression, persecution, and genocide. As I showed, one reason for this attitude was the touch with the Fourth World Movement that offered recipes as to how indigenous peoples should proceed in their anticolonial struggle. Further, it was only by these harsh and sensational methods that Aborigines succeeded to arouse a considerable degree of public attention in a time when Taiwan's constitutional reform was at its high-tide.[81] Third, the supporters of the aboriginal intellectuals—who mostly advocated a free and democratic Taiwan and therefore looked forward to a power change on the island—hardly intervened when the latter put forward their accusations, as these were mostly directed against the KMT regime. One exception was the "Cultural-head-hunting-raid of Aborigines" at the First Aboriginal Culture Congress in 1994 where nativist aboriginal elites also directed their criticism against Taiwan's anthropologists, especially those members of the older generation of anthropologists who had not supported the correction of the ethnonym—accusing them of collaboration with the KMT regime.[82] Many of the young anthropologists—themselves caught in an intergenerational conflict with the older generation of anthropologists[83]—at that time enthusiastically analyzed this outburst as the Aborigines' endeavor to detach themselves from the mental control of the Han. Actually, this was exactly the interpretation that aboriginal intellectuals—well informed in theories of postcolonial discourse—had aimed at: Not only the Han-Chinese in Taiwan had a right to construct and to display their undominated "subjectivity" (*zhutixing*) and mental independence vis-à-vis China, Japan, and the West, Aborigines had the same right in their forced juxtaposition to the Han people. In order to reach thorough emancipation one had to liberate oneself from the negative self-image that the dominators had forced upon the dominated. In working up to this aim, the transgression and subversion of commonly recognized rules were sometimes believed to be unavoidable.[84]

Another exception that has been presented is the criticism put forward by Liyijing in articles like "The degeneration of tradition." However, as I perceive it, the main function of Liyijing's charges of human rights violations was to construct a contrast between different groups of aboriginal intellectuals, that is, between those who did nothing to save their people from extinction and those who dedicated themselves to Aborigines' (cultural) survival.

Though it has become clear in the course of this chapter that human rights of Taiwan's Aborigines are very well respected today and that charges of violations of these rights—as it can sometimes still be seen on the internet—are merely polemic, this argument should not lead the reader to the following conclusions:

First, it should not be suspected that aboriginal society in Taiwan is living in a "golden age" today. As far as an emancipation from Han society occurred, it only involved the elite strata of this society. Any reforms carried out since 1990 were initiated within a very eliterian surrounding: Neither aboriginal commoners nor ordinary middle class–Han showed much interest in the indigenous status and human rights—debates pursued by aboriginal— and Han intellectuals and politicians in the 90s.[85] Thus, the aboriginal movement was far away from being a "bottom to the top" process. Instead, it was much more the expression of the commitment and the interplay of different elites all involved in what Xie Shizhong in 1987 had called the "re-adjustment of ethnic power constellations within Taiwan's society." This is one of the main reasons why—while the main political issues seem to be solved and the cultural status and cultural situation of Aborigines have changed dramatically—many of the most urgent social problems of Taiwan's aboriginal society still persist. One of these is the high percentage of unemployment: According to a study of the CIP, the rate of aboriginal unemployment (7.55 percent) in 1996 was almost three times as high as in Han society (2.7 percent), and it was rising rapidly.[86] Had the low standards of education, alcoholism, and the differing living habits of Aborigines formerly been the main causes for this phenomenon, the increase observed today must be attributed to an additional cause that is situated in the government's economic policy: the influx of large numbers of cheap guest workers from Southeast Asia.[87] Today, their working force is already exceeding that of Taiwan's Aborigines: by 2001, there officially lived 329,312 guest workers from Indonesia, Malaysia, the Philippines, Thailand, and Vietnam in Taiwan.[88]

On the other hand, Taiwan's nativist multiculturalism generates a situation that has strong similarities to what Roger Sandall describes in his book *The Culture Cult*. Focusing on the situation of Australia's and New Zealand's Aborigines, Sandall writes here:

> Empirically, the children of the old-time tribesmen are now citizens like the rest of us who have needs like the rest of us—for housing, education, jobs.

But their attempts to succeed are handicapped by the usual academic hostility to market society, and they are intimidated by a lot of newly invented "traditions" they are supposed to support. Combined with this a suffocating religiosity now descends on public discussion enforced by priests and judges, journalists and teachers, poets and politicians, all of whom claim that native culture possesses a "spirituality" found nowhere else.[89]

Under the impact of a real mass tourism into Taiwan's mountain areas in the last few years, more and more of Taiwan's Aborigines today feel motivated to recover, to restore, and to reinvent their cultural particularities and present them to the public in the way that sells best. In times of diminishing opportunities on the Han labor market, this new perspective seems to have come just in time. From a long-term perspective, however, it is doubtful whether these activities can prepare Aborigines for competition in modern Han society. Only if "romantic primitivism"[90] in Taiwan's Han society is more than only a temporary trend, the massive expansion of the aboriginal tourist sector observed in the last years might also have genuine future prospects for Taiwan's Aborigines.

Second, in spite of my emphasis that charges of genocide formulated by Taiwan's Aborigines in recent times were merely polemical and metaphorical, since there did not occur any intended mass murder on a grand scale in recent times,[91] I do not agree with Sautman's claim that people should avoid the term genocide except in such serious instances as Rwanda and Bosnia (Sautman mentions these two as the only cases that deserve to be defined as genocide in the late twentieth century). He argues that the inapt application of this term would not only lead to a language inflation, but would also additionally annoy the regime, like in the case of the PRCh government that merely tries to modernize Tibet and that believes that its modernization policy and cultural protection endeavors are righteous and positive for Tibet. I want to hold against this view that—if we take for instance the situation of Tibetan or Uighur activists—they would have a hard time in our medial age to arouse the world's attention for their peoples' physical and cultural subjugation by just stating that they are dissatisfied with the harsh measures of the PRC's "modernization policy." In my opinion, terms like genocide or ethnocide[92] should perhaps be much more understood as a kind of a "warning signal": in order to prevent things that amount to genocide or ethnocide; we as members of the "free world" are assigned to watch and scrutinize the situation. Where there appear charges of genocide, impartial scholars or experts have the task to make close examinations and to prove or falsify the charge.

Notes

1. The term *Yuanzhumin*—a direct translation from the English term "ab-originals"—has been chosen in 1984 by members of the aboriginal movement as a substitution for the official term "mountain compatriots." It took ten years until this new ethnonym was officially recognized by the third constitution amendment of June 28, 1994, and two more years until the government yielded to pressure from *Yuanzhumin*-legislators to establish a *Yuanzhumin*-representing committee on the central level (Rudolph 1996).

2. This is the revised version of an article originally written in 2002. For this reason, this chapter only covers the discourse on the issue of aboriginal genocide in Taiwan until that time. The terminology generally used for "genocide" in Taiwan is "*miezu (zhengce)*" / "*minzu huimie*" / "*minzu miejue*." There neither seems to be a clear distinction between genocide and ethnocide in the writings of aboriginal activists, nor does one explicitly speak of "cultural genocide" ("*wenhua miezu*" in PRCh sources). Only Gao Wanjin (1995) distinguishes the two categories "genocide" (translated as "*zhongzu miejue*") with reference to the physical extermination of Aborigines during Japanese colonization, and "ethnocide" (*zuqun miejue*), meaning the extermination of an Ethnie that can also be caused by forced assimilation. According to Gao, both the Japanese and the KMT—both of them colonial powers that forcibly assimilated Taiwan's Aborigines— are guilty for the latter.

3. The term which in Chinese is "*zhutixing*" can be best understood as "cultural, political and mental sovereignty."

4. Prior to Japanese rule over Taiwan, there had been constant clashes between Han and Aborigines, especially since the beginning of large-scale Han-immigration in the seventeenth century. Nevertheless, as both sides had casualties in these conflicts (Linck-Kesting 1979: 265ff), it would be inappropriate to refer to genocide here. However, Linck-Kesting also cites one of the few Western sources of that time where the author J.W.Davidson—consul of the United States in Taiwan—reports incidences of Han-cannibalism. According to Davidson, Taiwan's Han sold "savage flesh" on the open market and even exported it to Amoy on the mainland. Davidson concludes that "the Chinese ordinarily deserved all the punishment they received from the savages. Their treatment of these children of the forest [who were headhunters, but not cannibals, as Davidson explains earlier in the same passage] was always cruel in the extreme." (Davidson 1903: 254f (cited from Linck-Kesting 1979: 263f)).

5. Between 1896 and 1930, about 11 thousand Japanese lost their lives in confrontations with Aborigines (Linck-Kesting 1978: 70).

6. Linck-Kesting 1978: 71.

7. There existed still another term used by anthropologists: the "highsand people" of the Japanese were renamed into "high mountain people"

(*"gaoshanzu"* in Chinese). This term is still used by the PRCh referring to the *"gaoshanzu"* as one of China's fifty-six nationalities (including the Han). The "mountain compatriots of the flatland" (*pingdi shanbao*) shall not be confused with the "plain dwelling Aborigines" (*pingpuzu*) mentioned later, about ten different ethnic groups that had totally assimilated to the Han by the end of the nineteenth century.

8. As parts of the Paiwan in the East lived closely together with Han, they had been put into the category "flatland," while the majority of the Paiwan who lived in the West belonged to the "mountain compatriots of the mountain areas."

9. One major problem was the prostitution of under-aged Atayal women, who were often sold by their own parents and then became the victims of Han dealers and traffickers (see Rudolph 1993 for a detailed discussion of the prostitution problem in Taiwan).

10. Cai Zhonghan (ed.) 1996: 11. The percentage of alcohol abuse in Ami society was 38% in this study.

11. Hsu 1991.

12. For a detailed discussion of these issues see Rudolph 1993; Hsu Mutsu 1991.

13. "Hoklo" or "Minnan" constitute the majority of Taiwan's population (75 percent). The so-called mainlanders, who emigrated from the mainland with Chiang Kai-shek after 1945 and suppressed Taiwan's population in the following four decades until the lifting of martial law in 1987, make up only 14 percent of Taiwan's population. Another group of Han Chinese who settled in Taiwan before the arrival of the mainlanders are the "Hakka" (9 percent). The only non-Han on Taiwan are the Aborigines (*Yuanzhumin*), who today comprise no more than 1.6 percent of Taiwan's 22 million people.

14. There were two articles (§168 and 169) in the constitution of 1947 (this constitution was established at a time when the ROC-government was still on the mainland) that guaranteed special rights and status to so called "border region people" (*bianjiang minzu*).

15. See for instance the account of Atayal woman activist Liyijing Youma (1996).

16. After the recognition of the PRCh as the official China by the UN in 1979, the KMT regime faced a growing crisis of legitimacy in Taiwan.

17. In their first magazine published at National Taiwan University in 1983, the leading intellectuals of the movement claimed that Taiwan's high-mountain people (*gaoshanzu*) were threatened by racial extinction (*zhongzu miewang*). As this land was their land, it was necessary to found a movement that would help Aborigines to conscientize (*juexing*) and to realize their disadvantageous situation (Gaoshanqing No.1).

18. Stainton 1995. Actually, Jiang Kai-shek had signed the ILO Convention as early as in 1962. The only problem was that the ROC-government always refused to define Taiwan's "mountain compatriots" as "border region people," a status that would have vested them with special cultural and autonomy rights guaranteed in the constitution.

19. The first time that a member of the ATA took part in such a meeting was in 1988.

20. Yifan Yougan, "You bie yu 'tongpai', 'dupai' de 'yuanpai': *Yuanzhumin kan tongdu wenti*' " [The "aboriginal faction" that is different from the "unification faction" and from the "independence faction." How Aborigines look at the unification / independence-problem], in *China Times* January 4, 1989. Another reason to keep some distance to the political opposition at that time was the closeness of some aboriginal leaders to the KMT that paid them regular salaries for internal informations about the movement (see later).

21. These influences can be also seen by looking at the composition of the members of the ATA that was founded in the PCT's Mackay-Hospital: in 1985, 39 of the ATA's 53 members were Aborigines, among them 17 people from Christian colleges. The other 14 members were Han, many of them oppositionals and anthropologists. Until 1987, the ATA had 97 members, 22 of them Han, among them such prominent oppositionals like Gao Junming, Lin Zhengjie, and You Qing (Xie 1987b: 157).

22. The *Pingpu* comprise about ten different ethnic groups that all belonged to the Austronesian language family, but that were said to have become totally assimilated to the Han majority since the end of the nineteenth century.

23. Taiwanese folk religion is a syncretism of elements of folk Daoism, Buddhism, and Confucianism.

24. Stainton 1995. The publication of this declaration had severe consequences for the PCT. The state withdrew all exit permits for PCT representatives to travel overseas, and ordered the General Assembly to withdraw the resolution, which it termed illegal and exceeding the proper sphere of religion.

25. Within the PCT, Han and Aborigines are represented by two different branches: while the former are organized by the PCT's General Assembly, the latter are organized in the PCT's Aboriginal Mission Committee. In ideological issues, the two branches work closely together (Stainton 1995).

26. The number of demonstrators that participated in the "Return our land"—protests in 1988, 1989, and 1993 always exceeded 1,000.

27. Rudolph 1993.

28. Rudolph 2000.

29. A similar meaning was expressed by the reference to the Bible verse "Naboth's vineyard" that was frequently referred to by the preachers (Stainton 1995: chap.4.334). Actually, all these analogisms referring to ethnic identity and land were also part of the "homeland theology" of the Taiwanese PCT, but were re-contextualized for use in the mountain churches.

30. Huang Xiurong (Duo Ao), 1985, "Look how the civilized countries treat their indigenous peoples," in: *Yuanzhumin* 15.2.1985; also in: ATA 1987: 36–42.

31. Tong Chunfa (Jingruo Mashigeshige), 1985, "The Christian Mission and the local languages: Criticizing the ban on the use of dialects to missionize," in *Yuanzhumin*. 2.15.1985; also in: ATA 1987: 36–42. Jingruo Mashigeshige played a similar role in the movement as Duo Ao. Same as the latter who died in a car accident in 1994, he had been raised in the PCT's Aboriginal College in Hualian. Jingruo Mashigeshige later served as head of this college. Also see Lai Azhong in Li Renkui (ed.) 1995: 185 and Lin Jinbao in Li Renkui (ed.) 1995: 212.

32. Stainton 1995. In an unpublished statement in 1998, Stainton put it this way: "Though the ATA seemed to be the main actor to the outside, it only played a minor role as an executor: to the extent that the aboriginal movement had an organization, it was the Presbyterian Church, which provided an ideology [built on metaphors like 'chosen people' and 'promised land,'] a multilevel organizational network [for instance Urban Rural Mission-trainings in Japan and Canada] trained and paid workers [both clergy and staff at the national offices] and financial access to the Taiwanese donors and foreign grants through the World Church Council Program to combat racism."

33. See Xie Shizhong 1987a, b.

34. A full translation of this convention was printed in a 1987 publication of Taiwan's China Human Rights Organization entitled *Traditional society and culture of Taiwan's indigenous people and their contemporary human rights situation*. All articles were written by scholars from the Academia Sinica. (China Human Rights Organization 1987).

35. vgl. Xie 1987b.

36. In *Action-agenda for the fight for an "Aborigines-paragraph" in the constitution—* a publication by the ATA and the PCT—Xie pleaded for the right of Aborigines to choose their own ethnic symbols (ATA/PCT 1992: 12).

37. From the late eighties to 1993, there existed two controversial wings in the KMT, i.e., one constituted by mainlanders and their children (so called "second generation mainlanders"), the other by native Taiwanese that had been co-opted into the party since the mid-seventies when the first mainlanders died away and additional forces were needed in governmental offices. After the official election of the Taiwanese Li Denghui as president in 1990, the wing around him was named "mainstream-wing," the other wing was named "non-mainstream"-wing. After three years of fierce inter-factional fighting, the members of the non–mainstream-wing finally left the KMT and founded a new party—i.e., the "*China New Party*" (CNP).

38. For an understanding of how the "question of provincial origin" (*shengji wenti*) developed into an "ethnic question" (*zuqun wenti*) and finally into a "question of the four great ethnic groups" (*sida zuqun wenti*) see Zhang Maogui 1996a and Chang Mao-kuei 1996. See also Rudolph 2004. The greater efforts mainland China showed to obstruct Taiwanese elites' endeavors to construct a Taiwanese identity vis-à-vis the mainlanders, the more this identity construction was also directed against China.

39. Gao Deyi 1995: 14. At least until the mid-eighties, politicians as well as academic elites were strongly convinced that the development of Taiwanese society would proceed according to the models put forward by modernization theory, i.e., that social progress would be a priori accompanied by a diminution of ethnic, religious, and cultural factors. According to this view, the progressive transformation of traditional societal structures and the expansion of "modern" structural elements was an inevitable consequence of functional differentiation and the division of work.

40. ZMTYWFX 1994: 56. The setting up of such a program had been considered as early as in 1988 by the newly founded Committee for Mountain Compatriots Education, but it was not put into force until 1993. The program contained the following aims: the promotion of contact and communication of mountain-society with the main society; the promotion of marketableness; the preservation and promotion of aboriginal languages and cultures to build up self-dignity and self-respect; the promotion of talented people to develop the capability for autonomy.

41. *Zhonghua minguo Taiwan Yuanzhuminzu wenhua fazhan xiehui* (ZMTY-WFX) 1994: 55ff.

42. For a detailed discussion of different "aboriginal elites" in Taiwan see Xie 1992. Here, Xie works with the categories "resisting elites" (*kangzheng jingying*) and "KMT-loyal, political elites" (*zhengzhi jingying*). I prefer to use the expression "nativist aboriginal elite" instead of "resisting aboriginal elite," because during the 90s many aboriginal intellectuals—although opposed to the KMT's homogenization policy—did not actively take part in the aboriginal movement, but tried to express their convictions through aboriginal art and literature.

43. One of the shortcomings of the ATA had been that they had concentrated too much on the improvement of living conditions in the urban areas and neglected the rural regions. The tribalist movement hoped to be able to motivate the people to stay in their villages and find new modes of production in the tribal areas.

44. First efforts to implement multicultural education could be discerned in 1990/91. At that time, the DPP began to introduce lessons for the different vernacular languages of Taiwan in elementary schools of all counties ruled by the opposition party.

45. In 1992, Xie Shizong (1992b) already points to the fact that these categories were gradually disappearing.

46. Xie 1990: 177f.

47. Liu Wenxiong 1994.

48. Such demands had strong legitimacy: In 1993, the mortality rate of Aborigines was still twice as high as that of the Han. The most frequent death causes were—right after accidents owing to drunkenness—a very high suicide rate, tuberculosis of the lungs and liver-cirrhosis (Wang Minghui 1993).

49. Reservation land was state land. Aborigines had only user rights on this land.

50. Though the government had increased reservation land of Aborigines as a reaction of the protests of 1988 and 1989, this increase was considered too small.

51. The petition was also published in Taiwan's newspapers (see *United Daily* December 1993).

52. The incident took place in 1994 at the "First Aboriginal Culture Congress" with 50% of all participants being aboriginal, the other 50% being Han officials and anthropologists. Dressed in traditional cloth, intellectual members of the different ethnic groups of Aborigines interrupted the conference, marched to the stage and proclaimed a manifesto with the title "Cultural-head-hunting-raid." The spectacular title was supposed to be a warning to those Han who were not willing to accept the ethnonym "Taiwan Aborigines" and to grant more political and cultural rights to Aborigines. For a more detailed description of the incident see Rudolph 2003b.

53. *Austronesian News* No. 31; also see CHINA aktuell No. 2/1996: 194.

54. Webpage of the *Council of Indigenous Peoples*: http://www.apc.gov.tw/cip/index.htm.

55. *Austronesian News* No 1, 1.7.1995: 1f.

56. Liyijing Youma 1996: 168. "Young aboriginal intellectuals" (*Yuanzhumin zhiqing*) is another expression for "resisting aboriginal elite" or "nativist aboriginal elite."

57. Liyijing Youma 1996: 169.

58. Liyijing Youma 1996: 171.

59. The revelations about their previous role in the line-correction project harmed nativist aboriginal elites seriously. Even in 2002, Yifan Yougan—one of the main initators of the movement in the 80s who applied for a political office in 2002—was forced to justify his own role in the incident.

60. One rare exception is the *Working Group of the Tribes of Taiwan's Aboriginal Peoples (Yuanzhuminzu buluo gongzudui)* on the internet (www.watahope.org.tw), a neo-marxist organization that consists mainly of Han-activists unsatisfied with the new government. In their Watahope magazine, expressions like genocide, racial suppression, etc., are still very common.

61. All together, Aborigines had fourteen representatives in the parliament at that time. According to Lin Jiangyi (1996), this was twice as high as that of the Han. On the county and township levels, Aborigines had even 3.4 times as many elected delegates and representatives than the Han (Taiwan Indigenous Voice Bimonthly No. 11, 1/1996: 6f).

62. In 1996, the CIP had approximately 120 members (Freies China No. 5/1997: 11f).

63. Today, the Yami—a people of about 3000 individuals—insist on being called "Tao" again, which is their real ethnic name.

64. See for instance the webpage of Shiyman Feaien http://guhy.ee.
ntust.edu.tw/~lanyu/.

65. Besides the twelve aboriginal groups, these include the Hoklo, the Hakka,
and the mainlanders.

66. Minshengbao January 18, 2002: Yuanzhumin baoliudi jiang you zuqun
gongguan [Aboriginal reservation land will soon be administrated by
Aborigines themselves].

67. *The Taipei Times* January 22, 2005, p. 3.

68. Actually, the government in 1995 had passed a regulation according to
which Aborigines could apply for hunting permissions in those periods
when their specific ethnic group held traditional rituals. Few people however applied for permissions before going out hunting.

69. Rudolph 2003a. I discuss these issues in my Ph.D.dissertation that draws
on my fieldwork done in the villages of two different aboriginal groups
1994–1996.

70. *The Republic of China Yearbook* 2001 (http://www.gio.gov.tw/taiwan-
website/5-gp/yearbook/chpt02–2.htm).

71. "A multitude of tongues," editorial in: *The Taipei Times* January 10, 2000.

72. "A multitude of tongues," editorial in *The Taipei Times* January 10, 2000.

73. Chi Chun-chieh, "Utility key to new language policy," in *The Taipei
Times* February 7, 2000.

74. Chi Chun-chieh, "Utility key to new language policy," in *The Taipei
Times* February 7, 2000.

75. Mark Munsterhjelm, "Teaching native languages," in *The Taipei Times*
January 13, 2000. To be more convincing, Munsterhjelm points to the
fact that in 1948 the UN passed the Convention on the Prevention and
Punishment of the Crime of Genocide. What Munsterhjelm does not tell
us is that the UN did not pass Lemkin's definition. As we learn from
Sautman (see Sautman in this book), Lemkin in fact added to his
definition that a ban on cultural genocide must not be directed against
policies designed to assimilate a group into a larger society, but only
against "drastic methods, used to aid in the rapid and complete disappearance of the cultural, moral and religious life of a group of human beings."
The same author created a webpage on the internet with the title "*The
Taiwan Aboriginal Rights Webpag*" (www.taiwanfirstnations.org), where
human rights issues of Taiwan's Aborigines—though from an activist
perspective—are thoroughly discussed.

76. Matthew Ward, "To keep a mother tongue, teach it," in: The Taipei
Times of 1.22.2000.

77. On the county level, mother tongue education was begun much earlier.
Extracurricular Atayal language lessons made their debut in 1990 at Taipei
County's Wulai elementary and junior high schools, where the majority
of students are Atayal aborigines. Yilan County was the first to initiate
Hoklo courses in elementary and junior high schools. The program was

heralded by a county order in June 1990 that students should no longer be discouraged from or punished for speaking dialects at school. Pingtung County followed suit in September 1991. Since then, elective courses in Hoklo, Hakka, and the aboriginal languages were taught in selected schools of other counties as well (*The Republic of China Yearbook 2001*).

78. *The Republic of China Yearbook 2001*.

79. See Sautman in this book.

80. As for sources in Western languages, see for instance Wu Yau-Fong (1988) or Rin Hsien (1975), who is a representative of the older generation of anthropologists in Taiwan. At least until the mid-eighties, Han-politicians as well as academic elites were strongly convinced that the development of Taiwanese society would proceed according to the models put forward by modernization theory, i.e., that social progress would be a priori accompanied by a diminution of ethnic, religious, and cultural factors. According to this view, the progressive transformation of traditional societal structures and the expansion of "modern" structural elements was an inevitable consequence of functional differentiation and the division of work.

81. In an earlier article, I described the situation in which Taiwan's different ethnic groups fought for special political and cultural rights this way: "The frame in which social processes were organized before—i.e., the ROC national state that considered the political and cultural entities as identical—was undergoing thorough changes. Under the claim of bringing about a democratic transformation in a multicultural society, limits and rules were now newly determined; newly determined were the possibilities and the opportunities of the players and the distribution of political and cultural resources, social welfare and compensation and subsidizing measures." (Rudolph 2003b. In such a situation, the most important precondition for success was of course the recognition of a group's ethnic status).

82. Many members of the older generation of anthropologists were not only supporters of the modernization theory, but also believed in the superiority of Chinese culture and in the possibility that China one day could be unified if ethnic integration was successful (Rudolph 2003a: 253–180 (chap. V: "Die Rolle von Taiwans Ethnologen"), Chen Zhaoru 1994).

83. For a discussion of this conflict see Rudolph 2003a.

84. Fanon even suggested violence as the way to liberty—violence as an equalization (or compensation) for the violence one had endured in receiving the negative self-image (Fanon 1961). However, aboriginal elites in Taiwan never resorted to violence.

85. For a thorough discussion of this phenomenon that Xie Shizhong in 1992 (Xie 1992) had named "Elites without people" see Rudolph 2003a.

86. Scholars believe that the percentage had risen to approximately. 10% by 2000 (Pan Meiling 2001).

87. Guest workers earn only 70% of the lowest salary paid for cititzens of the ROC (Pan Meiling 2001).

88. The in-official numbers were much higher. For comparison: In 2001, there lived 412,444 Aborigines in Taiwan (Pan Meiling 2001), 53% of them Mountain-Aborigines and 47% Flatland-Aborigines, the latter including those who already had registered their households in the cities (after the correction of the ethnonym in 1994, the old categories "mountain" and "flatland" were preserved).

89. Sandall 2001: 181.

90. According to Sandall, "romantic primitivism"—a fashion that transferred many of Australia's Aborigines into a "new stone age"—is very much part of a larger phenomenon, i.e., the "New Age Movement." To what degree Aborigines in Taiwan are romanticized, we can observe in the discussions focusing on the questions of hunting or on the question of protection of intellectual property rights where Han- and aboriginal elites formulate their conviction of the spiritual wisdom of Taiwan's indigenous people and their potential in terms of ecological sustainability (see for instance the article of Yvonne Lin Mei-jung (www.taiwanfirstnations.org/TFNIPR.html)).

91. There are sources that claim that a large number of aboriginal intellectuals had been killed by the KMT in the "2-2-8 incident" of February 1947, where up to 20,000 Taiwanese Han were killed, and in the period of "White Terror" around 1955, but until now there is not enough substantial evidence to prove such charges (Chen Suzhen 1994).

92. Sautman apparently suggests that "ethnocide" is a more neutral term, as "unlike cultural genocide, which is invariably connected to mass ethnic murder on a grand scale, ethnocide as envisaged by proponents of the concept is not necessarily tied to killing. (Sautman in this book).

References

ATA/PCT Yuanzhumin xuandao weiyuanhui, 1992. *Zhengqu xianfa "Yuanzhuminzu tiaokuan" xingdong shouce* [Action-agenda for the fight for an "aborigines-paragraph" in the constitution]. Taibei: Presbyterian Church of Taiwan.

Cai Zhonghan (ed.), 1996. *Yuanzhumin jiaoyu congshu* [Article collection on aborigines' Education]. Taibei: Jiaoyu guangbo diantai.

Chang Mao-kuei, 1996. "Political Transformation and the 'Ethnization' of Politics in Taiwan." In Schubert and Schneider (eds.). Hamburg: Institut für Asienkunde (*Mitteilungen des Instituts für Asienkunde*, No. 270), 135–152.

Chen Suzhen, 1994. "Baise kongbu xia xisheng de Gaoshan zheren Gao Yisheng" [The high mountain philosopher Gao Yisheng who sacrificed his life during the "white terror"]. In: *Taiwan wenyi*, No. 2, 4/1994: 6–60.

Chen Zhaoru, 1994. "Shilun Taiwan renleixue de Gaoshanzu yanjiu" [Preliminary discussion of the research on high mountain peoples in Taiwan's social anthropology.] In *Taiwan Indigenous Voice Bimonthly*, No. 6, Taibei 9/1994: 27–36.

China Human Rights Organization (Zhongguo renquan xiehui) (ed.), 1987. *Taiwan tuzhu de chuantong shehui wenhua yu renquan xiankuang* [Traditional society and culture of Taiwan's indigenous people and their contemporary human rights situation]. Taibei 6/1987.

Davidson, J.W., 1903. *The Island of Formosa. Past and Present*. London 1903 (Reprint: Taibei 1972).

Fanon, Frantz, 1961. *Les damnées de la terre*. Paris.

Gao Deyi, 1995. "Maixiang duoyuanhua jiaoyu: Yuanzhumin jiaoyu xiangguan fagui de jiantao" [Toward a pluralist education: critical discussion of the regulations regarding aboriginal education.] In: *Convolute of the Symposium on Aboriginal Education. Taiwan*. Taiwan: Hualian Pedagogical College, 12–32.

Gao Wanjin (Buxing Dali), 1995. *Ningsi buqu de Yuanzhumin—Wushe shijian de gushi shenxue* [The aborigines who prefer to die than to submit—about the story and the theology of the Wushe incident.] Taiwan: Tainan Theological College.

Hsu Mutsu, 1991. *Culture, Self, and Adaption—The Psychological Anthropology of Two Malayo-Polynesian Groups in Taiwan*. Taiwan: Academia Sinica.

Li Renkui (ed.), 1995. *Taiwan nandao minzu muyu yanjiu lunwenji* [Research on the mother tongues of Taiwan's austronesian peoples.] Taiwan: Ministry of Education.

Linck-Kesting, Gudula, 1978. "Ein Kapitel japanischer Kolonialgeschichte: Die Politik gegenüber der nichtchinesischen Bevoelkerung von Taiwan" [A chapter of Japanese colonial history: the policy toward Taiwan's non-Han.] In: Nachrichten der Gesellschaft für Natur- und Völkerkunde Ostasiens Hamburg, No. 123, Hamburg 1978: 61–81.

Linck-Kesting, Gudula, 1979. *Ein Kapitel chinesischer Grenzgeschichte, Han und Nicht-Han im Taiwan der Qing-Zeit 1683–1895* [A chapter of China Frontier history: Han and Non-Han in Qing-Dynasty Taiwan 1683–1895,]. Wiesbaden.

Liu Wenxiong (Yijiang Baluer), 1994. "Taiwan Yuanzhuminzu yundong fazhan luxian zhi chubu tantao" [Preliminar discussion of the development of the social movement of Taiwan's aboriginal people]. In: *Taiwan Indigenous Voice Bimonthly*, No. 4, Taibei 5/1994: 23–38.

Liyijing Youma, 1996. *Chuancheng—zouchu kongsu* [Handing on the tradition: walking out to denounce.] Taibei: Yuanzhu minzu shiliao yanjiushe.

Pan Meiling, 2001. "Quanqiuhua yu ruoshi laodong zuqun: Taiwan de Yuanzhumin yu waiji laogong" [Globalisation and minority laborers: Taiwan's aborigines and guest workers in Taiwan.] Taiwan: http://home.kimo.com.tw/liutaho/A75.htm.

Rin Hsien, 1975. "The Synthesizing Mind in Chinese Ethno-Cultural Adjustment." In: De Vos, George/Romanucci-Ross, Lola (eds.), *Ethnic Identity, Cultural Continuities and Change*. Chicago, IL: University of Chicago Press, 137–155.

Rudolph, Michael, 1993. *Die Prostitution der Frauen der Taiwanesischen Bergminderheiten—Historische, Sozio-kulturelle und Kultur-psychologische Hintergruende* [The prostitution problem of Taiwan's mountain minorities: historical, sociocultural and psychocultural factors]. Hamburg/Muenster/London: LIT Verlag.

———, 1996. " 'Was heisst hier taiwanesisch?'—Taiwans Ureinwohner zwischen Diskriminierung und Selbstorganisation" [" 'Who's got the right to call himself

'Taiwanese'?—Taiwan's aborigines between discrimination and self-organization"]. In: Schubert / Schneider (eds). Hamburg: Institut für Asienkunde (*Mitteilungen des Instituts für Asienkunde*, No. 270), 285–310.

———, 2000. " 'Ethnic Power' oder 'gegenhegemoniale presbyterianische Aboriginalität'? Der Einfluß der Presbyterianischen Kirche Taiwans (PCT) auf die Ethnizitätsbildung taiwanesischer Ureinwohner" ["Ethnic power" or "counter-hegemonic Presbyterian aboriginality"? The influence of Taiwan's Presbyterian Church on the ethnicity of Taiwan's aborigines]. Ruhr-Universität Bochum 2000: *Cathay Scripten No. 17*.

———, 2003a. *Taiwans multi-ethnische Gesellschaft und die Bewegung der Ureinwohner: Assimilation oder kulturelle Revitalisierung?* [Taiwan's multiethnic society and the movement of aborigines: assimilation or cultural revitalisation?]. Hamburg/Muenster/London: LIT.

———, 2003b. "The Quest for Difference vs the Wish to Assimilate: Taiwan's Aborigines and their Struggle for Cultural Survival in Times of Multiculturalism." In: Rubinstein, Murray and Paul Katz (eds.), *Religion and the Formation of Taiwanese Identities*. New York: St. Martins/Palgrave, 123–156.

———, 2004. "The Emergence of the Concept of 'Ethnic Group' in Taiwan and the Role of Taiwan's Austronesians in the Construction of Taiwanese Identity." In: *Historiography East and West: A Multi-lingual On-line Journal for Studies in Comparative Historiography and Historical Thinking* (Leiden: Brill), No. 2:1 / 2004, 86–115.

Sandall, Roger, 2001. *The Culture Cult: Designer Tribalism and Other Essays*. Colorado: Westview Press.

Schubert, Gunter / Axel Schneider (eds.), 1996. *Taiwan an der Schwelle ins 21. Jh— Probleme und Perspektiven der Gesellschaft einer fernöstlichen Wirtschaftsmacht* [Taiwan on the step to the twenty-first century: problems and perspectives of a fareastern economic power]. Hamburg: Institut für Asienkunde (*Mitteilungen des Instituts für Asienkunde*, No. 270).

Stainton, Michael, 1995. *Return our Land: Counterhegemonic Presbyterian Aboriginality in Taiwan*. Canada: Ph.D.dissertation York University.

Wang Minghui, 1993. *Taiwan shandixiang de jiulei xiaofei yu yinjiu wenti* [Alcohol consumption and problems with alcohol in Taiwan's mountain townships.] Taibei: M.A.thesis at National Pedagogical University.

Wu Yau-Fong, 1988. "Taiwan's Aboriginal Administration Policy." In: *Southeast Journal of Social Science*, Vol. 16, No. 2, 1988: 61–75.

Xie Shizhong, 1987a. *Rentong de wuming yu Taiwan Yuanzhumin de zuqun bianqian* [engl. abstract: Ethnic contacts, stigmatized identity, and pan-Taiwan aboriginalism: a study on ethnic change of Taiwan aborigines]. Taipei: Zili wanbao cbs.

———, 1987b. "Yuanzhumin yundong shengcheng yu fazhan lilun de chengli: yi Beimei yu Taiwan wei li de chubu tantao" (engl. abstract: Toward dynamic theories of the origin and development of aboriginal movements: the cases of North America and Taiwan.) In: *Bulletin of the Institute of Ethnology Academia Sinica*, No. 64, 10/1987: 139–177.

————, 1990. " 'Disi shijie' de jiangou: Yuanzhumin shijie de qiji yu weiji" (engl. abstract: The establishment of the Fourth World: on the opportunities and crises of the indigenous world). In: Xie Shizhong, Sun Baogang (eds), 1990. *Renleixue yanjiu* [Ethnological Research]. Taibei: Nantian cbs., 177–215.

————, 1992. "Pianli qunzhong de jingying: Shilun 'Yuanzhumin' xiangzheng yu Yuanzhumin jingying xianxiang de guanxi" [Preliminary discussion on the relation between the symbol "Yuanzhumin" [aborigines] and the elites' phenomenon]. In: *Daoyu bianyuan* [Isle Margin], No. 5, Taibei 10/1992: 52–60.

Yohani (Song Guoxian), 1993. "Cong Lianheguo yuanzhumin quanli cao'an kan Taiwan yuanzhumin de chongjian" [The reconstruction of the Taiwan aboriginal people in the perspective of the draft UN declaration on the rights of indigenous peoples]. In: *Wilderness Magazine*: Daosheng cbs., 13–32.

Zhang Maogui, 1996a. "Taiwan zui cishou de zhengzhi wenti" [Taiwan's Most Urgent Political Problem]. In: *Cai Xun* (Wealth Magazine) No. 168, 3/1996: 152–163.

ZMTYWFX (Zhonghua minguo Taiwan Yuanzhuminzu wenhua fazhan xiehui) [ROC-Taiwan-Aborigines-Development-Committee] ed., 1994. *Yuanzhumin zhengce yu shehui fazhan* [Aboriginal Policy and Social Development]. Taibei: Executive Yuan.

CHAPTER 4

WEST PAPUA: THE DISCOURSE OF CULTURAL GENOCIDE AND CONFLICT RESOLUTION

John Otto Ondawame

Introduction

The Papuan ancestors are believed to have settled in Papua, known to many outsiders as New Guinea, around 60,000 BC. Since then, Papuan cultures have developed their own traditions, farming and other technologies, social structures, laws, and etiquette. Today there are Melanesian cultures from Fiji to West Papua, but each is unique. The two million indigenous West Papuans value their homelands and hundreds of cultures above any foreign payments. West Papuan languages are quite distinct from the peninsular Malay of Indonesia.

The Dutch claimed possession of parts of West Papua after 1828, though they had only charted the coastline from ships. It was the mid-nineteenth century before Dutch missionaries arrived to teach their language and sciences. When Germany claimed the north-eastern quarter of Papua in 1895, the Netherlands built Hollandia (now Jayapura) near the German border at Humboldt Bay. For 134 years. the Dutch claim was largely benign, and Papuans openly discussed their interest in forming a unified West Papuan government in the 1930s. Although the Imperial Japanese forces occupied Papua from 1941 to 1944, the Netherlands regained control after the war and, by the 1950s, its administration strongly supported the Papuan people's desire to create a Melanesian State.

Unknown to Papuans and Dutch, a 1936 Dutch geological team had sent its reports to Standard Oil in New York, instead of the Shell company in the Netherlands, and unknown to the Dutch or U.S. governments, Standard Oil discovered the world's richest gold and copper deposits in West Papua. After the World War II, Sukarno, who had worked with the Japanese war-time government, attempted to claim all Dutch possessions in South East Asia and the Pacific as part of a new Republic. In December 1949, Sukarno's Republic was included as one of sixteen autonomous States of a federated "United States of Indonesia." By July, 1950, Sukarno's Republic had dissolved or absorbed the other fifteen States and claimed the entire region as the "Republic of Indonesia."

Although the Moluccas islands, in the Australian Arafura Sea, had been one of the sixteen States, West Papua, which had been liberated from Japanese occupation over a year before Java, had not been included in the list of countries surrendered to the Indonesian federation in 1949. In support of his 1950 demand for possession of West Papua, Sukarno threatened to nationalize all Dutch and U.S. business assets, unless West Papua sovereignty was surrendered to his Republic. These threats continued throughout the 1950s. Then, in March 1959, the *New York Times* published an article that revealed the Dutch government was now searching for the source of the alluvial gold they had found flowing into the Arafura Sea, which was, of course, the Papuan gold and copper deposits Standard Oil had found in 1936. By January 1960, another Rockefeller interest, Freeport Sulphur, had signed an agreement with the East Borneo Company to mine West Papua.

In 1959, the Netherlands had begun to implement the United Nations decolonization process for West Papua and was presenting annual reports on West Papua's progress toward self-sufficiency and self-governance. Then, in April 1961, Sukarno visited the United States and informed President Kennedy that only if the United States supported his claim to West Papua would he oppose communism. In September 1961, UN Secretary General Dag Hammarskjöld died in an aircraft accident and shortly after the US–UN mission began to rally support for West Papua not to be decolonized, but for its colonial administration to be transferred from the Netherlands to Indonesia. In West Papua the Dutch promised the Papuans would have their independence by 1970, and in May 1961 inducted an elected Papuan National Council or *Nieuw Guinea Raad* into office. As the first national congress, the council officially recognized new Papuan state symbols, such as the national anthem *Hai Tanahku Papua*, a constitution, parliament, police, military force, currency, and the *Morning Star* flag. On December 1, 1961 the West Papuan and Dutch flags were raised side by side.

This bright future came to an end a few weeks later as the Indonesian military attempted the first of several invasion attempts. Although Indonesian paratrooper and naval attacks were successfully repelled, in New York, U.S. President Kennedy coerced the Dutch to succeed in secret negotiations designed to trade the sovereignty of West Papua to Indonesia without Papuan knowledge or permission. On August 15, 1962, the Netherlands and Indonesia signed the New York Agreement for the transfer of the administration of West Papuan rights from Dutch to Indonesian control.

On January 31, 1962, Indonesian Foreign Minister Subandrio promised that all Papuan interests would be protected, if West Papua's administration were transferred to Indonesia, including a guarantee that the Papuans could quit Indonesia after "ten or fifteen years," if they still wanted to. The New York Agreement confirmed this in writing and stated, in Article 22 item 1, that the parties "will guarantee fully the rights, including the rights of free speech, freedom of movement and of assembly, of the inhabitants of the area." From Article 14 to Article 21 the Agreement specified the international standards by which an "Act of Free Choice" was to be conducted, including the eligibility of all male and female Papuan adults to vote. The process was not to be started until one year after a UN Representative arrived in the territory to commence his duties.

On December 7, 1966, Indonesian Home Affairs Minister Lieut. Gen. Basuki Rahmat renounced the Indonesian pledge to allow an "Act of Free Choice." The next year, Indonesia sold a thirty year license to mine West Papua to the U.S. Freeport Corporation. To legitimatize the sale, it was decided that the Indonesian military should stage the "Act of Free Choice." On August 22, 1968, the UN representative, Ambassador Oritiz Sanz, arrived in West Papua; on January 9, 1969, NASA announced the Apollo 11 crew and that its expected mission date would be in the third week of July. On February 18, 1969, Indonesia accordingly proposed that the "Act of Free Choice" should begin in the third week of July, six weeks earlier than specified in the New York Agreement. The West Papuan people were no longer able to express their wishes via a voting system, such as they had used in their 1959 local elections or in the 1961 national elections. An Indonesian system, under which the military would select suitable male representatives to express everyone else's wishes, was to be used instead.

On July 5, 1969, Ambassador Oritiz Sanz gave an interview in which he criticized the Indonesian processes being used. He revealed he was still attempting to gain permission for a "one person, one vote" system to be used, a proposal which Jakarta continued to reject. The same *New York Times* report quoted a member of the Indonesian Parliament as saying, "We are going through the motions because of our obligations under the

New York Agreement of 1962. But West Irian (Papua) is Indonesian and must remain Indonesian; we can not accept any alternative." While the international media watched the Apollo mission and then followed Richard Nixon's whistle stop tour of South East Asia, the "Act of Free Choice" was conducted without any media coverage, except for that of a journalist, Hugh Lunn, who disobeyed Reuters' repeated instructions not to report on the West Papua election process. In West Papua, Mr. Lunn was shocked to discover that the people were not being allowed to vote, and that instead around 1,025 men were handpicked as "representatives" by the Indonesian military. When protesters arrived with signs calling for one vote per person, they were arrested. Since then, all of the selected "representatives" have testified they were coerced by threats to their families and villages. The UN, rather than commenting upon this shameful injustice, instead gave an almost silent approval by "taking note" of the Indonesian claim that the entire West Papua population had unanimously voted to be integrated into the foreign nation of Indonesia.

The 1962 New York Agreement and 1969 "Act of Free Choice" are shocking examples of disregard for the human rights of an indigenous population and of the ease by which such abuses could be hidden from the international community. Within West Papua, denial of the natural rights of freedom of expression and freedom of movement has been absolute since May 3, 1962.

As a colony, massive cultural genocide in West Papua has become routine, with devastating effects. Today, the international community finds such practices to be shocking and morally abhorrent, akin to the barbarism of the Nazi era or the racially prejudiced "White-Australia" policies. Yet Indonesia is still willing to throw Papuans aside to carry out these genocidal polices.[1] But unlike the overt colonial relationship declared by the Netherlands, Jakarta uses democratic terms to mask its colonial nature. Terms such as "regional development and stability" are commonly used. The rhetoric of "development" is used to obfuscate colonial discrimination, exploitation, repression, and genocide of the people and ecology of Papua for the benefit of Java and its transmigrant settlers. Consequently Papuans feel like foreigners in their homelands, becoming no more than smiling creatures or objects whose rights Jakarta willingly disregards.

This chapter examines "cultural genocide" in West Papua from a colonial context and Papuan perspective. The analysis will build on the concepts of colonialism, genocide, and practices of conflict resolution. The empirical dimensions of analysis are tested by examining the extent of the marginalization of Papuan culture over the last forty-three years of

Indonesian occupation. The claim will be supported through analysis of the impact of militarization, transmigration, social injustices, politics of denial, and political repressions, and the Papuan responses. The chapter then suggests a way toward a peaceful solution of the conflict. It will argue that as long as there is a lack of respect for and recognition of Papuan culture and political rights, including the rights to self-determination and independence, the escalation of conflict will likely continue. New viable alternatives are therefore required to end this conflict.

Colonialism as a Concept

Definitions of colonialism vary greatly, but the term is literally derived from the word "colony," or a piece of land, that is located abroad or far away from a center and that could be exploited. The suffix "ism" refers to a political ideology that influences the manner of political control over a colony. According to Jack Woddis, colonialism is "a direct and overall subordination of one country to another on the basis of state power being in the hands of the dominating foreign power."[2] The concept implies the use of force to expand territory, to control cheap labor and resources, to open land space for new settlement, and to maintain a market monopoly at the expense of local peoples.

Colonialism, as a political system, can be divided into two distinct types: neocolonialism and conventional colonialism, which may be distinguished by their origins. Neo-colonialism, which is also called internal colonialism, is defined as oppression that is perpetuated by a government over its own people within a nation-state. Typically it involves exploitation of resources in the periphery and enrichment of the center, the accumulation of power and wealth in the hands of a small central power elite, while the periphery remains poor, and affecting a direct and overall subordination of citizens for economic and political interests. Conventional colonialism is defined as domination by a foreign power, a concept I will explore further in this chapter.

Colonial ideology developed in association with the industrial revolution in Europe from the beginning of the seventeenth century. European capitalists needed new territory for raw materials, cheap labor, and markets. To control these vital assets, the elimination of entire populations of indigenous peoples, was the policy of colonial powers. The dominant power of the imperial nations was achieved at the expense of slaves, the working class, and the periphery. The mercantile symbols of wealth were gold and spices and the colonial powers occupied territories in order to open markets and have access to gold, supplies of raw materials, and "slaves" in Asia, Africa, the Pacific, and Americas.

Colonialism and imperialism are two sides of the same coin. Colonial power preserves imperial interests and vice versa. Both are characterized by territorial expansion, exploitation, and genocide. Colonial administrations preserved the interests of capital. Like Chilcote[3], Woddis describes the relationship between colonialism and capitalism as an integrated system, saying: "colonialism enabled the imperialist power to rob the colonial peoples in various ways. They were able to secure cheap land, cheap labor, and cheap resources".[4] The establishment of new trade centers and ports in Africa, America, Asia, and the Pacific by European colonists in the fifteenth and sixteenth centuries demonstrates how colonists preserved the interests of their imperial masters in their host countries.

Exploitation of the indigenous peoples is a common colonial practice, as is the extermination of their culture; through the following ways: the imposition of the colonial culture and language; the introduction of laws and orders that preserved the interests of the colonialists, the outnumbering of indigenous people by the planned resettlement of immigrants, the establishment of loyal, local puppet regimes, the large-scale exploitation of the colony's local natural resources, the imposition of a slave system involving social apartheid, the dispossession of the people and removal of their children, and the dishonest systematic denunciation of local cultures as primitive.

Over the past three hundred years or so, millions of immigrant colonists from Europe, the Middle East, and Asia have settled in the colonial territories of Australia, New Zealand, America, Asia, and Africa. This demographic movement has brought about serious socioeconomic, political, and ecological consequences for indigenous communities, in particular the Aborigines of Australia, the Indians of North, Central and South America, and peoples in Asia and Africa as well. The colonial ideology prevents any development of an autonomous economy, politics, and self-government within the colonized territories.[5] Thus, colonial expressions, such as "progress," "development," or "improvement" empowers the colonialist, but denies the rights of indigenous peoples. Colonialism is, therefore, a necessary component of capitalism, channeling the accumulation of capital to the capitalists; colonialism and imperialism are intertwined.

In brief, colonialism is an ideology that attempts to subordinate others for the purpose of protecting the interest of the colonizers. Territorial expansion, the use of cheap labor and other people's resources, and most importantly, the genocide of indigenous peoples marginalized in the perpetrator's mind, has been seen a necessary approach for colonial power. But what do we mean by "genocide"?

Genocide: Definition and Controversies

"Genocide is the policy of deliberately killing a nationality or ethnic group."[6] Article II of the Genocide Convention of 1948, which was adopted in January 1951, stipulated that genocide means any of the following acts committed with intent to destroy, in whole or in part, a national, ethnical, racial, or religious group, as such (a) Killing members of the group; (b) Causing serious bodily or mental harm to members of the group; (c) Deliberately inflicting on the group conditions of life calculated to bring about its physical destruction in whole or in part; (d) Imposing measures intended to prevent births within the group; (e) Forcibly transferring children of the group to another group. Furthermore, Article III stipulates that the following acts should be punishable: (a) Genocide, (b) Conspiracy to commit genocide, (c) Direct and public incitement to commit genocide, (d) Attempt to commit genocide, (e) Complicity in genocide. Article IV stipulates that persons committing genocide or any other act enumerated in Article III shall be punished, whether they are constitutionally responsible rulers, public officials, or private individuals.

Genocide is, therefore, one of the general characteristics of colonization. As the relationship between the colonized and the colonists inevitably becomes unhealthy, mistrust and disobedience become new social diseases. The relationship between the "core," referring to Jakarta, and the "periphery," referring to West Papua, becomes unbalanced, with an unequal distribution of goods and services.

Genocidal Policies and Their Implications

In light of the above articles, let me analyze the implications of the genocidal policies that have affected the lives of the people of West Papua. It is apparent that systematic genocide is going on in West Papua. The Albert Lowenstein International Human Rights Clinic at Yale University Law School has published their conclusions from an examination of documented human rights conditions in West Papua. In their paper entitled *Indonesian Human Rights Abuses in West Papua: Application of the Law of Genocide to the History of Indonesian Control*, they conclude that the historical and contemporary evidence strongly suggest the Indonesian government has committed proscribed acts with the intent to destroy the West Papuans, acts that violate the provision of the 1948 Convention on the Prevention and Punishment of the Crime of Genocide. In their conclusion, the research team states:

> Since the so-called [1969, UN-supervised] Act of Free Choice, the West Papuan people have suffered persistent and horrible abuses at the hands of the

Indonesian Government. The Indonesian military and security forces have engaged in widespread violence and extra judicial killings in West Papua. They have subjected Papuan men and women to acts of torture, disappearance, rape and sexual violence, thus causing serious bodily and mental harm. Systematic resource exploitation, the destruction of Papuan resources and crop, compulsory (and often uncompensated) labor, transmigration schemes, and forced relocation have caused pervasive environmental harm to the region, undermined traditional subsistence practices, and led to widespread diseases, malnutrition, and health problems among West Papuans. Such acts, taken as a whole, appear to constitute the imposition of conditions of life calculated to bring about the destruction of the West Papuans. Many of these acts, individually and collectively, clearly constitute crimes against humanity under international law.[7]

The study highlights the urgent need for heightened international attention to the grave human rights situation in West Papua. A similar study was conducted by the West Papua Project at the Centre of Peace and Conflict Studies, University of Sydney, entitled *Genocide in West Papua?: The role of the Indonesian state apparatus and a current needs assessment of the Papuan people.* Its concluded that there are serious threats to the survival of the West Papuans and stability of the region. Due to recent increases in large-scale military campaigns that are decimating highland tribal communities, the HIV/AIDS explosion, and persistent Papuan underdevelopment in the face of a rapid and threatening demographic transition, West Papuans will likely become a minority in their own land.[8]

Now, let me use Freeport Indonesia (FI), a giant mining company owned by a U.S.-registered mother company, as a case study to get a clear clue on the ongoing genocide in West Papua. Freeport McMoRan Mining's exploitation of West Papua in the last thirty-eight years of operation has brought serious implications, and the company has been criticized for its lack of social and environmental accountability.

Suharto's coup in 1965 and the establishment of a repressive right-wing dictatorship were a turning point in Indonesian history, and turned out to be a boon to Western corporations. Over the next three decades, a new oligarchic system formed, in which the Suharto family and its associated members, Indonesian political and military elites, and foreign corporations, were to play central roles.[9] In 1967, two years after Suharto seized power from the late President Sukarno, Freeport was the first foreign company to receive a permit to operate in Indonesia after the coup. It developed a close and mutually profitable relationship with Suharto.

Freeport has been rewarded with the right to exploit what turned out to be the third largest copper mine and the largest gold mine in the world, with up to US\$2 billion per year gross income, and up to US\$200 million per year in profits. Freeport has in turn been Indonesia's largest corporate taxpayer and has provided the crucial expertise needed to exploit the mineral resources seized from the Papuans.[10]

In 1984, Jim Bob Moffett, who was later to become a close friend and ally of Suharto, took over Freeport and invited former U.S. Secretary of State Henry Kissinger onto the board of directors, paying him U.S.\$500,000 a year.[11] The large-scale exploitation of the natural resources of West Papua brings little benefit to the Papuans, but provides an economic surplus for the government in Jakarta and for the capitalist owners, most often foreign multinational companies. Freeport McMoRan, a New Orleans registered mining company that today operates in West Papua, is one of many examples of such capitalist imperialism[12] and of the rewards that Henry Kissinger receives for the advice he has provided to U.S. Presidents to endorse Indonesia's colonial interests.

Killing of the Group

Used to protect colonial strategic, territorial and economic interests, a coercive approach and rapid militarization of West Papua has created serious political, economic, environmental, and social consequences ever since West Papua was declared a *Daerah Operasi Militer* (Military Operational Zone) in 1960s. Today, Jakarta deploys both organic and nonorganic troops, including the elite KOPASUS and KOSTRAD troops. The more than 50,000 troops deployed in West Papua today were formerly deployed in East Timor and Aceh. There is increasing fear that the history of East Timor in its post-referendum period will be repeated again in West Papua.

The Indonesian military has actively promoted terrorist activities in West Papua. Laskar Jihad, an extremist Muslim militia, has been given support to promote religious conflict. According to a human rights organization in Jayapura, 3,000 members of Laskar Jihad,[13] responsible for human rights abuses in Molucca's conflict five years ago, have established four bases in West Papua, including in the Fakfak and Sorong regencies. Their presence was confirmed by the commander of Laskar Jihad, Ja'far Umar Thalib.[14]

According to Global Security Organization (May 5, 2003), Laskar Jihad is being armed, funded and protected by the Indonesian military, and is reported to be particularly active in the highlands on the north of the island, along its border with Papua New Guinea. At the border town of Arso, Laskar Jihad members are said to be actively recruiting and training both local Papuans and migrants from the country's more populous western islands, such as Java and Sumatra.

The latest reports of Laskar Jihad's activities in the region confirm the fears of many Indonesians that Laskar Jihad is still active, despite its October 2002 announcement that it was disbanding. The same report said that its members began to arrive in the territory in 2000, and two years later established an office in Sorong. In the area of Fakfak, over 175 boats carrying Laskar Jihad personnel and equipment are said to have arrived along the coast between April and June 2002. Several Papuans reported discovering stockpiles of weapons. A number of Pakistani and Afghan mujahideen were sighted and believed to have joined the Jihad against local Christian populations. Laskar Jihad's magazine, which contains articles attacking Christians, Jews, and the U.S., began to be sold openly in markets in Papua, together with T-shirts, DVDs and books on Osama bin Laden.

In a joint statement, Papuan tribal council and youth organization leaders condemned these activities. It is strongly suspected that groups such as Laskar Jihad have links with Osama bin Laden's al- Qaeda terrorist network. The U.S. has strongly responded to this alarming development. It "believes that dozens, possibly hundreds of al-Qaeda fighters have slipped out of Afghanistan into Indonesia"[15] and that "Now, it seems that history might be repeating itself in the Indonesian province of West Papua—or Irian Jaya—where the locals are also after independence from Jakarta. There have been serious claims that Indonesian army-backed militias and Islamic extremists are working in tandem, provoking some damning allegations of ethnic cleansing and genocide."[16]

The Indonesian armed forces (ABRI), has used the classical policy of divide-and-rule as an effective strategy to destroy Papuan national unity. It has sought to create divisions among the people on the basis of ethnicity, religion, and region. The army (TNI) has actively promoted horizontal conflict among groups by orchestrating political and social unrest in many parts of the territory and then blaming the *Organisasi Papua Merdeka* (OPM) or Free Papua Movement. Many civilians have been killed during the occupation and the Rev. Sofyian Yoman stated in 2005 that TNI has been using humanitarian funds for military purposes.

There has been much evidence of TNI killing innocent people and entire townships. There have been killings of innocent people in the Tsinga and Hoa valleys of Mimika regency in 1969 and in Paniai Wissel Lake District massacre in 1985. There were the Biak massacres of 1989 and 1998, the Wasior massacre of 2002, Balim massacre in 2000, Abepura student killings in 2000, and killing of predominant Papuan leaders such as Arnold Ap in 1984 and Theys Eluay in 2001. There also was the killing in

Timika of two Americans and an Indonesian in 2002. A year ago, another mass killing occurred in Puncak Jaya. These are but a few examples of known systematic killings. Recently, Rev. Soratez Yoman, Head of Baptist Church in West Papua, provided a list of names of killings, tortures, intimidations and disappearances that occurred in the central and western highlands of West Papua in the last three years. In Nabire for example, eight civilians were tortured to death on January 17, 2005 by Indonesian soldiers from Battalion 753. Similar brutalities happened in Tokikara, the central highlands, where fourteen civilians were arrested and tortured and one was shot dead on January 21, 2005. There are many other killings and other forms of human rights abuses being committed across West Papua, but very few victims are able to report what has happened.[17]

Causing Serious Bodily or Mental Harm to Members of the Group

In West Papua democratic freedom has been regularly violated and the people subjected to oppression and exploitation. The Indonesian response to growing public pressure for political change has been to steadily increase the violation and repression of fundamental human rights. The occupation forces maintain their tight grip on the opposition partly through the new Criminal Code. Amnesty International, which has been observing the situation closely, has concluded:

> Opposition to Indonesian rule of West Papua, both armed and unarmed, has continued since authority over the province was transferred to the Indonesian Government in 1963. Protests, the occupation forces have responded to flag-raising and peaceful demonstrations with severe widespread human rights violations including arbitrary arrests, disappearances, extra-judicial executions, torture and the imprisonment of prisoners of conscience.[18]

Human rights abuses have intensified since Presidential Decree No 8, 1963, concerning prohibition of the exercise of political rights, was promulgated. It was later reinforced by Presidential Decree No. 11, 1963, which formulated an Anti-Subversion Law that legitimated the Indonesian armed forces' role in eliminating political opposition.[19]

The government has continued to impose severe limitations on freedom of assembly, association, demonstration and criticism, as well as social intimidation, through waves of arrests, torture, and expanded surveillance aimed at reining in political activities. The occupation forces place restrictions on public meetings of five or more persons, including academic or other seminars. All marches and demonstrations require permits from the police and several government agencies. Lectures and class discussion materials in schools, colleges and universities that might provoke government displeasure can lead to academic sanctions, if not expulsion or arrest. Any publications that contain the word "Papuan" were banned until late 1999, when former President, Gus Dur Abdulrahman Wahid allowed the use of the name. Old scholarly publications that deal with Papuan songs, literature, poetry, politics and culture are similarly barred from circulation on the basis that such items are relics of Dutch colonial rule and could encourage Papuan nationalism. The military is allowed to intervene on campuses and in schools to arrest and detain students who may have taken part in any form of "subversive" activity. The arrest and detention of members of the Papuan Youth Organization in 1968, 1975, 1996, and 1998, both in Timika and Jayapura, are classic examples of such military intervention.

Papuan human rights, environmental and social organizations, churches, and unions have all been subjected to systematic government crackdown and have become regular targets of intimidation. In the past few years, human rights activists in Jayapura, including John Rumbiak, Johannes Bonay, Dr. Benny Giay, and Rev. Socratez Yoman, have repeatedly faced death-threats from the Indonesian military. NGOs have faced harassment through police raids on their offices, surveillance by police or military intelligence, and cancellation of private meetings. In some cases, high-level government officials have been threatened with legal action because they are considered to be trouble-makers.[20]

The abuse of women's rights and family planning are two examples. The occupation forces use arbitrary arrest, detention, rape, torture, and intimidation as means to oppress women and members of the OPM. There are many cases of brutalities and human rights abuses occurring. Human rights violations occurred in Bela, Alama, Jila, and Mapnduma in 1996–1997,[21] where more than 138 civilians died in military reprisals; 166 buildings were burned down, including one traditional men's house, 13 church buildings, and two medical care centers. Twelve rape cases in Mapnduma were also reported. While some of these events have been widely reported, many more systematic human rights abuses are never reported in the world media.

The disappearance of many Papuans has also been reported. According to Zonggonau et al.,[22] K. Kwalik,[23] and B. Niwilingame,[24] many Papuans have disappeared without a trace. Following the Tembagapura incident, both the Australian Council for Overseas Aid (ACFOA) and former Bishop Jan Herman Munninghoff, OFM of Jayapura[25] reported five relatives of Kelly Kwalik missing. Mama Josepha Alomang, who was one of the detainees, has said that "Kwalik's relatives were taken away that night but never returned again."[26] A report made available by Amnesty International[27] records that people are missing; independent observers believe that most are dead, including the five relatives of Kwalik. Jakarta is also responsible for the murder of Chairman of the Papuan Presidium, Theys Eluay, on November 10, 2001, by death squad units of the military.

Torture and degrading treatment have been common practices in the detention centers and prisons. The Indonesian Criminal Code makes such practices a crime punishable by up to four years in prison and gives suspects or their families the right to challenge the legality of an arrest or detention. However, such legal protection is in practice both inadequate and widely ignored. Security forces continue to use torture and other forms of mistreatment on suspects, forcing them to make confessions.

Lack of civil liberties is another form of genocide. This includes the lack of respect for and recognition of freedom of speech, of the press, of peaceful assembly and association, and of movement within the country and overseas. Although the 1945 Constitution and the 1982 Press Law provide for freedom of the press, the government has consistently restricted public discussion. Critics of the president, senior officials, and influential local interest groups, for example, are at risk of harassment, arrest, or torture. In West Papua, news magazines and daily newspapers have been banned, and the authorities provide guidance to local journalists and editors on what they should write and print. Freedom of movement is restricted and special permits are required to visit certain places in West Papua, particularly sensitive areas, such as Tembagapura/Timika and surrounding areas. Even to visit their own relatives, Papuans are required to have an identity card, *Kartu Penduduk*, and a travel document, *Surat Keterangan Jalan*, a system little different from that under the apartheid regime in South Africa. In brief, militarization has negative implications for the lives of the people of West Papua.

Deliberately Inflicting on the Group Conditions of Life Calculated to bring about its Physical Destruction in Whole or in Part

For political purposes, a considerable number of transmigrants (whom the Papuans call immigrants) from the overpopulated islands of Java and Bali have been moved to West Papua and used as cheap labour. Most transmigrants are landless and poor. Since 1967, Indonesia has sponsored a massive transmigration program from Java and other densely populated islands in the archipelago. Its aim is to reduce population pressures in densely populated Java and other islands, and to secure Indonesian political and social dominance in an economically crucial area. The result is the political and social marginalization of the Papuans and ultimately a process of cultural genocide. In 1985 the Indonesian Minister of Transmigration said ominously that the goal is to "integrate all ethnic groups into one nation," so that "different ethnic groups will, in the long run, disappear" and there will be one kind of man, the Malay race.

Rapid population growth in the region through government-sponsored immigration (*transmigrasi*) is an integral part of the colonial process of territorial control, with the ultimate objective of Papuan genocide and ethnic uniformity in the entire Malay Archipelago. What has happened in West Papua since the 1960s is analogous with European colonization over the last four hundred years, when European peoples settled in America, Australia, and Africa, wiping out indigenous peoples and taking over their land and resources.

There have been official immigrants from Java and Bali, but also there have been "spontaneous" immigrants from Moluccas and Sulawesi. West Papua has become one of the major targeted territories of the government's transmigration program, with numbers 88.4 percent higher than in any other province. During the PELITA IV (Fourth Five Year Plan, 1984/85–1988/89), for example, West Papua was used to solve the overpopulation problem of Java, which was the major destination of transmigrants. In 1988/89 alone, 137,800 families, or 685,000 people, resettled in West Papua.[28] Apart from these official immigrants, "spontaneous" migrants came, looking for better[29] lives and job opportunities. In the last five years, Jakarta promised to stop the transmigration program, but in reality, Jakarta continues to support the program by encouraging spontaneous job seekers to enter West Papua. Every week, passenger boats from Java and Bali drop off newly arrived transmigrants in large numbers. Many fear the population of West Papua will double by the year 2050, threatening the future of the people of West Papua, with the serious consequences of becoming marginalized in their own country.

The confiscation of land and dispossession of landowners is another deliberate policy inflicted on Papuans. In order to extract the mineral wealth and build roads, airfields, bridges, and military posts, the lands of Papuans have been confiscated without any compensation. Many landowners have been and are being forcibly dispossessed and relocated to resettlement camps. In 1998, for example, the local government made public a plan to relocate considerable numbers of Amungme and other highland groups from Wa, Banti, and Utekini villages in the highlands.

Thousands, probably up to 40,000, of indigenous folk including Amungme people, were dislocated when Freeport McMoRan built the mining town of Tembagapura for its workers. Since the company started operation in 1967, unrest and riots have been reported in protest of mining operations. Amungme leader Tuwarek Karkime [Natkime] once said: "I am always angry at God and ask why He had to place these beautiful mountains here, because the Amungme people have received nothing from Freeport except problems."[30]

Dozens of villagers from Koperapoka in the south were also forcibly moved to settlement camps in Timika creating a buffer zone for mining expansion by FI and the dumping of mine wastes. Most importantly, there was a settlement program for transmigrants from Indonesia. The regime uses various justifications to dispossess the landowners, including the claim that a village is a center of OPM sympathizers. The most common practice is to claim the land on the basis that it is no-man's land and therefore the government and FI have the right to claim it as state land in according with Article 33 of the Indonesian state constitution 1945.

Imposing Measures Intended to Prevent Births Within the Group

The lack of accountability in combating health problems introduced to West Papua is another genocidal mechanism. For example, in 1980 it was claimed that 216 Amungme people in Kwamki Lama died in an epidemic.[31] In the highlands, the people now commonly suffer from poor nutrition, yaws or treponemal infection and also from respiratory ailments, skin infections and eye infections.[32] Many people die from diseases spreading inland from the coast, such as malaria, cholera, TB, tapeworm, diarrhea, dysentery, and tetanus.

Malaria is now endemic in the area. According to FI, malaria positive rates in Kwamki Lama in 1992 were as high as 68 percent.[33] Despite the well-documented existence of these health problems, and notwithstanding local demands for medical assistance, the state and FI initially did very little to improve the health conditions of the local people.

The spread of HIV/AIDS in West Papua has been an alarming issue since the virus was first detected in the territory eleven years ago. "In West Papua (Irian Jaya) the percentage of HIV/AIDS cases is much higher than the other provinces. It is regrettable, that regional government has not paid serious attention to these alarming issues."[34] In Timika, for example, this issue has very serious implications.[35] When I visited Timika in 1975, there were no brothels, but the economic boom has since attracted many sex workers, with centers of prostitution located in Kilo 10, Pisa, and a few bars in the city. Mostly, the prostitutes are Javanese and Menadonese (from North Sulawesi), from broken families, orphans, or driven by poverty. The sex industry is one of the faster growing developments in the area. In 1995, it was reported that there were six suspected HIV cases in the Timika area, but this number had jumped to forty in 1997. In Kwamki Lama alone, AIDS reportedly affected four people. Sorong is another hot spot for spreading this deadly virus. Out of Sixty-two persons infected with the HIV virus, twelve patients have died.[36] In a society where the use of condoms is taboo, a rapid spread of the virus is likely. There have been severe social consequences: the destruction of social structures and belief systems; the loss of traditional land; significant changes in traditional life styles; and the spread of coastal diseases such as malaria, cholera, and dysentery and recently; the alarming spread of HIV/AIDS virus. According to the Papuan Health Office in Jayapura, 1.910 cases have been detected by June 30, 2005, 1,133 HIV positives and 777 AIDS cases. This number is regionally distributed as follows: 700 in Merauke, 592 in Mimika, 173 in Jayapura and 146 in Sorong. Remote areas in the central highlands have also become infected to an alarming degree.[37]

Lack of environmental accountability has been a contentious issue for some time. Environmental destruction has intensified over the last thirty-eight years, with serious social, religious, and economic consequences. The high pollution of air, seas, and rivers with highly toxic substances has affected the level of births in West Papua. The Aijkwa River in southern West Papua has already become polluted to the extent that locals cannot drink from the river or swim in it.

The destruction of rainforest has also brought serious erosion and much reduced the fertility of land used for producing basic food crops such as taro, yam, and tapioca.[38] Erosion has caused major flooding, which has destroyed the gardens and houses of the lowland Kamoro people. Organisms in rivers, the sea, and forests along riverbanks are causing cont-amination. Currently 120,000 metric tons of tailings (including toxic chemicals) are discharged into the Aijkwa river system every day, killing fish, plankton, sago palms, and mangrove trees.[39] Jakarta has recently approved an increase in production to 300,000 tons of ore per day; this means that another 88 square miles of land will be smothered under the grey, sand-like tailings.

Clean drinking water is a continuing problem: "The main concern of the Amungme and Kamoro is their water supply."[40] The people along the Aijkwa, Minajerwi, and Kopi rivers cannot now drink the water because it originates in the Ertsberg and Grasberg mining areas and is heavily polluted by toxic wastes that could produce deadly diseases.

Problems during pregnancy have been related to environmental degra-dation. According to a Catholic Mission report, the rate of natural increase in 1936 was 1.9, but had dropped to 0.9 in 1989.[41] The low birthrate and high level of mortality among children in the region in the past twenty-eight years can be directly related to destruction of the environment.

Denying the Rights of the West Papuans: Social Injustices

Social discrimination on the basis of race, color, religion, and sex is an integral part of colonial policies of genocide. Discrimination in access to health services and in wages are examples. In order to understand the overall situation, let us examine in more detail discrimination in job opportunities, wages, educational opportunities, and cultural values.

Discrimination against Papuans in job opportunities and wages is disproportionate. Looking for new lives, traditional dwellers have moved into the cities and towns expecting to make their fortunes. However, few achieve their goals. Most small- and medium-sized business activities are in the hands of newcomers, primarily the Buginese, Makassans, and Javanese. As the former governor of Irian Jaya, Pattipi said: "Both Javanese settlers and 'spontaneous' migrants coming from Sulawesi have taken many jobs and secured a stranglehold on the urban economy."[42] For example, FI brought in Javanese and Buginese taxi drivers, ignoring the many Irianese with the skills to drive cars and trucks.[43] Today, there are 17,308 workers employed directly or indirectly by Freeport, of which only a small number are local unskilled workers.

My own analyses show an increase of 46 percent from the previous total of 670 West Papuan workers in March 31, 1997, caused mainly by FI's commitment to increase the West Papuan workforce in response to riots of March 10–12, 1996 and also to the demands of the Amungme Council, LEMASA. Freeport Indonesia and the government argue that this imbalance exists because of the lack of appropriate skills among locals and Papuans. But this defense merely raises the question of how many Amungme and Kamoro are given educational opportunities that would reduce this disadvantage. The Amungme and Komoro workers are employed as unskilled workers with low wages while immigrants dominate the semi-skilled and skilled jobs. This bias in the allocation of jobs has become one of the main factors fuelling widespread social resentment in the region. Marked differences in wages are a further problem. An unskilled Papuan worker in Tembagapura, for example, can earn Rp 464 per hour, while an Indonesian manager earns 220 times this. One basic problem is the lack of education and training for West Papuans. Consequently, working class families are faced with difficulties both in the workplace and in their domestic situation.

Unequal access to education is another form of genocide. The Indonesian Constitution of 1945 sets out the principle of equal rights and obligations for all citizens, both native and naturalized. Chapter 4 of the 1993 Guidelines of State Policy also states that all Indonesians have the same rights, obligations, and opportunities. Notwithstanding this, Papuans have consistently been discriminated against on the basis of their race and religion and excluded from high official posts because they are seen as an inferior race of lazy and unreliable people. Indonesians replaced the Papuan public officials who held government offices in the 1960s because Jakarta considered the locals to be incapable of holding positions of responsibility over the occupation forces. In Timika, for example, the Indonesians consistently look down on Papuans in general, and the local peoples in particular, as an inferior and "primitive" race; local people are not allowed to shop at the supermarket in Tembagapura and the company has built a wire fence around the city area to prevent local people from entering.

Discrimination against the people of West Papua, particularly highlanders, and in the current case, Amungme, has created deep social divisions. Stereotypes of West Papuans, notably the highlanders—that they are backward, primitive, OPM supporters, alcoholic, and resistant to progress—make it very difficult for the Amungme to participate in the development process and gain access to education. This attitude is clearly reflected in the way education and social services are distributed. Even though FI has been in the area for more than three decades, equal access to education and training for local people has been ignored. Following the signing of the January 1974 Agreement, only one elementary school was established, with classes UPT I–IV (primary educational Technical Service Units). In contrast, an Elementary School INPRES (Presidential Instruction Program) was built for 300 students, with eight teachers employed, to serve children of Freeport employees. Training and education centers established in Tembagapura in the 1970s served only children of expatriates and Indonesians; the children of the Amungme were excluded. More recently, again in response to LEMASA demands and local protests, Freeport has begun to realize the need to provide education and training for the Amungme and Kamoro. New elementary schools were established in Wa, Banti, and Timika in the 1990s and a dormitory for Amungme students was built in Kwamki Lama. New senior high schools were built in Timika and an international secondary high school was established in Tembagapura. Freeport Indonesia has also opened vocational training centers in both Tembagapura and Jayapura, and is now engaging in preschool education, literacy campaigns, and other educational and skills-based activities. A human resources program and a training center (*Balai Latihan Kerja* or BLK) are now located in Jayapura, and a primary school and dormitory have been established in Timika.[44]

Social disparities and crime remain major problems in the emerging towns and villages. Considerable numbers of students drop out of schools, and there has been an increase in social crimes and alcoholic problems among the local youth. Local competitors who are very ready to import cheap alcohol, pornography, and prostitution and engage in other forms of criminal activity have exploited this unhealthy situation. In Timika, for example, boats from Java and Makassar bring in cheap whisky, locally made *sagoer* (a fermented palm juice), and pornography, and sell these products to their willing customers at high prices.[45] Alcohol and drug policies are seen as an effective means of genocide. The same method was used against Aboriginals in Australia and Native Americans in the United States.

Political Repression

The Political administrative approach also been used in response to the failure of the purely military approach. The Indonesian government has introduced a new political approach in its attempt to destroy the influence of the OPM and most importantly; the marginalization of the people of West Papua. This may be termed an "administrative approach." The government plans to focus on particular strategic regions, creating new provinces or regencies in order to counteract the influence of the OPM and facilitate "Indonesianization." The first step in this plan is to divide the province of "Irian Jaya" into three provinces,[46] a northern province, with Jayapura as its capital; a western province, with Sorong as the capital; and a southern province, with Timika as capital. Each of these provinces will be under the authority of an assistant governor. Jakarta argues that such reorganization is crucial to the provision of development and services, and to improve infrastructure and create more job opportunities. But Papuans see the plan as a strategy for increasing political and military control. According to state law, a region can only be upgraded to a "province" if it fulfils certain criteria; one of these is that there must be a population of at least one million. The Papuans fear that if the plan were to be implemented, an even greater influx of migrants from Indonesia would be needed to increase the population in each of the newly created provinces and so the 1.5 million Papuans would very quickly become marginalized.

Following social unrest that occurred in the central and southern parts of the country in 1996, another administrative reform was put in place: four new regencies were created in East Timika (with Timika as capital), Puncak Jaya (with Mulia as capital), Paniai (with Enarotali as capital), and Nabire (Nabire as capital). Again, Papuans believe that such administrative rearrangements are part of a strategic plan. In order to restrict the movement of the OPM in the border areas, the military has built new outposts even in the most remote locations. In Akimuga district, for example, three times a week military aircraft drop troops from the military's new base in Aramsolki into Jila, Ilaga, Beoga, Hoea, Alama, and Bela. Each small village now has its own military post, with the main KODIM (military territory) in the region supplying manpower, food, and medicines.

Jakarta is proud of its current administrative policy, but Papuans remain extremely critical, believing that its real objectives are to restrict the movement of the OPM and to cut off its information networks and local support. The military has used the administrative reorganization to legitimate further forcible removal of landowners and increased militarization in the regions. Moreover, if the government continues to claim land in accordance with Article 33 of the Indonesian Constitution 1945, which concerns the state's right to ownership of all "no-man's-land," the Amungme, Komoro, and other Papuans will not have any right to claim compensation. In such circumstances, conflict between the Amungme and FI (and Nabire Bhakti) will drag on well into the future.

Another problem is the denial of social access in remote regions. Even the International Red Cross (ICRC), and Amnesty International, a nonpolitical organization with UN observer status, have periodically encountered difficulty in implementing humanitarian programs in the famine-affected areas of the West Papuan highlands. It is claimed that ABRI can only permit limited access to the area by nonresidents, for security reasons; it argues that such areas are very remote and there is a lack of materials and transport. But in 1997 the OPM International office in Sweden strongly criticized the government relief policy and stated that the relief program was intentionally protracted, leaving Papuans to die slowly; the delay in the relief program was, it argued, an integral part of its policy of genocide.[47]

During the drought of 1998, the military also used the social catastrophe as a means to hasten the extermination of the Papuans. Apart from delays in supplying food to victims in remote areas, such as Sinak, Mulia, and Geselama, the military set fire to the terrain. Landowners in Hoea were unable to save their crops, animals, houses, and land from the bushfire. According to an ICRC report (1998), the district of East Mimika was one of the areas worst hit by drought, with more than 250 people dying of hunger and drought-related diseases such as diarrhea, malaria, and cholera. Despite all the evidence compiled, Jakarta failed to assume accountability in this matter.

In brief, the evidence indicates that Jakarta continues to employ genocidal policies. The Papuans fear that they will be exterminated in a twenty-first century repetition of similar histories of Aboriginal Australians or Native Americans.

Resistance Movements

The Universal Declaration of the UN Political, Social, and Economic Conventions and Protocols, UN General Assembly Resolution 1514 and other relevant laws set out the criteria for entitlement to the right of self-determination. Persistent in their desire for self-determination and independence, the people of West Papua have carried out resistance against Indonesian domination for forty years. Under the coordination of the national liberation movement, an armed resistance, OPM, has been active. In turn, Indonesia quickly instituted and has continued for over four decades, a program of military and police repression, including widespread torture, intimidation, destruction of property, and killing. A considerable number of Papuans have been killed under Indonesian domination. In an attempt to protect such rights, the same resolution 1514-IV stipulated that "all armed actions or repression measures of all kinds directed against dependent people shall cease in order to enable the colonized peoples to exercise peacefully and freely their right to complete independence and the integrity of their nation territory shall be respected."[48] Despite the fact that Indonesia is a UN member, Jakarta continues to violate those principles and laws. Moreover, the presence of the Indonesian administration and FI in West Papua and Amungme land has not improved social and economic conditions or local infrastructure nor broken down the isolation of the people. West Papuans are still highly critical of it. As Professor Steven Feld argues:

> Like all indigenous West Papuans in Irian Jaya, Amungme have suffered from the brutal oppression of their Indonesian colonizers. They had no say in the takeover of their homelands for mining or in the resettlement programs that removed them for the benefit of Freeport Indonesia. Their lands have been annexed; their wealth has been absorbed. They receive no land rent and no royalties, and have virtually no legal, political, or economic recourse to this forced dispossession. When some Amungme rebelled in frustration in 1977 and blew up part of a pipeline, Indonesian military retaliations resulted. Gardens and houses were destroyed, people murdered and tortured. Indonesia claimed that "only 900" were killed. Others put the estimate at twice that number.[49]

West Papua's two major actors in the resistance movement are the OPM or Free Papua Movement and the Papuan Presidum. Both parties share the same objectives, but are different in strategic approach and historical experience.

Major Actors

The OPM/Free Papua Movement

The oldest national liberation movement (OPM),[50] was established on June 26, 1965 in Manokwari by the Mandacan brothers and Ferry Awom. Its primary objective has been to destroy Indonesian colonial power and establish a free and democratic state of West Papua. In its long journey, the organization has faced serious challenges. Despite all those attempts, the organization maintains its firm commitment to carry out the aspiration of the people and coordinate both political and military campaigns. People from all walks of life both Papuan and non-Papuan, who support the primary objective of the movement, are members of the OPM. A recent public opinion poll indicates that 90 percent of West Papuans claim to be members of the OPM who do not openly acknowledge membership.

The organization believes in both armed and political struggles. Due to this, the organization has both political and military wings. The political wing is responsible for political issues, at home and abroad, while the military wing is responsible for protecting civilians from the Indonesian military brutalities. Political struggle involves mass mobilization, diplomatic offensives, cadre training, networks, advocacy works, public awareness campaigns, and lobbying. Armed struggle is seen as a complementary approach to political struggle and is only used for self-defense, in accordance with UN conventions and resolutions, as mentioned elsewhere in this chapter.

The organization is well aware however that military means cannot defeat the occupation forces, for obvious reasons. The organization thus also advocates a peaceful solution of the conflict. A range of attempts have been made in this respect, ever since the new reform was implemented at the end 1967. Initiatives have included a call for a cease fire, third-party intervention, peaceful dialogue, and a review of the conduct of the Act of Free Choice in 1969.

Despite the organization having had some internal problems, it has a clear strategic plan. One of its main strategies is *regionalization* of the issue, as a stepping stone to internationalization. Collective Melanesian support is extremely important for gaining further support from the rest of the international community. In this context, the organization put all its efforts into gaining collective support in the immediate region and has been granted Permanent member status in the Melanesian Spearhead Group (MSG).

Papuan Presidium

The democratization of Indonesian politics opened up new opportunities to publicly express political desires and organize mass protests and rallies.

West Papuan national sentiment was channeled through an effective organizational system. The presidium[51] was established in 2000 as a result of what was called a "Second" National Congress, funded by the former President of Indonesia, Gus Dur Abdulrahman Wahid, attended by more than 3,000 people, and supported by more than 20,000 Papuans and non Papuans. This event demonstrated to the world that the aspiration of independence is deeply rooted in the hearts and minds of Papuan society, undermining the false claims made by Indonesia that the aspiration of independence is promoted by only a handful of people.

The Congress passed a 12-point resolution. It called on the UN Secretary General to review the conduct of the Act of Free Choice in 1969 and called on Jakarta to engage in peaceful dialogue. Thirty-one members of the presidium were appointed and in turn appointed Theys Eluay as president. A year later, Theys Eluay was assassinated by members of KOPASUS, on November 10, 2001 in Jayapura.

Unlike the OPM, the presidium is a mass-based organization and very young in experience. Some people claim it lacks mass support and that many members have served in the colonial administration and are opportunists or government spies. The organization has no clear strategic plan and direction. For those reasons and owing to the death of its president and its failure to compromise with other parties, the organization has declined in popularity. However, like members of OPM, members of the Presidium have often faced death treats. Thus, many members have left the organization and joined the enemy or hid themselves in what is known as *Dewan Adat Papua* (Papuan Traditional Council).

The presidium also promotes peaceful dialogue as a viable alternative in conflict resolution. In an attempt to express their aspirations openly, the presidium has, on different occasions, called for national dialogue to discuss key issues, including military withdrawal, regional development, human rights, land issues, and, most importantly, satisfying the people's aspirations for the future political status of West Papua, whether through autonomy, federation, or independence. Jakarta, however, has been very reluctance to take any further steps forwards.

Process of Conflict Resolution

The possible approaches to conflict resolution are many, depending on the type and level of the conflict to be resolved. To discuss the three options for resolution of the conflict in a cordial manner, the conditions suggested by FORERI (the independent Forum for the Reconciliation of Irian Jaya Society) and the other organizations must first be met. Among these, the most important are the presence of international peace monitoring groups, the participation of all layers of the West Papuan community, including leaders of the OPM abroad, and the withdrawal of the military from West Papua. These three conditions are vital in order to establish a basis from which to achieve a genuine consensus. In relation to West Papua, third party intervention, national dialogue, and special autonomy will be discussed briefly.

The Role of Third Parties

Third party intervention in negotiating a peace settlement has in many cases ended in success. Regional organizations, the United Nations, foreign governments, and sometimes NGOs, churches and academics commonly undertake such mediation. The role of mediator is to facilitate a peace accord by taking an active role in bringing the conflicting parties to the negotiating table.

West Papua has gone through a painful experience with international mediators. As argued earlier, the intervention of the United Nations and the United States as mediators in the conflict between Indonesia and the Dutch did not achieve a better outcome for Papuans.[52] Instead of playing a mediating role, both parties collaborated with the government of Indonesia, effectively denying the rights of the people of West Papua, and forcibly transferring power from the Dutch to Indonesia.

The United States and the United Kingdom have recently suggested that the Decolonization Commission of the UN (Committee of 24) should be abandoned, arguing that such a body is no longer necessary because the decolonization process in the world has been completed. These world powers see the Committee of 24 from a Eurocentric viewpoint, assuming that conventional colonialism ended with the departure of Western colonial powers in many parts of what is known as the Third World. However I disagree: "colonialism and imperialism are not only European diseases, but are a global human problem, relating to a capitalist mentality, regardless of race, social status and religion."[53] Special attention must be directed to the apparent sanctity of inherited Western colonial boundaries and the emergence of neocolonialism. A large number of peoples around the world are still suffering from both Western and indigenous colonialism, and international intervention to end colonialism is still important.

Some international intervention on behalf of West Papua has already taken place. The government of PNG, with Maori Kiki as Foreign Minister, offered to act as mediator in 1974. The government of Vanuatu in 1985 made a similar offer. However, both initiatives failed. The involvement of international peacekeeping forces is currently unlikely, but as West Papuan demands for independence escalate, the presence of such troops may be crucial. West Papuans would welcome a Pacific peacekeeping force, led by New Zealand. Members of the South Pacific Forum countries, particularly the Melanesian Spearhead Group, might be expected to take some initiative, though such an expectation has been unrealized so far. Intervention by the United States, the European Union, or the United Nations is currently unlikely.

With the process of democratization of Indonesia, however, the acceptance of peacekeeping forces, international monitoring groups, and foreign mass media in Indonesia, and in West Papua, is more likely in the future. New Zealand, for example, expressed its wishes to play a mediator role in the conflict in 2002, but Jakarta saw such intervention as interference in its internal affairs and rejected it. An attempt was made by the Government of Vanuatu in 2004 to facilitate a round-table discussion between the representatives of West Papua and the Government of Indonesia, but Jakarta rejected the proposal for the same reason. However, the call for third party intervention has been intensified and Jakarta must accept the political reality that West Papua is no longer an internal issue, but an international issue. In the Aceh case for example, Indonesia finally allowed third-party intervention that produced the Helsinki Accord in 2005. If such peace talks could happen with Aceh's GAM organization, why not with the OPM in West Papua? In this context, third-party intervention is likely to occur in the near future.

On July 18, 2005, the U.S. Congress attached a provision on West Papua to a foreign relations bill. The provision was moved by the Congressman for American Samoa, Eni Faleomavaega, and Congressman Donald Payne (D-NJ). This initiative was supported by the 38-member Congressional Black Caucus. During the vote, 315 congressmen supported the provision and 78 opposed it. The motion is still under consideration by the Senate. If it passes the Senate, it may encourage West Papuans to believe a positive outcome is possible in the near future. The ten-point provision called upon the U.S. Secretary of the State and UN Secretary General to review West Papua's political status and lends support to West Papua's right of self-determination.[54] Point 5 of the provision states that in July and August 1969, Indonesia conducted what was known as an Act of Free Choice, in which 1,025 selected Papuan elders voted unanimously to join Indonesia, in circumstances that were subject to both overt and covert forms of manipulation.[55]

National Dialogue

Over the past two years, the issues of peaceful dialogue and autonomy as viable paths to conflict resolution have been widely given serious attention.

A middle ground is needed where the aspirations of the people and the intentions of government can be heard, and alternative approaches can be discussed, with a view to narrowing the social and political differences until a consensus is achieved.

In an attempt to express their aspirations openly, FORERI recently undertook a new initiative. Three points of the position statement of the people of West Papua were contained in a final official communiqué of February 26, 1999, following a meeting with Indonesian President Habibie:

> Firstly, we, the people of West Papua want to separate ourselves from the Unitary Republic of Indonesia, to be fully sovereign and independent among other nations in the world.
>
> Secondly, to establish as soon as possible a Transition Government in West Papua under the auspices of the United Nations, democratically, peacefully and accountably at the latest in March 1999.
>
> Thirdly, if there will be no solution to respond to this Political Statement, specifically to the First and Second statements, then we demand: (i) to arrange an International Dialogue between the government of the Republic of Indonesia, the West Papuan People and the United Nations; (ii) We the people of West Papua hereby declare to abstain from the General Election of the Republic of Indonesia in 1999.

One hundred delegates representing various communities and social classes in West Papua signed the political statement.[56] This communiqué is significant for four reasons: first, it represented the true expression of the desires of the people without political orchestration or manipulation; second, it marked a new preparedness by the Indonesian government to listen to the voices of opposition; third, the Papuans clearly affirmed their political commitment, self-respect and confidence in proposing to take over political power, if Jakarta agrees; finally, it informed the world community that independence is the last chance for West Papuans, in order to save their people, culture, traditions, and ways of life from extinction.

The former President Jusuf Habibie in 1999 welcomed the statement, saying that he honored the demands because he saw them as being very honest and true, arrived at without any pressure, and reflecting a civilized and ethical approach to the principles and issues in dispute.[57] Even though the response of the Indonesian government remained unclear, the president's statement was significant for future debate.

A majority of West Papuans, including those overseas or in Jakarta, and the OPM have welcomed the initiative and support the aims and objectives of national dialogue. Such initiative has a number of advantages. It creates and contributes to any type of consensus concerning the future of West Papua. Inside West Papua the growing wave of Papuan nationalism cannot be underestimated; however, the OPM has generally distanced itself from the calls of FORERI for political reasons. The two forces are agreed on broad objectives, but divided on the choice of approach as mentioned earlier. There is a fear that Jakarta will use the outcome of the dialogue as confirmation of the people's opinion, and that the mistakes of the consultation process during the Act of Free Choice in 1969 will be repeated. Another concern is that the lack of involvement of all layers of Papuan society will fuel popular opposition. The organization of Second National Congress of West Papua in 2000 was seen as a further step toward national dialogue, but in fact little progress has been made toward this goal.

In the past five years, a range of peace initiatives have been taken but without achieving any result. Political observers argue that power change in Indonesia in itself has direct implications. However, the call for peaceful dialogue has also greatly intensified in the last five years. Civil society in West Papua calls for creating a *Zone of Peace* in West Papua. Another peace initiative has been taken by the Center of Peace and Conflict Studies at University of Sydney, which established a West Papuan Project whose primary objective is to promote peaceful dialogue between the government of Indonesia and the people of West Papua. In a constructive approach, the Project has been able to build trust and common understanding with Jakarta through the Indonesian Ambassador to Australia, Budi Sudjadman. However, since the political change in Indonesia, after the Magawati Sukarnoputri regime, this initiative has not received much attention. Rather, Jakarta promotes more violence in the territory by deploying more troops. There are other peace initiatives of equal importance; however, Jakarta continues to downplay them. Since 2000, the Pacific Islands Forum, in its final communiqués, has called for peaceful dialogue as a viable alternative in conflict resolution.

"Special Autonomy"

Old Saga: An Empty Promise

Any solution to the problem of West Papua must recognize that the cultural and religious identity of West Papua is distinctive, and that cultural differences have been used to create socioeconomic and political imbalances in society between center and periphery (Indonesians and "spiritual" non-Indonesians). So far, there is no clear acknowledgment of these differences by either side.

Debate about an autonomous status for West Papua took place even before annexation began, back in the 1950s, when the government of Indonesia first declared its objectives. A report prepared by the Research Institute for Oppressed People (RIOP) in Amsterdam[58] and a study by Djopari[59] have both reviewed this early discussion.

Article 6 of decree MPRS No.XXI/MPRS/1966 placed West Irian (West Papua) in the position of an autonomous region. It stated, "as soon as the AFC is over, we will immediately start the realization of the autonomous province of West Irian." The New Guinea Parity Commission's 1950 report also affirmed that "when Indonesia has control of the sovereignty of the area, an autonomous provincial administration will be quickly set up, according to the principles of decentralization within the Indonesian state."[60]

To be seen to fulfill these promises, when West Papua was forced to become a part of Indonesia, President Sukarno immediately announced a Presidential decree 1962/1, which declared West Papua an autonomous region in accordance with the spirit of Article 18 of the State Constitution 1945. The people of West Papua were to be "fully autonomous," with the appointment of Papuans to officials' posts such as governor and the establishment of a regional parliament.[61] This meant that all powers, except foreign policy, defense and financial powers would be in the hands of the regional government. In August 1962, Sukarno made his intention clear that "only self-determination within Indonesia would be recognized"[62] in other words, autonomy. What was called "fullest autonomy" was then spelt out in three presidential decrees during the period of the UN Temporary Executive Authority (UNTEA) in 1962–1963: Pen Pres 1963/1 (which regulated the powers, responsibilities, and functions of the governor, vice governor, parliament, and executive council), In Pres 1963/2 (secret) and Keep. Pres 1963/57.[63]

The West Papuan parliament was installed on May 2, 1963; it consisted of forty-two members of whom thirty-three were Papuans.[64] Unlike the other regions of Indonesia, the parliament in West Papua was not given the essential powers to draw up a budget or make provincial by-laws; instead such legislation must be approved by the national government. It must be in accordance with national legislation and must follow nationally established guidelines. An additional problem has been that under Pen Pres 1963/1 the governor is deemed to be head of the parliament, which is unusual, as it means the governor, who is a political appointee, is head of the executive, with power over the members of the parliament, who are chosen through direct election. Thus, autonomy has never been implemented in any real sense in West Papua. It has been more a case of de-concentration than decentralization.

New Saga, Old Rhetoric

The question remains: Why was the Indonesian government so reluctant to implement "fullest autonomy"? Jakarta argued that *Irian Jaya* qualified for "special consideration." But from the viewpoint of the central government, without West Papua having the appropriate levels of technical and administrative skills, giving it autonomy would be an empty symbolic act that would foster corruption in West Papua and present a real threat to Indonesian national unity. In short, the national government was worried that the "special status" of the region would lead to "self-government," undermining the political and moral integration through which Jakarta retains centralized power.

However, the new special autonomy arrangement allows for a change of name (from *Irian Jaya* to West Papua), as well as changes in regional symbols. It also offers economic benefits for the West Papuans. The percentage of profit from the region's enterprises retained by the Papuans would be increased, with 80 percent of revenues from forestry, fisheries, and mining industries and 70 percent of revenues from oil and gas exploration to be apportioned to the province. Of the latter, a minimum of 30 percent is earmarked for education, with a minimum of 15 percent allotted to health care programs. After twenty-five years, the West Papuans' share of their own oil and gas revenues will be reduced to 50 percent[65]. These concessions are a small victory for the West Papuans, as they will open up new opportunities for capacity building and the development of administrative skills required for self-governance.

On the other hand, the special autonomy arrangement has many weaknesses. Jakarta regards the existing national symbols of the Papuans as representative of their "cultural identity" only and explicitly refuses to recognize them as "symbols of independence." And the central government retains strong influence over the provincial government. Article 34 of Chapter III regarding regional division, stipulates: "the provincial government has the right to propose any changes to the central government, but the central government has the right to overrule the decision of the regional government. The central government also retains the dominant role in police and security issues."

Jakarta continues to undermine the land rights of Papuans, which are regulated by Article 43 of Chapter XI, which regards traditional rights and stipulates: "traditional rights are subordinated to national law and regulations." The phrase "subordinated to national law" means that these rights are overruled by Indonesian law. The law does not recognize the land rights of the people of West Papua. The power of Article 33 of the

Indonesian Constitution of 1945 is seen as resurrecting the "New Order Period" in the contemporary context. Moreover, Jakarta continues to reject an independent human rights body. Article 45 of Chapter XII, regarding Human Rights, says "a Special Commission for Human Rights [is] to be set up by the central government, not by the provincial government of West Papua."[66] Under these conditions, a credible report by this commission, regarding human rights violations by the Indonesian government, would seem highly unlikely.

Under the new arrangement, the current transmigration program would continue in West Papua. In the final document, the program is still included, contingent on approval by the provincial governor. Such prolonging of the old policy may encourage new and even worse horizontal conflict between Papuans and non-Papuans. This unhealthy situation may be used as an excuse by the military to justify its presence in West Papua.

A coercive approach is used in dealing with security issues. Under Article 68 of Chapter XXI, regarding supervision, the central government is given the right to "supervise" any decisions, regulations, and so on, and settle any conflicts in the region. It is permitted to use coercive force. Article 68:2 states that "the government has the right of repressive control over *Perdasus* (special regional law), *Perdasi* (provincial laws) and *Keputusan Gubernur* (the decision of the governor). The use of the word "repressive" in the final document suggests the central government has far-reaching authority.

The autonomy proposal itself does not reflect the desires of Papuans, but rather, reflects the desires of certain groups of Papuan society, which hold inordinate influence and power. Despite Jakarta having ratified Special Autonomy Law in 2001, it fails to implement it in accordance with the aspirations of the people of West Papua. Instead of implementing Special Autonomy, Jakarta promotes a divide and rule policy by carving West Papua into three provinces. This policy has serious social and political implications. Clashes between pro- and anti-division supporters have occurred in many parts of the territory. The killing of five civilians in Timika in 2003 is an example.

Due to these problems, reactions are mixed. The OPM, the Presidium and the majority of West Papuans have distanced themselves from the new arrangement. Western countries, including the European Union and the United States, as well as the Pacific Islands Forum consider this approach as a best alternative to end the current conflict. In the final communiqué, the Forum said: "Forum Leaders reiterated their support for special autonomy for Papua which they considered to offer realistic prospects for peaceful resolution of the situation in Papua. Noting that the 2001 special autonomy law had yet to be fully implemented, they urged the sovereign authority, Indonesia, to expedite promulgation of the necessary regulations and to take other steps needed to give effect to special autonomy"(paragraph 43).[67]

In a direct response, the people of West Papua protested the Special Autonomy Law (SAL) package on August 12, 2005 and urged Jakarta to engage in the peaceful dialogue. In response, Jakarta formed a new team, consisting of Papuan loyalists who have been trusted to investigate the Law. If Jakarta persists in continuing with the old paradigm of control through coercion, they cannot hope to sustain good relations.

Conclusion

Compiled evidence indicates West Papua is indeed a colony of Indonesia. In that colony, a policy of genocide has been imposed, with substantial consequences. Unequal distribution of wealth and power, lack of respect for and recognition of the rights of the colonized people, widespread human rights abuses, environmental destruction, dispossession of the population, and cultural domination—all encourage stronger national sentiments. In such circumstances, the emergence of West Papuan nationalism has been inevitable, and will remain a major problem for the Indonesian government.

The fact is West Papuans have suffered countless violations of the most fundamental human rights. Gross and systematic human rights abuses against the people have intensified. In the last thirty-nine years, the situation in West Papua is characterized more than ever by an increasing level of violence provoked by local militias and the occupation forces. Mass killing, summary execution, detention, imprisonment, disappearances, rapes and all forms of torture and intimidation, and also cultural genocide have been routine. These systematic human rights abuses have occurred in many parts of West Papua, resulting in the death of a considerable number of West Papuan civilians.

The future of West Papua must be seen within the general political context of Indonesia. The repercussions from the current democratization process have serious consequences for political change in West Papua. The advancement of the mass movement, the escalation of protests, limited demilitarization, and policy change of the OPM are some of the positive developments. On the other hand, negative consequences include the effects of economic crisis, widespread orchestration and manipulation of mass protests against change, and divisions created within the Papuan community concerning political options for peace. There are signs of hope that the aspirations of the West Papuan people for self-determination can be channeled in

peaceful ways and through a process of dialogue with the government of
Indonesia. To strengthen this process there is a need for international support
and commitment to prevent further bloodshed in West Papua.

In the absence of constructive peace initiatives, however, the persisting
conflict between Jakarta and West Papua on the one hand, and within
Papuan society, on the other, are contributing to renewed violence with
serious political implications. Promotion of a dialogue for peace over West
Papua is therefore an urgent need of the region. A priority is to understand
the historical background of the problem and the previous peace initiatives
promoted by the OPM and FORERI.

In a desperate attempt to save Indonesia from total collapse and placate
the people of West Papua, the old saga repeats itself, but with new rhetoric,
offering "special" autonomy, which was ratified by the central parliament
as a last-ditch attempt to resolve the conflict in West Papua. But the people of West Papua have summarily rejected the autonomy package, view-
ing it as nothing more than "lip-service" on the part of the Indonesian
government. Direct central interventions in the drafting of the Special
Autonomy package, which resulted in substantial changes and restrictions,
demonstrated that the old paradigm repeats itself. There is a lack of recognition of fundamental and decisive issues, such as the rectification of history,
the referendum and national dialogue, and human rights. Immigration and
militarization policies will likely continue, which may fuel more violence in
the near future, even if Jakarta and its local royalists would like to choose
different strategies to achieve the same objective.

The rectification of the history of West Papua is important to all conflicting parties, both to restore a good image and credibility for Indonesia
and to develop West Papua. If the result of the examination finds fraud,
then there is an urgent need to organize a new just, democratic, and peaceful referendum under direct UN supervision. That may save the
Indonesian republic from total collapse.

A new consensus needs to be developed in order to save Papuan culture,
traditions, and ways of life from total obliteration. Through peaceful dialogue, this issue must be addressed and a referendum on options called. It
must be carried out in a manner that upholds the principles of democracy. It
must be just, peaceful, secret, and conducted under international supervision.

Notes

1. John Clark (2001). "Cultural Genocide and Ecocide as Responsible
   Corporate Policy: The Case of Freeport McMoRan in West Papua,"
   Conference paper, Loyola University New Orleans, pp. 2–3.

2. Jack Woddis (1967). *An Introduction to Neo-Colonialism*. New York: International Publishers, p. 147.

3. Ronald H. Chilcote (1984). *Theories of Development and Underdevelopment*. Boulder, CO: Westview Press, p. 16.

4. Woddis, 1967: 16.

5. Robert, Petersen (October 25, 1992). *Colonialism as Seen from a Former Colonized Area*, Working Paper presented at the 8th Inuit Studies Conference at Laval University, Vol. 32, No: 2, pp. 10–11.

6. Diana Treffry, Alan Isaacs, and Sheila Ferguson (eds) (1999). *Collin Concise Dictionary*, Fourth Australian Edition, Glassgow: Harper Collins Publisher, p. 592.

7. Paul W. Khan, James J. Silk, and Elisabeth Brundige (December 10, 2003). "Confirms Crimes Against Humanity by Indonesia in West Papua," New Haven, CT: Research Paper, Yale Law School, p. 1.

8. John Wing and Peter King (July 2005). "Genocide in West Papua?" Report, The West Papua Project at Center for Peace and Conflict Studies, University of Sydney, p. 1.

9. Clark, 2001: 2.

10. Ibid.: 2–3.

11. Ibid.: 3.

12. Ibid.: 3.

13. ELSHAM News Service, (March 13, 2002). "3000 Laskar Jihad Now in Papua (Irian Jaya)," Jayapura.

14. "Sepak Terjang Laskar Jihad di Papua," Jayapura (March 25, 2002), www.infopapua.com/papua/0302/2411.html.

15. Gay, Alcon (March 22, 2002). "US Push to Chase Terrorists Melting into the Indonesian Island Maze," *Sydney Morning Herald*, Sydney, p. 1.

16. Nick Lazaredes (March 16, 2005). "West Papua Militia," *SBS-Dateline*'s Report, Sydney.

17. Socratez Sofyan Yoman (May 14, 2005). "Systematic Genocide of the Indigenous People of West Papua under Special Autonomy," *Report*, Jayapura, p. 2.

18. Amnesty International (1997). "Urgent Action Request about Recent Events near the Freeport Mine." *AII Index*: ASA.21/61/97, p. 2. [See also: http://www.cs.utexas.edu/users/boyer/fp/amnesty-970829.html.]

19. C.Budiardjo and Soe Liong Liem (1984), *West Papua: The Obliteration of a People* London.:TAPOL, pp. 24–52.

20. Australian Council for Overseas Aid (ACFOA), April, 1995. Trouble at Freeport: Eyewitness Accounts of West Papuan Resistance to the Freeport-McMoRan Mine in Irian Jaya, Indonesia and Indonesian military repression: June 1994–February 1995, Melbourne.

21. Isak Onawame, Nato Gobay, and A.B.M. Hutapea (1998). *Human Rights Violations and Disaster in Bela, Alama, Jila and Mapnduma, Irian Jaya*, Melbourne: Indonesian Evangelical Church, Mimika, Catholic Church,

Three Kings Parish, Timika, Christian Evangelical Church of Mimika, ACFOA Human Rights Office, pp. 2–34.

22. Wim Zonggonau et al. (1997). Accuses: The Case of West Papua, Port Moresby, (unpublished), p. 88.

23. Kelly Kwalik (May 3, 1996). *Fakta-fakta Pengorbanan jiwa bangsa Melanesia Barat sejak tahun 1962–1996 Dalam Wilayah KODAM III, Fakfak, Puncak Abadi Jaya, Laporan*, MAKODAM III, FakFak.

24. Bonifasius Niwilingame (1984). Niwilingame, Bonifasius (July 24, 1985). Bersama ini Kami Laporkan Beberapa Perisitiwa Penting Antara Lain Pembunuhan Masal Atas Rakyat Papua Barat Diderah Pegunungan Tengah Dibagian Barat Dari Papua Barat Oleh Pemerintah Republic Indonesia, Laporan, Markas Besar Nasional-OPM.

25. Jan Herman Munninghoff, OFM (1995). "Violations of human rights in the Timika area of Irian Jaya, Indonesia," Report by the Catholic Church of Jayapura.

26. Josepha Alomang and Juliana Magal (1997), interviewed by Mark Enger, German TV Journalist, Timika.

27. Amnesty International (1995). "Irian Jaya: National Commission on Human Rights Confirms Violations," Document No: AI Index: ASA 21/47/95, London, pp. 1–13.

28. Prayan Purba, Anna M. Massie et al. (1987). *Irian Jaya: The Land of Challenges and Promises*, PT Alpha Zenith, p. 39.

29. Mus Pigai (1996), interviewed by the author, Timika.

30. Andreas Burdani, in article: "Environment-Indonesia: As Big Mines Settle in, Indigenous Folk Crowded Out," *Inter Press Service World News*, December 11, 1998, Jakarta.

31. Chris, Ballard, (1996). *Chronologies of West Papuan History*, Research School of Pacific and Asian Studies, Australian National University, p. 8.

32. Carolyn, Cook, (1995). *The Amungme Way: the Subsistence Strategies, the Knowledge and the Dilemma of the Tsinga Valley People in Irian Jaya, Indonesia*, Ann Arbor, MI: UMI, pp. 345–348.

33. *Warta Freeport* Vol.XIV (Ist quarter of 1995) Indonesian Government, The Community and Freeport: Working Together Toward Sustainable Development in Irian Jaya, Jakarta, p. 12.

34. Komisi Penanggulangan Belum Peduli HIV/AIDS, July 30, 2001, http://www.infopapua.com, Jayapura.

35. "Sex workers in Timika and Nabire are those in a high risk group," *Cenderawasih Post*, June 5, 1993, p. 3.

36. http://www.infopapua.com, February 2, 2002, Jayapura.

37. Nethy Dharama Somba (Spetember 27, 2005). Papuans Educated on HIV/AIDS, Jakarta.

38. Podzolic and latozolic soil structures are found in southern mountain ranges and lowlands respectively. Both are characterized by softness and lack of keasaman and are particularly vulnerable to erosion. Ronald G. Petocz,

(April 1987), *Konservasi Alam dan Pembangunan di Irian Jaya: Strategi Pemanfaatan Sumber Daya Alam Secara Rasional*, World Wildlife Fund, *Grafitipers*, Jakarta, p. 28.

39. An independent environmental audit concluded that Freeport mining operations have significant impacts upon the environment, and called for an immediate improvement (Ros Kelly, Paul Whincup and Soeharto Wongsosentono 1996), PTFI *Environmental Audit Report*, Dames and Moore, p. 2.

40. Cook, 1995.: 424.

41. Forum Studi dan Pengembangan Mimika-Akimuga di Jayapura (Mei 22, 1993). "Laporan Keadaan Lingkungan dan Social Penduduk Koperapoka, Tipuka dan Iwaka Dalam Kaitannya dengan Aktivitas Freeport Indonesia Inc," *Report*, Jayapura, p. 17.

42. *Pacific Islands Business* April 1994, p. 34. See also *Far Eastern Economic Review*, March 10, 1994, p. 50.

43. *Forum Keadilan* No.11, Thn IV, September 11, 1995.

44. Freeport Indonesia Incorporated (1992). *Program Yayasan Freeport Cenderawasih*, Jakarta, pp. 27–32. See also George A. Mealey, (1996). *Grasberg: Mining in the Richest and Most Remote Deposit of Copper and Gold, in the World, in the Mountains of Irian Jaya*, Indonesia, Freeport McMoRan Copper & Gold Inc. New Orleans, pp. 312–345.

45. *Far Eastern Economic Review* December 26, 1996– January 2, 1997, p. 105.

46. Yusril Ihza Mahendra "Irian Jaya Agar ijadikan Tiga Provinsi," *Republika*, June 25, 1998, Jombang.

47. J.H. Prai *Press Release* (October 14, 1997). OPM-International Office, Malmö.

48. Otto, Ondawame (2000). "One People, One Soul," West Papuan Nationalism and the Organisasi Papua Merdeka (OPM)/Free Papua Movement, PhD Thesis, Australian National University, Canberra, p. 46.

49. Steven Feld (1995). *"Let's Call It Amungme Hall," University Press*, University of Austin, p. 3.

50. Otto Ondawame (May 1, 2005). "West Papua: New Prospect for Change," A Briefing Paper No.:1, West Papua Representative Office, Port Vila, pp. 17–18.

51. Ibid.: 18.

52. C. McMullen (1981). *Mediation of the West Guinea Dispute in 1962, A Case Study*, Washington, DC: Georgetown University, p. 79. [See also RIOP (1984: 50); M.C. Terrence (1996). *The West Irian Dispute, How the Kennnedy Administration Resolves the "other" Southeast Asian Countries*, Baltimore, MD: The Johns Hopkins University, p. 63.]

53. Otto Ondawame (1997). "Impact of Freeport Mining's Activities On The Amungme and Kamoro Peoples in West Papua," in Susan Wareham (ed.), *Vision and Actions for Peace*, Conference Paper, International Physicians and Actions on Nuclear War and the Medical Association for Prevention

of War (Australasia), Canberra: Panther Publishing & Printing, pp. 227–228.

54. Eni F.H.Faleomavaega (July 1, 2005). "International Relation Committee Passes State Department Authorization Bill with Mr. Faleomavaega and Mr. Payne's Language About West Papua," *Press Release*, U.S. House of Represenatives, Washington, DC: p. 1.

55. Ibid.: 2.

56. Forum Untuk Rekonsiliasi Bagi Rakyat Irian Jaya. *"Pernyataan Politik Bangsa Papua Barat Kepada Pemerintah Republik Indonesia,"* Document, February 26, 1999, Jakarta.

57. Pius Urbanus Adi (1999). "Rangkuman Dialog Bapak Presiden Republik Indonesia dengan Masyarakat Irian Jaya," *Report of the Representative of Nabire Regency to the National Dialogue*, Nabire, p. 2.

58. Research Institute of Oppressed Peoples (1985). *The Tragedy of the People and the International Political Order, RIOP Report No.1.* Amsterdam: Makula, Boskoop, pp. 23–29.

59. John R.G. Djopari (1993). *Pemberontakan Organisasi Papua Merdeka,* Jakarta: Grasindo, pp. 65–70.

60. Ibid.: 28.

61. Ibid.: 23–29 (see also pp. 60–71).

62. Chris, Ballard, 1996: 1.

63. RIOP, 1984: 24.

64. Ibid: 27.

65. Theo van de Broek (December 2001). "Special Autonomy, its Process and Final Contents," Sekretaria Keadilan and Perdamian Keuskupan Jayapura Seri Socio-political Notes, No:5, Jayapura, p. 10.

66. Ibid.: 11.

67. Pacific Islands Forum (August 14–16, 2003). "Decisions of the Forum Leaders' Retreat, Papua," Thirty-Fourth Pacific Islands Forum, Document, Auckland, p. 11.

CHAPTER 5

EDUCATING THE NAGA HEADHUNTERS: COLONIAL HISTORY AND CULTURAL HEGEMONY IN POST-COLONIAL INDIA

Dolly Kikon

The mission to civilize the "savage" Naga headhunters inhabiting the Northeastern frontier of India was accidental. The primary concern for the British administration was centered on protecting their lucrative tea trade and oil explorations in the Brahmaputra valley. Colonial regulations and expeditions systematically encroached upon community lands for tea plantations and pushed back the Nagas into the hills. The Naga Hills were declared *Excluded Areas*, which restricted movements of both outsiders entering the hills and the Nagas from coming out of these enclosures. Such regulations cut off trade and communication with the neighboring communities. Instead, military barracks, educational institutions, and mission churches came up in Naga villages. What was the process of conquering and educating the "Naked" Nagas? Was there any clash of interests between the British administration and the American missionaries? Most importantly, how did the Nagas see the transition of power in 1947? Have postcolonial nation-building processes been accommodative of the histories of peripheral regions? These are some of the questions that animate this chapter.

Introduction

The Naga peoples struggle for the right to self-determination has been a contentious issue in postcolonial India. Within modern India indigenous peoples of North East India like the Nagas have developed a distinct political identity and have also laid claim to being a nation. The concept of a Naga nation can be defined to consist: (1) a reference group, to which the nationality claim is attached; (2) the claim to self-determination, which may or may not mean the right to establish their own state; (3) a territorial definition, and (4) the claim that the reference group constitutes or aspires to be a global society, containing within itself the full range of social institutions and the mechanisms for social regulation, as opposed to a mere fragment of a larger society, making specific claims for cultural recognition, or for special policy measures. A political issue, which has received some attention in recent times, concerns the need to protect cultural diversity in contemporary societies. Almost all large states today face a plurality of ethnic demands for self-determination. While there may be sympathy for ethnic demands within a state, they may also be viewed with some fear as posing a possible threat to the integrity of the nation-state. They are perceived as posing a threat to the orderly conduct of international relations. The political responses of nation-states to ethnic demands have been therefore somewhat ambiguous (Joseph 1998: 18). While India has agreed with the fact that the issue of culture and the Naga people's struggle has a very strong political dimension, it has consciously worked toward policies especially in the field of education that will finally identify the Naga people as one with India culturally. The area of education has recently become a contentious one for Indian citizens.

One believes that it is on such notions of a problematic collective self upon which state policies are initiated. The textual content of the syllabi used by the education department in Nagaland and dictated by the national policy makers in India are geared toward reworking this collective self. It shows how the careful construction of a "new" Naga identity precludes the possibility of an imaginative sense of history for Naga students. The irrelevance of the syllabi shows it to be completely different from the situation that exists outside the classrooms. One is therefore trying to draw a link, no matter how tenuous, between different experiences of militarization and the policy of wiping out the history (and memory) of Naga struggles via the medium of state-sponsored education.

Describing a People: The Nagas

The Naga people inhabit a contiguous hill range, from Barail in northeastern India, to parts of the Arakan Yoma, in present day Myanmar. As such they encompass the North Eastern region Indian states of Nagaland, Manipur, Arunachal Pradesh, and Assam. In Myanmar, the Naga inhabit the North West regions that include the Somrah Tract bordering India that is further divided into two administrative units—Kachin State and Sagaing Sub-Division. The population of Naga people according to the 2001 India censuses stood at 1.9 million.[1] However, there are disagreements. Naga political and civic organizations tag the total Naga population at around 3–4 million,[2] which includes Nagas both in India and Myanmar.[3] British colonial surveys of the nineteenth century, and British administrators like Mackenzie, while charting out the unadministered frontiers of northeast India in 1835 referred to the Burmese Nagas as "Patkoi Nagas"[4] and cited their population as "under 5,000 souls" without specifying the number of tribes (Mackenzie 1995: 88–89). However, during the creation of the state of Nagaland in 1963, the Naga population stood at roughly 1. 2 million with the total number of Naga tribes quoted at eight. Today, an official document published by the state of Nagaland asserts that sixteen Naga tribes inhabit Nagaland[5] (Kikon 2005: 2833–2837).

Building the British Empire and a "Frontier"

With the commencement of the nineteenth century, British colonialism reached its peak with territorial expansion and exploitation of resources in the Indian subcontinent. The territorial expansion toward the northeastern frontier of India was the fact that China and Burma figured prominently in the British-Indian politics in the beginning of the nineteenth century when they made all-out efforts to promote their mercantile interests (Sladkovsky 1981: 158–162). The declining fortunes of the monarchy in the Brahmaputra valley proved to be an advantage for the British colonial expansion. The Anglo-Burmese War of 1824 led to the emergence of the British colonialist as the dominant power by the Treaty of Yandabo in 1826. Under the terms of this treaty the king of Ava on the Burmese side surrendered among other things his claim over Assam and the neighbouring states of Cachar, Jaintia, and Manipur to the British (Barpujari 1977: 7). The British occupation of the indigenous territories bordering Assam was a strategic move.

The British aimed at using the tribes on the eastern fringes as a buffer between the newly acquired territories and the kingdom of Burma. The discovery of tea (1823), coal and petroleum (1825), (further) impressed upon the British the prospects of promotion of its commercial interests (Bhattacharjee 1980: 178). The first British contact with the Nagas was established in 1832 when Francis Jenkins and R. B. Pemberton traveled through Naga territory in search of a route between Manipur and Assam.

The British expeditions in the Naga Hills were conducted under various civil officers and military lieutenants from 1833 to 1879. By 1878 the British established Kohima as the chief Administrative Centre for the Angami area and Wokha as a subcenter for the Lotha tribal area. The killing of Dament, the first Deputy Commissioner of Kohima, by the Angami Nagas in 1879 sparked off the Battle of Khonoma. The occupation of Kohima by the British was the turning point of the last War of Independence of the Nagas against British Imperialism.

Enclosing the Nagas within a Territory: The Colonial Process

From 1874 to 1878 the British Government conducted surveys and operations for the purpose of demarcating the territorial boundary and extending political consolidation of the Naga people. By March 1880 the (former) Assaloo subdivision was reconstituted to extend the jurisdiction of the Political Officer of the Naga Hills. A line was drawn from the Manipur frontier through the Kopamedza Hills and hence northward from the junction of the Sijjo and Zuloo rivers to the Wokha and Golaghat road which included the Lotha territory within the district. However, by July 1882, the British Government laid down the boundaries of the Naga Hills District.

From the beginning, the British colonialists were clear that they would not gain anything profitable from the Nagas. The Nagas fitted the colonialist's definition of savage inhabitants and barbarous people who were best to be left undisturbed. According to Lord Dalhousie, "our [i.e., British] possessions [i.e., Naga Hills] could bring no profit to us, and it would be costly to us (and) unproductive" (Mackenzie 1884: 113–115).

Thus in 1851, Dalhousie laid down the policy of noninterference, which lasted for fifteen years. However, the British government viewed the frequent Naga raids in the tea plantations and the tribal feuds in the hills as a hindrance to the British administration in the plains of Assam. The British introduced the Forward Policy that not only aimed at preventing feud and extracting reparations for past losses but also led to the establishment of British administration in the Naga Hills. In 1866, the Naga Hills District was set up to look into the administrative and political functions of the British government. However, no demarcation of any geographical area was laid down. To control the inhabitants of the Naga Hills the British introduced a series of laws and regulations that aimed at creating a territorial enclosure for the Naga people. While massive alienation of land and immigration of indentured labor occurred in the plains, the administration implemented laws to sequester the hills and secure the plantations in the plains from raids (by hill men). The Inner Line Regulation (1873) was introduced to prevent incidents of friction between the Naga people from the hills and the plainsmen. The regulation was drawn up to prescribe a line, to be called the "Inner Line," in each or any districts affected (by the feuds), beyond which no British subject of certain classes or foreign residents could pass without a license. Rules regarding trade, the possession of land beyond the line, and other matters were also laid down (Mackenzie 1884: 141). The Inner Line separated some tracts inhabited by the tribal people from the districts of Assam Administration and journey beyond the inner line was restricted (Gait 1963: 385–386). The Inner Line regulation of 1873 was the first of laws promulgated in Assam under the authority conferred by the Statute 33 that had given the Government of India power of summary legislation for backward tracts. Such laws are made to distinguish them from the Acts or Laws passed after discussion in the legislature.

In 1874, the Naga Hills District was declared a Scheduled District under the Scheduled District Act, 1874. The purpose of this act was to enable a simpler and personal administrative policy in the Naga Hills District. The British Government further passed the Assam Frontier Tract Regulation II of 1880 (as amended by the Regulation III of 1884) and extended it to the Naga Hills District. Under this regulation the Naga Hills were excluded from the operation of enactment relating to elaborate Codes of law, the Code of Criminal Procedure, and the Civil Procedure Code. In short, the history of promulgation of special laws to restrict and contain the Nagas to a territory had several dimensions. First and foremost, the basis upon which these laws were formulated was rooted in notions of racial and ethnic bias that proclaimed the Nagas as a savage and primitive race. This dual characteristic attributed to them resulted in the implementation of a peculiar policy, wherein the "savage" was contained within an area that could be administered tactfully, while the "primitive" could be protected from the pitfalls of their own simplicity. A selective reading of the past coupled with the strategic interests of the British framed the basis of this policy (Baruah 1999: 43).

Second, it severely affected the existing economic base of the Naga people. Their natural trade routes and trading partners were cut off. In pre-British times, many Naga tribes enjoyed a special tribute (sometimes paid as ransom) from the Ahoms in the Lohit (Brahmaputra) Valley. This included food grain, cotton, and other items. This relationship had survived over centuries and had transformed itself into one of mutual respect and development (Devi 1968: 38–45). The discontinuance of this relationship meant that the Nagas had to rely on a scarce economic base. While earlier it was possible to rely on the relationship of cooperation from other ethnic groups, the new laws made it that much more difficult for any economic interaction for the Nagas. This translated into the cultural sphere and consolidation of a Naga identity as well.

Moreover, what constituted tradition for the British administration was actually fuelled by strategic concerns of governance of such so-called backward areas. The vacuum that was created by the promulgation of these colonial laws was far reaching in terms of creating a sense of siege amongst the Nagas. A social and cultural system that could address the alienation of the people from their past and reorient their productive capacities toward the creation of a new identity was not there. In such conditions, it was the advent of Christianity that radically changed the course of Naga history.

The Advent of Christianity and Education

British military expeditions and missionary activities commenced almost simultaneously. Describing the process, Major Jenkins elaborated how the tribes on the Assam frontier should be brought within the scope of missionary activities as early as possible as the influence of persons skilled in the languages of these tribes and devoting all their time and attention to humanize these rude races could not fail of being useful to both the colonial administrators and the missionaries. The first military British expedition to the Naga Hills took place in 1832; by 1836 the first group of Christian missionaries had made their appearance in that area. The missionaries were members of the American Baptist Mission, who arrived in Sadiya in 1836 to take up missionary work in Assam (Downs 1983: 33). The first center of Christian activities was set up around 1876, one year after Rev. E. W. Clark arrived in the village of Molungyinchen in the Ao Naga area. Missionaries taught the Nagas to read the bible and sing western Christian hymns. Such processes initiated the first elements of Western education. Consequently, the missionaries introduced the Roman alphabet, which translated the Bible and Western hymnbooks in various Naga languages during the latter part of the nineteenth century.

The first Christian converts among the Nagas became preachers in their respective villages. However, colonial writers like Elwin also point out that the colonial missionaries with a moral burden to civilize the Naga people followed a culturally destructive policy and robbed them of the things that gave vitality to their lives (Elwin 1997: 62). In that respect, the British Government left matters of education entirely in the hands of the missionaries and refused infrastructural assistance, as they would not gain anything profitable by spending money on education in the Naga Hills. However, after educational institutions were set up by missionaries in the Naga Hills, the British administration saw the benefit and necessity of starting secular educational institutions in order to enable Naga men avail of jobs in the colonial job-market. By 1913–1914 mission institutions were transferred into the hands of the colonial government. Nonetheless, it was only on the eve of their exit from India that the British government granted financial aid to the schools in the Naga Hills. The educational system of that period was not an instrument for imparting knowledge to the people. The primary objective for introducing formal education was to start off a process of cultural colonization, producing mainly a service class of petty officials and clerks to run the clogs of the system. To quote the Administrative report of the Naga Hills for 1883–1884:

> As soon as any of the boys are educated (they will) get an appointment as a copyist or clerk, the Nagas will see the advantage of education, and will send the boys willingly to school, which is not the present case. (Foreign Political Proceedings 1884)[6]

However after twenty-two years, the Administrative Report of 1906–1907 written by the Deputy Commissioner Lieutenant Colonel Woods, stated that education was not popular among the Nagas. In this regard, he quoted a letter of A. W. Davis, the former Deputy Commissioner of the Naga Hills, which described the Naga people's views regarding education. Some of the questions raised by the Nagas were

> What is the use of education? I want my boy to work in the fields with me, I want him to work in the house, to draw water and to cut wood; if he goes to school he cannot work for me, and what will be gained afterwards? (General Department (M) October 1908, Nos. 29–34)[7]

The village chiefs regulated the students' attendance in the formal educational institutions that were set up by the British administration. Monetary compensation was paid to parents who sent their children to schools. Such measures were taken up because a decreasing attendance in these educational institutions also meant a reduction of the number of Christians in the respective villages. By the early part of the twentieth century a new curriculum was introduced which included regular classes for teaching Naga folklore, dancing, and singing. However, there was an absence of a formal educational policy in the Naga Hills. By 1938–1939 there were around ninety-one Naga boys and girls studying in high schools in different places outside Naga Hills. Some colonial administrators felt that the prevailing educational system put the Nagas in a disadvantaged position. C. R. Pawsey, the Deputy Commissioner of the Naga Hills stated:

> The education which they are receiving is purely theoretical and will certainly unfit them for life in the Naga Hills . . . they have become totally incapable of earning a living by cultivation in the hills. There are practically no

government jobs available for them and the only future for those unfortunate boys will be a life of discontent, for which most of them have prepared themselves by the sale of their land. (Excluded (B), programs: September 1939)[8]

Changes in the Colonial Period and Its Impact on Naga Society

Naga society underwent a drastic social, political, and cultural transformation as a consequence of colonization. Among other things, Christianity and Western education significantly influenced the Nagas. Education emerged as an important instrument that brought them together to form a pan Naga identity. It also provided employment for a section of educated Nagas who raised issues concerning the future development of the Naga people. This new class of educated Nagas emerged as an important factor that molded the political history of the Nagas. The participation of the Nagas in World War I led to the formation of the first Naga political forum—The Naga Club.

The Naga Club, formed in 1918 can be seen as a reaction to the process of colonial domination. As alluded to earlier, part of its formation had its genesis in the war effort that brought a section of the Nagas together. The greater thrust to its formation had to do with the severe changes that had taken place in the lives of the Naga people in the matter of a few decades under colonial subjugation. Initially this conscious solidarity, as expressed by the Naga Club, was centerd on the concerns of the people living in the hills and later on, was transformed into a political force, which spearheaded the struggle of the Naga nation. The first meeting of the Naga Club showed that the Naga elders were apprehensive about "the introduction of foreign laws and customs to supersede their own customary laws" (Mankekar 1968: 32). By this time, Indian independence was a forgone conclusion. Only the nitty-gritty details of the transfer of power remained. Hence, within a short period of time the Naga Club became engrossed with political issues concerning the future of the Naga homeland once the British left the Naga Hills. The nationalist doctrine of the Nagas was that, racially and ethnically, the different Naga tribes were much closer to one another than to the rest of India. The racial differences may have been insignificant but culturally and politically they were important markers of the desire for autonomy amongst the Nagas. Culturally they were different and Hindu influence, so crucial to the identity of the Gangetic Indian heartland, by-passed them. Politically administered along with India, Burma, and Sri Lanka by the British, the Nagas never claimed to have been an integral part of India. By the same token that Burma and Sri Lanka are sovereign states today, the Naga people began a struggle to establish their separate political identity (Horam 1988: 34).

Culture played a significant role in stirring up doubts about the contributions of the colonial rulers in the lives of the Nagas. While it was true that knowledge of modern science and technology benefited the people, it was also seen as a way through by which the colonial rulers also gained more power and legitimacy in relation to the system that existed in the Naga society. It became a domain of political conflict where the dominant power was equated with knowledge while the existing system of the Nagas was seen as barbaric and inferior since it was defined and projected by the outsider as the prevalence of superstition and myth. In this regard, the introduction of administrative offices and regulations over which Nagas had no control was of little help to them. Culture did not belong to the civil society. It did not stop at the manner of defining a people's way of life, language, their worldviews, and belief systems. Culture became the basis of a struggle for an identity amongst the Nagas, which they felt was being drowned by the direct intervention of the colonial power structure. A system that said that progress was equal to Western/modern way of life and barbarism was equal to the Naga way of life.

The Naga Hills District Tribal Council was established in 1945 with an aim to unite the Nagas and repair the damages done during the war in the Naga Hills. By 1946 it was rechristened as the Naga National Council (NNC). Its functions gradually widened and it took up issues of the political aspirations of the Naga people. By 1947, the Naga people demanded that the Naga Hills should cease to be a part of India once the British transferred power to India. The Naga National Council declared independence of the Naga Hills on August 14, 1947 and conveyed the declaration to the Government of India and the United Nations Organization by cable. Meanwhile India became independent on August 15, 1947.

This history is central to the creation of a Naga identity. The complex effect that colonial institutions had on the social fabric of the Naga people cannot adequately be addressed in the scope of this chapter. However, one has tried to relate the changes in administrative patterns and the introduction of education, to show the instrumental relationship between events in modern history and the ways in which the Nagas reacted to them. While this itself may be a shortcoming, one has to reiterate that such an exegesis is necessary to set the foundation for the role that education played in the colonial past and more importantly, how it affects the colonial realities of the present.

Re-Colonizing the Colonized

While the British rulers decided what should be taught according to the concrete conditions of the subjects they governed, postcolonial India was characterized by the introduction of uniform principles that were applied to all the governed, regardless of their differences and similarities. Themes such as "Unity in diversity" notwithstanding, the major concern of the newly independent Indian State was one of nation building. Little, if any, consideration was spared for regional sensibilities (Baruah 1999: 113). While political issues about sovereignty and freedom from foreign rule were being discussed in the Naga Hills, the situation in the Indian subcontinent was following a slightly dissimilar route. Committees were set up for framing the Constitution of India and policies for territorial integration were taken up. This process involved much academic engagement and political negotiations. The post independence years witnessed an important aspect of educational development that ushered in large-scale changes in school education leading to evolve a national system of education, which looked at education as an integral part of national development and nation building.[9] Professionalization of the school curriculum, syllabus design, preparation and evaluation of textbooks continue to be some of the important issues taken up by the Indian state. This was necessitated mainly to face the challenges brought about by the magnitude and complexity of the problems involved in changing the established structure of education and pattern of curriculum. Policy makers felt that the existing system created by the British was detrimental to the process of nation building itself. The express intention of the policy makers was to rid education of its colonial baggage. Hence, the national Policy on Education in India continues to reflect almost every element included in the Fundamental Duties enshrined in the Constitution of India.

Designing a National Curriculum: The Hegemonic Construction of "Modern Indian History"

The framework for an education policy was laid out, keeping in mind its strategic role in the nation-building exercise. The Indian state by and large retained the existing (British) framework but initiated a cut and paste policy where the history of India as a nation would be emphasized. The tricky question was how to construct the history of another nation like the Nagas as part and parcel of a pan–Indian historiography? Some scholars like Joshi suggested that the tribals and other indigenous peoples of the subcontinent were actually aboriginal Hindus (Joshi 2000: 6–10) while those like Verrier Elwin said that their difference from Hinduism itself was the basis on which they ought to be treated as citizens of a postcolonial India (Elwin 1997: 37–48).

In other words the pedagogic process seemed to say, "then British now Indian." For the Nagas, the introduction of the Indian curriculum and textbooks was a glorification of a foreign nation. It was clear that the continuity of the idea of an Indian nation steamrolled the aspirations of smaller nations in postcolonial India. More importantly, a hegemonic nation appropriated the monopoly over historical events and processes. The proponents of the one-nation theory, all but did away with the populist slogan of "Unity in diversity," when it came to addressing the national question of smaller, ethnically different people.[10] Yet, India also has laws that recognized and protects minorities. Article 29 of the Constitution of India lays down the protection of the interest of minorities and guarantees that "Any section of the citizens residing in the territory of India or any part thereof having a distinct language, script or culture of its own shall have the right to conserve the same."

However, this protection laid down for minorities is rather weak. First of all, it does not devolve any concrete measures and powers to minority communities whereby their systems of knowledge and cultural existence may be reproduced. No culture is static, but India's idea of a people's culture has never gone beyond the national museums where handicrafts, artifacts, and indigenous clothes are framed. There is often a yawning gap between the noble principles of democracy and the political reality in India. The contradiction between a commitment to democracy and the actual practice of governance, the gap between existing legal provisions and their implementation, along with the State's unwillingness to devolve power, are probably nowhere more evident than in the way it deals with its indigenous people.[11] Indian society is of a bewildering complexity and heterogeneity. The heritage of thousands of years of movements of people, goods, and ideas in and out of the subcontinent is reflected in the presence of hundreds of languages and distinct cultures. To integrate such a culturally heterogeneous population of one billion people undoubtedly poses a formidable challenge to the State. India's way of tackling this is through a federal system of government (Erni 2001: 57). According to Baruah, India's commitment to federalism has been rather tame. India's Constitution-makers even shied away from actually describing the polity as federal and settled for a phrase they found safer: the Union of India (Baruah 1999: 1–20). The central Government of India retains extensive powers over the union states and the union territories. Article 3 of the Constitution of India states that the Parliament may by law:

1. Form a new state by separation of territory from any State or by uniting two or more States or parts of States or by uniting any territory to a part of any state;
2. Increase the area of any State;
3. Diminish the area of any State;
4. Alter the boundaries of any State;
5. Alter the name of any State:

The central government further has the right to dismiss elected state government according to Article 356 of the Constitution of India which state that.

1. If the president, on receipt of a report from the Governor of a State or otherwise, is satisfied that a situation has arisen in which the Government of the State cannot be carried on in accordance with the provisions of this Constitution, the President may by proclamation—
   a. Assume to himself all or any of the functions of the Government of the State and all or any of the powers vested in or exercisable by the Governor or any body or authority in the State other than the legislature of the State;
   b. Declare that the power of the legislature of the State shall be exercisable by or under the authority of parliament;
   c. Make such incidental and consequential provisions as appear to the president to be necessary or desirable for giving effect to the objects of the Proclamation.

Electoral democracy brought into existence a class of powerful Naga elites who became managers for New Delhi. Such democratic mechanisms also defined citizenship, rights, and politics and brought along several cleavages in the Naga society. The formation of Nagaland as the sixteenth State of the Indian Union in 1963 split up the Naga inhabited areas into various political boundaries. The historical disruption of national formation in the region was further exacerbated by the systematic dissolution of the basis upon which the Nagas had waged their struggle for self-determination. Yet, such political expediency was backed up by sops in the form of special provisions. Article 371 (A) of the Constitution states

1. Notwithstanding anything in this constitution:
   i.   Religious or social practices of the Nagas,

ii. Naga customary laws and procedure,

iii. Administration of civil and criminal justice involving decisions according to Naga customary law,

iv. Ownership and transfer of land and its resources,

Shall apply to the State of Nagaland unless the Legislative Assembly of Nagaland by a resolution so decides.

However, Clause (b) of the subsequent paragraph also states:

> The governor of Nagaland shall have special responsibility with respect to law and order situation in the state of Nagaland for so long as internal disturbances occurring in the Naga hills . . . in discharge of his functions in relation thereto the Governor shall, after consulting the Council of Ministers, exercise his individual judgment as to the action to be taken.

Issues of security and territory have defined the relationship between the Nagas and the government of India. Even though the Indian state promises policies, development and autonomy of the tribal hills, and the preservation of their cultural and political autonomy, the law itself gives way to the state to have the final say.

Governance and Suppression through Cultural Dominance

One can argue that the role of education introduced by the Indian state has been instrumental in perpetuating forms of cultural dominance that seek to institutionalize the hegemony over Naga culture and identity. It is widely accepted that the state authorities rigidly control the state educational system in any oppressive governing system. Thus, the first step for the government was to "educate" the Nagas and tell them what they "need" to know. The discourse on Naga culture, history, and people cannot take place in a vacuum keeping in mind rows of handicrafts and dances that are presented as the key elements of Naga culture in state sponsored functions and national televisions. No culture is static. But the general definition used to describe the culture of a community or a group of people through their value systems, their eating habits, language, songs and dances, food habits have actually contributed to the perpetuation of cultural stereotypes. The idea of culture for the state has been reduced to the circulation of "cultural products" through commercial exchanges, thereby living up to the notion of the State as the capitalist exploiter (Kikon 2005a: 36–39). This is at odds with the Naga people's political resistance against the Indian state and the demand for the right to self-determination, which is very strongly linked to the resistance of cultural dominance in the socio- and political sphere and the field of education.

Admittedly, education (in the narrow sense) has been more effective than military sorties in a protracted armed–struggle situation. Therefore the introduction of a national syllabus by the state was a process that recolonized the Naga mind, to an extent where Nagas have lost the ability to construct their own past. This has resulted in misinterpretation and misappropriation of the Naga's indigenous knowledge and perspectives. It is in this context that education has become a ground of political struggle between the Indian State's aggressive policies to obliterate the Naga people's history. For many Naga nationalists, such projects are linked to the effort to suppress the political resistance movement. It is true that the Indian state has not only used the education policy to rewrite Naga history but it has also resorted to using repressive laws and military operations which has led to widespread violations of human rights amongst the Nagas. As we have seen earlier, the existence of Constitutional safeguards are in no way indicative of the existence of an open and democratic milieu in Naga society. These safeguards have been instrumental in creating enclaves of collaboration that have been effectively utilized to reproduce the military discourse of insurgency and counter-insurgency which remains the framework of the Naga national question today. Spelling out this strategic concern more clearly, Rajesh Sachdeva highlights the concerns of Indian educationists in Nagaland. His dialogue with the Director of the Central Institute of Indian Languages shows how the policy makers are obsessed with the Indo-Naga armed conflict. The result of this obsession is the fact that even the medium of instruction, English, becomes a tool for creating doubts about a shared identity between Nagas and Indians. In the same set of interviews, a Naga politician steeped in the fortunes of the Indian Parliamentary system pointed out "(Whether the Nagas are) Independent or not, Hindi will continue to play an important role" (Sachdeva 2001: 14–20). Other Indian writers like Joshi stress "there is a certain degree of psychological aversion to Hindi, but sustained efforts to propagate it should gradually erode the barriers of prejudice" (Joshi 2001: 151–52).

"History and Civics": A Look at the Contents of a Class VIII Textbook

It is significant to analyze the pedagogic tools utilized in the denial of a Naga history. While the Nagaland State Council of Educational Research and Training Nagaland may have added few pages about the Naga people, all the contents of history textbooks follow a similar pattern that is overloaded with Indian history. The Class VIII Social Science Book on History and Civics developed by the State Council of Educational Research and

Training Nagaland, Kohima has been taken up to show how history is studied. The first eight sections deal with India's role in the modern world, the colonization of the subcontinent and the anticolonial struggles. This section has an explicitly north Indian focus and the struggles of the peoples of the frontiers of the colonial state are excluded. In civics the syllabus is entirely oblivious of the challenges to the nation-building process and includes sections such as (a) National Goals and Democracy of India (b) The society in India (c) Economic reconstruction (d) National Integration (e) Defense of the country (f) India and the World and (g) World problems. While the history textbook manages to add a chapter on Naga society, it is extremely cursory. It is interesting to observe how there is an overemphasis on the qualities like "simplicity, honesty and hard working." These attributes are repeated to describe Naga people in the past.[12]

One sees the total transformation of the complex history of the formation of Naga identity, into a complete travesty of what social sciences profess as the objective reality of social process. The glorification of Naga past is done by creating a stereotype of the simpleton Naga that is at once condescending and reductionist. Interestingly, modernization is equated with the coming of keys and locks—symbols of the dishonesty that plagues Naga society today. In an amazing display of mental gymnastics, the perceived ills of modernization are blamed on the oppressed themselves. The passage goes on to attribute the ills to the fact that the present generation of Nagas is not hardworking enough—at least not in the same league as their "simpleton" forefathers. They "lie, steal and are lazy." This is actually a direct reference to the changes that Naga society has undergone during the past five decades of militarization. The Indian State has been a part to this process of brutalization of the civil space but this fact is not at all clear from the passage. Instead, the textbook avoids the political questions entirely and moves on to what it sees as the fallout of these "ills"—AIDS, alcoholism, and drug addiction—not necessarily in that order. Remarkably, the passage still finds it prudent to venture back to the unresolved civil and political questions that have caused this "decay" and subtly equates what it sees as a "moral ineptitude" of Naga society, to the dangers of modern life.

Education is a fundamental right of every person regardless of gender and is also widely accepted that it is the most important factor for social development meaning a better life. This kind of characterization and description of marginalized people and tribals in India have contributed in conditioning the minds of the Nagas toward development. Such a notion would justify more subsidy-oriented policies, more reforms and yes, more NGOs bringing more food, more roads, more money, and more lessons on "what is to be done." As a matter of fact, education is a major sector where both the State and non–State actors, like the church and private educational trusts, have made significant contributions. The matter that is imparted to students remains the same.

Even non–State actors are not empowered to take the community into confidence in framing the curricula. Hence, the reiteration of colonial constructs has survived well. While such description of communities by school textbooks raises unexamined questions about the kinds of teaching and the objectives of an educational system prevailing in the Naga society, development through education has become a dominant discourse. So hegemonic are its effects that it seeks to embrace the hopes and aspirations of all. Saigol aptly points out that most development experts cite statistics to prove that countries with high literacy rates or better-educated populations are more developed or more prosperous than those with low literacy rates. The number crunching approach is often used to intervene in societies where there is a dearth of modern education and that are lagging behind economically, politically, and socially. The general impression created by this discourse is that education is some kind of panacea for all ills afflicting societies, and that once education is delivered to the maximum number of people at the fastest possible rates, all will be well (Saigol 2000). Whatever rhetoric may be used by the Indian state to explain their concerns or justify the implementation of such chapters about the Naga people's society in history textbooks, it is evident that such representation of a people's society is aimed at eliminating the sociopolitical and cultural history.

The entire expression of education is wrapped up in the language of rights and development. But the hegemonic structure that delivers education to the people violates the fundamental rights of the people to develop and discuss their social, cultural, and political history. Thus, education has forced the Naga people to acquire a national identity that is detached from their sociopolitical and cultural history. Textbooks that teach the students the characteristics of their own people as inhumane and retrograde because of their laziness, dishonesty, and drug addiction is not empowering and rights based. Thus, the usual assumption (as seen in the school textbook discussed) is that social and economic problems that characterize modern societies, for example crime, drug abuse, poverty, violence, sectarian and ethnic conflict, and religious intolerance, will vanish by means of education. Saigol points out that notwithstanding the experience of highly industrialized and developed countries where education rates are high along with high crime rates, rampant violence, racism, sexism, and classism, the uncritical purveyors of education repeat their faith in the progressive and emancipatory power of education. Seldom has the downside of education been examined with critical veracity and the result is that there has been little effort to understand what kind of education is capable of producing thinking and emancipated persons, necessary for guiding the development project toward liberation (Saigol 2000).

Education has conditioned the present Naga generation to loathe their history. It is no longer important to know about the past because doing so would mean engaging with the repression, exploitation, and subjugation of their people. This has resulted in a great deal of frustration, especially amongst youth, at not being able to understand the milieu. Added to this is the sheer handicap that one has to contend with in order to communicate a sense of self, which can critically engage with the historical movements and the struggle of one's own people. While the Indian Government's educational policy may have been very focused on "conditioned education" as to what needs to be taught, its result is that the state's educational intervention has produced a society filled with complexities. It has developed a classic "victim's mentality" of blaming the past for the entire crisis of the present. Education has given rise to systems and structures that nurture a culture of destruction and despair. It has started off a systematic process of cultural assimilation and political domination in which Nagas have become unwitting accomplices (Longchari 2001). Many of the younger generation of Nagas, who would otherwise consider themselves "modern" and adequately educated, have become dismissive and intolerant, when it comes to engaging with political and civil ground realities.

With an emphasis on discipline, obedience with behavior-alteration tactics, the school syllabus has created an educated society that tries to imitate the mainstream societies, their culture and way of life. While modern State-aided education has allowed the people entry into a make-believe world of rights and awareness, to dream and hope about their futures, the reality for the Naga people is different. Tuensang is a Naga district in the Indo-Myanmar border. In this town, students of the fourth standard in a Christian mission school study about "Different Birds of Prey" during school hours. By sunset as these children do their homework at home; they try to identify the different types of guns from exchanges of fire between various Naga insurgent groups and Indian security forces. In their social science period, they draw the Indian flag (saffron, white, and green). The military camps in the town have the same flag flying at the gate as do the politicians' cars that come to this small town; the moral of the story is that this flag gives one money and the power to bully.

Wokha is another Naga district bordering Assam. Here, students of Seventh standard study about the "Right to Equality," in their civics lessons. Is this applicable to them? They have heard from their parents and elders that the Naga people are governed by special laws[13] which do not permit them to seek justice in any court of law, either their own or outside. On their way back home, they are frisked like thieves, by the security personnel. This is embedded in the very structure and system of an oppressive education that works toward destroying one's self-respect and dignity. By the time these students become adults, they will, like their seniors, accept inhumane treatment and torture by the security personnel who will continue to humiliate them with their racist abuses. They will hear (maybe even campaign for) the politicians who will come with false statements to win votes. The scene here is that of a people who will be dependent on external forces for any help, including the resolution of their problems. These school textbooks are not true. The life that Nagas have to live is not commensurate with the obtuse notions of justice that the textbooks seek to perpetuate. In the evening when families sit around the hearth in the kitchen to share their stories, parents talk about issues and events, which the Class VII student does not understand. When children try to discuss the lesson taught in the school about "Equality in the eyes of the law" they feel foolish. The very symbols of authority and that of the state, such as emblems and insignia, courts, police, are military symbols for these children. Hence, in the civic space the state represents a military machine, rather than the provider of security and protection that it aspires to be.

Education as a Tool for Conflict Transformation

At this point one may argue that textbooks are never meant to reflect reality. Hence, the Naga case may seem like a minor trifling in the political discourse of subjugated nations. There may be some truth in that. Yet, it is at the realm of widely accepted standards of rational behavior and governance where we exist as citizens and as people. It is this same neoliberal belief that equates education with a fundamental right for all citizens. What makes the Naga case so special is the wide discrepancy that exists between "what is taught" and "what is out there." One has briefly tried to point toward the high levels of military engagement that goes on within the civil and political sphere in Naga areas. All along, one has also seen the desire amongst Indian policy makers to try and adapt the existential conditions of routine violence into another "problem" that needs another solution—preferably bureaucratic.

However, while it is true that the pedagogic structures are incapable of handling the issue of violence and its roots, it is in the adaptation to social realities that lay bare an interesting phenomenon. The education system in Naga areas is seen to mediate, rather than clarify when the issue of conflict arises. It is in this mediation that its role in the political conflict is clarified.

It is largely due the political history of the confrontation between Naga national aspirations and a larger Indian nation-building process that education policies have taken its present form. Yet there are at least three internal sources of strain that are visible in the process of mediation that education seeks to play. These strains are instrumental in the process of retarding the capacity of education to deal with the existing realities.

First and foremost, one notices that there is an enormous amount of pressure being exerted for adaptation (to existential situation) arising from the philosophy of education itself (Corwin 1965: 397). The tradition of decentralized control over education supports a pervasive belief amongst educators and policy makers alike, that the public ought to determine education policy. This is an argument that has been used by certain sections in India itself, for continuing with a policy that allows for religious control over educational establishments. Yet, when this argument is extended to include areas where the State has waged a fifty-year-long war against ideas that it seeks to have a monopoly over, namely, the politics of self-determination, then a certain degree of subterfuge comes into play. Educators and educational establishments turn their backs on the violence, while ironically upholding the liberal values that education itself seeks to impart to the people. The idea that the Nagas can exert some pressure on the educational policies is only taken seriously after they (the Naga people) have been suitably "conditioned."[14]

The second strain comes in the form of legal sanctions that control education. The fact that education also leads to some form of "awakening" (for the lack of a better word), leads to a certain fear and to a realistic adjustment to the power structure. The result, according to many in the State apparatus, may be reprisal and resistance. It is perhaps the fear that this awakening may lead to a condition of greater space for change, by using the legal and political structures, leads to the implementation of cautious policies by the State apparatus. This caution does not run both ways however. While on the one hand there has been considerable hesitance in including a comprehensive reading of the creation of Naga political consciousness, the manner in which Indian history and concerns have been incorporated, override this sense of caution.

The adjustments that come about as a result serve to transform the realities into something that people can have no control over. Legally speaking, there is little that can be done in the realm of transforming the education system in Naga areas. Along with military exigencies, it remains a strong bastion of State control.

The third source of strain comes in the form and the manner in which educational institutions are organized. The rules that govern the functioning of schools and shape their curricula, also provide a way of resisting pressures from within Naga civil society. The responsibility that is entrusted to the pedagogic structures is never rotated to include civil society initiatives. Another important aspect of the manner in which the educational institutions are organized, is the physical/geographical one. Most schools in Naga areas have (para) military armed presence that drives home the point that education itself is a matter of national security for the Indian State apparatus.

Ironically though, the government of India spends very little on social welfare schemes, including education. Amartya Sen and Jean Dreze have computed that India needs to spend at least 10 percent of its Gross Domestic Product (GDP) on education. Even then, one finds that this spending rarely goes over 6 percent and with the current climate of "liberalization" of the Indian markets, government spending on education has reduced even further. So there is a condition that may lead us to believe that the State is simply not interested in social spending and wishes to concentrate on defense instead. It would be borne out of the proliferation of private schools all over India. Yet, at another level, the situation of the Naga people is going in the opposite direction. Rather than retreat from the social sphere, as many commentators in India have rued, one is given the impression that the State apparatus is out to seek more control. Only, what seems to be routine in other parts of the subcontinent have to be qualified in Naga areas. Therefore, while the State may be moving out and reducing its budgetary allocation for education, it is also a fact that it is spending a lot more on defense.

In the Naga areas, defense has always been the primary concern for policy makers. At the same time, the State also allowed concessions to non-State actors like the church and Hindu missionaries to carry on with their welfare activities amongst the peoples of the "backward" regions. Hence, functionaries of the Roman Catholic church run most of the premier academies of the region. Many intellectuals in India saw the Ramakrishna Mission as the Hindu equivalent of Christian missionaries. The dual policy of allowing the growth of private schools, while continuing with the policy of tightening the contents of the syllabi was followed during the period of consolidation by the Indian State. Yet, it was in the realm of what was imparted to students outside the curriculum that shows an interesting side in the pedagogic exercises of the period. Students in Roman Catholic schools acquired a label of their own. They were deemed to be Westernized and modern. Their uniforms and mannerisms were picked out from manuals of public school education in Britain. The Ramakrishna Mission and its affiliated schools were more intent on imparting an Indian education. This ipso facto implied the rejection of anything Western. Nevertheless, the important matter of the content of the syllabus remained more or less the same for both.

However, the notion that the State has moved away from its welfare role, while being an axiom of sorts in the Indian subcontinent, can be misleading. Education, when posed as a right, becomes a part of the welfare activities of the State. Hence, it is not surprising to see that the Indian administration often quotes the amount it has spent on schools and textbooks for marginalized people like the Nagas as proof of its obligations as a welfare state. It is true that much money has been spent in paying wages and designing the curricula of education in Naga areas. Part of the reason why such copious amounts of funds are available for education-related activities has to do with the strategic role that the administration sees in the promotion of certain modes of knowledge. As already seen earlier, what constitutes a Naga past in the textbooks is actually a rehash of old colonial stereotypes, added as unwanted appendages to the end of the chapter. What is more interesting are the instrumental reasons that are attached to this kind of spending by the government of India, in an area that it has itself marked out as "backward" and does not intend to loosen its political and military stranglehold. To be sure, the special provisions that are outlined in Article 371 (A) have a built-in mechanism that allows the Indian state to maintain its grip over changes, while appearing to allow for maximum autonomy. The role of the governor in deciding the political climate and its implications is crucial for us to understand the kind of freedom that is permissible. In the same manner as the governor finally decides when and how the terms of political engagement between the Nagas and the Indian State needs to be transformed, the business of education is also a concern that the state apparatus is not willing to relinquish its hold over. So, it is hardly surprising that the two areas that this window-dressing autonomy does not apply are (a) civil and political rights and (b) education. Education has also become another area of contest between those seeking further militarization of civil society and those who are in favor of more consensual forms of engagement between the Indian state and the Naga people.

It is evident that the purpose of education for the Naga people is to cover the past, rather than allow the Naga student to discover their own history. The kind of instrumental rationality that one sees in the communiqués and missives, regarding the role of education in Naga society, bears this out. This is the worst kind of liberal tradition that Indian policy makers have inherited from the Enlightenment. The idea that education can be something like filling a vessel with water, thereby fulfilling a loose commitment to welfare politics and also condition minds into obedience, is so evident in the schooling of the Naga mind. One wishes to consider the role of the Central Institute of Indian and Foreign Languages that came into existence in 1969. This Institute aimed at playing a pivotal role in the development of the state by working on the tribal languages, as for Indian policy makers, language development is a prerequisite to educational development and in turn both are needed for socioeconomic development of the people. Since language permeates all social life and it is the most important tool for communication, educationists can ignore it only by risking education itself, for it cannot be denied that education is undoubtedly concerned about transmission of content, as well as values, and words embody both. The eventual work that has been conceived of by the Institute has sought to inculcate concepts of multiple identities amongst a people who have been demanding their political freedom (Sachdeva 2001: 20).

Conclusion

The Indian state mass education for the Nagas was designed to achieve much the same ends as the British education system. Today, the primary purpose of education policies for the Nagas seems to be the desire to domesticate the erstwhile "wild" Nagas into a pliant segment of the Indian republic. This single-minded objective, of deferring the political resolution to the Naga resistance movement, itself forms a hegemonic system, where anyone questioning the dominant modes of production of knowledge is forced into more and more marginalized positions. India has evolved its own laws and acts that can pass off as those designed to protect the interests of its minorities. However, in the analysis of the education system for the Nagas, these provisions stand negated by the deeper philosophy that informs these policies. For the Naga people, this silent and insidsious process continues unabated and the fear that it may be a while before its implications are understood is one that they shall have to live with. One believes that it is at the level of educational institutions and educational policies that the next phase of the Naga's struggle for self-determination will be waged.

Notes

A draft version of this paper titled, *Schooling Consent Destroying Differences: A Critical Analysis of education in Indian Administered Nagaland* was presented at the annual meeting of the Association of Asian Studies, Washington DC, United States of America, April 4–7, 2002. A revised version was published in the Inter-Asia Cultural Studies Journal, Volume 4, Number 2, 2003.

1. This accounts only the Nagas of Nagaland.

2. See <http://www.nscn.com> (accessed December 12, 2004).

3. This is a rough estimate since there has never been an attempt to bring out a joint census of the Nagas residing in India and Myanmar. Yet, the Naga civic and political bodies frequently use this figure. In such instances Naga nationalist myths not only circulate around one blood/one people theory, but also graft onto modern nation state practices of censuses and number games to mobilize and demand for a homeland.

4. "Patkoi" refers to the Patkai hills situated between India and Myanmar.

5. Government of India Census Report 2001.

6. Foreign Political Proceedings (1884) Nos. 23–60, National Archives of India, New Delhi (unpublished).

7. General Department (M) October 1908, Nos. 29–34, from Lieutenant colonel A. E. Woods, Deputy Commissioner, Naga Hills, to the Commissioner of Sumra Valley and the Hill Districts.

8. Excluded (B), progs. September 1939, No. 3240, Assam Secretariat Proceedings, Record Office, Assam Secretariat, Shillong.

9. Romantic notions of intellectuals involved in building bridges to integrate the country ought not to sway one. The fact that the first decade after the transfer of power in 1947 also coincided with the aggressive expansion of territory by the Indian state is a matter that recurs in the history of nationality movements in the northeast. The bitter fact remains that hardly any democratic voice outside the region has raised this issue in public.

10. The idea that India is a "foreign" nation is a recurring motif in any expression of dissent by the indigenous peoples of Northeast India. Slogans like "Indian by accident, Naga (or Assamese, or Khasi, or Boro, or Dimasa, or Mizo) by blood" and "Down with Indian Colonialism" continue to be painted on whitewashed walls in the region. In the last decade, one of the major tasks of the administration has been to ensure that such graffiti is cleaned over. Instead, one finds "Save Indian Unity" displayed prominently along the national highways. Interestingly, these new billboards are designed and produced by the administration's publicity department.

11. Government of India rejects the use of the term "indigenous" for any of the people living within its boundary. It argues that the complex and age-old history of migration and exchange and mixing of cultural and physical traits makes it impossible to distinguish any group as "indigenous" in relation to other groups; therefore everyone in India has to be considered indigenous.

12. The standard school textbook: Social Sciences, Book Four, Part One (History and Civics) for Class VIII students has all this and more. The State Council of Educational research and Training, Kohima, Nagaland has developed the book.

13. These following laws and regulations are annexed:

   Appendix 1. Punjab Security of State Act: 1953
   Appendix 2. The Assam Maintenance of Public Order (Autonomous Districts) Act, 1953

Appendix 3. The Armed Forces (Special Powers) regulation, 1958 No: 2 of 1958

Appendix 4. The Armed Forces (Assam And Manipur) Special Powers Act, 1958 No: 28 of 1958

Appendix 5. The Armed Forces (Assam And Manipur) Special powers (Amendment) Act, 1972

No: 7, 1972

Appendix 6. Regulation 5 of 1962 (The Nagaland Security Regulation) 1962.

14. School children are routinely rounded up to proclaim their desire to live in peace through several state-sponsored rallies and functions. These events are generally held at the behest of the government and under the watchful eyes of the security forces. Such cases are an instance of using children and other non-combatants in the war against rebels. This is a sore point for Naga civil and political rights activists. In neighboring Assam as well, Human Rights groups have been very critical of such "staged" marches for peace.

References

Barpujari, H.K. (1977) *Political History of Assam (1826–1919), Vol. 1*, Gauhati: Spectrum Publications.

Baruah, Sanjib (1999) *India Against Itself*, New Delhi: Oxford University Press.

Bhattacharjee, J.B (1980) "The Eastern Himalayan Trade of Assam in the Colonial period," North East India History Association, First Session Proceedings, Shillong.

Corwin, Ronald G (1965) *A Sociology of Education*, New York: Meredith Publishing.

Devi, Lakshmi (1968) *Ahom-Tribal Relations (A Political Study)*, Gauhati: Lawyers Book Stall.

Downs, Frederick. S (1983) *Christianity in Northeast India*, Delhi: Indian Society for Promoting Christian Knowledge.

Elwin, Verrier (1997) (First published in 1961 by the research Department Secretariat, North East Frontier Agency, Shillong) *Nagaland*, Guwahati: Spectrum Publications.

Erni, Christian (2001) *Indigenous Peoples' Self-Determination in Northeast India*, International Work Group for Indigenous Affairs, Copenhagen.

Gait, E.A (1963) [1905] *A History of Assam*, 3rd rev. ed. (Calcutta: Thatcher Spink).

Horam. M. (1988) *Naga Insurgency-The Last Thirty Years*, New Delhi: Cosmo Publications.

Joseph, Sarah (1998) *Interrogating Culture, Critical Perspectives on Contemporary Social Theory*, New Delhi: Sage Publications.

Joshi, Hargovind (2001) *Nagaland: Past and Present*, New Delhi: Akansha Publishing House.

Kikon, Dolly (2005a) *Operation Hornbill Festival*, Seminar Magazine, June 550.

Kikon, Dolly (2005b) Engaging Naga Nationalism: Can Democracy Function in Militarised Societies? In *Economic and Political Weekly*, Vol. 40, No. 26, June 25.

Longchari, Akum (2001) "Towards and Indigenous Ethical Discourse" (unpublished).

Mackenzie, Alexander (1884) *History of the Relations of Government with the Hill Tribes of the Northeast Frontier of Bengal*, Calcutta: Home Dept. Press. Reprinted as Mackenzie, Alexander, The Northeast Frontier of India (New Delhi: Mittal, 1979).

Mankekar, D.R. (1968) *On the Slippery Slope in Nagaland*, Bombay: Manaktalas.

Sachdeva, Rajesh (ed.) (2001) *Language Education in Nagaland*, New Delhi: Regency Publications.

Saigol, Rubina (2000) *Symbolic Violence*, Lahore: Society for the Advancement of Education.

Sladkovsky, M.I (1981) *The Long Road: Sino- Russian Economic Contracts from Ancient Times to 1917*, Moscow: Progress Publishers.

The Constituent Assembly, *The Constitution of India* (1991) New Delhi: Universal Law Publishing Co.

CHAPTER 6

TIBET AND THE (MIS-) REPRESENTATION OF CULTURAL GENOCIDE

Barry Sautman

If anyone finds a reason why there's something wrong with a sacred cow, what they should do is find some really good proof that there is something wrong with it and then publish it.

—Prof. Robin Warren, 2005
Nobel Laureate in Physiology and Medicine[1]

Introduction

Ideologues of all stripes elaborate myths in order to mobilize a following. Nationalists, however, often openly eschew intellectual integrity in justifying their mythmaking. A leading proponent of liberal nationalism contends that if nationalist myths suppress what is negative in the history of a nation, they do so to facilitate moralizing that encourages its members to live up to ancestral virtues.[2] A conservative defender of nationalism argues that even deliberate falsehoods should be condoned where mythmaking is essential to a merited nationalist project.[3]

Nationalists magnify ethnic differences to bolster national identities:[4] in the Tibet case, the claim is that Tibetans and Han Chinese are "completely different."[5] They also seek to activate a nation and garner external support by invoking myths of moral grievance, even where there is no clear pattern of ethnic oppression or a mixed record.[6] They typically assert that the claimed oppression is indisputable. For example, a U.S. Tibet Committee board member has said "By now, the oppression of the Tibetan people, their culture and their religion by the Chinese government is a proven and accepted fact." She also noted, however, that middle-class Lhasa Tibetans—the only Tibetans she reported observing —were not unhappy.[7]

The result of nationalist hyperbolizing is pervasive political mystification. A quick example concerns the claim that Tibetans must be oppressed because annually 2,000–3,000 of them illegally travel from Tibet to India via Nepal.[8] It is said these Tibetans "flee" or "escape persecution."[9] What is seldom revealed is that most such "refugees" are not motivated by "persecution" or "oppression." Dorjee, director of the Refugee Reception Centre in Dharamsala, India, where the Tibet Government-in-Exile (TGIE) is headquartered, has stated that 10–15 percent of such new arrivals are "released prisoners and other people with political problems," 25 percent come only to see the Dalai Lama and then return, while 60–65 percent come for secular or monastic education and an uncertain percentage of these return to Tibet.[10]

The core of Tibetan nationalist ideology is that Tibet has been occupied and colonized by China for five and a half decades.[11] The Dalai Lama has said "Tibet was an independent country before its occupation by China. . . . There is no justification claiming that Tibet was 'part of China' "[12] and that Tibet "is an issue of colonial rule: the oppression of Tibet by the People's Republic of China and resistance to that rule by the people of Tibet."[13] The TGIE and "Tibet supporters," including major media, also argue there is a Chinese colonial effort to exploit Tibet and destroy the Tibetan nation and its culture,[14] even though every state in the world recognizes that Tibet is part of China and none deems Tibet a colony.[15]

Émigré leaders attribute a malign purpose and effect to all actions of "the Chinese" in Tibet, especially as to culture, and assert their demarches to China seek only to preserve Tibet's culture.[16] The Dalai Lama has said: "The Chinese authorities view Tibet's distinct culture and religion as the source of threat of separation. Hence as a result of deliberate policies an entire people with its unique culture and identity are facing the threat of extinction."[17] He acknowledges that the claim that Tibetanness is threatened by an undermining of Tibetan Buddhist culture is a drawing card for his cause among Buddhism's international following[18] and he mobilizes this following by telling converts that support for Tibetan nationalism is a religious obligation.[19] The TGIE also endorses the commercialization of Buddhism because it attracts foreign support for the "cause of Tibet's liberation."[20]

To magnify the appeal, the Dalai Lama emphasizes the redemptive features of Tibetan culture, stating: "My main concern is the protection of Tibetan culture because [it] has the potential to create a peaceful human society, a compassionate society at peace with nature and the environment."[21] Despite TGIE claims,[22] there is no basis however for concluding Tibetans are more environment-friendly than other peoples in terms of forest protection,[23] animal rights,[24] or landscape preservation[25] or that Tibetans are especially compassionate.[26] Supporters of the émigré cause moreover make such claims even though the Dalai Lama terms old Tibet feudal[27] and holds that Tibetans are being punished for bad karma acquired by practicing feudalism, just as a disabled child is punished for past life sins or communities suffer disasters, such as earthquakes and tsunamis, because of common negative karma.[28] They do so while speaking positively of Tibet's former theocracy[29] and even though the Dalai Lama's most long-standing foreign supporter called that monastic supremacy "a stern dictatorship"[30] and old Tibet's leaders limited the cultural sphere through an underdeveloped and skewed educational system. The Dalai Lama's eldest brother has approvingly explained that

> A secular education corresponds only to secular needs, and in Tibet these are minimal. The son of a nomad knows all there is to know about the life before him by the time he is nine or ten years old. So with the son or daughter of a farmer . . . Reading and writing are virtually unnecessary for there is no such thing as secular literature in Tibet . . . What intellectual development any layman wants he wants in terms of his knowledge and understanding of the scriptures, and [because monks can read to laymen] this is always open to him. Further knowledge, to anyone with so clear a sense of direction, is meaningless.[31]

Contemporary émigré discourse, as one Western Tibetologist observes, has "adopted a Western-style rhetoric that emphasizes human rights issues (a concept unknown in traditional Tibet culture and suspect to most Chinese politicians), lack of freedom (as if the traditional Tibetan government would have ever granted any freedom to commoners), and economic and environmental issues."[32] The discourse is framed in the starkest terms to force the hand of international elites. Introducing a study of a purported PRC plan to "crush an ancient civilization" in Tibet,[33] Kalon T.C. Tethong stated that "Tibet today is in the throes of a second Cultural Revolution as the Chinese authorities step up their long-term strategy to exterminate Tibet's distinct cultural and ethnic identity" and "accomplish their Final Solution to the Tibet problem."[34] The Kashag or TGIE cabinet has said that China is committing "systematic destruction" of Tibet's culture[35] and the

Dalai Lama has stated "The Tibetan nation is dying."[36] A leading Western "Tibet supporter" has put it that the very fabric of Tibet's religious and cultural identity is threatened every day by the occupation of China.[37]

Invocations of the Holocaust[38] have caused Western leaders—even those who do not endorse Tibetan independence—to demand China refrain from actions that imperil Tibet's culture, the assumption being that the émigrés veritically point to a clear danger to Tibetans from PRC cultural or migration policies. After the Dalai Lama visited the U.S. President in 2001, his representative averred the United States offered "moral and material support to help preserve Tibet's unique linguistic, cultural, and religious identity."[39] Secretary of State Colin Powell stated that Han Chinese migration to Tibet "seems to be a policy that might well destroy that society" and pledged "solidarity with the Dalai Lama and the people of Tibet."[40] In introducing a "Tibet Policy Act"[41] bill in 2001, U.S. Senator Diane Feinstein said she crafted the legislation to support the émigré cause because "Beijing has repeatedly ignored promises to preserve indigenous Tibetan political, cultural and religious systems."[42] A Canadian newspaper has editorialized that China is "flooding Tibet with hundreds of thousands of Chinese migrants in an obvious attempt at cultural assimilation."[43] Concomitantly, émigré leaders try to foreclose responses to their charges by establishing a binary of "pro-China/pro-Tibet" and dismissing critics as "pro-China." Gabriel Lafitte, a "Tibet activist" and scholar, notes that for émigré leaders.

> The picture is black and white, without ambiguities. China is often viewed monolithically, so the multivocality of Chinese elite contestation goes unheard. Chinese data is dismissed wholesale as propaganda—even the data used by China's still enormous machinery of central planning.[44]

This essay analyzes the émigré claim that China is directly or indirectly extirpating Tibetan culture. It examines the state of culture in Tibet, especially religion, language, and the arts. The essay concludes that the discourse of cultural genocide in Tibet is intended as incitory, rather than as an intellectually meaningful conceptual framework for assessing state policy.[45] Designed to bolster the legitimacy of the émigré ethnonationalist movement, it misreads the effects of cultural transformation, ascribing to Tibet's subsumption into China changes connected to late modernity that affect people throughout the world. It is used by émigré leaders to foster a polemical polarity between themselves as the torchbearers of "authentic" Tibetanness[46]—and thus rightful rulers of an independent or quasi-independent Tibet—and "the Chinese," who as negators of Tibetanness, are disentitled to exercise sovereignty in Tibet. The discourse casts Han Chinese as materialists and Tibetans as spiritual;[47] Han as immoral and Tibetans as moral.[48] In doing so, it follows a well-worn path. As a scholar of German history notes, "The thread that links all historical forms of anti-Semitism, whether religious, economic, political, or racial, is the identification of Jewishness with materialism and immorality."[49] The argument to be made here is not that Tibet's cultural life is unproblematic;[50] there are few places in the world where that is so. Almost all cultures are fast being changed by a globalizing modernity of Western (especially American) origin. As Dibyesh Anand has observed, moreover,

> The entire project of preserving a culture and civilization is theoretically problematic since it considers culture as something that can be identified, mapped, practiced, and preserved. Such a conceptualization of culture essentializes and naturalizes what is socially and politically constructed and contested.[51]

What is argued is that cultural change, not cultural genocide, is proceeding in Tibet and, for the most part, is a result of the intrusion of Westernized modernity, mediated through China proper. In PRC minority areas, Han are viewed as "conduits of western globalization"[52] and not as transmitters of such traditional cultural elements as Confucianism or Han folk arts. The argument is not that this intrusion is generally positive, but that Tibetans are not subjected to a concerted, state-backed effort to destroy their culture.

Throughout the world, cultural life is particularly problematic in poor and minority areas. Although more embedded in "traditional culture," the populations of such areas have fewer defenses against the negative aspects of globalizing modern culture and many fewer options than richer and larger populations to preserve or revive key elements of traditional cultures. In all respects, the claim of cultural genocide in Tibet is misleading and inaccurate and this is so even if one assumes—in contradiction to its conceptualization in international law—that the cultural genocide at issue is unintentional.

The Claim of Cultural Genocide in Tibet

Unquestioned Cultural Genocide

As the International Olympic Committee met in Moscow in 2001 to award the 2008 Games, the Dalai Lama's envoy in Russia, Ngawang Gelek, told a journalist that Beijing should be denied the Games because "China has been executing a policy in Tibet of ethnic and cultural genocide against the Tibetan people" intended to "erase the Tibetan people from the face of the Earth." He added that there "has not been one single [terrorist] incident in all the 50 years of [Tibetan] emigration," and endorsed Russia's policies in Chechnya, stating that "Chechens within the Russian Federation have a hundred times more freedom than the Tibetans inside the PRC," and that "Russia has given the Chechen people full autonomy."[53]

The Dalai Lama's representative could not help but know of Tibetan guerrillas who fought China for almost two decades[54] and have been repeatedly praised by the Dalai Lama.[55] Despite attempts to portray him as a pacificist,[56] the Dalai Lama's stance on violence is pragmatic: "Buddhists believe if the motivation is good and the goal is good, then the method, even the apparently violent kind, is permissible. But here in our situation, in our case whether it is practical or not, that I think is the big question."[57] He has said that use of force by an elected government is better than by an authoritarian one.[58] His support for or agnosticism about wars waged by the United States since World War II, including praise for U.S. efforts in Korea, Vietnam, and Afghanistan,[59] has drawn disappointment or criticism from pacificists.[60] He upholds India's acquisition and testing of nuclear weapons.[61] An 8,000-strong commando group of Tibetans in the Indian army daily affirms its fealty to the Dalai Lama and desire to "liberate Tibet."[62]

Gelek must have been aware of nine bombings in Lhasa from 1995–2000 and of endorsements of terrorism by the largest émigré organization, the Tibetan Youth Congress (TYC).[63] Presidents of the TYC of the late 1980s and early 1990s held that, because no Chinese in Tibet is innocent, war should be waged on civilians there.[64] Indian intelligence agencies reportedly believe the TYC is planning guerrilla warfare in Tibet and have contacted retired officers of a Tibetan unit of the Indian army to be trained in insurgency. The TYC president stated in 2003 that the organization was planning to train members in guerrilla warfare and hinted also at assassinations: "I want to ask the Dalai Lama: 'If you could achieve Tibetan independence in a day by killing 100 Chinese would you do it?' If he says no, he cannot be the leader of the Tibetan people."[65] The Dalai Lama has himself allegedly encouraged extreme nationalist expressions "to make him[self] look more conciliatory."[66] "A steady hate-China diet" and talk of martyrdom through violence are noted in India's Tibetan settlements.[67]

A faction of émigré notables fantasizes about terrorism—without public rebuke from exile leaders—but accuses China of "state terrorism."[68] For example, an ex-guerrilla leader has called for a "force [to] rise up in Tibet, killing Chinese one by one."[69] After the September 11, 2001 terrorist attacks, a journal fostered by mainstream émigré leaders published a missive, by a proponent of the discourse of cultural genocide,[70] who urged émigrés: "In future, if any individual is determined to take his or her life, why not use this final act in a gesture of heroism? For example, like those Palestinians, carrying suicide bombs, in their freedom struggle."[71] Meanwhile, the TGIE's "moderate" faction, exemplified by Samdhong Rinpoche, argues there should be an "evacuation" of "Chinese" from Tibet.[72]

The Dalai Lama's representative must also know that specialists find Chechen autonomy much less than full. Chechen separatists are up in arms because Russia does not permit in Chechnya what Tibetan émigrés seek in Tibet—a regime based on a preferred religion.[73] Gelek sought Russian support by implying that Tibetan émigrés, in contrast to Chechens, uniformly practice nonviolence, a notion linked to the essentialist discourse of the unique magnanimity and equanimity of Tibetans.[74]

The Dalai Lama has said "peacefulness and compassion are part of Tibetan culture."[75] Samdhong Rinpoche speaks of "Tibet's gentle civilisation"[76] and asserts "the struggle of Tibet has always been a nonviolent one."[77] Power struggles among Tibet's spiritual and temporal lords however were often violent. For example, although the Khambas of eastern Tibet are among the most religious of Tibetans, "the history of Kham was marked by endless feuds between warrior chieftains in deadly competition for supremacy over Kham's remote hinterlands."[78] The seventeenth century Dalai Lama called the Great Fifth by émigré leaders, ordered his enemies, their families, descendants, and servants annihilated without a trace.[79] The present Dalai Lama's immediate predecessor instigated violence against Tibetan and non-Tibetan opponents.[80]

Émigré leaders have only recently claimed that nonviolence is essential to Tibetan culture and underlies their strategy.[81] Apart from armed uprisings in Tibet in the 1950s and émigré armed incursions into Tibet in the 1960s and 1970s,[82] there has also been violence against critics of the administration or their exclusion from the émigré polity.[83] The same has held true of religious dissenters.[84] A discourse of democratization exists in which the TGIE is presented by itself and "Tibet supporters" as having all the attributes of a "free democratic" or "fully-functioning democratic government."[85] There are however no institutional mechanisms for dissent, as even the top émigré leadership is subordinate to an unelected supreme leader, in accord with the Tibetan Buddhist idea of rule by the enlightened.[86] Thus, publications that "do not conform to the desired image of traditional Tibetan society" have been suppressed.[87] Tibetans in India have also engaged in violence against their local neighbors:

> Sometimes the local population has attacked the refugees in mobs and ransacked their property. In retaliation, Tibetans too have used violent methods and even killed individuals thought to be responsible for such acts of vandalism. Rivalry among gangs of youth breaks out into violent physical

clashes, which on many occasions end up in murder. In 1999 in Manali two murders took place due to a conflict between the local population and the Tibetans . . . [A]ccording to local sources, the reason may have been the fact that Tibetans were buying large tracts of land through *benami* transactions (that is, land purchased by the Tibetans in the name of local citizens), something which irked the local population.[88]

Ngawang Gelek's other assertion—that unlike Chechens, Tibetans are deprived of any say in how their region is run—is also a political myth. Tibetans are numerous at all rungs of the Tibet Autonomous Region (TAR)[89] political hierarchy, except as Regional Party Secretary.[90] Their political participation is unlike the situation in Ladakh, the largely Tibetan Buddhist area of India, a country whose political system émigré leaders fulsomely praise.[91] Ladakhi Buddhists agitate for direct rule by New Delhi because they lack autonomy in Indian Jammu and Kashmir.[92] There, New Delhi's Indian Administrative Service has never employed any of the many Ladakhi Buddhists who have passed its examinations.[93]

The disregard by the Dalai Lama's representative of well-understood aspects of the politics of the place where he is from and the place where he is stationed did not lead the interviewer to question his assertion of "ethnic and cultural genocide." The mass media curb their skepticism where émigré representations of the Tibet Question are concerned, both to avoid accusations of being tools of the PRC and out of awe of a world religious leader and Nobel Prize winner. The Dalai Lama himself observes that the Western "media is very favourable, very supportive" of his cause. Public opinion, as expressed through the media, "gives inspiration for more support, and more concern in Parliament or Congress."[94]

The media is highly receptive to claims of cultural genocide,[95] despite a consistent lack of evidence proffered by émigré leaders. Western media reflexively allude to the concept even when not using the phrase. Thus, in a report on a German parliament human rights committee invitation to testify, extended to actor Richard Gere as "someone who is 'knowledgeable about the political situation' in Tibet," a wire service stated, "Under Chinese rule, the Tibetan language and culture have been suppressed."[96] In that and other cases, Westerners, aware of the histories of genocides and cultural effacements perpetuated by their own states,[97] may readily accept claims of similar oppression elsewhere.

The Émigré Conception of Cultural Genocide

In the first years after the 1959 emigration, the Dalai Lama charged China had "a view to the total extermination of the Tibetan race,"[98] had brought "the danger of total destruction" to Tibetans,[99] and had instituted a form of oppression "a thousand times worse than the system of apartheid."[100] At the same time, he implied China's aim was not physical annihilation, but assimilation and subordination: China "seems to attempt the extermination of religion and culture and even the absorption of the Tibetan race."[101] In 1959 and 1960 reports, the CIA-funded International Commission of Jurists (ICJ) claimed China was committing genocide through restrictions on religion that were destroying Tibetans' way of life.[102] Émigré leaders took up the term "genocide,"[103] but at times fixed on the idea of an effort to destroy Tibetan culture. The Dalai Lama said in 1973 "our unique culture is being deliberately undermined."[104] The émigrés' first use of "cultural genocide" dates back at least to the return of an émigré delegation from a 1980 "fact-finding" trip to Tibet.[105] Cultural genocide has since been the centerpiece of émigré discourse, with many documents referring to it. North American politicians sympathetic to the émigré cause also refer to cultural genocide and occasionally to genocide *tout court*.[106] Many of these politicians are critics of China in every respect and charges of genocide are their heaviest rhetorical clubs for "China bashing."[107]

Statements about cultural genocide in Tibet rarely involve an examination of the concept and almost never include direct evidence that the PRC intends to de-culture Tibetans. The one instance in which a claim was made of direct evidence of "planning cultural genocide"[108] concerned a "secret meeting" dubbed "512," after the May 12, 1993 date on which it was convened near Chengdu, Sichuan, by the Chinese Communist Party's (CCP) United Front Work Department (*tongzhan bu*). "Tibet supporters" were still referring to this meeting more than a decade later.[109] Conferees were said to have decided to " 'transfer' large numbers of Chinese settlers into Tibet with the aim of making it demographically 'impossible for Tibetans to rise,' " to break the unity of the Tibetan émigrés, and to manipulate "international figures and religious personages in Tibet for propaganda purposes." The émigré Tibet Bureau in Switzerland asserted that realization of these aims would "destroy the cultural and national identity of the Tibetan people and amount to a form of cultural genocide."[110] Neither the existence nor the content of the "512" meeting has been independently verified. The claims about the meeting do, however, exemplify how the émigré leaders seek to own the idea of cultural genocide by assimilating to it almost every policy or action undertaken or permitted by the state in Tibet. As to the "512" meeting, their all-inclusive conception of cultural genocide encompassed ordinary political acts of mobilizing allies and dividing and discrediting opponents.

Only the implication of ethnic swamping raises the issue of cultural genocide.[111] Population transfer has played a role in genocide against small groups of indigenous peoples, as in the settler infusion into the Amazon.[112] A state plan of migration of Han to Tibet would amount to cultural genocide if three conditions were present: (1) an intent to organize a transfer (as opposed to merely permitting migration); (2) an intent to use transfer to damage Tibetan culture, as opposed to securing Tibet politically and developing it economically; and (3) if transfer were an adjunct to the physical extermination of Tibetans as such (as opposed to undertaking repressive action to curb separatism). None of these conditions apply.

First, there is no evidence of a "government program to promote mass emigration of Chinese to water down the native Tibetan population," or an "official effort to shift the ethnic balance" in Tibet, as the Dalai Lama and "Tibet supporters" claim.[113] The PRC government has not transferred most Han migrants who live in Tibet today, either by ordering their migration or offering inducements to settle. Annual net migration rates from the 1950s to the 1970s were low, from three to fourteen Han Chinese per thousand Tibetans.[114] The number of Han with household registration (*hukou*) in the TAR peaked in 1980 at about 122,000,[115] but fell to 70,000 by 1985.[116] Ironically, in 1985 also, the Dalai Lama complained Tibetans were threatened with "the complete assimilation and absorption of our people by a vast sea of Chinese settlers streaming across our borders."[117] The U.S. government however disparaged as "inaccurate, incomplete and misleading" claims that Tibet was being swamped with migrants.[118]

From 1964 to 1994, there was a net inflow of 98,500 migrants who transferred their *hukou* to the TAR, but 70 percent were ethnic Tibetans from adjacent provinces.[119] Han with TAR *hukou* in 1999 numbered almost the same as in 1985,[120] and many Han who formerly lived in Tibet keep their *hukou* in the TAR, even though they no longer live there.[121] Han transferred to the TAR are a small part of recent migrants to Tibet. About 1,950 were sent in three batches from 1995 to 2001, according to government statements, and a fourth batch of 800 were dispatched in 2004.[122] Most are assigned for three years, but spend only half that time in Tibet, due to extended leaves.[123] There were 17,000 Han cadres in the TAR in the mid-1990s,[124] while TAR Han in 2000 (all Han civilians who had lived there for six months or more, regardless of place of household registration) numbered 155,000.[125] Those transferred thus amount to about a tenth of all TAR Han. It is inaccurate to say that "[m]ost of the Han people in Tibet are there on government order, not out of choice,"[126] while reasonable for a leading demographer of China to conclude "there has been no policy of promoting massive permanent migration of Han Chinese people to the TAR."[127]

The vast majority of Han who go to Tibet migrate on their own initiative and struggle to get by. They are surprised to hear that they are represented in the West as induced by state incentives to settle in Tibet, as some claim,[128] and that they are well off, since only the few transferred cadres receive incentives that raise their pay to a level already provided to Tibetan cadres in Tibet.[129] Most Han in Tibet have less than a high school education,[130] are from peasant and worker backgrounds, have blue-collar or lower middle-class jobs, and are ill regarded by the ethnic Tibetan and *lao Xizang* (old Tibet-based Han) elites.[131] Most of this "floating population" (*liudong renkou*), moreover, are not "settled" in the sense of expecting to live long-term in a place. Many Han come to Tibet's cities for only the summer months to work on construction projects or engage in small businesses, such as repair work or making and selling handicrafts, and then return home for the rest of the year.[132] Others secure employment or set up businesses for longer periods of time, but seldom intend to stay for many years. As one scholar who has studied the Han in Lhasa observes, "Most Han migrants stay for a period of perhaps five or six years and then go back taking with them the money they have accumulated."[133] Another has noted that, in Tibet, "many of the young [non-Tibetan] traders are not families but single men; professionals also will try to keep the *hukou* of at least one key family member in their place of origin."[134] A Western journalist conducting interviews among Han in Lhasa concluded that "the influx seems neither to be well planned, nor permanent. As soon as the Chinese arrive, they are scheming to leave."[135] Sociologists who carried out extensive fieldwork among Han migrants to Lhasa concluded that because market saturation was reached in a short time after the TAR was opened to small businesses, competition is fierce and profit margins and prices tend to fall. As a result, conflicts among competitors are common, and business' turn-over rate is high; about 85 percent of migrants choose to leave Lhasa within two years' arrival; only about 5–10 percent would stay five years and more.[136] Similarly, Han traders from outside Qinghai, most of whose territory is on the Tibet Plateau, are said to generally stay there only for a year or two.[137]

The lack of evidence that the PRC government planned large-scale population transfers to Tibet at a "secret meeting" in 1993 is underscored by the absence of ethnic swamping since then.[138] In PRC Tibetan autonomous areas as a whole, a comparison of the 1990 and 2000 censuses[139] shows the number of Han *fell* slightly and their proportion diminished significantly. It is even likely the TAR non-Tibetan population did not rise from 5 percent to 7.8 percent, as census figures seem to show, because the 1990 census included only persons who had lived in the TAR for a year or more. The 2000 census included those present for six months or more as did the 2005 one percent sample census, which found that there were about 180,000 Han resident in the TAR or some 6.5 percent of the population.[140] The census results call into question claims of a strategy "to flood Tibet with more Chinese settlers"[141] and to "drown the Tibetans in a sea of Chinese."[142] The apparent increase in Han in the TAR derives from observations of Lhasa, where TAR Han concentrate,[143] a city that accounts for less than a tenth of the people of that still very rural region[144] and such observations are mainly done in the summer, when Han short-term merchants, construction workers, and tourists swell.[145] In rural areas, according to a Western scholar who did fieldwork over six years, Han cadres are usually limited to an accountant or agronomic expert at county level and a few medical personnel; in some cases, their relatives run road-side restaurants or other petty-trading facilities, but there is little presence, if any, at the township level or below.[146] Samdhong Rinpoche has acknowledged that the ethnic demographic balance has changed "only in towns, not in the rural areas of Tibet" and not at all in nomadic societies.[147]

While there is no evidence of a state endorsed "ethnic swamping" of Tibet, that concept has been supported by a ruling party in a country adjacent to Tibet, a party regarded well by Tibetan diaspora elites.[148] The Bharatiya Janata Party (BJP), the Hindu nationalist party that ruled India in 1998–2004, "stands for large-scale settlement of Hindus in the Vale of Kashmir, to overcome the Muslim majority."[149] The Tibetan émigré leaders fully backed their Kashmir policy.[150] If privately organized migration of people of another ethnicity who settle in a region and dominate its trading sector is "ethnic swamping," then ethnic Tibetans in India's Ladakh have been "swamped" by Indian Muslims.[151] A senior Chinese analyst has also pointed to another instance where, impelled by a political agenda, "ethnic swamping" might have taken place, even though, as in the Tibet case, there is no evidence of a state plan. He noted that in the 1940s native Alaskans were more than half the population in what would become the United States's largest state, while today they constitute about 15 percent. The analyst asked his American interlocutor, "So are we both guilty of cultural genocide?"[152]

Second, there is no evidence that the PRC intends to eradicate Tibetan culture through population transfer. Émigré reports on the "secret meeting" claim that the plan was to change the demographic balance in order to avert a separatist uprising, not to extirpate Tibetan culture. Under international law, a state-organized population transfer (a "settler implantation" or "settler infusion") into an area that is neither a colony nor under alien occupation[153] resulting from international war, is not unlawful, let alone genocidal.[154] Claire Palley, a leading international jurist and specialist on population transfers, has stated that "no international standard specifically addresses and outlaws the act of population transfer itself and its various forms."[155] The Dalai Lama has compared Han migration to Tibet with the Soviet-era "population transfer"of Russians into the Baltic states,[156] but Palley and other scholars have concluded that it is not clear Russians were unlawfully settled in the Baltic states after their 1940 annexation by the Soviet Union.[157] This is so even though Baltic independence was well established and several states (including the United States) refused to recognize the annexation, and even though many Balts opposed Russian migration, which was largely individual but altered the demographic balance and undercut Baltic nationalism.[158] Although there is no indication "settlers" were ever sent to Tibet to change the region's ethnic composition in order to stabilize it politically, even were that the case, it would not violate international law, as long as the program was premised on national consolidation, and not ethnic discrimination.

Third, there has never been a credible showing that physical genocide has been committed in Tibet.[159] Claims that a fifth of the Tibetan population was annihilated from 1959 to 1979 through executions, famines, imprisonment, and other means are without any evidentiary basis. The TGIE never publicly revealed its sources for the assertion that 1.2 million Tibetans died state-caused, unnatural deaths from the 1950s through 1970s, a claim constantly reiterated by Western politicians and media.[160] The ex-head of the UK Free Tibet Campaign, Patrick French, did gain access to the data file on which the claim is supposedly based and found it consists of "seemingly random figures" and "constant, unchecked duplication," with death tolls in sparsely populated northern and eastern Tibet "unfeasibly high." Most tellingly, French discovered that of 1.1 million deaths listed, only 23,364 were females, indicating 1.07 million of the approximately 1.25 million Tibetan males would have died. French judged the data file "statistically useless."[161] Far from being decimated, the Tibetan population of the PRC has doubled in a half-century.[162] The 1953 PRC census estimated 2.75 million Tibetans; by 1990, there were 4.6 million, and there were more than 5.4 million in 2000.[163] The still-large Tibetan families—averaging 5.25 members in 1999, compared to 3.63 in China as a whole[164]—have caused a few advocates of Tibetan independence to repudiate the discourse of "demographic annihilation." Barbara Erickson, US academic journalist, for example, concludes, "Tibetans are more numerous today than at any time in recent history. Population growth has been rapid and continuous and there is no sign that China wants to wipe out the Tibetan race."[165]

Absent a nexus to genocide per se, a claim of cultural genocide is a mere rhetorical device. Therefore, some advocates of Tibet independence base assertions of cultural genocide not on killing, but on a limitation of births among Tibetans. As Article II(d) of the Genocide Convention states: "[I]mposing measures intended to prevent births within the group" is genocide if carried out with intent to destroy the protected group as such.[166] Article II(d) arose from the Nazis' mass sterilizations and forced abortions against Jews and others, while more recent mass rapes involving ethnic animus are also deemed "biological genocide." Measures to prevent births need not be calculated to accomplish the destruction of a group in whole or in part, but must be at least ancillary to a plan of physical genocide.[167]

Paul Ingram, in a book circulated by the émigrés, states that *population transfers + coercive birth control = cultural genocide*.[168] A lawyer with the U.S.-based Tibet Justice Center advances the same formula.[169] The Dalai Lama has said China is "forcing strict family planning rules on my people" in order "to make us [a] minority in our own land," while a U.S. Congressman in 2006 spoke of "the use of genocide against Uighurs and the Tibetans as part of their family planning program."[170] Family planning, however, even where coercive, can be based on many objectives other than changing the ethnic balance, including improving the well-being of those coerced.[171] China's policy links fewer births with increased prosperity [*shao sheng kuai fu*].[172] In Tibet, rapid population growth—PRC ethnic Tibetans increased by 40 percent in 1982–2000[173]—has been an obstacle to rural economic improvement. Arable land makes up only 0.31 percent of the TAR's land area.[174] A TAR family-planning document indicates the average landholding per capita in Tibet was 2.5 mu "in the early years after liberation," but has been reduced to 1.5 mu per capita due to population growth,[175] which has also offset two-thirds of the increase in TAR grain production in 1952–1992.[176]

Coercive birth control, moreover, cannot be related to a genocidal intent where the purported perpetrators subject themselves to greater coercion than is applied to alleged victims. In Nazi-occupied Europe, state pro-natalism for Germans accompanied efforts to end or reduce births among victim groups.[177] Family planning in the PRC, however, is stricter for Han than for Tibetans and other minorities.[178] Urban TAR Tibetans are limited to two children, but urban Han to only one child.[179] There can also be no plan to reduce the Tibetan population through coercive birth control if most Tibetans are not coerced, either because they are exempt (most rural TAR Tibetans) or want no more children than the state allows (urban Tibetans).[180] For these reasons, most claims of genocide based on coercive birth control have focused on forced sterilizations, abortions, and implantations of birth control devices. Such practices would not imply genocidal intent—they are well documented for Han areas[181]—but focusing discussion on such distasteful practices as they supposedly affect Tibetans is useful to the émigré leaders in their effort to invoke visions of biological genocide.

An analysis of birth control policy in Tibetan areas by the UK-based Tibet Information Network recounts one refugee's allegation of forced sterilization of 300 women in sparsely populated Ngamring County and another refugee's claim of coercive implantation of birth control devices in thirty-five women in Chamdo County.[182] A four-year study in the rural TAR by U.S. and Tibetan scholars, unaccompanied by PRC officials, found no evidence of forced abortions or forced sterilizations in Ngamring County or other sites. In Ngamring, visited many times by Melvyn Goldstein and co-researchers, including after the TIN report appeared, there was no two-child limit, as claimed by the refugee, nor, according to local nomads and officials, had fines been imposed for having four or more births. In villages studied by Goldstein, while villagers complained to researchers about many aspects of rural life and government regulation, "[n]o formal or informal discussions with villagers about family planning, birth limits or local problems revealed even a hint of forced abortions." The study did find, contrary to TAR officials' claims of no restrictions on rural births, that in the four townships studied, officials mandate a modest fine for bearing more than three children. But in three of the townships, the fine had never been imposed and in the fourth it was imposed at one-third the specified level.

Birth rates in the TAR have fallen from very high to moderate over the past two decades. The total fertility rate (TFR) of PRC ethnic Tibetans in 1999 was still 2.6 however, as against 1.4 for PRC Han. In 1999, the Tibetan TFR was 1.86 times the Han TFR; in 1975, ratio had been 1.44. In 2000, more than one in four births were third-child births among Tibetans, as opposed to less than one in 20 among Han.[183] Birth rates of PRC Tibetans are comparable to those among ethnic Tibetans in Nepal, with voluntary contraception becoming more widespread since the early 1990s, due largely to the effect of high population growth on the land-to-people ratio.[184] Access to contraceptives has also caused similar fertility transitions among Tibetans in Tibet and those in exile.[185] Erickson found TAR peasants and nomads to be unaware of any restraints on family size. She adds: "The Tibetans I met never spoke of birth control as a Chinese plot to exterminate their race. Many of them, in fact, supported family planning."[186]

A spokesman for the International Campaign for Tibet (ICT), the émigré leaders' arm in the United States, responded to Goldstein's findings by asserting that coercive birth control occurs mainly in cities and Qinghai province, on the northeast Tibet Plateau, where Tibetans are a minority.[187]

The statement tacitly admits the accuracy of PRC government assertions of no limits on rural TAR Tibetan births.[188] In Qinghai, where birth rates were traditionally low,[189] family-planning regulations since 1992 allow urban and agricultural Tibetans to have two children and pastoral area Tibetans to have three.[190] A study conducted in a mixed agricultural/pastoral part of Qinghai mainly inhabited by Tibetans found that government policy allows three children and average family size was 6.2 people.[191] Tibetan Information Network did not report any Qinghai cases of forced measures. The Independent Tibet Network UK, the group most adamant in making such claims, has reported a single, anonymous "eyewitness testimony" of forced sterilization among Tibetans in a Qinghai village, a report provided by an affiliate of the émigré administration.[192]

The head of the TAR Committee for Family Planning, Purbu Zhoima, states that, in Shigatse prefecture, sterilization is mainly available to Tibetans with more than four children and abortion is not available at all. Meanwhile, more than 30 percent of TAR women have three or more children, and the region's birth rate in farming and pastoral area stands at a high twenty per thousand.[193] Among urban Tibetans and in the émigré community, as elsewhere in the world, increases in education and more secular and consumerist values have produced decreases in family size.[194] In China as a whole, "[a]s far as [most city residents] are concerned, there is no need to enforce a strict birth-control policy" because few parents want more than one child.[195] Survey results presented in PRC media indicate 30 percent of Lhasa Tibetans want one child, 40 percent want two, and 19 percent want three or more.[196]

Because physical genocide of Tibetans is clearly not evident, the Dalai Lama no longer speaks of genocide per se—either with respect to the past or present;[197] however, Samdhong Rinpoche does, as do many prominent Western "Tibet supporters," including journalists.[198] The Dalai Lama does often state that the Tibetan nation is "facing extinction,"[199] sometimes implying that he means physical extinction.[200] At other times he conveys that what he refers to is the dissolution of the Tibetans as an ethnic group through the evisceration of their culture.[201] He frequently uses the term "cultural genocide" and has said that it must end for peace to prevail in Tibet.[202] In discussing his claim that "[t]here is an attempt to destroy the integral core of Tibetan civilization and identity," he has cited "[n]ew measures of restrictions in the fields of culture, religion and education."[203]

Since the early 1990s, the Dalai Lama has wavered between arguing the cultural genocide he alleges is deliberate[204]—in line with claims by other émigré leaders of "calculated 'cultural genocide' "[205]—and arguing China may or may not intend cultural genocide.[206] Using phrases like "intentional or not"[207] and "intentionally or unintentionally,"[208] he insists "some kind of cultural genocide is taking place."[209] He contends China commits intentional cultural genocide by controlling and restricting Buddhism through political study in monasteries and allowing bilingual university students to be more successful than monolingual ones. He avers unintentional cultural genocide involves "population transfer and sinicization policies" that result in there being Han artisans and shopkeepers in Lhasa and Tibetans who speak Chinese among themselves, eat rice rather than barley, and are unruly.[210]

Émigré leaders thus term as cultural genocide any action that introduces Han or "Han culture" into Tibet or that "interferes with" practices the émigré leaders deem traditional. The phenomenon of deploying the most conservative interpretation of the "traditional culture" of their homelands as a standard against which to measure "modernizing" change is common among other upper and middle class transnational migrants. In her study of identity among well-off Indian immigrants in New York, Monisha Das Gupta found that first-generation migrants, by distancing themselves from what they perceive to be American, invent what they understand to be appropriately Indian. They do so in order to control their children by labeling as "American" any behavior of which they disapprove. In interviews with the second generation, Das Gupta found that

> [t]he notions of "Indian tradition" that emerged from the tension between cultures ironically bore few resemblances to contemporary middle-class attitudes in India. What the first-generation immigrants rigidly enforced as "Indian" ways were, in fact, specific to the context they were familiar with before they left India. My respondents were only too aware of this museumization of practices.[211]

It is one thing for a migrant elite to choose to museumize an ethnic group culture,[212] but quite another to charge cultural genocide if others have a less "pure" and more hybrid conception of the culture. This inflated view of cultural genocide bears no resemblance to the crime that proponents of a ban on cultural genocide have sought to eradicate. There is moreover no evidence of a substantial erosion of the key elements of Tibetan culture.

The Empirical Basis of "Cultural Genocide" in Tibet

The propagandist's purpose is to make one set of people forget that certain other sets of people are human.

—Aldous Huxley[213]

Most studies of cultural genocide of indigenous peoples or minorities concentrate on religion and language.[214] Charges of cultural genocide in Tibet have primarily focused on how migration,[215] family planning,[216] and political repression[217] are supposedly leading to cultural extinction.[218] When they have been directly about culture, charges have concerned religion,[219] language[220] or both.[221] There have also been allegations that changes in the performing arts aim to eradicate Tibetan culture and that such "vices" as prostitution, drug use, billiards, and karaoke are promoted in Tibet to wean Tibetans away from their culture. There is, however, no evidence of an ongoing state plan to destroy religion in Tibet, nor any indication Tibetan religious institutions or religiosity are in sharper decline than those in other societies. Available evidence does not indicate Tibetans are losing their language or that PRC authorities intend it to erode. Finally, the process of cultural hybridization in Tibet is not unusual or negative in a world context.

Tibetan Buddhism and Cultural Genocide

The Dalai Lama has alleged that "the Chinese are anti-religion"[222] and that "the Chinese have made it nearly impossible for Tibetans to practice their Buddhist beliefs."[223] The perception that Buddhism is suppressed in Tibet is common in the West,[224] so much so that it affects even a few otherwise sober Tibetologists, one of whom has claimed the PRC government's assertion of freedom of religion in Tibet is "a complete lie."[225] Other specialists disagree. Another respected Tibetologist has said that "China does allow freedom of religion. But when it perceives state interest to be at issue it clamps down."[226] The U.S. State Department has reached a similar conclusion: "In Tibet the authorities permit many traditional religious practices and public manifestations of belief; however, activities perceived by the government to be vehicles for political dissent, such as religious activities considered to be advocating Tibetan independence or any form of separatism, [are] not tolerated by authorities."[227]

Contrasting views of PRC policies on religion stem in part from different conceptions of freedom of religion in China and the West. A high Australian foreign affairs official has complained that state registration of religious bodies and their alignment to state institututions in China "is not what we understand by freedom to practice religion."[228] There is however a centuries-old practice of state-religion imbrication in China proper and Tibet.[229]

The Dalai Lama distinguishes between culture and religion—the former relating to society, the latter to the individual—and argues Tibetan Muslims exemplify that one can be Tibetan, through language and customs, without being Buddhist.[230] Thus, if Tibetans were to cease being Buddhists, other cultural elements would continue Tibetan ethnicity.

In any event, an attempt to extirpate a religion through conversion to another faith or atheism is not cultural genocide, no matter how pious those affected or how central religion to their ethnic self-identity, unless forced conversion is accompanied by physical destruction of the religious group. For example, the Myanmar junta forces conversions to Buddhism of Burmese Muslims who return from exile, assigning Muslim children to Buddhist monasteries. Despite these acts, there is no evidence the junta seeks to destroy the seven-million strong Muslim minority as such and thus no proof of genocide or cultural genocide.[231]

Physical genocide based on the conjunction of ethnicity and religion have been accompanied by cultural genocide. During and after World War I, Turkish forces massacred between 500,000 and 2 million Armenians, sparing the 200,000 who converted to Islam.[232] In the process, the Armenians sustained huge cultural losses.[233] In World War II, Croatia's Ustashe killed a half-million Serbs, but those who converted to Catholicism from Orthodoxy were generally spared.[234] Croatian fascists also attempted to extinguish the part of Serbian culture that differs from Croatian culture.[235] Tibet presents no parallel with these paradigmatic examples of ethno-religious genocide and no evidence for the claim that state restrictions aim at cultural extinction.

Tibet Autonomous Region leaders recognize that theirs is "a region with a long religious history, where religion has great influence."[236] Alongside the pious majority, there are a significant number of Tibetan cadres, intellectuals, and businesspeople detached from religious practice.[237] Some agree with official pronouncements that claim that Tibetan Buddhism adversely affects development[238] or with assertions that there is harm to development from separatist activities that use religion to justify their cause.[239]

The state in Tibet demands that the devout "adapt to socialist society" and "establish a normal order [of] traditional Tibetan Buddhism."[240] State ownership of industry and socialist welfare practices are not at issue; indeed the Dalai Lama has often said there are good aspects to Marxism, that it has some common ground with Buddhism, and that he is a "true socialist" and "more Marxist than the current Chinese leadership."[241] What is in question is the CCP historical teleology, in which secular modernist rule has supplanted that of feudal theocrats. "Socialist society" means a society shaped by the nominally socialist, but fulsomely nationalist CCP. To adapt to it is to reconcile it with a CCP-led Tibet, rather than an independent state led by the Dalai Lama, the highest figure in the *sangha* (the community of monks and nuns) and an ex-officio aristocrat. Acceptance of this status "normalizes" Buddhism in the PRC leaders' view. Despite their occasional antireligion fulminations,[242] they are concerned with Tibetan spirituality only insofar as it impinges on the sovereignty question and, to a lesser extent, as it may raise barriers to "rational" economic activity. Allegations of cultural genocide in Tibet that focus on religion concern freedom to participate in religious activity, efforts to alienate Tibetans from the Dalai Lama, and regulation of monasteries, particularly in terms of admissions.[243]

Participation in Religious Activities

Views on what constitutes freedom of religion are often culture-bound, but some observers transcend cultural boundaries when considering questions of religious freedom abroad. Billy Graham, the U.S. evangelist visiting the Soviet Union in 1982, stated, "I think there is a lot more freedom here than has been given the impression in the United States because there are hundreds, thousands of churches open."[244] For Graham, the existence of many sites of worship indicated a modicum of freedom of practice, even though Soviet law limited religious activity to registered entities and barred religious activities that undermined the state and social system[245] and even though U.S. culture tolerates virtually no state regulation of religious practice and allows religious bodies to adopt any political stance.[246] In contrast, "Tibet supporters" apply Western (especially U.S.) standards of religious freedom,[247] allowing them to represent that there is no freedom of religion in Tibet.

Émigré leaders claim "Tibetans are not even permitted to undertake routine religious activities."[248] They assert that 6,000 monasteries were destroyed before or during the Cultural Revolution[249] and that "the handful of surviving monasteries are being used as public toilets and barracks [while] monks and nuns in Tibet have been forced by the Chinese to desecrate religious objects."[250] Such claims are anachronisms designed to impart that a "second Cultural Revolution" is ongoing in Tibet. Yet mass participation in routine religious activities is evident to even sceptical U.S. officials and journalists.[251] A top émigré official has also stated that Tibetans are "allowed to say prayers, worship at temples and monasteries, make offerings at these places and to take the sacred walk around holy places."[252]

The PRC claim that every year more than one million people visit the Jokhang temple[253] has not been challenged. A U.S. journalist noted in the late 1990s that "The most striking aspect of daily life in Lhasa today is the passionare worship by Tibetans of every station."[254] Speaking of the major monasteries outside the TAR, Western reporters have noted that Labrang "teem[s] with signs of religious activity,"[255] and Kumbum "appears to thrive."[256] According to Chinese sources, the abbot of a monastery in

Nagqu prefecture has stated that there are 1,787 "sites for Tibetan Buddhism" in the TAR.[257] A scholar in Qinghai puts the number of "Tibetan temples" in the PRC at over 3,000.[258] Tibetan scholars assert there are now 300 more monasteries and temples in the TAR than existed in the region before 1951.[259] The PRC government also claims that from 1978 to 2002 it contributed 300 million yuan (US$37 million) and much gold and silver to TAR monasteries.[260] Again, such figures are not disputed.

The involvement of Tibetans in quotidian religious activity belies claims of cultural genocide through suppression of religious elements of their culture. Some Tibetologists are aware this is so. For example, Glen Mullin, a leading specialist in Tibetan Buddhism and translator of the Dalai Lama's works, has said "This is a boom time for Buddhism in China. Many of the monasteries that were shut down and destroyed during the Cultural Revolution are being rebuilt, along with new ones."[261] If freedom of religion is conceived as more plenary than freedom of worship, the former exists in Tibet, except as a platform for advancing nationalism. In certain avowedly Buddhist countries however, for example, Bhutan and Myanmar, there is generally freedom of worship, but not freedom of religion. Religious minorities are severely constrained in propagating their faith. Proselytization and conversion are illegal and it is difficult for Hindus, Muslims, and Christians to gain permission to hold public ceremonies and build places of worship.[262]

Attacks on the Dalai Lama

State authorities seek to curb support for the Dalai Lama, especially in monasteries, the prime sites of pro-independence sentiment.[263] They insist this effort is not connected to his devotion to Buddhism, but to his refusal to acknowledge Tibet has been part of China and campaigns for "independence in disguise."[264] Public displays of his image have been banned in the TAR since 1994,[265] and in monasteries prayers for his longevity are not offered. Efforts to compel monks to criticize him were carried out during the Patriotic Education Campaign of 1996–2000,[266] although in some places, resistance to denouncing the Dalai Lama caused work teams to back away from the demand.[267] In the mid- to late 1990s, monks were in essence told to "distance yourself from the Dalai Lama, and we can offer you the freedom to pursue your religious studies."[268] State authorities thereby conveyed that official hostility toward his persona was not hostility to Buddhism per se. The TAR CCP did at one point intemperately label the Dalai Lama a "hooligan politician" [*liumang zhengke*].[269] People's Republic of China media have also quoted "eminent monks" who question the Dalai Lama's bona fides as a religious leader, based on his separatism.[270] They do sometimes concede, however, that most Tibetans respect the Dalai Lama and hope for his return.[271] By 2005, with "talks about talks" between the PRC's and Dalai Lama's representatives, the TGIE noted the mildness of criticisms of the Dalai Lama while the Dalai Lama's representative to the talks said of PRC Premier Wen Jiabao "We know that the present Prime Minister has much reverence for Buddhism."[272] Officials of the TAR also made positive statements about Buddhism: Governor Jampa Phuntsog said "The vast majority of Tibetans are Buddhist followers . . . they are supposed to be benevolent and do good deeds. There is a role for Buddhism to play in creating a harmonious society."[273]

The level of the campaign to alienate people from the Dalai Lama depends on the authorities' perception of the degree of local separatist sentiment.[274] There has been a more liberal attitude in eastern Tibetan areas than in the TAR,[275] and in the TAR itself, attacks on the Dalai Lama have eased up after extended periods of political quiescence. At monasteries where monks are not involved in politics, "they face minimal interference from local authorities in their religious life" and the authorities overlook displays of respect for the Dalai Lama.[276] In any case, attacks on the Dalai Lama are not tantamount to an attempt to destroy Tibetan Buddhism, let alone Buddhists as such, even in the eyes of the Dalai Lama. He has made clear that he does not regard his position as essential to Buddhism or to Tibetan culture, even stating, "I do not want to preserve the institution of the Dalai Lama. But only the Tibetan people can abolish it."[277] The Dalai Lama regards as "nonsense" that people revere him as a "god-king"[278] and terms it "ignorance" that his position is seen as central to Tibetan culture. He has stated that "Tibet's formal civilisation has lasted for 4,000 years, 6,000 to 8,000 by some historical findings. The Dalai Lama institution has only been around for 300 years. It is just a part of Tibet's history."[279]

The Dalai Lama, if not his supporters, recognizes that attacks on him are part of Tibet Question politics, not an attempt to eradicate Buddhism.[280] The same holds true of PRC leaders' supposed policy of waiting for the Dalai Lama to die, alleged by émigrés and others.[281] Even if such a policy were uniform—which is doubtful[282]—it would more likely arise from hope that the event improves Beijing's position in the Tibet dispute, not an expectation that Tibetan Buddhism will diminish. The Dalai Lama similarly hoped late supreme leader Deng Xiaoping's death would improve the Tibetan émigrés' position in the dispute.[283] Tibetan Youth Congress leaders are also waiting for the Dalai Lama's passing to change émigré opinion to favor violent struggle against China.[284]

Regulation of Monasteries

Official regulation of PRC religious institutions was liberalized in the 1980s but was tightened in the 1990s, in part because religious organizations played a key role in the downfall of Communist rule in Eastern Europe.[285] In Tibet, tightened regulation came after demonstrations in Lhasa from 1987 to 1989 and eventually affected monasteries. Tolerance of monastic expansion from the end of the 1970s to the mid-1990s led the authorities in 1997 to complain that because they had no standard for their restoration, there was "uncontrolled development of lamaseries and temples."[286] The late 1990s thus saw an imposition of greater control over the expansion of monasteries. Democratic Management Committees (DMC) have run the monasteries since the late 1970s[287] and are supposed to be politically vetted.[288] However, scrutiny was superficial through the mid-1990s, when authorities concluded that many DMCs had "assum[ed] an ambiguous political attitude," "persecuted lamas who love their country and religion," and "showed no concern for the monks and nuns," (i.e. engaged in favoritism and financial malfeasance). In the mid-to-late 1990s, work teams were posted to monasteries to carry out political indoctrination and administrative tasks.[289]

The main factor affecting the degree of regulation of the monasteries is the state leaders' perception of the extent to which religion is being used to foster separatism. Monasteries relatively far from Lhasa are for that reason subject to less scrutiny than those in or nearer to the city.[290] Heightened separatist activity by monks linked to the émigrés or to successes of their internationalization campaign generates political campaigns in monasteries and expulsions or arrests of recalcitrant monks and nuns.[291] Regulation of monasteries is thus in part attributable to actions of the very émigré leaders who complain that regulation is part of "cultural genocide." The waxing and waning of regulation of monasteries throughout Tibet in turn indicates that there is no concerted campaign to eradicate Buddhism per se.

In recent years there has been an easing of regulation of religion in Tibet and in China.[292] At the Fourth Tibet Work Forum in 2001, President Jiang Zemin said: "We must . . . lawfully protect people's freedoms to hold religious beliefs and conduct regular religious activities."[293] Guo Jinlong, TAR Party Secretary from 2000–2004, initiated "a somewhat softer line on some religious conflicts than his predecessor," including relaxation of pressure on state employees and their families to stop practicing Buddhism.[294] At a 2001 conference on religion attended by top leaders, Jiang recognized religion's contribution to upholding moral behavior and helping cope with crises.[295] Leaders and commentators have spoken of *mutual* adaption of religion and socialism and have recounted contributions made by religion[296] and underground groups and foreign missionaries operate a bit more openly.[297] State Religious Affairs Bureau director Ye Xiaowen has indicated that "simple methods," such as repression, do not work with "complicated religious problems" and are generally counterproductive.[298]

When he was in Tibet, the Dalai Lama imposed limitations on the numbers of monks.[299] Today he "is against an overproliferation of monasteries" in Tibetan settlements in India.[300] For over a dozen centuries, Chinese authorities restricted the number of monks.[301] That practice and almost every aspect of present-day regulation of Buddhism in China resemble regulatory practices of emperors from the Tang to Song dynasties, who were also concerned about antistate activities and economic harm from an unbridled expansion of monasteries and the *sangha*'s complete freedom to preach.[302] Tight imperial regulation of monasteries coincided with official patronage of Buddhism, indicating that regulation per se does not evince a destructive design. There are still countries today with governments that employ and regulate the conduct of clergy. In Denmark, for example, all Lutheran ministers are state employees who can be dismissed if their expressed beliefs diverge sharply from accepted doctrine.[303]

Tibet Autonomous Region officials have said that the number of monks and nuns "satisfies Tibet's religious needs" and have kept it in a steady state since the mid-1990s.[304] The 46,000 monks in the TAR[305] are much less than the 114,000 or so there were in 1959.[306] As a percentage of adult males, however, they are more numerous than monks in all other Buddhist lands, and far exceed the density of priests in Catholic Poland and Ireland.[307] Among 61 million Catholics in the United States in 2000, there were 45,000 priests,[308] a ratio of about one priest per 2,500 Catholics. In the TAR, there was one monk for every 52 Tibetans. The Tibetan autonomous areas outside the TAR, which have slightly more than half the PRC's ethnic Tibetans, have over 100,000 monks—twice the "clerical density" of the TAR—or about one monk for every 25 Tibetans.[309] These figures include only "official" monks, who reside in monasteries with state approval. There are also monks with long-term residence in monasteries who are "unofficial." In Labrang, for example, there were in 2001 about 1,100 official monks and about 1,200 unofficial monks.[310] Besides monks resident in monasteries, there are also a significant number of "monks in society." The count of nearly 150,000 Tibetan monks in the PRC may then be a substantial underestimate. In any event, Tibetan Buddhism's hierarchy in various lands stresses that they are "more interested in the intellectual quality than the numerical quantity of its priests."[311]

With such a large number of monks and monasteries in Tibetan areas, no credence can be given to claims "the Chinese" only allow monasteries to "serve as museums to attract tourists rather than living cultural and religious institutions" or that "the limited number of monks allowed to join these monasteries serve more as showpieces for tourists and, in most cases, caretakers rather than true religious students and practitioners."[312] There are scarcely a dozen monasteries in Tibetan areas, with a small percentage of monks, attracting many tourists. The PRC government lists a wide range of activities of monks and nuns learning and propagating the dharma.[313]

Because there are few ethnographies of monastic life in contemporary Tibet, it is difficult to gauge the depth of Buddhist study in these settings, but anyone who visits the region's monasteries sees monks studying *sutras* and debating.[314] In contrast to old Tibet, where many monks did nothing to advance their learning,[315] today monks at monasteries such as Drepung must be either full-time scholars of a fixed Buddhist curriculum or do productive work on behalf of the monastery. If they choose to be scholars, their monastery subsidizes them. A U.S. anthropologist who did fieldwork at Drepung from 1989–1995 found hundreds of monks engaged in full-time study,[316] belying claims that monasteries in Tibet are not mainly places for transmission of Buddhist thought and philosophical debate.[317]

Conditions for religious institutions in Tibet are much better than in China proper. About half of China's 300,000 "clerics" in 2003 were Tibetan Buddhist monks, even though Tibetan Buddhists made up less than 4 percent of the estimated 200 million believers in China.[318] Three-fourths of China's Buddhist monks are in Tibetan areas, leaving just 50,000 monks for an estimated population of 95 million non-Tibetan Buddhists.[319] In Beijing, once the religious capital of the world's most extensive empire, most monasteries and temples were closed in the 1950s and 1960s. Many Beijing people are now interested in Buddhism,[320] Daoism, or Christianity, but because of "a longstanding policy designed to prevent Beijing [from] recovering its identity as a centre of religion remains," the state blocks religious bodies from reclaiming former monastery and temple buildings.[321] In Beijing before 1949 there were several hundred Buddhist temples; in 2003, among a population of 14 million that includes hundreds of thousands of Buddhists, there were only five functioning temples.[322] In Zhejiang province in 1999–2000, 1,200 temples or churches were closed for carrying out "superstitious" activities or operating without permission.[323]

In old Tibet, most monks were sent to monasteries by their parents at between seven and ten years of age without regard to their wishes.[324] There were then only a handful of schools in the region. When monasteries were revived in the 1980s, many parents enrolled their children.[325] Religious motives played a role, but so too did a desire to secure the livelihood of children from impoverished areas and the lack of secular schools.[326] After the disturbances in Lhasa in the late 1980s, TAR monasteries were supposedly prohibited from recruiting children,[327] but during a 1994 visit to Tibet, the UN Special Rapporteur on Religious Intolerance was told that child monks could be admitted if their act was voluntary and they had parental permission.[328] There is a regulation stating that one has to be at least eighteen years old to take vows,[329] but it is irregularly applied, both according to reports of abbots, who state that they admit boys at age sixteen, and those who say they became monks at that age.[330] In Lhasa, the Religious Affairs Bureau "turned a blind eye" at underage monks at Drepung, which in the mid-1990s was "replete with young monks in the under-18 age bracket." Although the minimum age was supposed to be enforced since 1996,[331] the U.S. State Department has observed that "many younger boys in fact continue the tradition of entering monastic life."[332] It may not be unreasonable, now that there are more schools, to allow only adults to become monks, but in any case, where schools are lacking or support for separatism is thin, the authorities tolerate the admission of underage monks.[333] Some monasteries have also set up schools or the authorities have hired monks as teachers.[334]

A minimum age of admission to a religious vocation is not necessarily a violation of international law. A UN declaration calls for children to have access to religious training in some form, but access can be regulated in "the best interests of the child."[335] In any case, the prohibition on the admission of child monks and nuns has not held back the growth of the *sangha*, let alone amounted to cultural genocide.

The Tibetan Language and Cultural Genocide

Language is often intimately connected to an ethnic group's culture, although there are groups with several mother tongues, such as China's Yi minority[336] or whose members mainly do not speak the mother tongue. In 1990, only 200,000 of China's 5.7 million Tujia minority members could speak Tujia, with the vast majority speaking *putonghua* ("Mandarin Chinese"). But in other respects, Tujia people share common cultural elements and an ethnic consciousness.[337] It is also uncertain whether ethnic groups that have a language in common fully share the same culture. A Canadian political philosopher, for example, has queried whether a common culture exists for a Montrealer and a Quebec rural village dweller.

They have the same language, but different modes of recreation, different architecture, divergent career paths, dissimilar tastes, and so on.[338] In few places in the world are differences between rural and urban society more visible than in Tibet. Within Tibetan urban society, there are striking cultural differences between social strata, including language differences.[339] This is not to deny that an overarching Tibetan culture exists, but rather to underscore the idea that language and culture do not necessarily have a determinative relationship.

European colonialism eliminated at least 15 percent of all languages spoken at the time and "language murder" is recognized as "one of the basic tools of ethnocide, of the deculturation of peoples, which has always been perpetrated by colonization and is still the semi-official aim of governments which do not recognize the rights of their native ethnic minorities."[340] The Dalai Lama claims that "migration to Tibet threatens to cause the eradication of the Tibetan language"[341] and has said, "Our own language no longer has any value in our own land."[342] A U.S. Congressman has stated that "Tibetan Buddhists face virtual extinction. There is cultural genocide today taking place in Tibet. Their language is being stripped out."[343] These assertions misrepresent that "linguicide" is part of a plan to destroy Tibetan culture.

China's minority tongues are seen as preservative of ethnic cultures, while *putonghua* is viewed as a bridge to urban areas.[344] The law in the PRC states that minorities enjoy freedom to use their own languages in autonomous areas[345] (where 95 percent of Tibetans live). Most do so, although bilingualism is also promoted, especially in education.[346] Regulations encourage local language use in primary instruction,[347] with *putonghua* introduced in upper primary or lower middle school grades.[348] Most minority areas, including Tibet, follow this practice.[349] Some rural TAR counties however have unilingual Tibetan education, due to a lack of *putonghua*-speaking teachers.[350]

Claims that Tibet's primary schools teach in *putonghua* are in error.[351] Tibetan was the main medium of instruction (MOI) in 98 percent of TAR primary schools in 1996; *putonghua* is introduced in early grades only in urban schools.[352] In six years of Tibetan primary school, pupils are said to spend a total of 1,598 hours studying in Tibetan and 748 hours studying in Chinese, a two-to-one ratio.[353] Because only four of ten TAR Tibetans reach secondary school,[354] primary school matters most for their cultural formation. In other Tibetan areas, primary schooling may be in Tibetan, and in some places, parents choose the primary school MOI.[355] Most Tibetan students outside the TAR are taught in *putonghua* because of parental choice or because Tibetan language instruction is unavailable due to a shortage of Tibetan instructors or high percentage of other groups living among Tibetans.[356]

Each Tibetan autonomous area has its own policies on bilingual education, but secondary education in Tibetan is generally more common outside
than inside the TAR. In some areas it is possible to study in Tibetan from
primary school through university.[357] Authorities in the TAR in 2000
asserted that "local junior middle schools are gradually turning to teaching
subjects on natural sciences with Tibetan language" and that "Tibetan language is the only teaching language for 102 classes in some local middle
schools in [the TAR], while the Tibetan language is partially used in some
other local middle schools."[358] In Lhasa Middle School, the region's best,
there are six classes a week on the Tibetan language, five on *putonghua*, and
four on English.[359] Many parents want instruction in *putonghua* for children
who go on to middle school; thus, the TAR regulation requiring middle
schools to use Tibetan has not been enforced.[360] Tibetan students in the best
secondary schools in Lhasa often prefer Chinese as MOI,[361] while those elsewhere would benefit from having Tibetan as the main language of schooling.[362] The TAR introduced secondary school Tibetan language texts in
1999 and Tibetans are now half of TAR secondary school teachers.[363] The
greater availability of instructional material in Tibetan[364] clashes however
with the desire of many Tibetan parents for bilingual education, even at
the primary level, so they can compete with native *putonghua* speakers in
secondary school.[365] That attitude also obtains in the émigré community:
"Tibetan students fear that a Tibetan medium primary education will
reduce their chance of success in secondary schools as well as their career
prospects."[366]

Studies in many parts of the world indicate bilinguals fare much better
in earnings than unilinguals. A Miami, Florida study found unilingual
English speakers earn less than two-thirds what English/Spanish bilinguals
do; unilingual Spanish speakers earn barely more than one-third.[367] Where
a native tongue is not one of the world's main languages, unilinguals are
also disadvantaged in other ways: after the Soviet breakup, the younger
generation in Turkmenistan was deprived of learning Russian by the
switch to Turkmen unilingualism and now knows little of the outside
world.[368] The same holds true in Georgia, plus young ethnic Georgians
cannot even communicate with their countrymen of other ethnic
groups.[369]

At the tertiary level, many Tibetans major in humanities, and, at two
universities, they can study humanistic disciplines in Tibetan.[370] At that level
it is unlikely that *putonghua* instruction contributes to language erosion. At
universities around the world where much instruction is not given only in
the national language, but also in English (Hong Kong, Netherlands,
Sweden, etc.), students still speak their mother tongue fluently.

There often are predictions that Chinese will become the main (although not sole) MOI in more TAR primary schools,[371] but this fear has not been realized,[372] while there are counter-indications that the TAR government is reconsidering its bilingual education policies.[373] MOI issues are debated around the world, with no easy choice among mother tongue, bilingual, or national language instruction. Where the outcome is use of a national language, the choice may be wrong pedagogically. It may even impinge upon the language rights of an ethnic minority, without being part of a purposeful effort to stifle the minority language, let alone commit cultural genocide. After all, it was not until 1994 that the émigré administration endorsed Tibetan as the MOI for primary schools in Tibetan settlements in India and it "may have been no more successful than the Chinese government in providing Tibetan-medium education for the children in the refugee community in India, even though the preservation of Tibetan culture is one of its primary goals."[374] Tibetans in India now complain that "Tibetan education is useless for the current prospects of a life in India or abroad."[375] Mother tongue instruction in Tibet also compares favorably to the situation for ethnic Tibetan natives of India's Ladakh. Schooling there is largely only for boys and monastic. The Ladakh state schools' MOI is Urdu, an unknown language for Ladakhi Tibetan children, 90 percent of whom fail to finish school.[376]

The émigrés have contended that "Chinese-built schools teach Chinese history and culture in the Chinese language and propagate communism while denigrating religion" and education is aimed at "erasing cultural identity."[377] However, a study of a Sichuan Tibetan secondary by a U.S. anthropologist found textbooks used in the school "do contain a fair amount of material drawn from Tibetan sources and relevant to Tibetan cultural life in the broad sense," that lessons based on the texts "play an important role in establishing a sense of unified Tibetan culture and identity among young Tibetans," and that religious concepts are treated respectfully by the Tibetan teachers.[378] A field study led by a U.S. educationalist notes "TAR primary school texts do have pictures of yaks, agricultural tools and names familiar to local people. The Tibetan epic Gesar is also taught in school."[379] Tibetans themselves, however, do not necessarily consider Tibetan their first choice as an MOI, because it narrows career choices compared to Chinese.[380]

The TAR issued regulations in the late 1980s on the use of Tibetan,[381] with the aim to "make Tibetan the dominant language in Tibet."[382] A TAR law to protect the Tibetan language was passed in 2002.[383] While Tibetan is not dominant in urban Tibet, it is in rural areas, where 85 percent of Tibetans live. Regulations provide that public signs and documents issued by public institutions at or above the county level be bilingual and that documents at the township and village levels be in Tibetan only.[384] Since 1991, a regulation has allowed lower-level bodies to forgo implementing orders specified in any document that does not have a Tibetan version,[385] even though regional authorities admit lacking a sufficient pool of translators.[386] There has been an effort in the TAR to ensure notices are bilingual. The émigrés' Minister for Information and International Relations has said that with 80% of television programming in Tibet being in Chinese, the Tibetan language is no longer the prominent language in the region.[387] However, some 76% of households in the TAR had television sets in 2000, and 16 hours a day of Tibetan TV broadcasts are reportedly aired. In 2006, the almost half the Tibetan population that speaks Amdo dialect gained access to 17 hours-a-day of television broadcasts in that dialect.[388] A "Tibet-Xinjiang Project" was launched in 2000 to set up more TV and radio relay stations in rural areas so as to reach almost all Tibetan villages. Tibetan-language newspapers, radio, films, and other media also exist in all Tibetan areas, although much of what they produce is translated from Chinese, due in part to limited funding.[389]

The Dalai Lama has claimed that "young Tibetans are compelled to speak Chinese rather than Tibetan,"[390] but except for some persons living at the edge of the Plateau,[391] Tibetans speak their mother tongue and associate it with both social status and group solidarity. In the TAR, an ethnic Tibetan who cannot speak Tibetan is practically unheard of.[392] In the whole PRC, 92.5–94% of Tibetans speak Tibetan and the remainder speak another ethnic minority language or a Chinese dialect. Outside the TAR, 10–30% of Tibetans can also speak such a dialect, but in the TAR, apart from Lhasa, only about 5% of Tibetans can do so.[393] Even if all urban TAR Tibetans were bilingual, they are only some 15% of the TAR Tibetan population.[394] In fact, surveys show only about half of urban Tibetans have mastered spoken Chinese and little more than a third have mastered written Chinese.[395]

Members of a Western "mission" dispatched to Tibet by the émigré administration have claimed that "Chinese is the dominant language which everyone is expected to speak," but this assertion, based only on a visit to a secondary school and university in Lhasa, is inacccurate.[396] So too is the assertion, with regard to Mandarin's use in Tibet, that "such enforcement most clearly represents the operation of colonialism in Tibet."[397] Tibetan peasants are not expected to speak Chinese and urban Tibetans only if they work with non-Tibetans. In this regard, the situation of Tibetans differs from that of minorities in many Western liberal democracies until the last half century: the teaching of Breton was banned in France from 1902 to 1951, while in the United States, Canada, and New Zealand, Mexican-American, First Nations, and Maori students who spoke their native languages at school were punished.[398]

None of the many studies of endangered languages deems Tibetan imperiled[399] and even scholars concerned about the impact of Chinese in (urban) Tibet advocate bilingualism.[400] Tibetan Autonomous Region authorities are not entirely unconcerned either: "Regulations on the Study, Use and Development of the Tibetan Language" were enacted in 2002.[401] Although the extent to which they are implemented is still unclear, the regulations do state that Han cadres and workers must learn Tibetan. The language is also a required subject in the first nine years of education. Government offices and state-owned enterprises must give hiring preference to bilinguals.

Language maintenance among Tibetans contrasts with language loss in even remote areas of Western states.[402] In the United States, all indigenous languages are nearly extinct in California,[403] only 3 percent of the Sioux on the famous Pine Ridge Reservation speak their native tongue,[404] French is found increasingly less in Louisiana,[405] and there is official and popular hostility toward other "ethnic" languages and bilingualism.[406] The United States is described as "a veritable cemetery of foreign languages"—only 16 percent of second-generation children of Asian and Latin American immigrants report fluency in their parents' tongues.[407] Among third-generation Americans of Asian ancestry, only 5–10% can speak their ancestral language and not necessarily fluently.[408] Even among U.S. Hispanics, who in theory share a language with a bordering country, 72% of third-generation children speak English exclusively.[409] Of all U.S. territories, only the people of Puerto Rico retain their language, while one-fourth of them have the very bilingualism decried by the Dalai Lama.[410]

Language loss is found in many parts of the world. In Taiwan, 95% of Hakka, an ethnic group who are 15% of the population, speak fluent Hakka, but only 12% of Hakka under age thirteen do.[411] Some scholars argue that Tibetans in India are at risk of losing their language[412] and many émigré leaders point out that this loss is already proceeding among younger Tibetans there.[413] Thubten Samphel, a TGIE official, has observed that in Tibetan settlements in South Asia, "the current trend is that everyone wants to migrate to the West."[414] Tibetans in South Asia generally find however that Tibetan communities in the West are losing not only their language, but their identity as well.[415] In Canada, "young Tibetans lead Western lifestyles and speak little Tibetan."[416] Most Tibetans in Switzerland do not speak or have only a limited command of Tibetan.[417] Young Tibetan-Americans generally do not speak Tibetan and the ability to read Tibetan has disappeared in some U.S. Tibetan communities.[418] Tibetans who migrate from Nepal to New York tend to favor speaking Nepali rather than Tibetan.[419] The Dalai Lama has had to urge Tibetans in the United States to speak Tibetan in their homes.[420]

Regulations in Tibet require that laws, official notices, commercial signs, and the like be bilingual; that Tibetans be allowed to interact with government in their own language; and that mass media have substantial Tibetan components.[421] To increase the utility of print media, adult Tibetan literacy seems to have risen in recent years.[422] Official policies thus go beyond the respect for minority languages required by international law or practiced in European "rights-based" states.[423] Most of these states have not ratified the European Charter for Regional or Minority Languages, even though its obligations are fairly minimal. In education, for example, it is satisfied by making available pre-school education in minority languages.[424]

"Mandarin" and most local Chinese dialects are mutually unintelligible. In most parts of China, *putonghua* is however the sole language of mass communication and is needed by those who want to advance, while, in places where the local dialect is quite distinct, it is often used to exclude outsiders from employment and educational opportunities.[425] In this respect, Tibetans' language predicament is not radically different from that of other PRC citizens. Tibetans who do learn *putonghua*, moreover, are acquiring a more valuable asset than, for example, a Greenland Inuit who learns Danish. Chinese is spoken by more people than any other language in the world and, because of China's rise, it is the "must learn" language of the future.[426] Thus far, Tibetans who have learned Chinese retain Tibetan language competence and, like other people who become bilingual, are creating their own version of their second language. Europeans who need a lingua franca to communicate have done this with English. They use it in multinational business and political settings, but members of each group "nationalize" English's syntax and vocabulary.[427] In Qinghai province something similar has already happened to Chinese: the local dialect, *Qinghai hua*, has a Tibetanized syntax and includes many Tibetan words.

Arts, Vices, and Cultural Genocide

Because they conflict with the idea of saultural genocide, state efforts to preserve and popularize Tibetan culture are ignored in émigré discourse, even as they are touted in PRC statements.[428] Thus, the publication of literary works[429]—large-scale efforts such as compilations of the many-volumed, encyclopaedic *Tripitaka* and the world's longest epic, *King Gesar*—go unacknowledged by émigré leaders. This is so even though Western observers note them.[430] One study states that "despite the constraints, a thriving indigenous literary scene persists. This encourages young Tibetans to master their own language and participate in the development of modern Tibetan literature."[431] That literary scene includes debates within a body of Tibetan-medium literary criticism.[432] An eminent émigré historian has spoken of a renaissance of Tibetan publications, including rare texts and novels and short stories by Tibetan writers, whose "work does not always merely follow the diktats of the Party, even when it is written in Chinese and published under the eyes of the censors . . . [and who] are able to bring burning issues into the foreground."[433] The same studious ignorance is feigned concerning Tibet's cultural centers and performances, although the International Campaign for Tibet (ICT) director in Washington has acknowledged he enjoys watching the annual Losar (Tibetan newyear) programs on Lhasa TV, featuring the Lhasa City Performing Arts Troupe and TAR Performing Arts Troupe.[434]

Émigré leaders often represent the performing arts in Tibet as polluted and have stated that "[i]n this calculated 'cultural genocide' the Chinese ma[ke] every effort to remove any vestige of Tibetan character in the performing arts." Lobsang Samten, artistic director of the Dharmasala-based Tibet Institute of Performing Arts (TIPA), avers that TAR troupes cannot "put on an authentic performance" and instead stage Tibetan operas that are "like a Chinese drama with monkey kings or something."[435] He argues that there has been an "annihilation of Tibetan opera, folk dances, monastic music, Buddhist writings, and literature" in order to allow the PRC government to claim that Tibet never had a separate cultural identity.[436] The Dalai Lama's representative in Australia asserts that "[c]ulturally Tibet is being strangled to death. There is no room for the Tibetans to carry on any independent cultural activities without interference and influences from the Chinese."[437]

An Australian scholar who has visited Tibetan areas many times to observe Tibetan performance arts, found however that scores of troupes, religious and/or secular, traditional and/or modern, continue to draw large audiences. In the TAR at least, troupes are if anything overly conservative in their attitude toward innovation.[438] A U.S. anthropologist has stated

> A generation of Tibetans has now grown up under Chinese rule, and among them the performing arts are again flourishing. Amateur folk troupes organized privately by Tibetans far out-number state-run "professional" troupes in most Tibetan regions, and most are run by those dedicated to reviving "traditional" Tibetan performing arts.

She adds that both state and amateur folk troupes have "been the source of much creativy among Tibetans" and points out that while émigré activists, complain of "sinicization" of Tibetan performances in Tibet, "no mention is ever made of the influences of Hindi or Euro-American cultures on Tibetan performers growing up in India, Europe or North America." Observing a TIPA performance in the United States, she notes that while it claims to be the only source of "authentic" Tibetan culture, it gives "radically recontextualized performances," often adapted to Western audiences.[439] An example of such a purportedly "authentic" performance is provided by another anthropologist, who witnessed it being put on at a Tibetan school, for members of a European "Free Tibet" group that sponsors the school:

> At the Atisha School, what the students performed as the traditional Tibetan culture is a curious mix of behaviors and practices. Their performance included fife and drum music (instruments introduced by British army officers only after the turn of the twentieth century), the Tibetan national anthem (invented, again, only after the turn of the century), yoga exercises (adopted from India and Nepal only after the exile), British school uniforms (again, adopted only after the exile).[440]

There is a burgeoning school of modern painters in Lhasa, who produce impressive works and receive state support through the artists' union or teaching positions.[441] In 2005, it was estimated there was "a thriving community of about 200 artists—half of them ethnic Tibetan, the other half mostly from China's Han majority—who are trying to push the frontier of cultural expression."[442] Western scholars have also described an "artistic renaissance"[443] and "resurgence of Tibetan cultural production."[444]

One prominent émigré, former Kalon Tripa Tenzin N. Tethong, who now teaches at Stanford University, declared in 2005 that

> Tibetan Buddhist art continues to thrive once again, in exile and back in the Tibetan homeland . . . [T]he state of Tibetan Art is alive and well; traditional Tibetan Buddhist Art is firmly anchored once again at its roots and in its homeland and in the Diaspora, and the new emerging art is blessed with limitless potential in the global village.[445]

Most émigré leaders, however, consider *thanka* (religious scroll) painting to be the only authentic Tibetan style and disapprove of paintings produced by TAR Tibetans as corrupted by Chinese influences. Even artists educated in contemporary Tibet who emigrate to India, such as Gongkar Gyatso, are spurned as inauthentic in Dharmasala, where authorities are unhappy that the main trend in Tibetan art, in or out of Tibet, has been modernistic, that is, from religious or ritualistic to secular.[446] Younger émigrés however have become attracted to aspects of nontraditional culture, such as secular theatre, as "the new generations have turned to Western cultural models, transmitted especially through music and cinemas, as well as through direct contact."[447]

The émigré discourse of the arts and cultural genocide is a classic nationalist opposition of the inauthentic in "occupied Tibet" to a "pure" preserved culture in emigration.[448] Tibet specialists and artists have a different view: they recognize that Tibetan arts retain their own Tibetan form in Tibet; that Tibetan culture has long been a hybrid;[449] that traditional Tibetan art forms can profit from a further melding; and that, in the arts, the competing culture is not "Chinese" per se, but global. A Tibetan musicologist in the United States has written that the Tibetan singing style in Tibet continues to differ from the Chinese style.[450] Tseten Dorjee, a folk singer who performs in Tibetan and Hindi with a Tibetan opera troupe in Lhasa, has commented that "all Tibet is a mishmash of influences from the eastern and western tips of Asia." Asked about the popularity of discos with young Lhasa Tibetans, he ventured that "[j]ust about every point on the planet is becoming more global, and Tibetan musicians have to compete with that if they want to survive."[451] Concomitantly, "in the fields of literature, art, film, and music alike, Chinese intellectuals and artists have been turning more and more frequently to Tibet as a source of inspiration."[452]

Tibetan diaspora performativity is no longer based on unalloyed traditionality: "Some of the public gatherings or celebrations have little in common with authentic Tibetan culture; often it is a strange mixture of a political meeting, a Tibetan ceremony, with elements of popular folk dance performances, in the style popularized by the Chinese army in Tibet in the 1950s."[453] The singer Yungchen Lhamo, in emigration in Australia, has said that she likes to experiment, that her albums include songs with an electronic accompaniment, and that if old and new are joined together, our culture will live."[454] Other Tibetan émigré performers who have "experimented with fusion styles" include Techung, Nawang Khechog, and Coying Drolma.[455] Some Tibetan monks in India also listen to Western pop music.[456]

The authorities in Tibet's cities have replaced many Tibetan-style structures with inelegant, dysfunctional "Chinese" (read: faux-Western) buildings.[457] To label the result "the scars of cultural genocide,"[458] however, is extreme: the same process of destroying traditional buildings to make way for "development" has occurred throughout China. For example, only twenty-five of the original 6,000 *hutongs* (narrow alleys) of Beijing have been preserved; the rest having been bulldozed by developers, and that despite a UNESCO declaration of inner Beijing as a world heritage site.[459] There is no evidence that Tibetans did not join with Han in the similar pseudo-modernizing affront to the eyes in Lhasa and other Tibetan cities.[460]

As anyone who has been to Lhasa in recent years can attest, there has also been some effort to correct past mistakes by putting up more attractive and well-adapted Tibetan-style buildings. Since 2004, there has been a "massive effort to renovate a recently reconstructed section of Lhasa" to "reverse the sinicisation of architecture."[461] The damage done to architecture in Lhasa, where buildings central to the cultural heritage of the city have been either preserved or destroyed, stands in stark contrast to more overt attacks on buildings in other parts of the world that are part of a national heritage.[462] Architecture in the Tibetan diaspora is also not unproblematic, with one Western authority noting that the way in which buildings are constructed often reduces the distinctive elements of traditional Tibetan architecture to "cosmetic clichés." He also finds that not only is there a lack of traditional Tibetan buildings in Dharamsala, but many "resemble the box-like concrete structures which are now found over most of India."[463] Indeed, a Canadian journalist has described Dharamsala as a "polluted dump filled with tourists" where Tibetans are now forsaking their culture. An Australian journalist has observed that in Dharamsala "tourists gaze out, not over a verdant valley but onto hillsides covered with garbage."[464]

The émigrés try to attribute "vices" found in Tibet's cities to cultural corrosion due to the Han presence. Lhasa, like cities elsewhere, has abundant outlets for prostitution, gambling, and drugs.[465] The ICT director has stated, "We are concerned that more and more young Tibetans are being tempted by the very worst aspects of Chinese culture."[466] However, none of the "vices" complained of are particularly "Chinese." Billiards is a Western invention, karaoke was born in Japan, and prostitution, drugs, and alcoholism are universals. When questioned about Lhasa's nightclubs, the TAR's Tibetan vice-chairman referred to them as part of "Western lifestyle" and said they add diversity to the Tibetan and Han cultures.[467] Authorities in the TAR do denounce gambling and prostitution and the police stage raids, although concerted efforts are precluded by corruption, as in many countries.[468]

The "vices" in Tibet decried by the émigrés are for the most part present in Dharamsala and elsewhere in the Tibetan diaspora[469] (including the Tibetan diaspora in China proper),[470] so much so that the head of a center for substance dependence in Dharamsala has said "We have seen a rise in the number of AIDS patients in our society and drug addiction and alcoholism has become a commonplace today."[471] The same problems appear in the holy city of Kathmandu.[472] They are not uncommon among Buddhist monks in some countries[473] and were not unknown in Tibet before 1950: a famous Japanese visitor to Lhasa in 1914 learned that prostitution was legal there, while German visitors to the city in the late 1930s found a great many prostitutes.[474] Many local Indians are said to resent the "vices" of their Tibetan neighbors.[475] Many also resent their privileges.[476]

"Cultural erosion," including the adoption of words of foreign origin, is as prevalent in Dharamsala as in Lhasa.[477] It has been said of Tibetans in India that "[d]aily life is laden with markers of reified Tibetanness, and a nagging anxiety that the necessary accommodation to the Indian host society dilutes more and more the Tibetanness of each generation of exile."[478] Additionally, "[i]n daily life people speak English and Hindi more than Tibetan, and even if people speak Tibetan, they pepper their conversation with many English and Hindi words." In contrast, Tibetans in India who attended school in Tibet "even if they didn't finish middle school, are often better in both their spoken and literary Tibetan than exile students, even those who finish university."[479] This outcome is expected, as Tibetan settlements in India have "secondary schools struggling to integrate Tibetan curricula into a mandatory Indian syllabus."[480] In the famous Tibetan Children's Village in Dharamsala, for example, pupils take all classes in Tibetan until around age ten, but all subsequent classes are in English.[481]

Émigré and Western leaders are usually much less concerned about Western than Han influence on traditional Tibetan culture.[482] Young Tibetans, however, have become more attuned to "a Western dress sense and a greater awareness of life outside" than Han Chinese.[483] In ethnic Tibetan Bhutan, a student has commented, "Sometimes the young people here copy the Westerners so much that they are almost Westerners themselves."[484] At the émigré Sera monastery in south India,

> Reeboks are standard gear, and the strains of Pearl Jam not unknown in these regions. And the tuck [snack] shop outside the monastery is a slice of Middle America, well stocked with chips, chewing gum and soft drinks.[485]

Sonam Chophel, Tibetan Welfare Officer in Dharamsala, notes "western music, jeans and related western mores" are common among Tibetans in India, but "does not blame the Indian social fabric for these influences. "If we cannot safeguard our own culture, it is our own fault.' "[486] In effect, he recognizes that the "Indian social fabric" and Western cultural elements are imbricated and that acculturation need not be a function of state imposition, but may be welcomed by elements of the community. A journalist interviewing young Tibetans in India described the teenage Dolma who "instead of speaking Tibetan . . . uses a smattering of Hindi, English, and the local Kanadda language. She prefers Indian movies, Western clothes, and rap music to Buddhist poetry."[487] Tempa Samkhar, an émigré cabinet secretary, has noted that 60 percent of Tibetans in India were born there and

> These youngsters are more Indian than Tibetans. They are fond of Indian food . . . and Hindi is their second mother tongue. Tibetan girls often wear *salwar kameez*. . . . The young are more fond of Hindi films and film songs than Tibetan songs."[488]

The Dalai Lama himself has said that "I have spent the better part of over 43 years of my life here in India. I'm practically Indian."[489] The Dalai Lama recognizes that Tibetan culture has synthesized many different cultures. Tibetans, he points out, have "adopted Chinese food, Indian philosophy and the Mongolian way of dressing."[490] Another émigré leader has said "the custom of drinking tea, eating vegetables . . . wearing silk, and aspects of astrology, art and musical traditions are some examples of many influences happily borrowed from China."[491] The art of Tibetan religious painting resulted from Han/Tibetan interaction.[492] As in the Tibetan diaspora, Tibetans in Tibet today are undergoing cultural hybridization in the context of the state in which they live. Even some severe critics of state policy in Tibet acknowledge this hybridization is not compelled. One Western reporter has noted, "It might offend Western romantic sensibilities, but young Tibetan men adore kung fu movies and karaoke."[493] Another journalist (and longstanding "Tibet supporter") has noted in Lhasa "Tourists are generally horrified by the Italian ice-cream parlour and the signs for Giordano and Jeans West on every other plate glass window, but the Tibetans don't seem to object to them, or mind the better facilities and the cleaner streets they accompany."[494] As in the diaspora, Tibetans learning the national language to partake of economic opportunities and communicate with non-Tibetans, as well as their cultural adoptions from the state's dominant ethnic group (generally of elements of Western culture) hardly amount to forced assimilation. There is, however, a Tibetan-ruled Himalayan land, Bhutan, where minorities are required by law to speak the national language and, despite widespread illiteracy, to write it as well. They are required to wear the dominant people's traditional dress in public. Minority people who entered the country after the late 1950s are not admitted to citizenship. Forced assimilation is a factor in tens of thousands of minority people fleeing the kingdom.[495] The Tibetan émigrés have not, however, criticized this "cultural genocide" and have friendly relations with the government of Bhutan.

Words Matter: "Cultural Genocide" and the Qinghai Resettlement Project

Tant de gens se sont crus traqués et ont écrit une littérature de traqués sans tracas. [So many people have believed they were persecuted and have written a literature of persecution, without any persecution taking place.]

—Jean Genet[496]

Language inflation is targeted to affect policymaking by altering perceptions and limiting the options of political actors. Confronted by accusations from a world spiritual leader that China is committing cultural genocide in Tibet, many people, especially Westerners, unquestioningly accept the characterization or are reticent to challenge it and face obloquy. In doing so, they diminish their capacity to aid in a compromise of the Tibet Question by signaling to the PRC that they are in the thrall of separatists[497] and by strengthening those Tibetan émigré forces that oppose compromise.

The long-term, diffuse effects on the Tibet Question of the discourse of cultural genocide have been accompanied by more immediate and direct consequences for a group of poor and mainly ethnic minority Chinese. In March 1999, China announced it would match US$40 million of a World Bank (WB) loan over the next five years to relocate 57,750 peasants from one county belonging to Xining City (population density 337 persons per square km) and five ethnic minority autonomous counties (ACs) in Haidong prefecture, eastern Qinghai (114.3 persons per square km; arable land per capita .157 ha).[498] They were to move 550 kms to the "oasis" of Xiangride, the second largest town in Dulan County, Haixi Mongolian and Tibetan AP (one person per square km), in western Qinghai.[499]

Some 65% of Qinghai's population is packed into the 2% of provincial territory designated as Xining City and Haidong Prefecture.[500] Haixi Prefecture's area, in contrast, is 45% of Qinghai and contains 7% of the province's population. The WB reported in 1999 that Haixi's population was 76% Han, 11% Tibetan, 7% Mongol, and 5% Hui, although these figures were likely out-of-date.[501] Average annual per capita income in the fourteen national poverty counties of Qinghai, which include all six move-out counties, was Y755, which is about half that of the rural TAR.[502] Some 170,000 persons applied for resettlement, and 34% were selected, with a selection rate of 40% among Tibetans.[503] Peasants had made repeated resettlement applications in the 1990s, and those not selected told journalists they were disappointed. About 90% of the selected had a yearly per capita income of less than Y580 (US$70), with many earning Y200–300 ($24–36). They suffered from malnutrition, relied on the government or others for food six months a year, complained they lacked water, schools, medical facilities, transport, and electricity; and said local roads are little more than dirt tracks.[504] Western journalists who visited the move-out area found "[e]thnic Tibetans in Ka Village have no school, no doctor and little more than bare rooms papered in newspaper"[505] and the Tibetan village of Shangchia has no school, no electricity and no medical facilities. There is no transport, and an illness would mean a 20 km hike to the nearest hospital. Everyone interviewed in the village, home to these dirt poor people for generations, expressed eagerness to leave, a sentiment echoed in other villages.[506]

The move-out counties' population was 1,333,484, of which 124,842, or 9.4%, were Tibetan.[507] Only 6% (3,466) of selected settlers were Tibetans, so the Tibetan share in these counties would have increased to 9.5% after the move. Han were 48.7% of the move-out counties' population, but only 42.3% of total people to be moved. Thus, 57.7% of the settler group were minority members, yet some project opponents claimed that it involved "moving nearly 60,000 Han Chinese farmers."[508]

Before the proposed "move-in," Dulan County reportedly had 52,669 people. The move would have doubled the population, while Tibetans in the county would have increased from 11,952 to 15,418.[509] After move-in, the percentages of three ethnic groups in Dulan were to drop: Han (from 53.1% to 47.5%), Tibetans (from 22.7% to 14%), and Mongols (from 14.1% to 6.7%), while those of three other groups were to increase: Hui (from 7.2% to 22.1%), Salar (from 1.5% to 4.2%), and Tu (from 1% to 5.4%).[510]

The percentages of ethnic change from resettlement would have been different if an area larger or smaller than the county were the unit of measurement—for example, the entire move-in prefecture or the project specific area, a 200-square km part of Dulan County where settlement was to take place. Haixi Prefecture Tibetans were 11.1% of the population and set to fall to 10.3% as a result of the move. Haixi Han would rise from 236,918 to 261,375,[511] but, the prefecture was 76% Han before the move-in and only 42% of those resettled were to be Han, so Han in Haixi would fall to 70.7%.

The project specific area had some 4,000 people, of whom 26.3% were Han, 69.1% Mongols, and 4.6% Hui. There were no Tibetans. In project townships, the rural area that included the project specific area plus adjacent lands (2,000 square km), there were 5,736 people. This number included 276 Tibetan herders who lived 120 kms from the project specific area in the summer and autumn and 60 kms from it at other times. After settlement, Tibetans in the project specific area would rise from 0% to 5.6% and Han would grow from 26.3% to 41.3%. The number of Mongols would remain the same, but their percentage would drop to 4.5%. If the project townships were considered instead, Han would rise to 41.8% and Tibetans to 5.9%, with Mongols falling to 4.9%. No Tibetan or Mongolian farmers already in the project specific area were to be relocated or displaced.[512]

In opposing the project, the ICT adopted two disparate figures. It highlighted the decrease in the proportion of Tibetans in Dulan County from 22.7% to 14% and the increase in Han in the project specific area from 26.3% to 41.3%.[513] It never disclosed the obverse effect—that Tibetans in the project specific area would rise from 0% to 5.6% and that Han in Dulan County would fall from 53.1% to 47.5%—even though this effect would probably be more meaningful, since Tibetans would for the first time have a presence in a part of the county where they were hitherto absent, while the proportion of ethnic minorities in the county would increase. Almost all Western news sources relied on ICT and other "Tibet support group" press releases, rather than detailed WB statistics. An unproblematic impression was created that Han were to increase in the relevant political jurisdictions and thereby threaten whatever influence Tibetans may have over local decisionmaking.[514]

The ICT also sought to create an impression that it was mainly Tibetans living in an indisputably Tibetan area who would be affected by the project. The ICT president stated, "This is an area where Tibetans have lived for generations. . . . It's like moving people from Denver to a [N]ative American reservation in Colorado."[515] While Tibetans have long lived in Dulan, they were scarcely present in project townships. Mongols and other peoples have also been present for generations, including Hui and Han who have been settled there since the 1920s, although an influx of Han also arrived in the 1950s.[516] Denver moreover is a generally prosperous city, while the population to be moved to Haixi came from one of the poorest rural areas in China. The analogy with a Native American reservation was also flawed, as reservations are generally populated by one Native American *ethnie*, not a variety of "tribes" and reservation authorities have the power to exclude anyone, including Native Americans of other tribes, not only from settlement, but even from entry for most purposes.[517] In contrast, at every level from project specific area to prefecture, the Qinghai project move-in area was already ethnically diverse. In addition, compared to the sovereign-nation status that Native Americans enjoy under U.S. and international law, in practice PRC minority groups cannot exclude other ethnic groups from living in ethnic autonomous areas unless the central government agrees.

The move-in area is one of the last, largely unsettled areas of Qinghai suitable for irrigated agriculture. The economic benefits touted by the WB for the project were largely undisputed. Crop yields near the move-in area were already three to four times higher than those in the move-out area, and the WB estimated that, in a few years, settlers would be able to triple or quadruple their incomes and have better health care and educational facilities than they had in eastern Qinghai.[518] While there were no schools for many settler group children in eastern Qinghai,[519] ten schools that would reflect the ethnic and language background of students were to be built for ethnic minority transmigrants.[520] Because the settlers were to live in twenty-four compact villages in a small part of the county, they would have left the rest of it undisturbed.[521] Tibetans were to live in a separate area, near villages inhabited by fellow Buddhist ethnic Tu people.[522] The projected increase in economic activity in the county would likely provide some opportunities for those already living there. As pointed out by the Dalai Lama's nephew, who lives in his uncle's hometown in Ping'an County (part of the move-out area), those remaining in the move-out area would also benefit from an increase in available land there and from less strain on resources.[523]

The Tibetan Centre for Human Rights and Democracy (TCHRD) in Dharamsala claimed that no Tibetans were included among the settlers, although there were to be some 3,500 Tibetans, and that Tibetans farming in the region would be displaced by the migration, although no forced displacement was to take place. They contended that the project "directly contributes to the assimilation and dilution of the Tibetan culture and destruction of the Tibetan way of life."[524] Other opponents among Tibet support groups argued that the project was "part of a Chinese effort to dilute and eventually destroy Tibetan heritage"[525] and would "desecrate unique local Tibetan culture."[526] Knowing that most settlers were not to be Han and many were to be Hui, the TCHRD nonetheless claimed that "the Hui Chinese are not different from the Han Chinese except for the fact that they are Muslims,"[527] contradicting the findings of Western scholars who have done fieldwork among the Hui.[528] Traditional Hui culture not only differs from Han culture with regard to religion, some aspects of language, folklore, and customs, but Hui ethnogenesis has accelerated under the PRC.[529] The Hui regard themselves as descended from Arabs, Persians, and Central Asians who came to China over the course of hundreds of years and intermarried with locals.[530] Ironically, the TCHRD assertion also conflicts with the outlook of eastern Tibetans, who sharply distinguish between Han and Hui and have a much greater animus toward the latter,[531] as a major clash in Qinghai between Hui and Tibetans in 2003 demonstrates.[532]

The TCHRD reported that "Tibetans in Dulan" had written to express a fear that "tens of thousands of Muslim Chinese" would come to Dulan and complained that "the Chinese" already in the county were "eroding the Tibetan religion, national identity, traditional dress and customs . . . [and] . . . [b]y doing so they [were] trying to sinicize [Tibetan] people."[533] The report, however, distorted the contents of the purported letter, which did not speak of an influx of "Chinese," or even Muslim Chinese, but of "tens of thousands" of Salar, although only 3,853 Salar were to move-in. A reference in the letter to the possibility of Tibetan casualties if resettlement went forward was an allusion to disputes between Dulan Tibetan and Salar herders over pastureland.[534] Herder disputes in Amdo can indeed be violent: in skirmishes from 1997–1999 between Tibetan herders (the "Ngulra tribe") of Maqu County, Gannan Tibetan Autonomous Prefecture (TAP),[535] Gansu, and Mongolian herders (the "Arig tribe") of neighboring Henan Mongolian AC, Huangnan TAP, Qinghai, twenty-nine people were shot dead.[536] However, the worries expressed about Salar were highly speculative. There were no Tibetan herders in the project specific area, but only Mongols, who were to receive better pastureland through the project. Few people in eastern Qinghai work primarily as herders. There was no reason to suppose settlers would do so or to conclude the project would deepen resentment between Tibetans and others, as opponents claimed.[537]

Having assimilated Hui with Han the TCHRD then designated the Salar as part of "the Chinese" as well.[538] Salar number some 100,000. Most live in the Xunhua Salar AC, Haidong Prefecture, Qinghai, where the tenth Panchen Lama was born. They are a Turkic people who migrated to the northeastern Tibet Plateau in the thirteenth Century from present-day Uzbekistan.[539] Pre-modern Salar social structures incorporated Tibetan and Hui elements.[540] The Salar language is Turkic, but has a vocabulary 30–40 percent Chinese and Tibetan. About 50 percent of Salar also comprehend Amdo Tibetan.[541] Some Salar cultural forms, such as singing, are influenced by Tibetan culture.[542] Thus, the ethnic group said to be the most threatening of "the Chinese" coming to Dulan to commit "cultural genocide" against Tibetans were a people who derive much of their own culture from Tibetans.

Another ethnic minority among the migrants that the émigrés designated as part of "the Chinese" also share their religion with Tibetans. The settler group was to include 5,431 Tu,[543] also known as Monguor. The Tu descend from Mongol soldiers who first came to what is now northeast Qinghai in the thirteenth century and intermarried with locals. Like the Dalai Lama and Panchem Lama, they traditionally adhere to the Gelugpa school of Tibetan Buddhism. Numbering over 200,000, they live mainly in Qinghai's Huzhu Tu AC, in the move-out area, as well as Minhe Hui and Tu AC.[544]

Opponents, including U.S. Congress members, argued that the Qinghai project would result in "cultural genocide" against Dulan's Tibetans.[545]

The ICT called the project "part of a larger Chinese policy which is now the greatest threat to the continued existence of the Tibetans as a distinct people and culture."[546] It is also said the project was "evidence of the Chinese policy of ethnic cleansing,"[547] even though ethnic cleansing typically involves mass ethnic murder and forced transfer of minority peoples from their traditional area of settlement. The Qinghai case, however, involved no forced transfers, let alone killings, and the ethnic groups who were to be transferred in were mostly from the diverse array of *ethnies* already there.

It was also erroneously claimed that "Dulan is officially designated an area of Tibetan autonomy within Qinghai."[548] It is Haixi Prefecture—not Dulan County—that was the relevant unit of autonomy: a county within an autonomous prefecture may have its own separate autonomy only if the county's ethnic minority or minorities are substantially different from the eponymous minority or minorities of the prefecture. This situation is not the case with Dulan County and Haixi Prefecture. Opponents stated that they feared that if resettlement went forward, attendant demographic changes would result in "tipping the ethnic balance so heavily against Tibetans and Mongolians that the region's autonomous status ultimately could be stripped"[549] from an area one-tenth of the Tibet Plateau.[550] These opponents spoke of how losing autonomous status would result in "fewer government posts for minorities and less support for bilingual education and cultural preservation."[551] They did so without a hint of the irony involved: émigré leaders have always argued that autonomous status brings no benefits whatsoever to minorities and that, in autonomous areas, "Tibetans have little or no say in running their own affairs" and "are completely deprived of their political identity."[552] "Tibet supporters" outdo each other in being dismissive of autonomy in Tibetan and other PRC minority areas.[553]

The PRC government pointed out that "[o]nce [an area is] granted autonomous administrative status, there is no constitutionally explicit mechanism for 'decertifying' such status, and there is no triggering method for such a process even when the percentage of ethnic people in an autonomous area falls low."[554] Officials have stated that no autonomous area of China has ever lost that status because of changes in the ethnic population balance.[555] There are large APs where the eponymous ethnic group is a small and declining percentage of the population and yet retain its autonomous status, for example, the Bayingol Mongolian AP in Xinjiang, where in 1990 Mongols were 13.6 percent of the total population and in 2000 only 4.1 percent.[556] The Party Secretary of Haixi pointed out that, as it stands, "[t]here are only a little over 20,000 Mongolians and 30,000

Tibetans among the 320,000 population of Haixi, but it is a Mongolian and Tibetan autonomous prefecture."[557]

Sixty U.S. Congress members opposed the Qinghai resettlement project.[558] The issue arose just after Lawrence Summers was nominated to be Secretary of the Treasury and was to go before a Senate panel for confirmation. The ICT had already organized senators to ask him questions about the Qinghai project.[559] While it was reported that U.S. officials clearly had their doubts about the argument that the project would dilute Tibetan culture, "they were unwilling to defend the loan and [thereby] appear to be siding with Beijing."[560] UK Minister for Development Clare Short observed that [t]he Tibetan lobby in the United States is very strong, in Hollywood and so on . . . I do not accept the allegations that were made and I think it is wrong that a sort of fashionable cause can be traduced to make people, for political reasons . . . force you to vote wrongly.[561]

In July 2000, the United States and Germany voted against the WB Qinghai project; France and Italy abstained. After an Inspection Panel issued a negative report, indicating the WB failed to follow its own procedures, especially in terms of assessing the project's environmental impact,[562] China withdrew its loan application, rather than await more studies.[563] In 2002, it was announced that hundreds of households had already left for Dulan on a "trial basis," that 17,000–20,000 settlers would move there in small groups, that US$80 million would be spent on irrigation and farmland improvements and that the ethnic composition of settlers was to remain close to the WB plan.[564] Almost all buildings in Xiangride were marked for demolition and a new townscape was to be created to receive the migrants.[565]

The outcry over "cultural genocide" in 1999–2000 in opposition to the Qinghai project had succeeded in reducing the number of the eastern Qinghai poor to be moved to western Qinghai, a result that may be best for the environment of the project area. The overall effect, however, on the impoverished of Qinghai was not as sanguine. Whatever the deficiencies of the plan, the leveling of the untenable charge of cultural genocide foreclosed the possibility for an open-minded evaluation of the plan's utility and thus denied tens of thousands of mainly minority people, including thousands of Tibetans, an opportunity to better their lives through the planned move. "Tibet support groups" offered no convincing evidence that the plan would have had an adverse effect on the culture of local Tibetans, but merely represented that this was inevitable once "the Chinese" had arrived. The opposite, however, could well be argued. With the planned increase in the number of Tibetans in Dulan and the addition of partially Tibetanized Salars and Tu as well, Dulan Tibetan culture might have been strengthened. That was the view implicit in the comment to a Western reporter by Gongbu Danzhou, a Dulan Tibetan, who stated, with Tibetans from eastern Qinghai slated to arrive, "Perhaps we will be able to build a temple."[566]

Conclusion

[I]n ten years there won't be a Tibet anymore.
    —Samdhong Rinpoche, 1994[567]

Tibetologist Elliot Sperling observes that "within certain limits the PRC does make efforts to accommodate Tibetan cultural expression" and "the cultural activity taking place all over the Tibetan plateau cannot be ignored."[568] Other supporters of the émigré cause, including Tibet scholar Robert Barnett and German Green Party leader Antje Vollmer, also recognize the inaccuracy of the cultural genocide claim.[569] The former head of the Dalai Lama's London office and a member of the Tibetan exile parliament has said that the PRC government's motivation in integrating Tibet into the national economy "may not necessarily be the destruction of the local economy or local culture as is often alleged."[570] By all accounts, Tibetanness remains robust. As a U.S. reporter has observed: "[F]or all the change in styles and attitudes—mostly among the small minority of Tibetans living in cities—Tibetan identity remains strong."[571]

If the concept of cultural genocide in Tibet is inapposite legally and empirically, the charge also has baleful political effects. The application of the concept exemplifies language inflation that disserves the urgent struggle against destruction of peoples and their cultures. It has been said that "the notion of genocide is marked by conceptual confusion, often compounded by its rhetorical use on the part of those seeking to inflame and stigmatise social and political discourse."[572] Scholars have catalogued many misuses of the term[573] and rhetorical inflation does affect the general public's view of key issues. For example, there has been a discourse, especially in Europe, of Israel's "genocide" of Palestinians. A poll found that 51 percent of Germans believe "there is not much difference between what Israel is doing to the Palestinians and what the Nazis did to the Jews."[574] One scholar has concluded that "when one needs a catch-all term to describe 'oppression' of one form or another, one often resorts to labelling it 'genocide.' The result is the debasement of the concept."[575] Another has deplored that "genocide" has been used as a "validation of every kind of victimhood."[576]

That the Dalai Lama continues to speak of cultural genocide[577] is especially anomalous, given that in 2005 he stated that "Tibetan culture and Buddhism are part of Chinese culture" and "we are willing to be part of the People's Republic of China, to have the PRC govern and guarantee to preserve our Tibetan culture, spirituality and our environment."[578]

The Dalai Lama notes that as globalization proceeds, "some communities have gained power over other communities." He has added, however, that "the interference of Western culture is not a bad phenomenon when taking this process separately, but it always depends on the strength of the affected culture and the cultural heritage."[579] He wants diasporic "future leaders of Tibet," to learn about Western cultures[580] and relies upon Westerners to "help save Tibetan culture from annihilation" and preserve it in their museums.[581]

The Dalai Lama thus does not seem particularly concerned that "cultural genocide" might be carried out under the aegis of Westerners or Westernizing influences. The situation with Tibetan cultural artifacts is exemplary in this regard. Émigré leaders claim "China" has "plundered and sold priceless statues and religious objet's art [sic]."[582] In 2001, they accused Chinese authorities of "looting" the Potala Palace and "emptying Tibet of its religious treasures" because artifacts were shipped to Shanghai, although there was no indication that the artifacts were to remain permanently out of Tibet. They have also asserted China earned over US$80 billion from selling artistic and religious objects in Hong Kong, Shanghai, and Tokyo during the Cultural Revolution, although they have offered no basis for this fantastical amount.[583] While many Tibetan artifacts were shipped to Beijing during the Cultural Revolution and some were scrapped, an essay on the émigré administration's own website states that PRC leaders stopped this practice in the early 1970s when they learned of it and that thousands of artifacts were returned to Tibet in the 1980s.[584]

In contrast, émigré leaders have in effect sanctioned the flood of Tibetan artifacts to the West. Tibetan objects on offer in the West equal in number India's offerings, with annual revenue in the tens of millions of dollars for Western auction houses and galleries that sell works they cannot prove left Tibet legally. Dealers claim that if these artworks are returned to Tibet they might be destroyed and, therefore, that applicable UN treaties on repatriation of pilfered national treasures do not apply.[585] They make this claim even though the world's greatest collections of Tibetan art are in Tibet's Potala Palace (which has 600,000 registered objects), the Jokhang Temple (10,000 tankas), and Drepung.[586] Artifacts sold to Western collectors include pieces taken from monasteries during the Cultural Revolution, but most have been removed in recent years, often it seems by Tibetans.[587]

Tibetan dealers market stolen artifacts in London, Paris, and New York and some end up in large Western, especially U.S., collections of Tibetan artifacts.[588] The Dalai Lama, however, has raised no objection to the vast Tibetan artwork collections of Western museums and wealthy owners. In his introduction to the 1990's Royal Academy catalog of "The Sacred Art of Tibet" exhibition in London, he "gave the trade his blessing," stating, "We have treasured these works of art for centuries in Tibet and are deeply moved that they are . . . treasured by the open-minded people of the whole world."[589]

The accelerated flow of stolen Tibetan artifacts follows the journey to the West taken by looted Chinese art: up to a million Chinese *objets d'art* not acquired legally, including some of the greatest relics of Chinese antiquity, are now lodged in Western museums or in the hands of rich denizens of New York, London, Tokyo, and other cities. The curator emeritus of the Shanghai Museum has said of the treasure trove of artifacts pillaged from China, "It is a real pity that right now, if Chinese people want to study their own history they must go abroad to do so." It is sometimes argued such art is better off abroad, where it will be preserved, but art taken to Europe before World War II is now in ashes from bombings and the Dalai Lama admits Tibetan art is stolen for money, not to preserve it.[590] The high prices paid by Western collectors stimulate thefts of Tibetan artifacts and "the Tibetan art heritage remains seriously threatened—not by Beijing but by the art markets of the West."[591] There have been repatriations of Tibetan artifacts by émigrés, but only one case involving a Westerner,[592] yet "Tibet supporters" are aiding an ultra-conservative U.S. Congressman's investigation into "systematic looting of Tibetan art and objects by Chinese authorities."[593]

The émigré leaders do not hesitate to imply that Chinese culture is a polluting influence in Tibet, almost always speaking of it in the negative, despite its many attractions for people around the world. A range of themes invoked by émigré leaders against "the Chinese" call to mind diatribes that took place a continent away and a half-dozen decades ago when it was falsely charged that one ethnic group sought to corrupt and destroy another through promotion of irreligion, prostitution, pornography, drugs, intermarriage, nontraditional art forms, and demographic catastrophe.[594] Those who advance the theme that a particular ethnic group or nation are "corrupters of peoples," fervently hold this conviction, and claim to have "proof" of its validity, make their claim all the more pernicious. Those subject to such accusations moreover will feel fully entitled to resent it and treat with the utmost suspicion those who make it. That is in fact the reaction of Chinese leaders, including ethnic Tibetan leaders in Tibet, who especially resent the émigrés'charges. Words do matter with regard to whether there will be negotiations over the Tibet Question as well. For example, a PRC spokesperson has acused the Dalai Lama of "deliberately poisoning the the atmosphere for his future contacts with the Chinese government" by "vilify[ing] the Chinese central government's policy toward Tibet."[595]

The existence of émigré leaders' ties to U.S. politicians, alongside the émigré administration's unsupported charges of cultural genocide in Tibet, fuels suspicions of PRC and TAR officials that the Dalai Lama is hypocritical in his pronouncements about Tibetan culture.[596] Furthermore, by extension, his claims raise suspicions about other matters, including his desire to arrive at a solution to the Tibet Question that respects the territorial integrity of China. If such a solution is indeed contemplated by the émigré leaders, a retreat from the discourse of "cultural genocide in Tibet" is warranted as one of the many steps needed to smooth the way to negotiations. In this way, the émigré leaders and "Tibet supporters" would better position themselves to engage in a credible and productive critique of the deficiencies of cultural policy and of human rights in Tibet.

Notes

1. "Nobel Researchers Tell of Years of Ridicule," Agence France Presse [AFP], Oct. 4, 2005.
2. David Miller, *On Nationality* (Oxford: Clarendon Press, 1995), p. 38.
3. David Archard, "Myths, Lies and Historical Truth: A Defense of Nationalism," *Political Studies* 43 (1995): 476–477.
4. K. Anthony Appiah, "The Multiculturalist Misunderstanding," *New York Review of Books*, Oct. 9, 1997.
5. See, e.g., Dakpa Tendar Bhailan, *Tibet and China: Two Distinct Nations* (Dharamsala 2002); "Thubten Jigme Norbu at the University of Rochester and Nazareth College," www.rangzen.or/march/days/040497.html; Lobsang Tsering and Kunchokj Tsering, "Open Letter to Florida Governor Lawton Chiles" (1996), www.caccp.org/stats/fiul/html.
6. Brian Fawcett, "Some Questions and Issues about the New Nationalism, *Journal of Canadian Studies* 31 (Nov. 1996): 189–92 (1996).
7. Terence Clarke, "Tibet: Lost in the Himalayas," *Salon*, Feb. 4, 2002.
8. Tibet Information Network (TIN), "Tibetans Sent Back Across the Border as Pressure Increases on Nepal," (News Update), Dec. 20, 2000.
9. Tibet Justice Center (TJC), *Tibet's Stateless Nationals: Tibetan Refugees in Nepal* (Berkeley, CA: TJC 2002):2; Tenzin Tsundue, "No Compromise on Tibet," *Tehelka*, Apr. 9, 2005, www.phayul.com/news/tools/print.aspxx?id=9445&t=1.
10. Linda Anderson, "Home Straits," *South China Morning Post (SCMP)*, July 3, 2004: C5.

11. "Dalai Lama Calls for Afghan Plan," Reuters, Nov. 28, 2001; Unrepresented Nations and Peoples Organization [UNPO], *China's Tibet: The World's Largest Remaining Colony* (1997).

12. Dalai Lama, "Tibet was an Independent Country (speech of Apr. 3, 1991)," in A.A. Shiromany (ed.), *The Political Philosophy of his Holiness the XIV Dalai Lama: Selected Speeches and Writings* (New Delhi: Tibetan Parliamentary and Policy Research Centre 1998), pp. 60–63.

13. Dalai Lama, "Address by His Holiness the Dalai Lama at the Palace of Westminster (July 16, 1996)," http://www.tibet.ca/wtnarchive/1996/7/16_5.html.

14. " 'Altar of the Earth' used as China's Dustbin: exiled Tibetan Government," AFP Apr. 25, 2000 (exile government argues Han migration to Tibet is part of colonial strategy); "Tibetan Activists Target British Energy Giant," Inter-Press Service (IPS), July 7, 2000 (Students for a Free Tibet head says China seeks to make Tibet economic colony); Isabel Hilton, "Will Tibet's Culture Simply Fade Away?" *New Statesman* 1344:4720 (Jan. 1, 2005):27 (PRC strategy is "to encourage Chinese colonization and to promote economic development in the hope that Tibetan culture will be obliterated, and with it Tibetan memory"); "A Narrow Stand on Human Rights," *Independent* (London), Nov. 23, 2005 (Tibetans "for years have been the target of a deliberate and cruel policy of Han Chinese colonization" and face "annihilation as a nation").

15. Émigré leaders do not generally abhor colonialism, Samdhong Rinpoche, Kalon Tripa (chief minister) of the TGIE Kashag (cabinet) described colonial Britain as "a civilized nation which had a rule of law and a parliament . . ." Isabel Hilton, "Tibet: Desperate Nation Prepares to Defy Might of Peking," *Independent*, Oct. 20, 1997:14. On the pro-British imperial stance of Tibetan émigré writers such as WD Shakabpa, including as to the 1904 British invasion of Tibet, see John Powers, *History as Propaganda*: Tibetan Exiles versus the People's Republic of China (Oxford: Oxford University Press, 2004): 84. Although many Puerto Ricans argue unequal political rights make their homeland a U.S. colony, the Dalai Lama has said "Puerto Rico is associated with the United States in many aspects . . . that helps with Puerto Rico's progress." "Dalai Lama Praises Puerto Rico for Rejecting Death Penalty," Associated Press [AP], Sept. 23, 2004.

16. "Sino-Tibet Relations: Dalai Lama Pushes Middle Path," *Bangkok Post* [BP], May 25, 2001: 14; "Address of Kalon Tripa Prof. Samdhong Rinpoche . . . ," World Tibet Network (WTN), Nov. 22, 2005 ("Our conflict is neither a conflict of political ideology nor for political power. It is neither fight for territory nor a struggle between nationalities. The Tibetan people do not ask neither separation nor larger share of political or economic power. Our sole objective is to retain the identity of Tibetan people as non-violent society in order to preserve and promote the unique Tibetan cultural and spiritual heritage.")

17. Dalai Lama, "Speech of His Holiness the Dalai Lama to the European Parliament (Oct. 24, 2001)," http://www.tibet.ca/wtnarchive/2001/10/24_1.html. He has said "the Tibetan people . . . are being gradually wiped out from the face of the earth," "Thousands Gather for Tibetan's Funeral," AAP Newsfeed, Apr. 30, 1998.

18. Robert Thurman, "The Realpolitik of Spirituality: An Interview with His Holiness the Fourteenth Dalai Lama," *Shambhala Sun*, Nov. 1996, www.Shambhalasun.com/archives/features/1996/Nov96/dalailama.htm.

19. Dalai Lama, "Buddhism in Practice," *Snowlion Newsletter & Catalogue* (Spring, 1993), http://www.sacred-texts.com/bud/tib/dl-usa.htm. "Tibet supporters" often quote the Dalai Lama on this score. See, e.g., "Socially Engaged Buddhism," *Odyssey*, Oct. 9, 2004, in WTN, Oct. 10, 2004. Guru devotion is a foundational practice of Tibetan Buddhism. See Daniel Capper, "Enchantment with Tibetan Lamas in the United States," *Journal of Contemporary Religion* 19:2 (2004): 137–153. It is thus problematic for adherents to not accept that support for Tibetan nationalism is religiously required.

20. Manpreet Singh, "Spirituality on Sale in India's Little Lhasa," *Seoul Times*, Oct. 19, 2005, in WTN, Oct. 18, 2005.

21. Dalai Lama, "Keynote Address at Tibet Support Group Conference (June 14, 1996)," in Shiromany, 1998: 118–25.

22. On Tibetans' supposed special "harmony with nature" see Department of Information & International Relations [DIIR], "Tibet's Environment and Development Issues," www.tibe.net /diir/eng/enviro/overview/; Tibetan Centre for Human Rights and Democracy [TCHRD], *Southeast Asia: Human Rights Seminar on Tibet* (Dharamsala: 1998).

23. "Excitement and Concern over Karmapa Move," *Statesman (India)* [S(I)], Jan. 16, 2000 (Indians in Dharamsala allege "rampant deforestation and encroachment on forest land" by Tibetans); Kevin Platt, "Tibet's Environmental Good Samaritans: Saving a Valley and a Village's Livelihood," *Christian Science Monitor* [CSM], Nov. 18, 1999 (Tibetans have stripped some forests in central Tibet.)

24. P. Phatarphekar, *Outlook*, Sept. 24, 2005, in WTN, Sept. 24, 2005 (Tibetan involvement in illegal trade in tiger skins from India to Tibet); "Tibetan Antelope Poachers Given Harsh Penalties," Xinhua, Sept. 4, 1999 (Tibetans and killings of Tibetan antelopes); "Human Competition Edging Out Those Lovable Icons of Wildlife," *New York Times* [NYT], Apr. 6, 2001: A6 (Tibetans and pressure on pandas in their reserves).

25. Poor Indian peasants near Bodhgaya, where Buddha realized enlightenment, have protested the erection by Tibetan Buddhists (endorsed by the Dalai Lama,) of a US$150 million, 150-meter high copper clad statue of the future Buddha Maitreya, as degrading their habitat. Eva Neumaier, "Missed Opportunities: Buddhism and the Ethnic Strife in Sri Lanka and Tibet," in Harold Coward and Gordon Smith (eds.), *Religion and*

Peacebuilding (Albany: State University of New York Press, 2004): 69–92; Christopher Titmuss, "The Unhappy Prince and the Maitreya Statue Project," *Bodhgya News*, May 10, 2002, http://www.bodhgayanews.net/statue/statue05.htm. Despite assertions that Tibetan Buddhism opposes extraction of minerals, see "Sino Gold Digs Itself a Hole in Tibet," *Sydney Morning Herald* [*SMH*], May 17, 2003 (Dalai Lama's representative in Australia says "Tibetan principles . . . oppose mining,") the Dalai Lama has said "In the economic field we must develop industry, using the vast Tibetan mineral wealth." *Shambhala Sun*, 1996.

26. Assertions of the special compassion of Tibetans are common among "Tibet supporters." See, e.g., Will Parrinello, "Dreaming of Tibet," WTN, Oct. 29, 2005 ("Tibetan lives are the embodiment of compassion.")

27. Dalai Lama, *My Land and My People: The Original Autobiography of the Dalai Lama of Tibet* (1962): 38. The Dalai Lama has praised the old society. Robert Coles and Steve Lehman, *Tibetans: A Struggle to Survive* (Umbrage Press, 1998):Flyleaf ("As I remember my childhood and youth, we Tibetans lived a delightful and peaceful life. We were free and contented . . .); Robert Thurman, "The Rolling Stone Interview: The Dalai Lama," in WTN, May 8, 2001 (in old Tibet nomads and peasants had light work and ample land and food). Within émigré society, "most people will refer to 'the old Tibet' as a happy country." Wangpo Tethong, "Between Cultures: Young Tibetans in Europe," in Dagmar Bernstorff and Hubertus von Welck, *Exile as Challenge: the Tibetan Diaspora* (London: Orient Longman, 2004): 409–418. Whether Tibet (or any place) was feudal is debatable, but it did conform to the concept as used in common parlance, i.e. a political entity ruled by and for aristocrats and leading clergy. See Lobsang Sangay, "Tibet: Exiles' Journey," *Journal of Democracy* 14:3 (2003): 11–130 ("Before 1959, Tibet was ruled under a two-tiered feudal system . . . with roughly equal numbers of *Tsidrung* (monk-officials) and hereditary *Kudrak* (aristocrats) controlling the government"); A. Simpson, "Where the Soul Calls Home," *Herald* (Scotland), Aug. 2, 1999 (émigré historian Tsering Shakya terms old Tibet "abysmally feudal"); Eva Dargyay, *Tibetan Village Communities* (Warminster: Aris & Phillips 1982): 16–21 (power in old Tibet exercised by central government of noble and monastic officials, monasteries with estates given by government, and nobilility with hereditary estates, to whom subject classes had many obligations). While many émigré leaders and supporters deny old Tibet was feudal, they nevertheless claim the "Tibetan people have become veritable serfs of the Chinese colonial masters." DIIR, "Response to Xinhua Interview of Apr. 28, 1994," in WTN, June 3, 1994.

28. Johann Hari, "The Dalai Lama: a Life Less Ordinary," *Independent* [London], June 7, 2004; Shekhar Gupta, "On the Record," *Indian Express* [*IE*], Oct. 25, 2005.

29. "Manifesto by Tibetan Leaders," in International Commission of Jurists, *The Question of Tibet and theRule of Law* (1959); Kyabje Gelek Rinpoche, "Life in Old Tibet: A Clear-eyed Reminiscence," WTN, Dec. 27, 1999; DIIR, *Tibet: Proving Truth from Facts* (Dharamsala: DIIR, 1996): 40–44. Old Tibet has been said to have been close to an "absolutist theocratic state, " while today "Opposition, criticism and dissent—essential aspects of democracy—currently have no place in the Tibet government-in-exile" because any challenge to the Dalai Lama's political authority may be interpreted as antireligious. Jane Ardley, "Learning the Art of Democracy? Continuity and Change in the Tibetan Government-in-Exile," *Contemporary South Asia* 12:3 (2003): 349–363.

30. Heinrich Harrrer, *Seven Years in Tibet* (London: Rupert Hart-Davis, 1953): 89 An "unrepentant Nazi," Harrer knows something of stern dictatorships. See Orville Schell, *Virtual Tibet: Searching for Shangri-La from the Himalayas to Hollywood* (New York: Henry Holt, 2000): 271. Despite his refusal to acknowledge his past as an SS man, the International Campaign for Tibet presented its 2002 Light of Truth award to Harrer. "Henrich Harrer and Petra Kelly to be Honored for Contributions to Tibet with Award Presented by the Dalai Lama," ICT, Sept. 27, 2002, in WTN, Sept. 27, 2002. The 2006 Light of Truth Award was presented to the Herge Foundation, established in the memory of the racist and anti-Jewish Belgian author of the Tintin comic book series. ICT, "Tutu and Tintin to be Honored by Dalai Lama," in WTN, May 17, 2006; Benoit Peeters, "A Never-Ending Trial: Herge and the Second World War," Rethinking History 6:3 (2002): 261–271; Phillipe Met, "Of Men and Animals: Herge's Tintin au Congo: a Study in Primitivism," *Romanic Review* 87:1 (1996): 131–142.

31. Thubten Jigme quoted in Audrey Topping, *The Splendors of Tibet* (New York: Sino Publishing, 1980): 140. Before 1951, the overall literacy rate was about 5 percent. There were some twenty public schools and about 100 small private schools, mainly for aristocratic children. Total enrolment was about 3,000 in a population of one million. About 10 percent of the population were monks and nuns, but only a fifth of them studied. In schools and among monks and nuns, education mainly focused on religion. N. Ram, "Educational Takeoff in Tibet," *Frontline* 17:19 (2000). Some Tibetan monasteries in South Asia now combine religious and secular education. Ellen Bangsbo, "The Tibetan Monastic Tradition in Exile: Secular and Monastic School of Buddhist Monks and Nuns in Nepal," *Tibet Journal* 29:2 (2004): 71–82; Samdong Rinpoche, however, opposes monks taking up any secular subject. V. Chinvarakorn, "The Long Road to Freedom," *BP*, Mar. 31, 2001.

32. Neumaier 2004.

33. DIIR, *China's Current Policy on Tibet: Life-and-Death Struggle to Crush an Ancient Civilization* (Dharamsala: DIIR 2000).

34. UNPO, "New Study Reveals China's Plans for Total Destruction of Tibetan Culture" (Sept. 29, 2000), http://www.unpo.org/press/000929tibet.htm. Samdhong Rinpoche has referred to China as a "terrorist state,"a "slave nation," and a "totalitarian system." "China is a Terrorist State," *Times of India* [*TI*], Sept. 24, 2001; "Tibetan Riddle: After the Dalai Lama, Who?"*TI*, Mar. 20, 2004; G. Rozenberg, "Exiled Tibetan Prime Minister Warns Against Armed Uprising," *Times* [London], June 1, 2004: 4. The Dalai Lama has said China practices the "rule of terror," that all Communist governments will "become a thing of the past soon," and that PRC officials in Tibet are "guests without proper invitations, guests with guns."; K. Scott, "Dalai Lama Laments 'Rule of Terror' in Tibet," *Guardian*, May 31, 2004; "Dalai," Press Trust of India, Jan. 13, 2003; Bob Hepburn, "A Meeting with the Dalai Lama," *Toronto Star* [*TS*], May 8, 2004. For all such talk, his envoy Lodi Gyari stated, after visits to China in 2002–2003, "We have been impressed by the dedication and competency displayed by many of the Tibetan officials" and "The current Chinese polit-ical structure is not a top-down affair with policy dictated from above but is instead being run by professional career politicians with an understanding of democratic processes" "Statement by Special Envoy Lodi Gyari." *Tibetan Bulletin* [*TB*] 6:3 (July–Sept. 2002); "The Happy People," *The Witness* (South Africa), Feb. 11, 2004, in WTN, Feb. 17, 2004. Such statements contrast with the Dalai Lama's earlier opinion of officials in Tibet: "The local authorities are very narrow-minded, very ignorant and ruthless." E. Gleick, "Dalai Lama," *People*, Apr. 6, 1998: 106.

35. "Kashag's Statement on the 14th Anniversary of the Conferment of the Nobel Prize to His Holiness the Dalai Lama," Dec. 19, 2003 in WTN, Dec. 20, 2003.

36. Martin Cohen, "Time Running Out for the Dalai Lama," *TS*, Dec. 6, 2003.

37. Minnie Cancellaro, executive director, TJC, Berkeley, California, quoted in Gloria Goodale, "When Art and Politics Collide," *CSM*, Jan. 9, 2004.

38. John Colvin, "Books: Peking's Destructive Rage," *Daily Telegraph* (London), Dec. 5, 1992: 21; Lynne O'Donnell, "China's Frontier Stacking Borders on the Genocidal," *Australian*, Oct. 2, 2000:37 (leading Tibet activist calls economic development in Tibet "Final Solution"); Dalai Lama, "Buddhism in Practice" (speaking of " 'the Buddhist holocaust' of the 20th century"); S. Awanohara, "Lukewarm Welcome," *Far Eastern Economic Review* (*FEER*), May 6, 1993 (Dalai Lama says results for Jews under Nazi Germany and Tibetans under China similar). The Tibetan Parliament-in- Exile has said Beijing is guilty of "brutal methods not less than Hitler's atrocities." J. Tyson, "Chinese Tighten Up Grip in Tibet," *CSM*, Oct. 7, 1987: 7. In 1997, the TGIE termed China "the eager stu-dent of Nazi's [*sic*] genocide culture." DIIR, "Nazis of Asia Set Out to Hoodwink the Free World," www.ibiblio.org/reg.burma/archives/199710/msg00147.html. The TYC has said the PRC state "resembles the

Nazi regime in every respect, including the manner of mass massacres, cultural genocide, arbitrary executions and the intended extermination of the Tibetans like the Jews and the maintaining of large concentration camps throughtout Tibet." "Tibetan Groups in India Protest Lhasa Arrests," UPI, May 23, 1993. While invocations of the Holocaust affect people generally, the Dalai Lama's Jewish constituency is especially strong. A Jewish outreach program in Dharamsala estimates three out of every four western visitors to the town are Jewish. An Israeli news service has said "Little Lhasa" seems like "Little Israel." In some areas of Dharamsala, the signs and menus are only in Hebrew. There is an Israeli-initiated museum in Dharamsala that documents the "tragedies of the Tibetan people." A third of all Western Buddhist leaders are said to have Jewish roots. Tibor Krausz, "Shalom Haverim," *Jerusalem Report* [*JR*], Mar. 12, 2001: 26; C. Halle, "How do you say Tikkun Olam in Tibetan?" *Haaretz* (Israel), July 5, 2003 in WTN, July 5, 2003; T. Krausz, "Magical Mystery Tour,"*JR*, March 12, 2001: 24. "A Diverse Spiritual Journey Through India's Dharamsala," Chiang Mai City Life, Jan. 31, 2006, in WTN, Jan. 31, 2006. Jewish support has allowed the Dalai Lama to make comments that otherwise might meet with criticism, such as that he found "a seed of human compassion" in the Nazis and that Heinrich Harrer probably became a Nazi out of patriotism. "Dalai Lama's Belief Nazis Have 'Seed of Human Compassion' Called 'Unconscionable' by Israeli Minister," AP, Mar. 22, 1994; Suzanne Goldenberg, "Cheers and Fears of the Dalai Lama," *Guardian*, Nov. 24, 1997. Harrer actually joined the Austrian Nazis in 1933, at a time when they advocated his country's annexation by Germany.

39. "Bush Meets Dalai Lama over China's Objections," AFP, May 24, 2001.

40. "Senate Foreign Relations Committee Questions Secretary of State Designee, Colin Powell," Cable News Network [CNN], Jan. 17, 2001.

41. Tibetan Policy Act of 2001, H.R. no. 1779, 107th Cong. (2001).

42. "U.S. Congress Considers New Tibet Charges against China," AFP, May 9, 2001.

43. "Meet the Dalai Lama," *Globe & Mail* [*G &M*] (Toronto), Apr. 7, 2004.

44. Gabriel Lafitte, "Tibetan Futures: Imagining Collective Destinies," *Futures* 31 (1999):155, 165. The author Patrick French, ex-head of the UK Free Tibet Campaign, has said of the émigré leaders, "While many feel that the romanticizing and exaggeration of the Tibetan cause has bolstered their battle against the Chinese, they also know that it's not quite right." "Cooking Up More Trouble?" *IE*, Apr. 30, 2000.

45. For example, in 1995, the Dalai Lama gave a speech accusing the PRC government of "total disrespect for the traditions and customs of the Tibetan people." His illustration of "total disrespect" was that the Chinese government had designated as the new Panchen Lama—the second highest figure in the Dalai Lama's Gelugpa sect of Tibetan Buddhism—one of three young finalists, while the Dalai Lama had chosen another boy.

"Dalai Lama Addresses Chinese Students and Scholars," www.tibet.com/DL/boston.htm.

46. See Lafitte, 1999: 159 ("The [émigré] Tibetans appeal to the nostalgia and yearning inherent in modernity, presenting themselves as bastions of authenticity in a world seduced by materialism").

47. Jonathan Watts, "The Railway Across the World," *Guardian*, Sept. 20, 2005) (Tibet independence supporters contrast "Han materialist pollution" with Tibetan spirituality); Gerry Baker, "Why Tibet?" *Rangzen Voice* (Spring 2004): 3 (a leader of International Tibet Independence Movement contrasts Chinese materialism with Tibetan spirituality); Joshua Glenn, "The Nitty Gritty of Nirvana: an Interview with Robert Thurman," *Utne Reader*, Dec. 15, 2002 (leading academic advisor to Dalai Lama says most Tibetans are spiritual and as yet "haven't succumbed to Chinese materialism"). The stereotype of Chinese materialism and Tibetan spirituality is present in Tibet as well. See, e.g., "China's Boom Spurs Migration into Tibet," Reuters, June 6, 1993 (Lhasa Tibetan says that "The Chinese are good at business, because all they think about is money. All Tibetans think about is religion.") First-hand observers of Tibetan communities generally do not find that Tibetans particularly eschew materialism, however. "Young Tibetans Embrace Development, but Opportunities Lacking," AFP, Sept. 11, 2003 (U.S. anthropologist who works in Tibet states that "Tibetans are very materialistic"); "Seven Months in Tibetan Outpost," *SCMP*, Apr. 14, 1998 (British teacher of English to monks in Bylakuppe, India states that "Everyone wants to go to the United States. They think they will be able to pick up a job that pays megabucks. They are money-oriented.") The Dalai Lama has said "I think all Tibetans want more prosperity, more material development," "For Our Own Interest, We should remain Part of China," *TB* 8:3 (2004): 10. A controversial Tibetan lama with a Western following argues that "material pursuit has become one of the top priorities among Tibetans in general and certain lamas in particular. Big Tibetan [émigré] settlements compete over everything from the largest monasteries to the latest and most prestigious brands of car. If some high lamas were just to sell their gold and silver teacup holders, they could feed hundreds of starving Ethiopians for days." Dzongzar Kyentse Rinpoche, "Tibetan Buddhism in the West," Oct. 2002, www.american-buddha.com/dzong/khentse.htm

48. TCHRD, "Briefing Paper for Travellers to Tibet" www.tchrd.org/publications//topical_reports/ travellers_to_tibet-2003/ (claim that prostitutes are housed around sacred circumambulation path in Lhasa with political aim of "corroding Tibetan morality"); "Educational Plans for Tibet Slammed," UPI, Oct. 3, 1996 (TGIE official states "Whatever they do, Chinese people and policy in Tibet undermine our culture and values").

49. Roderick Stackelberg, *Hitler's Germany: Origins, Interpretations, Legacies* (London: Routledge 1999): 47.

50. For example, PRC officials contend old Tibet was an especially backward and cruel society—"even darker and more backward than medieval Europe." State Council Information Office, "Regional Ethnic Autonomy for Tibet" (Beijing: 2004): 1. No study has compared old Tibet and medieval Europe in terms of "backwardness" and "cruelty," however, nor is it evident that Tibetan society was crueler than contemporaneous Han society. There is, moreover, no strict relationship between "backwardness" and cruelty, as "advanced" societies have carried out massive genocides and crimes against humanities.

51. Dibyesh Anand, "(Re)imagining Nationalism: Identity and Representation in the Tibetan Diaspora of South Asia," *Contemporary South Asia* 9: 3 (2000): 271–287.

52. Laurence Brahm, "Economics with Tibetan Characteristics," *SCMP*, Nov. 20, 2004: A13.

53. "Dalai Lama's Envoy in Russia Urges Opposition to Beijing's Olympic Bid," Ekho Moskvy Radio, July 11, 2001, in British Broadcasting Corp. Monitoring [BBC/M], July 14, 2001.

54. Jamyang Norbu, "The Tibetan Resistance Movement and the Role of the CIA," in Robert Barnett and Shirin Akiner (eds.), *Resistance and Reform in Tibet* (London: Hurst 1994): 186–96.

55. Dalai Lama 1962:190; Dalai Lama, "March 10 Statement 1970," in Shiromany 1998: 376–77; Claudia Dreifus, "The Dalai Lama," *NYT*, Nov. 28, 1993:6: 52; Dalai Lama, "March 10 Statement 1994," in Shirormanny 1998: 441, 443.

56. See, e.g., Christopher Gibb, *The Dalai Lama: Peacemaker from Tibet* (Austin, TX: Raintree Steck-Vaughn, 2003); Janet Sirotta, *The Dalai Lama's Pacificism in Tibet's Struggle with China* (unpublished MA thesis, College of Staten Island, 2002).

57. Tenzing Sonam and Situ Sarin (dirs.), *The Shadow Circus: The CIA in Tibet* (1999) (Video). See also "The Priest, the CIA, and their Guerillas," *Gold Coast Bulletin.* (Australia), June 7, 2001: T31; Gupta 2005 ("Any action carried by a sense of concern or compassion, no matter what its appearance, even if it looks harsh, is essentially nonviolent"). Kalon T.C. Tethong, indicated "The Dalai Lama is very concerned about the consequences of violence. The final result would be a massacre of Tibetans." "Dalai Lama Celebrates Golden Jubilee as Tibetan Head of State," AFP, Dec. 3, 2000. The Dalai Lama's pragmatic statements could be read as contradicting his assertion that "For us Tibetans the path of non-violence is a matter of principle." Dalai Lama, "March 10 Statement 1997," in Shiromany 1998: 455. His stance on Tibet becoming a "zone of peace" is also pragmatic: "Defence should be the responsibility of the Chinese central government because of the long border between India and China. If there is a problem along this border then we Tibetans, as Buddhist students of India, cannot open fire on Indians, let the Chinese do that!" D. Bernstorff and H. von Welck, "An Interview with Tenzin Gyatso, the Fourteenth

Dalai Lama," in Bernstorfff and Von Welck, 2004: 107–121. The 13th Dalai Lama in his "Political Testament" stated, "Use peaceful means where they are appropriate, but where they are not appropriate, do not hesitate to resort to more forceful means." John Billington, "Power before Prayer," *Independent*, Oct. 12, 1997: 5. Robert Thurman, the Dalai Lama's academic advisor, observes, "There is a Buddhist theory [that] sometimes you have to do a little violence to prevent a larger violence." B. Crossette, "The World: Searching for Tibet; the Shangri-La that never was," *NYT*, July 5, 1998: 4:3.

58. "His Holiness, the Dalai Lama Speaks Out on U.S. Foreign Policy . . ." www.democracynow.org/article.pl?sid = 03/09/25/1443250. It was the Dalai Lama's unelected government that deployed a 10,000-man army in 1950 to battle China's People's Liberation Army (PLA). His monk body-guards also went armed when they escorted him from Tibet in 1959. M. Strobel, "A Good Heart Counts,"[*TS*], Feb. 23, 2004. He has said "if someone has a gun and is trying to kill you . . . it would be reasonable to shoot back with your own gun." H. Bernton, "Dalai Lama Urges Students to Shape World," *Seattle Times*, May 15, 2001.

59. "America Honors Dalai Lama," *UPI*, Apr. 17, 1991; "US Supportive of our Cause: Dalai Lama," *TI*, Oct. 6, 2003; "Dalai Lama Warns War on Terrorism could Backfire," *AAP Newsfeed*, May 21, 2002; "Tibetan Leader Reserves Judgment on whether Iraq War was Justified," AP, Sept. 11, 2003; "Fight Violence with Peace, Poverty with Compassion," AP, Sept. 12, 2005; Dalai Lama Endorses Just Wars, but not in Case of Tibet," AFP, Nov. 5, 2005. In *The Art of Happiness at Work: a Handbook for Living* (New York: Riverhead 2003): 164, the Dalai Lama said "for defense purposes for the society, or even on the global level, nations do need weapons for secu-rity purposes. Especially in the American case, you look at the fact that in the world there are totalitarian regimes who are against democracy. I think so long as those nations are there, the American military power must remain." He has praised George W. Bush as an "old friend," "good friend," a "very sincere human being" and "very straightforward." N. Morrisand & M. Woolf, "Blair Provokes Outrage Over Refusal to Meet with Dalai Lama," *Independent*, Jan. 10, 2004; "Dalai Lama Keen to Revisit China after 50 Years," AFP, Nov. 4, 2004; "Dalai Lama Calm Amid Excitement that he Generates," *Arizona Daily Star*, Sept. 16, 2005; Alice Thompson, " 'Westerners are too self-absorbed,' " Daily Telegraph, Apr. 1, 2006. On Bush and Iraq, he has said "I am an outsider and an out-sider may not fully understand the reality he faces . . . So you can't blame everything on President Bush, poor Bush!" Gupta, 2005. He likes the US political system because "it is the real rule of law, that all are equal" and because the US "enjoys its global stature because, in addition to its power, it is a champion of democracy and liberty." S.Yoon, "The Young Show Signs of Impatience and Frustration," *Nation* (Thailand), June 19, 1999;

E. Greenspon, "Giggle like the Dalai Lama with the New Funnies Page," *G&M*, May 8, 2004. He has pronounced US policy on the Tibet issue "quite satisfactory and quite encouraging." Amitabh Pal, "The Dalai Lama," Progressive (Jan. 2006): 35–39. The Dalai Lama also admires ex-UK Prime Minister Margaret Thatcher, a leader also not known for her nonviolence. "Lama of God," *SMH*, Apr. 9, 1988.

60. Veteran U.S. pacifist leader Colman McCarthy has said the Dalai Lama is "a pacifist between wars, akin to being a vegetarian between meals" and "nowhere close to being in the company of Gandhi who said 'I do not believe in any war'. . ." "The Dalai Lama is no Gandhi," *National Catholic Reporter*, Oct. 2003: 22. McCarthy has added that the Dalai Lama's "message is cliché-ridden and compared with other people in the peace movement, he's politically shallow . . . Why doesn't he condemn the US government? It's the world's most militaristic and most violent nation and it needs to be said by . . . people like him who have an enormous audience . . . but the Dalai Lama fritters it away with hot tub spirituality— searching for inner peace while the world is in chaos." "Ordinary as Daylight," *TS*, May 10, 2004. As a regular *Washington Post* columnist, McCarthy had been a vigorous "Tibet supporter." See C. McCarthy, "Tibet Overrun by Wheels of Progress," *WP*, May 18, 1993: C10. See also Adrian Zupp, "Why Won't the Dalai Lama Pick a Fight?" *Humanist* 64:1 (2004): 5–6 (deploring the Dalai Lama's failure to oppose the Iraq War and general lack of a social critique); Chris McGillion, "It is So because the Dalai Lama Said So," *SMH*, May 28, 2002: 13 (stating that the Dalai Lama, on international problems, makes "generalized statements [that] tend towards the naivety of a primary school pupil at an end-of-year speech night").

61. The Dalai Lama supported India's refusal to ratify the Comprehensive Test Ban Treaty and its "right" to test nuclear weapons. "Dalai Lama Backs Indian Stance on Test Ban Treaty," AFP, Aug. 17, 1996. See also "Tibetans Condemn Chinese Daily Smear of Dalai Lama," AFP, Dec. 6, 1998 ("every nation does have an opportunity or right to obtain its own nuclear weapon for national security"). India's nuclear tests spurred "wild rejoicing by Tibetan exiles in Dharamsala." Ajay Singh, "Letter from little Lhasa," *American Spectator*, Apr. 1999: 62, yet the Dalai Lama "laud[s] the spirit of non-violence that India has always upheld." *S(I)*, Nov. 8, 2001.

62. Subramanian Swamy, "The Fundamentals About Tibet," *Hindu*, Apr. 29, 2001. India's rightwing forces are generally appreciative of the Dalai Lama's support. The Vishwa Hindu Parishad (VHP), the most extreme among them, tried to get the Dalai Lama to be featured speaker at its world congress. Shashi Thaoor, "Growing up Extreme," *WP*, July 2, 1993: C5.

63. "Explosion Hits Tibet's Tense Capital: Report," AFP, Nov. 9, 2000; Singh, 1999 (TYC support of violence in furtherance of Tibetan

independence); "Officials Say Martial Law has Thwarted Plans for Riots," AP, Mar. 21, 1989, (TYC calls for violence); "China's 21st Century Soft Underbelly," BBC Summary of World Broadcasts [BBC/SWB], May 4, 1999 (TYC's plan to use violence to induce "Chinese" to flee Tibet). The Dalai Lama has acknowledged nine bombings in Tibet. "Newshour with Jim Lehrer: Zone of Peace" (PBS broadcast, Apr. 22, 1997), http://www.pbs.org/ newshour/bb/Asia/Apr.97/Tibet_4–22.html.

64. Pierre-Antoine Donnet, *Tibet: Survival in Question* (1994): 186; John Gittings, "Tibetan Exiles Defy Dalai Lama in Call to Arms," *Guardian*, July 22, 1988. A well-known U.S. "Free Tibet" advocate has said "Chinese" who live in Tibet are "the purveyors of Tibet's destruction . . . ." John F. Avedon, "The Rape of Tibet," *WP*, Mar. 29, 1987: C7. TYC leaders continue to speak of using force. "Young Tibet up in Arms," *S(I)*, July 4, 2003 (TYC president Kalsang Phutsok states "We will resort to any action, violent or non-violent, if it is necessary for our cause,") "China Tightens Yoke 40 years after the Tibet Uprising," Deutsche Presse Agentur [DPA], Mar. 8, 1999 (TYC member Pema Lhundup states "Unless and until we do any forceful action there won't be any chance for the Tibetan issue to get up onto an international level").

65. Rituparna Bhowmik, "Young Tibet Up in Arms," *The Statesman* [India], Jul. 3, 2003; Jehangir Pocha, "Tibet's Gamble: Can the Dalai Lama's China Talks Succeed?" *In the These Times*, Dec. 1, 2003.

66. Robert Barnett, "Violated Specialness: Western Political Representation of Tibet," in Thierry Dodin and Heinz Rather (eds.), *Imagining Tibet: Perceptions, Projections and Fantasies* (Boston: Wisdom Publications, 2001): 315 fn. 82. TYC head Kelsang Phutsok has said the Dalai Lama uses the TYC as the stick to convince China he is the carrot. Pocha 2003.

67. Sudeep Chakravart, "Tibetan Refugees: Restless Rage," *India Today*, May 18, 1998. Leading pro-independence activist Tenzin Tsundue has recounted that Tibetan émigrés regard Han Chinese as "a cunning race, untrustworthy, unethical and absolutely cruel" and continue to represented them in that way in émigré theatrical productions. "Gyami: Our Chinese Imagination," *Tibetan Review* (July 2004). Dzongzar Kyentse Rinpoche (2002) contends that Tibetan émigrés also do not respect Westerners and that this attitude stems from "a long-held assumption that Westerners are barbaric."

68. "Briefing on the Changing World Order: The Human Rights Situation in Tibet," *Hearing before the Congressional Human Rights Caucus*, WTN, Dec. 6, 2001 (statement of Buchung Tsering, Director, International Campaign for Tibet).

69. Arthur Max, "Unity Behind Dalai Lama's Campaign Begins to Unravel," AP, May 31, 1998.

70. Yangchen Kikhang, "Coercive Birth Control: Women Face Cultural Genocide on the Roof of the world," in Ronit Lentin, *Gender & Catastrophe* (1997):110–116.

71. Yangchen Kikhang, "A Letter to my Fellow Tibetans," *Tibetan Review* [*TR*], Oct. 2001: 28. For a discussion of "human bomb" tactics, see Pimmi Pande, "Guns Over Faith," *TR*, Jan. 2002:19. Pocha 2003, reported that some young Tibetan exiles told him "they don't mind taking help even from Al Qaida." Ironically, the Dalai Lama's comments on the Israel-Palestine conflict have mainly been criticisms of Palestinians' use of violence. "Dalai Lama Foresees Free Tibet in 10 Years," AFP, May 11, 1992. Asked how Tibetans could look to Jews to preserve their culture in exile and regain a country, The Dalai Lama, referring to the most famous Israeli commander, exclaimed, "We need a Moshe Dayan!" Molly Gordy, "Everyone Benefits from a Democratic China," *Newsday*, Apr. 27, 1994: A31.

72. "Tibetans Reconciled to Chinese Sovereignty: Rinpoche," *The Tribune* (Chandigarh), Sept. 10, 2005.

73. Wendy Atrokhov, "The Khasavyurt Accords: Maintaining the Rule of Law and Legitimacy of Democracy in the Russian Federation Amidst the Chechen Crisis," *Cornell Internationall LawJournal* 32 (1999):67; John Dunlop, *Russia Confronts Chechnya: Roots of a Separatist Conflict* (1998):49.

74. The Australian Tibetologist Gabriel Lafitte (1999:57) has put it that "Tolerance and forbearance are classic Tibetan strengths, taught at mother's knee."

75. Wendy Singer, "The Dalai Lama's Many Tibetan Landscapes," *Kenyon Review* 25:3–4 (2003): 233–256.

76. "Height of Darkness: Chinese Colonialism on the World's Roof," *TB* 5:5 (2001): 12.

77. Angus Mcdonald, "Tibetan Leader says Iraq War is all about Business," AP, Mar. 24, 2003.

78. Fred Lane, "The Warrior Tribes of Kham," *Asiaweek*, Mar. 6, 1994.

79. Elliot Sperling, "Orientalism and Aspects of Violence in the Tibetan Tradition," in Dodin and Rather 2001: 317–329. See also Samten Karmay, "The Great Fifth," WTN, Jan. 6, 1006. For a recounting of politico-religious violence in Tibet from the fourteenth to eighteenth centuries, see Michael von Bruck, "Tibet, the 'Hidden Country,' " in Bernstorff and von Welck, 2004:13–44.

80. Melvyn Goldstein, *A History of Modern Tibet 1913–1951: The Decline of the Lamaist State* (Berkeley: University of California, 1989): 42–43, 513–515.

81. Barnett 2001: 308 n.23. The first instance in which the Dalai Lama mentioned nonviolence in his annual March 10 Lhasa Uprising commemorative speech was in 1988. Shiromany 1998: 421.

82. See Jane Ardley, "Violent Compassion: Buddhism and Resistance in Tibet," paper prepared for the Political Studies Association—UK 50th Annual Conference, Apr. 10–13, 2000: 7–8 (many monks fought with guerrillas, with permission of their monasteries).

83. Toni Huber, "Shangri-La in Exile," in Dodin and Rather 2001: 357–371; Vanessa Baird, "Exit the Dragon: is Dissent in the Exile Community a

Sign of Nascent Democracy or Disintegration?" *New Internationalist* no. 274 (1995) pp. 28–30. (death threats against dissident emigrés); David Tracey, "Tibetan Sherlock Shakes Up the Movement," *International Herald Tribune [IHT]*, Mar. 28, 2002 (death threats impel Tibetan exile dissident to go armed in Dharamsala); J. Gearing, "Wrangling Hinders Talks with Beijing," *SCMP*, Dec. 12, 2003 ("Those who speak out [to criticize the Dalai Lama], or who are suspected of being critical of him, risk being attacked."); Powers, 2004, p. 129 (among exiles, "those who deviate [politically] risk being ostracized); Dawa Norbu, *Red Star Over Tibet* (New York: Envoy Press, 1987):10–11 (Tibetan émigré scholar's life threatened for criticizing some TGIE policies); George Dreyfus, "Tibetan Religious Nationalism: Western Fantasy or Empowering Vision," *Tibet and the Tibetan Diaspora: Voices of Difference* (Leiden: Brill 2002):54 (those perceived as opposing Dalai Lama, "denounced, threatened and at time[d] physically abused").

84. Deepak Thapa, "It's Dalai Lama vs. Shugden," *Himal* (Sept, 1996), www.south-asia.com/himal/Sept./dorje.htm; Martin Mills, "This Turbulent Priest: Contesting Religious Rights and the State in the Tibetan Shugden Controversy," in Richard Wilson and Jon Mitchell (eds.), *Human Rights in Global Perspective: Anthropological Studies of Rights, Claims and Entitlements* (London: Routledge, 2003): 54–70.

85. Friedrich-Naumann-Stiftung, "Tibet's Parliament in Exile," www.fntst.org/webcome/show_article.php; "An Introduction to the Central Tibetan Administration," www.tibet.net/tgie/eng/.

86. Ann Frechette, *Tibetans in Nepal: the Dynamics of International Assistance among a Community in Exile* (New York: Berghahn Books, 2002): 65. See also Asa Dahlstrom, "Belonging in Nowhere Land: the Tibetan Diaspora as Conflict," in Paul Richards (ed.), *No Peace No War: an Anthroplogy of Contemporary Armed Conflicts* (Athens: Ohio University Press, 2005): 173–192 (to the émigrés, the Dalai Lama "embodies all leadership by virtue of his divinity and knowledge"). Samdhong Rinpoche has said that "His Holiness is the head of the government, as well as the head of state [and] has the final authority to make any executive decision . . . If we propose anything as advice to His Holiness, the convention, the tradition is that the advice of the *kashag* [cabinet] is not binding on His Holiness. He has the free will to take any decision and that would be binding on the *kashag*." TGIE regulations require the consent of the Dalai Lama. Tsewang Phuntso, "Government in Exile," in Bernstorff and von Welck, 2004: 125–149. Samdhong Rinpoche has asked the Dalai Lama to carry out his traditional role as political leader and said he will draw direction from him. He noted that all policies would be made by the exile parliament and Dalai Lama. "Text of Tibetan Prime Minister, Samdhong Rinpoche," WTN, Sept. 5, 2001. He has said that feedback from people who voted for him indicates he was trusted to not disobey the Dalai Lama and that "they have chosen me as a faithful follower of His Holiness." "Satyagraha in Exile," *Himal* (Sept.

2002). In 2006, he indicated that he did not want to run for a second term, but would have to abide by the Dalai Lama's wishes. "Tibetan 'Prime Minister' not for Second Term," Indo-Asian News Service (IANS), Feb. 12, 2006. Even the TYC, which criticizes the TGIE for abandoning complete independence, makes "allegiance toward His Holiness the Dalai Lama . . . a fundamental prerequisite of one's membership to the Organization. TYC, "Quote, Unquote," Apr. 22, 2005, WTN, Apr. 22, 2005. The Dalai Lama has reciprocated by stating that the TYC's "struggle for complete independence is a rightful demand and that the notion of the TYC's fight being anti-Dalai Lama is wrong." "No Significant Change in China's Policies: Dalai Lama, *Phayul*, Oct. 17, 2005, in WTN, Oct. 17, 2005. "Democratization" among the émigrés may be related to a desire for greater U.S. support. Frechette 2002:75. Despite claims of democratization, the existing system of power in the émigré community calls to mind the one that existed in 1940: "The Kashag makes its recommendations to the Prime Minister [who] makes further reference to the Dalai Lama or Regent, who, in matters of importance and especially in any matter of major foreign policy or affecting the interests of the monasteries, consults the National Assembly, in which the monasteries are strongly represented." Khemey Sonam Wangdu, et al., *Discovery, Recognition and Enthronement of the 14th Dalai Lama* (New Delhi: Paljor s.d.) (excerpt: http://www.buddhapia.com/tibet/14_dalai_lama.html).

87. Heather Stoddard, "Tibetan Publications and National Identity," in Barnett and Akiner 1994: 152; Huber 2001: 371.

88. Rajesxh Kharat, "Gainers of a Stalemate: the Tibetans in India," in Ranabir Samaddar (ed.), *Refugees and the State: Practices of Asylum and Care in India, 1947–2000* (New Delhi: Sage, 2003): 281–320.

89. The TAR is "political Tibet," the area the thirteenth and fourteenth Dalai Lamas ruled in the first half of the twentieth century. Other Tibetan areas were not then ruled by Dalai Lamas and now make up ten Tibetan autonomous prefectures and two counties in four PRC provinces. They are "Cultural Tibet," "Tibetan Cultural Areas," or "Ethnographic Tibet." See Melvyn C. Goldstein, "The Dalai Lama's Dilemma," *Foreign Affairs* (Jan./Feb. 1998): 83; Anthony Anderton "Monlam Chenmo: The Great Festival, "*Asian Geographic* no. 17 (2003), in WTN, May 25, 2003, http://www.tibet.ca/en/wtnarchive/2003/5/25_6.html

90. See Barry Sautman and Irene Eng, "Tibet: Development for Whom?" *China Information* 15 (2001): 57. In the TAR in 2002, eight of fifteen members of the regional party committee were Tibetan. "On the Defensive About Tibet, China Launches Campaign to Change Foreign Views," AP, Aug. 9, 2002. In 2002–2004, five of the seven TAR prefectures had Tibetan party secretaries, including Lhasa (Lobsang), Nyingchi (Baima Namgyai), Shigatse (Jampa Phuntsog, later Lhasa Party Secretary, now TAR governor), Ngari (Doje Cering); and Nagchu (Gombo Tashi, now Lhasa Party secretary). "Injured Workers Moved to Prefecture-Level

Hospital in Tibet," Xinhua, Nov. 22, 2004; Verna Yu, "New Tibet leader after Reshuffle in Party," *SCMP*, May 17, 2003; "Tibet's Ngari Expects 100,000 Tourists this Year," Xinhua, May 23, 2002; Indira Lakshamanan, "Fearing a Road to Ruin Tibetans Say Beijing Railway Poses Latest Threat to Minority Culture," *Boston Globe* [*BG*], Aug. 26, 2002: A1; "CPC Members Pin Hopes on Party Congress," *S(I)*, Nov. 7, 2002. In 2003, the TAR governor (Legqog and then Jampa Phuntsog) and seven of twelve vice-chairmen, as well the People's Congress head (Raidi and then Legqog) and thirteen of its fifteen vice-chairmen were Tibetans. "China's Tibet Elects New Leaders," Xinhua, Jan. 27, 2003; "Leaders of Tibet Government Elected," Xinhua, May 16, 2003. Raidi "is said by observers to have taken the centre stage at political meetings even when [Han Party Secretary Guo Jinlong] was present." Kate Saunders, "New Tibet Party Chief in Leadship Reshuffle," WTN, May 11, 2003. Jampa Phuntsog was acting Party secretary in Tibet in fall 2005, after then Party Secretary Yang Chuantang suffered heart problems. "TAR Party Secretary Yang Chuantang Hospitalized, Jampa Phuntsog Running 'Daily Work,'" Foreign Broadcast Information System, Oct. 4, 2005.

91. Pritish Nandy, "Encounter: India is our Guru!" *TI*, Mar. 21, 2000; Dalai Lama calls India a "Model Country," AFP, Aug.14, 1997.

92. Sumantra Bose, *Kashmir: Roots of Conflict, Paths to Peace* (Cambridge, MA: Harvard University Press, 2003):188, 192.

93. "If Justice is not Done to Us, This Northern Frontier will go," *S (I)*, Sept. 25, 2001.

94. Thurman 1996. In a speech "Buddhism in Practice," the Dalai Lama told U.S. Tibetan Buddhists in 1993 that "Our friends in the Congress of the United States have acted powerfully to express their support for our cause, urging China to cease her attempts to eliminate the Tibetan race, erase the Tibetan nation from history, and eradicate the Tibetan culture. These senators and representatives will increasingly need your help." In 2006, he noted "both houses and the administration all are very supportive [and] willing to help." "A Conversation with the Dalai Lama, Part 1" *Charlie Rose Show Transcripts*, Nov. 16, 2005.

95. "Dalai Lama says China Pursuing 'Cultural Genocide' in Tibet," AFP, Nov. 25, 2001; Peter Ellingsen, "The Art of Oppression," *The Age* (Australia), Nov. 17, 2001; Tristam Hunt, "How Britain helps China destroy Tibet," *Observer* (London), Sept. 11, 2005.

96. "Richard Gere Invited to Appear before German Human Rights Panel," AP, Feb. 4, 2002.

97. Robert Clinton, "The Rights of Indigenous Peoples as Collective Group Rights," *Arizona Law Review* (1990) 32: 745.

98. Dalai Lama, "Letter to Secretary-General, United Nations," in Shiromany 1998: 8.

99. Dalai Lama 1962: 30.

100. Dalai Lama, "March 10 Statement 1964," in Shiromany 1998: 359.

101. International Commission of Jurists [ICJ], *The Question of Tibet and the Rule of Law* (1959): 61 (quoting The Dalai Lama, June 20, 1959).

102. ICJ 1959; ICJ, *Tibet and the Chinese People's Republic: A Report to the International Commission of Jurists by its Legal Inquiry Committee on Tibet* (1960).

103. Dalai Lama, "March 10 Statement 1961," in Shiromany 1998: 49; Barnett 2001:11 N.43. In the early years of emigration, this claim was largely ignored internationally. Donald Jensen, *World Apathy to Genocide in Tibet* (unpublished M.S. thesis, George Washington University, 1970).

104. Dalai Lama, "March 10 Statement 1973,"In Shiromany 1998: 384.

105. "Tibet Delegation Returns from Interrupted Tour of Tibet," AFP, Aug. 14, 1980.

106. Lorien Holland, "Chinese Poor 'Invade' Tibet," *Independent*, June 27, 1999: 23 (quoting U.S. Sen. Connie Mack's description of China's resettlement project in Qinghai province as "appalling act of cultural genocide"); U.S. Senator Paul Wellstone, "March 10th Observed in Washington D.C.," in WTN, March 12, 1997; 143 Cong. Rec. H6957 (Sept. 5, 1997) (statement of U.S. Rep. Frank Wolf); Hearing of the Asia and Pacific Subcomm. of the House Internat'l Rel. Committee, "China's Anti-secession Law and Developments Across the Taiwan Strait," Federal News Service [FNS], Apr. 9, 2005 (statement of Rep. Dana Rohrbacher); "Canadian Parliament Begins Probe of China's Human Rights Record," AFP, May 6, 2004 (statement of MP David Kilgour); "Canadian Parliamentarian Vows to Support Tibet," WTN, Jan. 1, 2005 (statement of MP Yvan Loubier).

107. Tibetologist Robert Barnett has noted "Tibet is a paradise for lazy thinkers, hazy Buddhists and romantic novelists, and also sometimes a platform for crude anti-Chinese rhetoric." He has added that " 'There is something in the Chinese view that people use this issue to get at them.' " "Leader of a Losing Cause," *Weekend Australian*, Sept. 21, 1996: 23.

108. Claire Nullis, "Tibetans Accuse China of Planning Cultural Genocide," AP, Aug. 29, 1993.

109. Vijay Kranti, "Ethnic Changes in Occupied Tibet—Consequences for South Asian Security," in K. Santhanam, S. Kondapalli (eds.), *Asian Security and China: 2000–2010* (Delhi: Institute for Defence Studies and Analyses 2004).

110. "Secret Meeting in China Decides on 'Final Solution' for Tibet," in WTN, Aug. 30, 1993.

111. Member of the European Parliament and prominent "Tibet supporter," Olivier Dupuis has used the eliding phrase "genocide by dilution." "Tibet: Summary of the Public Meeting: What Future for Tibet, What Future for the Tibetan Cause?" July 7, 2003, in WTN, July 10, 2003.

112. Frank Chalk and Kurt Jonassohn, *The History and Sociology of Genocide* (New Haven, CT: Yale University Press, 1990): 28. A large state-organized population transfer program was said to be circumstantial evidence of genocidal intent in the Indonesian regime's massive killings in East Timor.

Christopher Goebel, "A Unified Concept of Population Transfer," *Denver Journal of International Law & Policy* (1993): 24–26. Indonesia's early transmigration program, however, aimed at diminishing social tensions around Jakarta and populating border areas, not extirpating ethnic groups. Riwanto Tirtosudarmo, "Demography and Security: Transmigration Policy in Indonesia," in Myron Weiner and Sharon Russell (eds.), *Demography and National Security* (New York: Berghahn, 2001): 209–210. The Dalai Lama has recognized that there are substantial differences between the East Timor and Tibet cases. "Dalai Lama Backs Tibet Autonomy," AP, Oct. 10, 1999.

113. "Dalai Lama Urges U.S. to Befriend China," UPI, Sept. 10, 1995; Jay Taylor, "Understanding Tibet," *WP*, Dec. 10, 1997: A25; Karen Parker, "Understanding Self-Determination: the Basics," in Y.N. Kly and D. Kly, *In Pursuit of the Right to Self-Determination: Collected Papers & Proceedings of the First International Conference on the Right to Self-Determination & the United Nations* (Geneva: Clarity Press, 2001): 63–73 (claim of "ethnic dilution" in Tibet); "On Record," *Strategic Affairs* [India], Aug. 1, 2001: 12 (Dalai Lama asserts "In the next 30 years, the Chinese are planning to settle 20 million Han Chinese in Tibet,") "Protest Theatre in Dharamsala Against Chinese Railway," WTN, Nov. 2, 2005 (émigré and supporter groups in India claim China plans to resettle 200 million people in Tibet). The Dalai Lama is not necessarily opposed to settlement projects if they do not take place in Tibet. Arriving in Melbourne, he noted "he had flown over 'a large empty area' of Australia that could house millions of people from other densely populated continents." The area is, of course, not wholly empty, as it contains Aborigines. To them, the Dalai Lama has proffered the advice that "black people 'should appreciate what white people have brought to this country, its development.' " R. Callick, "Dalai Lama Treads Fine Line," *Australian Financial Review*, May 22, 2002.

114. Judith Banister, "Impact of Migration to China's Border Regions," in Weiner and Russell 2001:289.

115. "Tibetan Population Grows by 19 percent in 10 years," Xinhua, Mar. 30, 2001. The TAR had 1.9 million people in 1982. "Backgrounder: Population of Tibet," Xinhua, Sept. 4, 2002. In 2000, all civilians who had resided there for six months or more numbered 2.61 million, of whom 205,200 were non-Tibetans.

116. Wang Lixiong, *Tian Zang: Xizang De Mingyun* [Sky Burial: The Fate of Tibet](1998): 28.

117. Stewart Slavin, "Dalai Lama Hopes for Return to Tibet," UPI, Nov. 9, 1985.

118. "Beijing is Backed by Administration on Unrest in Tibet," *NYT*, Oct. 7, 1987: A1.

119. Ma Rong, *Xizang de Renkou yu Shehui* [Population and Society in Tibet] (Beijing: Tongxin chubanshe 1996): 65. Some 122,800 Tibetans moved to the TAR in 1965–1990. Ma Rong and Pan Naigu, "The Tibetan

Population and their Geographic Distribution in China," in Per Kaverne (ed.), *Tibetan Studies: Proceedings of the 6th Seminar of the International Association for Tibetan Studies* 1 (Oslo Institute for Comparative Research in Human Culture, 1992): 507–516. Many were rural or small town people who migrated to Tibet's cities. Tibetan rural-to-urban migration is ongoing, facilitated by reform of the household registration system and other measures. See Susette Cooke, "Merging Tibetan Culture into the Chinese Economic Fast Lane," *China Perspectives* no. 50 (2003): 42–55. Ironically, the TGIE's vision of a future independent Tibet, written by Samdhong Rinpoche, includes the interdiction: "Migration of people from towns and villages to industrial areas will be strictly forbidden." Samdhong Rinpoche, *Tibet: A Future Vision* (1997): 23–24.

120. *Xizang Tongji Nianjian 2000* (Beijing: Zhongguo Tongji Chubanshe, 2001): 33.

121. Sheng Lijun, *China's Dilemma: The Taiwan Issue* (2001): 45.

122. "Tibet Secretary Addresses Tibet Party Congress on Economy," Xinhua, Sept. 10, 2001, in BBC/M, Dec. 17, 2001; "Personnel-Aid Scheme for Tibet to Continue," Xinhua, Sept. 30, 2003. The PRC government has stated that from 1994–2004 "well over 2,000 cadres" had been selected to serve in Tibet and that "about 1,900 officials and experts from some 17 provinces and municipalities and 59 ministries" were sent to Tibet. "China Spares No Efforts Promoting Tibet Development: White Paper," Xinhua, May 23, 2004; "State Aid Promotes Tibet's Development," Xinhua, Apr. 13, 2006. Of these, 1,268 came during the 10th Five Year Plan (2001–2005). Zheng Qingdong and Kang Shouyong, "Common Target," http://info.tibet.cn/en/newfeature/witness/vicissitudes/t200050428_2680 6.htm.

123. Wang Lixiong 1998: 32.

124. *Zhongguo Xizang Dangshi Da Shiji* [Great Events in the History of the Chinese Communist Party in Tibet] (1995):212.

125. "Chinese Officials Prepare 2000 Census of World's Most Populous Nation," AFP, Oct. 13, 2000; "Tibetan Population grows by 19 percent in 10 Years," *Xinhua*, Mar. 30, 2001.

126. Dawa Norbu, *China's Tibet Policy* (Richmond, UK: Curzon Press, 2001): 391.

127. Banister 2001: 289.

128. Loretta Tofani, "Tibetans Under Chinese Rule," in William Dudley (ed.), *Genocide* (2001): 151 ("China offers economic incentives for working-class Chinese to emigrate to Tibet.")

129. Peter Hessler, "Tibet Through Chinese Eyes," *Atlantic Monthly*, Feb. 1999, http://www.theatlantic.com/issues/99/feb/tibet.htm; "Tibet Leader Legqog on Assistance from Chinese Regions," *Ta Kung Pao* (Hong Kong), Aug. 10, 2001 in BBC/SWB, Aug. 13, 2001.

130. Wang Shuxin, "Xizang Lhasa Shi Liudong Renkou He Shehui Jingji Fazhan" [*Lhasa City, Tibet's Floating Population and Social and Economic Development,*] *Renkou Yu Jingji* no. 6 (1998): 3–9.

131. Some 64.2% of a 1997 sample of 137 households of Han migrants to Lhasa
      were peasants or herders before migrating, but 73.7% migrated to Tibet to
      work in commerce. Those with a junior middle school and primary edu-
      cation were 51.8% and 27% of the Han sample. Among 162 non-Han
      (overwhelmingly Tibetan) migrated-to-Lhasa households sampled, 79%
      had been peasants or herders. Only 37% worked in commerce in Lhasa and
      those with a primary education or no education were 42.6% and 43.8%.
      Robyn Iredale, et al., *Contemporary Minority Migration, Education and
      Ethnicity in China* (Cheltenham: Edward Elgar, 2001):156–160; interviews
      with Tibetan cadres, in Lhasa (July 2000).
132. Banister 2001: 292.
133. Iredale 2001: 157–158.
134. Graham Clarke, "The Movement of Population to the West of China:
      Tibet and Qinghai," in Judith Brown and Rosemary Foot (eds.), *Migration:
      The Asian Experience* (1994)::246–247; Graham Clarke, "Some Statistical
      and Other Issues in Migration to Tibet and Qinghai," Paper presented at
      the Oxford Workshop on Chinese Migration (July 3–7, 1996). It is a com-
      mon practice for Han in Tibet to have their children raised in their home
      area by grandparents. Yue Gang, "Echoes from the Himalayas: the Quest
      of Ma Lihua, a Chinese Intellectual in Tibet," *Journal of Contemporary China*
      13:38 (2004): 69–88.
135. "Chinese Flock to Tibet Seeking Fortunes," Reuters, July 5, 1999.
136. Hu Xiaojiang and Miguel Salazar, "Dynamic Change of Migrant
      Networks: How Migrant Networks Change Under Changing
      Environment," Paper presented at the Summer Institute on International
      Migration, UC Irvine, June 2005: 5.
137. "Qinghai: Developing Status," *China Economic Review*, Mar. 13, 2001. The
      lack by most Han of an intent to settle permanently in Tibetan areas distin-
      guishes Tibet from areas under alien occupation, like the West Bank. Han
      in Tibet also receive no privileges in law; Tibetans instead benefit from
      some preferential policies. For example, where Tibetans are qualified for
      construction work, they are to be given priority over others. "Statement of
      Arthur Holcombe, President, Tibet Poverty Alleviation Fund," *Ethnic
      Minorities in China: Tibetans and Uighurs: Roundtable Before the Congressional-
      Executive Commission on China* (Washington: GPO, 2002): 10; interview
      with an official of the United Front Work Department, Beijing, Dec. 12,
      2004. In contrast, in the West Bank, for Jewish settlers, there is "a vast net-
      work of special roads labeled for 'settlers only'. . . along with an enormous
      water and electrical power infrastructure. Tel Aviv also subsidizes the
      220,000 settlers (plus the 200,000 in East Jerusalem). Mortgage rates in the
      occupied territories are one quarter of those in Israel, education is subsi-
      dized, and settlers receive a 10% break on their income taxes plus a 7% dis-
      count on their social security." Conn Hallinan, " 'Coin of Empire' Too
      Costly for Israelis, Palestinians, and the U.S. Taxpayers," *Foreign Policy in
      Focus*, Mar. 7, 2003, www.fpif.org/ commentary/2003/0307coin.html.

138. In the late 1980s and early 1990s, Tibetan émigré leaders already claimed two million "Chinese" were in the TAR, compared to 1.8–1.9 million Tibetans, and that "Chinese" outnumbered Tibetans in Lhasa by ten to one. "Dalai Lama Cautious about Tibetan Independence," Japan Economic Newswire [JEN], Oct. 15, 1987; Yojana Sharma, "China: Dalai Lama Presence at Rights Meet will Anger China," IPS, May 7, 1993. Even after several more years of alleged "ethnic swamping," however, a U.S. journalist could say of Lhasa that "claims by Tibetan exiles that Chinese are now in [the] majority appear to be overstated." Dele Olojede, "Tibet Slowly Succumbs to Beijing's Influence," *Newsday*, Nov. 7, 1999: A7. Far-fetched claims by émigré leaders continue however, e.g., that China's "Great Opening of the West" (*Xibu da kaifa*) program is in Tibet designed to solve China's unemployment problem. See "Statement by Mr. Pema Jungney, the Chairman of the Assembly of Tibetan People's Deputies (Tibetan Parliament-in-Exile) to the World Parliamentary Forum," WTN, Jan. 22, 2004. Because 15 million new jobs must be created in China each year to avoid increasing the jobless rate, migration to the Tibetan areas, where only about 1.5 million Han live, could hardly make a significant difference.

139. "[T]he 2000 census went to great lengths to record temporary residents and represents the most accurate portrait of effective provincial population since the beginning of the reform period." Andrew Fischer, "Urban Fault Lines in Shangri-La: Population and Economic Foundations of Inter-Ethnic Conflict in the Tibetan Areas of Western China" Crisis States Programme Working Paper no. 1 (London: Development Studies Institute, 2004): 9.

140. Barry Sautman, " 'Demographic Aggression' and Tibet," (2004); unpublished ms. under submission; "Tibet's Resident Population Reaches 2.76 Million," Xinhua, Mar. 21, 2006. Census takers in 2000 also did not count among the TAR population those Tibetans not in Tibet at census time. Tens of thousands of Tibetans are now studying or working in China proper. "Official says Ethnic Chinese still Minority in Tibet," Xinhua 4 Sept. 2002, in BBC/WM Sept.5, 2002.

141. DIIR, *Survival under Surveillance: A Brief Overview of the Human Rights Situation in Tibet, 1994–1995*, http://www.subliminal.org/tibet/exile/ striving95/survival-a.html.

142. Dalai Lama, "March 10 Statement 1995," in Shiromany 1998:445–453.

143. Some 55 percent of Han with *hukou* in Tibet in the late 1990s lived in Lhasa Prefecture. Wang Lixiong 1998: 28. In 2000, half the Han in the TAR for six months or more lived in Lhasa. *2000 Nian Renkou Pucha: Zhongguo Minzu Renkou Ziliao* [2000NRKPCZGMZRKZL][2000 Population Census: China Ethnic Population Data] (Beijing: Minzu Chubanshe, 2003): 632.

144. Some 81.1 percent of the TAR population lived in rural areas in 2000. Xizang Zizhi Qu Tonji Ju, "Guanyu Xizang di wu ci quan guo renkou pucha zhuyao shuju gongbao" [A Public Report on the Main Statistics from the Fifth National Census in Tibet], *Xizang Ribao* [*XZRB*](Tibet),

Mar. 30, 2001: 1. The 2005 one percent sample census put the rural population at 73.35 percent of the total. Xinhua, March 21, 2006. Rural areas have few short-term migrants; cities have many. The rural proportion of long-term residents is thus higher—85 percent or more.

145. Fischer 2004: 11.

146. Clarke 1996: 9.

147. "Non-Violent Movement the Only Option—Samdhong Rinpoche," in WTN, Feb. 14, 2002.

148. See "That Tightrope Called Tibet," *IE*, Aug. 21, 2003.

149. John Cooley, *Unholy Wars: Afghanistan, America, and International Terrorism* (London: Pluto Press, 2000): 235.

150. "Statement of his Holiness the Dalai Lama," Aug. 7, 2001, WTN, Aug. 8, 2001, http://www.tibet .ca/wtnarchive/2001/8/8_1.html. Émigré leaders strongly supported Indian state policy under the BJP. The Dalai Lama's one sharp criticism of the United States has concerned India's interests: he has said that the "US attitude towards Pakistan is a disgrace." "On Record" 2001:12. He has also said "the world could learn from the long experience of India where many faiths and traditions lived side by side for centuries." "His Holiness the Dalai Lama in Rome," WTN, June 6, 2004 and joined the VHP and other militant anti-Islamic organizations in India in a statement deploring missionary efforts by Muslims and Christians. Muqtedar Khan, "Dalai Lama Condemns Islamic and Christian Practice of Conversions," www.beliefnet.com/story/64/story_6448_1.html. The TGIE has said it hopes the twenty-first century will be an Indian century. "Kashag's Letter to Prime Minister Manmohan Singh [May 22, 2004]," TibetNet, May 25, 2004, www.phayul.com/news/article.aspx?id = 6966.

151. H. Norber-Hodge, *Ancient Futures: Learning from Ladakh* (London: Rider, 1991) (large-scale migration of Muslim Indians to Ladakh).

152. John Pomfret, "A Less Tibetan Tibet: Many Residents Fear Chinese Migration will Dilute Culture," *WP*, Oct. 31, 1999:A31.

153. On alien occupation, see *Protocol Additional to the Geneva Convention of 12 Aug. 1949 and Relating to the Protection of Victims of Non-International Armed Conflicts*, adopted June 8, 1977, 1125 U.N.T.S. 609. It is established in law through recognition by the UN, as in the West Bank and Gaza case. G.A. Res. 3236, U.N. GAOR, 29th Sess., Supp. No. 31, At 4, U.N. Doc. A/9631 (1974). Alien occupation is a special case of colonialism. Anwar Frangi, "The Internationalized Noninternational Armed Conflict in Lebanon, 1975–1990: Introduction to Confligology," *Capital University Law Review* 22 (1993): 990. A regional organization may validate a claim of alien occupation. L.C. Green, "Strengthening Legal Protection in Internal Conflicts: Low-Intensity Conflict and the Law," *ILSA Journal of International and Comparative Law* 3 (1997): 504. Neither the UN nor a regional organization have judged Tibet to be under alien occupation or colonial domination; all states recognize it is part of China. "Final Report of the Special Rapporteur, Mr. Al-Khasawneh," U.N. ESCOR, Commission on Human Rights, Subcommission on Prevention of

Discrimination and Protection of Minorities, *Freedom of Movement, Human Rights, and Population Transfer*, 49th Sess., U.N. Doc. E/CN.4/Sub. 2/1997/23 (1997). Tibetan émigré leaders nevertheless continue to claim Tibetans are "people under occupation and foreign domination." "Speaker of Tibetan Parliament Attends Parliamentary Meeting," WTN, Jan. 19, 2004.

154. *Report of the International Law Commission on the Work of its 43rd Session*, U.N. GAOR, 46th Sess., Supp. No. 10, At 250, U.N. Doc. A/46/10 (1992) (banning population transfer if connected with wartime occupation or colonialism); Alfred De Zayas, "Forced Resettlement," in Rudolf Bernhardt (ed.), *Encyclopedia of Public International Law* 2 (1992): 422 (connecting forced resettlement, but not settler infusion, to genocide).

155. Claire Palley, "Population Transfers," in Donna Gomien (ed.), *Broadening the Frontiers of Human Rights: Essays in Honour of Asbjorn Eide* (Oslo: Scandanavian University Press, 1993): 231.

156. "Mclaughlin's One on One: Interview with the Dalai Lama," FNS, Apr. 19, 1991.

157. Palley, 1993: 240–241; Joanne Skolnick, "Grappling with the Legacy of Soviet Rule: Citizenship and Human Rights in the Baltic States," *University of Toronto Faculty Law Review* 54 (1996): 410–411.

158. Marc Holzapfel, "The Implications of Human Rights Abuses Currently Occurring in the Baltic States against the Ethnic Russian National Minority," *Buffalo Journal of International Law* 2 (1995): 345; Andrea Hanneman, "Independence and Group Rights in the Baltics: A Double Minority Problem," *Virginia Journal of International Law* 35 (1995): 493.

159. The London Office of Tibet head in the mid-1980s wrote that in Tibet killings had occurred on a scale comparable to that of the Khmer Rouge in Cambodia (more than a fourth of the population) and that population reduction in one Tibetan prefecture was 95 percent and "typical." No documentary support is provided for these claims however. Phuntsog Wangyal, "Tibet: a Case of Eradication of Religion Leading to Genocide," in Israel Charny (ed.), *Toward the Understanding and Prevention of Genocide* (Boulder, CO: Westview Press, 1984): 119–128.

160. "US Congresswoman Nancy Pelosi Statement on the 46th Anniversary of Tibetan National Uprising Day Rally," WTN, Mar. 14, 2005; D. Henderson, "Does China Execute 10,000 people a Year?" *Herald* (Glasgow), Oct. 12, 2004: 7; L. Scrivener, "Tibetans Find a Haven in Parkdale," *TS*, Feb. 22, 2004; "Jigme Phuntsok," *Times* (London), Jan. 12, 2004: 24; D. Thomson, "From Tibet, a 'Cry' to Melt the Heart," *WP*, Dec. 12, 2003:T49. There have been higher claims still. See, e.g., Jean-Francois Revel, "Disappointment of Post-Colonialism," *Society* (May/June 1990): 79–81 ("genocide in Tibet . . . has eliminated half the Tibetan population.")

161. Patrick French, *Tibet, Tibet: A Personal History of a Lost Land* (Hammersmith: Harper Collins, 2003): 288–292. The Dalai Lama acknowledged, in a 1998 interview with a Chinese dissidents' jounal in the US, the unreliability of the data on which the 1.2 million claim is based. Moli, "Dalai Lama fang tanlu"

[Dalai Lama drops by for an interview], *Zhongguo zhi chun* (China Spring) no. 60 (May):33-ff., http://bjzc.org/bjs/bc/60/33. The émigré leadership however has not repudiated the 1.2 million figure.

162. Barry Sautman, " 'Demographic Annihilation' and Tibet,' " in Barry Sautman and June Dreyer (eds.), *Contemporary Tibet:Politics, Development & Society in a Disputed Region* (Armonk, NY: ME Sharpe, 2005); Barry Sautman, "Is Tibet China's Colony?: The Claim of Demographic Catastrophe," *Columbia Journal of Asian Law* 15(2001): 81; Yan Hao, "Tibetan Population in China: Myths and Facts Re-Examined," *Asian Ethnicity* 1:1 (2000): 11.

163. *Zhongguo Minzu Tongji Nianjian* [China Ethnic Statistics Yearbook] (Zhongguo Tongji Chubanshe, 2000): 431.

164. *Zhongguo Renkou Tongji Nianjian 2000* [China Population Statistics Yearbook] (Beijing: Zhongguo Tongji Chubanshe, 2001): 473.

165. Barbara Erickson, *Tibet: Abode of the Gods, Pearl of the Motherland* (Berkeley: Pacific View Press, 1997): 194.

166. Genocide Convention 1948: Art. II(D).

167. William Schabas, *Genocide in International Law* (Cambridge: Cambridge University Press, 2001): 172–75.

168. Paul Ingram, *Tibet: The Facts* (Dharamsala: Tibetan Young Buddhist Association, 1990): 297.

169. Charles Burress, "Berkeley Waves a Flag for Tibetan Freedom—Only U.S. City to Do So," *SanFrancisco Chronicle [SFC]*, Mar. 9, 1996: 11.

170. "Tibet Issue 'Alive and Kicking,' Says Dalai Lama," AP, Sept. 13, 1987; "Hearing of the House International Relations Committee," FNS, May 10, 2006 (remarks of Congressman Christopher Smith).

171. States with high birth rates often find it difficult to maintain living standards. Saudi Arabia's population grew on average 4.4 percent per year, from 7 million in 1981 to 18 million in 2002. David Ottaway, "After Sept. 11, Severe Tests Loom for Relationship," *WP*, Feb. 12, 2002:A1. Incomes fell from over $28,000 per capita in 1981 (in current dollars) to below $8,000 in 2002. Elaine Sciolino, "Bored Saudi Youth Take Wild Side to the Street," *NYT*, Feb. 20, 2002: A6. While directly due to a drop in oil prices, the fall was facilitated by families averaging 6–7 children. "The Economy," *NYT*, June 23, 1981: 1; "Price Trough Endangers Saudi Arabian Economy," *Houston Chronicle*, Nov. 21, 1981:2. On the complex of motives and instruments of PRC family planning, see Gary Sigley, "Liberal Despotism: Population Planning, Subjectivity, and Government in Contemporary China," *Alternatives* 29 (2004): 557–575.

172. M. Grovanna Merlis and Herbert Smith, "Has the Chinese Family Planning Policy been Successful in Changing Fertility Preferences," *Demography* 39(2002): 577.

173. Nancy Riley, "China's Population: New Trends and Challenges," *Population Bulletin* 59:2 (2004): 36.

174. Li Tao, "Tibetan Rural Urbanization and the Desakota Model," *Perspectives* 6:1 (2005):8–25.

175. *Guanyu Xizang Zhizhiqu De Renkou Yu Jihua Shengyu Gongzuo* [On the Tibet Autonomous Region and Family Planning Work] (Lhasa: Mimeographed, 1998).

176. Zhang Tianlu, *Population Development in Tibet and Related Issues* (1997):70. See also Boris Cambreleng, "China plans to build railroad to Tibet," *G & M*, Aug. 16, 2002 (Tibetan party secretary of Nagqu prefecture notes population of prefecture grew from 200,000 in 1990 to 370,000 in 2000, with 90 percent of the population involved in herding, leading to overgrazing.)

177. Gisela Bock, "Racism and Sexism in Nazi Germany: Motherhood, Compulsory Sterilization, and the State," in Carol Rittner and John Roth (eds.), *Different Voices: Women and the Holocaust* (New York Paragon House, 1993): 166.

178. "Prepared Statement of Julia V. Taft before the House International Relations Committee," 105th Cong. (1999), FNS ("Tibetans receive preferential treatment along with fifty-four other minority ethnic groups, in marriage and family planning policies."); TIN, *Survey of Birth Control Policies in Tibet* (1994): 12 ("Chinese who work in the Tibet Autonomous Region face much stricter limits than Tibetans on family size.")

179. *Guanyu Xizang Zizhiqu de renkou yu jihua shengyu gongzuo* [On the Tibet Autonomous Region and Family Planning Work] (Lhasa: TAR government, mimeographed, s.d., circa 1998); "Tibet Provisional Procedures for Birth-Planning Management (For Trial Use)," *China Sociology & Anthropology* 32 (Tibet birth-planning document no. 6/1992): 82 [also in Xu Xifa (ed.), *Zhonguo Shuoshu Minzu Jihua Shengyu Gailun* [Outline of Birth Planning Among China's National Minorities] (Urumugi: Xinjiang Renmi Chubanshc 1995): 230.

180. *Tibet Provisional Procedures* 1992; Yan Hao, 2000: 11–20. Urban officials, factory workers, and military personnel are limited to two children. However, there is no serious attempt to enforce birth control among Tibetan farmers and herdsmen. Ibid., 27–28. Melvyn Goldstein and Cynthia Bell, *China's Birth Control Policy in the Tibet Autonomous Region, Asian Survey* 31 (1991): 294 (urban Tibetans not employed by state limited to two children); "New Generation of Tibetans Prefer Fewer Children," Xinhua, Sept. 4, 2001 (more than 60 percent of urban Tibetan choose to have only one child).

181. For examples of coercive birth control tactics in Han areas in the 1980s and 1990s, see Thomas Scharping, *Birth Control in China 1949–2000: Population Policy and Demographic Development* (2003); John Aird, *Slaughter of the Innocents: Coercive Birth Control in China* (1990).

182. TIN no. 29: *Reports from Tibet, 2000* (2001): 56, http://www.tibetinfo. co.uk/publications/news-reviews/nra29.htm.

183. Isabelle Attane, "Integration of Ethnic Minorities in China: Demographic Perspectives from the 2000 Population Census" (unpublished paper, s.d.): 21.

The TFR for the whole world in 2004 was 2.69; in 1970 it had been 4.48. Phillip Longman, "Everywhere, Even in Africa, the World is Running Out of Children," *New Statesman*, May 31, 2004: 27–28.

184. Melvyn Goldstein et al., "Fertility and Family Planning in Rural Tibet," *China Journal* no. 47(2000): 31.

185. Geoff Childs, et al., "Tibetan Fertility Transitions in China and South Asia," *Population and Development Review* 31:2 (2005): 337–351.

186. Erickson 1997: 195–196.

187. David Murphy, "Mother and Child: A New Study Disputes Charges by Tibetan Activists of Forced Abortions and Sterilizations by Authorities," *FEER*, Dec. 27, 2001: 35.

188. In 1990, as well as 2000, 86.7 percent of PRC Tibetans were from the agricultural workforce, though some were rural-to-urban migrants. In 1990, 7.1 percent of PRC Tibetans were urban residents, rising to 12.8 percent in 2000. Attane: 21–22. Percentages who work in agriculture likely remained the same over the decade because of much higher rural birth rates. It was planned that 15,000–25,000 rural Tibetans move to urban areas during each year of the 10th Five-Year Plan (2001–2005). TIN, "Lhasa Prefecture Encourages Rural Migration for 'Building a Middle-Class Society,'" *TIN News Update*, in *WTN*, Sept. 2, 2003. See also Kate Saunders, "Training for Tibetans to Compete in Chinese-dominated Job Market," Free Tibet Campaign, Dec. 2003, www.freetibet.org/press/specialreport 121203.html. This was to be facilitated by reforming household registration and upgrading some prefectures and counties to municipal status. Cooke 2003.

189. Samten Karmay, *The Arrow and the Spindle: Studies in History, Myths, Rituals and Beliefs in Tibet* (Kathmandu, Nepal: Mandala Book Point, 1998): 528.

190. Sun Jiangxin, *Zhongguo Zangzu Renkou* [China's Tibetan Population] (1994): 147.

191. Liu Yongsheng, *International Hunting and the Involvement of Local People, Dulan, Qinghai, People's Republic of China* (unpublished M.S. Thesis, University of Montana, 1993): 19.

192. Martin Moss and Jeffrey Bowe, *Orders of the State: Responsibility and Collaboration in China's Population Programme* (London: Independent Tibet Network UK, s.d. 2000).

193. "Tibetans Seek Family Planning," *China Daily* [CD], June 29, 1999; "Family Planning not Mandatory in Tibet," Xinhua, May 24, 2001.

194. Jayanti Alam, *Tibetan Society in Exile* (Delhi: Raj Publications, 2000):170. The birth rate in the émigré community in India in around 2000 was 16.8 per 1,000 and in decline. Shushum Bhatia et al., "A Social and Demographic Study of Tibetan refugees in India," *Social Science & Medicine* 54 (2002): 411. That compares with a birth rate among TAR Tibetans in 1995 of 16.1 per thousand. "Young Tibetans have new Concept on Marriage," Xinhua, Jan. 15, 2002. Between 1880 and 1940, even in the absence of most contraceptives now available, the average fertility rate of US Whites dropped from 4.4 children per woman to 2.1, and among

blacks from 7.5 children to 3. Barbara Seaman, "The Secret History of Sex," *The Nation*, June 11, 2001: 36.

195. Clara Li, "Beijing Relaxes One-Child Policy," *SCMP*, June 28, 2001: 1.

196. "Fewer, Healthier Births Valued in Tibet," Xinhua, March 22, 2001.

197. The last instance in which the Dalai Lama mentioned "genocide" per se in Tibet may have been his "March 10 Statement 1987," in Shiromany 1998: 419.

198. Angus McDonald, "Love Across the Divide," *SCMP*, Aug. 30, 2003: A5 (quoting Samdhong Rinpoche as stating "Inside Tibet there is genocide, there is enforced birth control and enforced intermarriage. So to protect a pure Tibetan race is also one of the challenges which the nation is facing"). On "genocide in Tibet," see also Maura Moynihan, "Genocide in Tibet," *WP*, Jan. 25, 1998: C7; "Giving Permanent Normal Trade Relations to China," Senate Committee on Foreign Relations, 105th Cong. (2000), in FNS, July 16, 2000; John Crace, "Forbidden Territory: The Dalai Lama has been in Exile for Forty Years," *Guardian* Mar. 9, 1999: 10; "God-King in Quest of a Lost Kingdom," *Sunday Times*, May 9, 1999: 17. U.S. Sen. Daniel Patrick Moynihan once referred to Tibetans as an "endangered species," 143 Cong. Rec. 58380 (July 30, 1997).

199. "Dalai Lama, Interview to '*The Times of India*,' " in Shiromany 1998: 201.

200. "Tibetan Dalai Lama has Audience with Pope," UPI, June 1, 1990; "Dalai Lama Asks Japan for Action," *Asahi*, Apr. 15, 1994, http://www.tibet.ca/wtnarchive/1994/4/17_1.html.

201. Pico Iyer, "Over Tea with the Dalai Lama," *Shambhala Sun*, Nov. 2001, www.shambhalasun. com/archives/features/2001/nov01/iyer.htm; "Dalai Lama Rails Against PRC Treatment of Tibetans," *China Post*, Apr. 3, 2001.

202. "China Must End Cultural Genocide," *TI*, Dec. 19, 2001.

203. Dalai Lama, "Statement of his Holiness the Dalai Lama on the Occasion of the 41st Anniversary of the Tibetan National Uprising (March 10, 2000)," at http://www.buddhapia.com/tibet/March10.html.

204. Dalai Lama, "Speech of his Holiness the Dalai Lama to the European Parliament (Oct. 24, 2001)," http://www.tibet.ca/english/index.html; Dalai Lama, "Statement of his Holiness the Dalai Lama on the 39th Anniversary of Tibetan National Uprising Day (March 10, 1998)," http://www.tibet.com/dl/10mar98.html; "Dalai Lama Accuses China of 'Cultural Genocide,' " AFP, March 9, 1998.

205. "China's Propaganda War on Tibet gets Cultural," AFP, June 29, 1999.

206. "Dalai Lama Supports Europe's 'Critical Dialogue' with China," AFP, May 13, 1996.

207. "Dalai Lama Meets Top French Officials," AFP, June 17, 1998.

208. Richard Ehrlich, "Taiwanese Spies, Reborn Mao Worry Tibet's Spiritual Leader," *TS*, Sept. 13, 1992:F3; Dalai Lama, "March 10 Statement 1993," in Shiromany 1998:439; Dalai Lama, "Dalai Lama Says in Internet Interview that he Dreams of Return to Tibet," in AP, February 23, 2000; "Dalai Lama Hopeful about Hong Kong, Despondent about Tibet," AFP, June 4, 1997.

209. "Rail link 'Cultural Genocide,' " AP, Sept. 12, 2005. It's AP
210. ICJ, *Tibet,: Human Rights and the Rule of Law* (1997): 352–354. See also the Australian Broadcasting Company [ABC] interview, "Dalai Lama Offers Compromise Over Tibet," May 22, 2002. www.abc.net.au/ra/asiapac/ features/AsiaPacFeautres_561611.htm (Dalai Lama says main aspects of "cultural degeneration" in Tibet is Chinese majority in Lhasa, which results in changing language, food, and singing among Tibetans.)
211. Monisha Das Gupta, "What is Indian about You?: A Gendered Transitional Approach to Ethnicity," *Gender & Society* 11(1997): 580.
212. On museumization, see Sharon Stephens, "The 'Cultural Fallout' of Chernobyl Radiation in Norwegian Sami Regions: Implications for Children," in S. Stephens (ed.), *Children and the Politics of Culture* (Princeton: Princeton University Press, 1995): 303.
213. *The Olive Tree* (New York: Harper & Bros., 1937): 101.
214. Robert Hitchcock and Tara Twedt, "Physical and Cultural Genocide of Various Indigenous Peoples," in Samuel Totten (ed.), *Century Of Genocide: Eyewitness Accounts and Critical Views* (New York: Garland, 1997): 373; Lonza Pagans, *Return of the White Buffalo: A Heuristic Study of Native American People Transcending Cultural Genocide* (unpublished PhD dissertation, Union Institute, 2000); C. Michael-Titus, *In Search of "Cultural Genocide"* (Upminster: Panopticum Press, 1976).
215. "Dalai Lama considers Taiwan visit: Tibetan Leader Tells Clinton that Occupation of Lhasa by Chinese is Equivalent to Cultural Genocide," *SCMP*, June 22, 2000; Geoffrey Varley, "Dalai Lama has 'Private' meeting with Mitterand," AFP, Nov. 16, 1993.
216. "Dalai Lama Denounces Chinese Efforts at 'Cultural Genocide' in Tibet," AFP, May 17, 1993.
217. "Dalai Lama Calls for Talks, Urges China to Stop Cultural Genocide," AFP, Nov. 28, 1996.
218. The émigrés have termed "population transfer" the "indirect means of attempting to change and control the nature of Tibetan culture and identity." TCHRD, "Impoverishing Tibetans," http://tchrd.org/pubs/impoverishing/ 3_economic.shtml#A_marginalisation [hereinafter *Impoverishing Tibetans*].
219. "Senior French Minister sees Dalai Lama despite Beijing's Warning," AFP, Oct. 29, 1996.
220. Ehrlich 1992 (Dalai Lama says "The Tibetan lanaguage is becoming a useless language in our own country because most urban shops in Tibet are Chinese").
221. Don Lattin, "Dalai Lama Speaks at Berkeley," *SFC*, June 13, 1997: A23.
222. D. Sharma, "Dalai Lama, I Pray for Change of Guard in China," *Jerusalem Post* [*JP*], Sept. 16, 1992: 1.
223. Diego Ribadeneira, "In Boston, Dalai Lama seeks support for Tibet Independence," *BG*, Sept. 19, 1995: 28. An International Campaign for Tibet spokesman has stated that "[Y]ou cannot practice Buddhism as a

dogma inside Tibet." "Jiang: China has Freedom of Religion," AP, Feb. 21, 2002.

224. See, e.g., Editorial, "The Distance Between Tibet and Quebec," *G&M*, Apr. 15, 2004, in which it is asserted that Tibetan Buddhism has been "outlawed" in Tibet.

225. Rod Micklburgh, "Tibet: in the Crosshairs and at a Crossroads," *G&M*, Oct. 23, 2004 (quoting Robert Barnett of Columbia University).

226. Elliot Sperling, "Ethnic Minorities in China," *Roundtable Before the Congressional Executive Commission on China*, June 10, 2002: 18–19.http://cecc.gov/pages/roundtables/061002/sperlingStatement.php

227. "Testimony of Gretchen Birkle, Acting Principal Deputy Asssistant Secretary, Bureau of Democracy, Human Rights and Labor, Department of State, Before the House Committee on International Relations . . . July 21, 2005,http://wwwc.house.gov/international_relations/109/bir072105.pdf

228. "China Invites Human Rights Delegation," AAP, Oct. 21, 2004, in WTN, Oct. 21, 2004.

229. In Tibet, there was a "combination of the religious and worldly" (*chos-srid-gynyis-idan*). It is still upheld by TGIE officials. Rebecca French, "A Conversation with Tibetans? Reconsidering the Relationship between Religious Beliefs and Secular Legal Discourse," *Law & Social Inquiry* 26 (2001): 99–102; Gray Tuttle, "Uniting Religion and Politics in a Bid for Autonomy: Lamas in Exile in China and America," in Linda Learman (ed.), *Buddhist Missionaries in the Era of Globalization* (Honolulu: University of Hawaii Press, 2005): 210–224. Religious figures are reserved ten of the forty-six seats in the exile parliament, a body that "oppose[s] negotiations with Beijing on any basis except independence for [the] homeland." Tibetan Parliamentary and Policy Research Centre, *Tibet's Parliament in Exile* (New Delhi: Friedrich Naumann Foundation, 1996). The Dalai Lama is "head of state." Samdhong Rinpoche, an incarnate lama (*tulku*), is "head of government" and "monks also feature in both the government executive and various departments" of the TGIE. Gyatso, 2004: 239. The Tibetan exile constitution endorses basing government on the dharma and the TGIE offers courses on Buddhism. Singh, 2005.

230. K. Sharma, "Call to Preserve Tibetan Culture," *The Hindu*, March 13, 2000; P. Chauhan, "Staunch Muslims, Tibetans at Heart," Tribune News Service (TNS)(India), Dec. 5, 2000, in WTN, Dec. 6, 2000. TAR Party Secretary Chen Kuiyuan also argued it is "utterly absurd" to equate Tibetan culture and Buddhism because the former preceded the latter's introduction into Tibet. "Tibet Party Secretary Criticizes 'Erroneous Views' of Literature, Art," *XZRB*, July 16, 1997:4 in BBC/SWB, Aug. 5, 1997. Although the Dalai Lama believes one can be Tibetan without being Buddhist, it is not clear whether he allows that one can be fully Buddhist without being a Tibetan Buddhist. See "Man, Monk and Then Leader,"

Budapest Sun, Oct. 25, 2000, in WTN, Oct. 26, 2000 (Dalai Lama states that "Tibetan is the only living language through which you can fully appreciate Buddhism.")

231. "Refugees Forced to Convert to Buddhism," *BP*, July 19, 1997: 3.

232. Vahakn N. Dadarian, "Genocide as a Problem of National and International Law: the World War I Armenian Case and its Contemporary Legal Ramifications," *Yale Journal of International Law* 14 (1989): 221; Steven Katz, "The Uniqueness of the Holocaust: The Historical Dimension," in Alan Rosenbaum (ed.), *Is the Holocaust Unique? Perspectives on Comparative Genocide* (Boulder: Westview Press, 1996): 34–35.

233. Yervant Azadian, *The Impact of the Holocaust on Armenian Culture: Armenian Cultural Losses During the Genocide* (New York: Diocese of the Armenian Church of American, 1982).

234. Jonathan Steinberg, "Types of Genocide? Croatians, Serbs and Jews, 1941–1945," in David Cesarani (ed.), *The Final Solution: Origins and Implementation* (London: Routledge, 1994): 180; Marcus Tanner, *Croatia: A Nation Forged in War* (New Have: Yale, 1999): 152.

235. Steinberg 1994: 175–93; Tanner 1997: 151–159.

236. "Gyaincain Norbu Stresses Tibetan Autonomous Laws, Religious Freedoms, Economic Development," (Central People's Broadcasting Station, Beijing, Oct. 30, 1994), in BBC/SWB, Nov. 21, 1994.

237. Erik Eckholm, "China Wins the Wallets of Tibetans, but Hearts are still Slow to Follow," *NYT*, Dec. 1, 2001: A8. Nonreligious Tibetans tend nevertheless to have high Tibetan ethnic consciousness, appreciate secular Tibetan culture, and promote prosperity for the region. Interviews with middle class Lhasa Tibetans, 2000–2003.

238. See remarks of ex-TAR Party Secretary Chen Kuiyuan "Communist Party Paper on Need to Clean up Tibetans Spiritually and Literally," *XZRB*, Nov. 5, 1996:3, BBC/SWB, Nov. 22, 1996; "Regional Party Leader: 'Narrow Nationalism' Creating 'Ideological Chaos,' " *XZRB*, Nov. 12, 1996, BBC/SWB, Nov. 27, 1996. See also Lynne O'Donnell, "Picking the Flesh off a Culture," *Australian*, Aug. 21, 2000: 8 (Tibetan businessman states "monks are contributing nothing to our economic development, they are holding us back in poverty").

239. "Tibet Leader says Dalai Lama 'Biggest Obstacle' to Economic Development," *Ta Kung Pao* (Hong Kong), Aug. 10, 2001, BBC/SWB, Aug. 13, 2001; "Police School Condemns Dalai Lama" (Tibet TV, Nov. 2, 2000), BBC/SWB, Nov. 8, 2000.

240. "Vice-Premier in Tibet Stresses Aligning Religion with Socialist Society" Tibet TV, Sept. 9, 2000, BBC/SWB, Sept. 14, 2000.

241. R. Harley, "Realpolitik from the Prince of Shangri-La," *CSM*, Aug. 20, 1981: B14; Sanjoy Hazarika, "Dalai Lama Urges Peaceful Protest against China," *NYT*, Oct. 8, 1987: A8; Yoon, 1999; "Mercy Balm for Terror-Prone," *S (I)*, Sept. 19, 2001; "Dalai Lama Renews Peace Efforts," *BP*,

Apr. 12, 2003; "An Opening for Tibet," *BG*, Sep. 18, 2003: A14. The Dalai Lama has recalled that after he visited China proper in 1954–1955 "I was so attracted to Marxism, I even expressed my wish to become a Communist Party member. Tibet at that time was very, very backward. The ruling class did not seem to care, and there was much inequality. Marxism talked about an equal and just distribution of wealth. I was very much in favor of this. Then there was the concept of self creation. Marxism talked about self-reliance, without depending on a creator or a God. That was very attractive, I still think that if a genuine communist movement had come to Tibet, there would have been much benefit to the people." "Exile his Journey," *Time*, Oct. 4, 1999, 78–79. In a 1969 interview, he said that "The Chinese have introduced many good reforms in Tibet. They are building roads, schools, and factories." Ved Mehta, "The Himalaya: Toward the Land of the Dead," *New Yorker*, July 26, 1969: 40–66. In a letter to Deng Xiaoping in 1981, he stated "I have a liking and belief in the ideology of Communism aiming to improve the lot of human beings and . . . was satisfied with the late Mao Tse-tung over the ideology and policy on nationalities. Had this ideology, with its related policies, been implemented, it would have brought happiness and contentment to all concerned." Quoted in Amar Jasbir Singh, "How the Tibetan Problem Influences China's Foreign Relations," *China Report* 28:3 (1992): 261–289. He has recently averred that the CCP is "too much liberal. Therefore, the Communist Party [is] without a Communist ideology." Charlie Rose Show Transcripts, 2005.

242. The PRC maintains it "has not conducted atheist propaganda in places of worship or among the faithful." *Interim Report by the Special Rapporteur of the Commission on Human Rights on the Elimination of all Forms of Religious Intolerance and of Discrimination Based on Religion or Belief*, 55th Sess., Item 116 (B), ¶ 59, U.N. Doc. A/55/280 (2000). The CCP is no longer wholly negative about religion and now interprets Marx's phrase "religion is the opium of the people" to mean "a medicine that calms, relieves pain, and anesthetizes." Huang Zhu, "An Historical Study of the Chinese Communist Party's Theory and Policy Concerning Religion," *Renmin Ribao*, Nov. 14, 2003, BBC/M, Nov. 25, 2003. Because Buddhists do not recognize a creator or interventionist god, the Dalai Lama has said "From the theistic viewpoint, Buddhists are atheists." N. Collias, "Dalai Lama Speaks up for Prisoners, Non-Believers," *Boise Weekly*, Sept. 21, 2005.

243. TCHRD, *Annual Report 2001: Human Rights Situation in Tibet*, http://www.tchrd.Org/Pubs/2001/ Chapter2.1.html [TCHRD, *Annual Report 2001*].

244. Walter Wisneiwski, "Graham Winds Up Soviet Visit," UPI, May 14, 1982.

245. Janet Domowitz, "Graham Calls Soviet Church 'Free,' " *CSM*, May 14, 1982: 2.

246. The U.S. legal system restricts some religious actions, e.g., the former Mormon practice of polygamy. *Reynolds v. U.S.*, 98 U.S. 145 (1878). The legal system is thus used to change beliefs expressed through religious practices. Phillip Hammond, "Conscience and the Establishment Clause: The Courts Remake the Sacred," *Journal for the Scientific Study of Religion* 35 (1996): 356–367.

247. Different standards of religious freedom exist among Western states. In Germany, for example, the Church of Scientology is under close government scrutiny. Scientologists, protesting this scrutiny, compared it to the Nazis' treatment of Jews. The UN special rapporteur on religious freedom called the comparison "childish." Gerhard Robbers, "Religious Freedom in Germany," *Brigham Young University Law Review* 2001: 662.

248. "The China Syndrome," *Asiaweek*, Oct. 26, 2001: 8.

249. "Dalai Lama's Envoy . . ." 2001. Tibetan émigrés formerly claimed there were 2,300 monasteries in all of "historical Tibet." Harley 1981. There was a wave of dismantling of monasteries and temples after the Lhasa Uprising of 1959. According to Ma Chengyuan, founder of the Shanghai Museum, who was in Qinghai and Central Tibet at the time, "[T]he locals destroyed the temples themselves" and sold artifacts to the Cultural Relics Bureau. Jasper Becker, "Guardian of the Past," *SCMP*, Jan. 3, 2001: 1. The Cultural Revolution destruction of monasteries was largely the work of Tibetan Red Guards. A dissident scholar who conducted extensive interviews among Han and Tibetans who lived in Tibet then found Tibetans were the most extensive and enthusiastic destroyers of monasteries. In Lhasa and other areas under PLA (i.e., Han) control, less damage was done. Wang Lixiong 1998: 314–323; Wang Lixiong, "Cultural Introspection of the Tibet Issue," *China Affairs* 1 (2000): 79. See also Stanley Karnow, *Mao and China: Inside China's Cultural Revolution* (New York: Penguin, 1984): 305 (Beijing and local PLA efforts to restrain and recall Red Guards in Tibet). A Canadian journalist reached the same conclusion based on interviews. Jan Wong, "Life at the Top of the World," *G&M*, Dec. 10, 1994: D1. An anthropologist who studies Labrang Monastery, Gansu, has stated that "Some of the most zealous activists . . . during the Cultural Revolution were young Tibetan women." Charlene Makley, "On the Edge of Respectability: Sexual Politics in China's Tibet," *Positions* 10 (2002): 600. See also Shakya 1999: 376 (Tibetan Red Guards enthusiastically destroyed monasteries). The destruction in Tibet was part of a China-wide anti-religion campaign. In 1949, there were 200,000 Buddhist monasteries and temples in China as a whole; in 1976, there were barely 100; Sun Shuyun, "Buddha's Back," *China Review* no. 27 (2003): 19–20.

250. Abdul Qadir, "Why Peace Eludes Tibet: Photographs Tell Tales of Tibetans' Plight," *TI*, Jan. 19, 2002, in WTN, Jan. 19, 2002. See also Khedroob Thondup, "Tibet's Cause through Tibetan Eyes," *Taipei Times*, Aug. 20, 2005 (Dalai Lama's nephew claims that Tibet has only 70 monasteries and 7,000 monks and nuns.)

251. Michael Lev, "Inside the Kumbum Monastery," *Chicago Tribune*, Dec. 9, 2004; Kent Wiedenmann, "Prepared Testimony before the Senate Foreign Relations Committee Subcommittee on East Asian and Pacific Affairs (Sept. 7, 1995)," FNS.

252. "Address of Mr. Pema Jungney . . . ," WTN, Nov. 22, 2005.

253. Olojede 1999; "Religious Activities," Xinhua, Jan. 24, 1999.

254. Seth Faison, "Buddha vs. Beijing," *NYT*, Nov. 11, 1998: A1.

255. Rena Miller, "Hard Choices," *FEER*, Nov. 26, 1998: 84. See also Steven Marshall and Suzette Cooke, *Tibet Outside the TAR* (CD-ROM) (Hong Kong: Alliance for Research on Tibet, 1997): 1430 (Labrang "almost seethed with animation"); Charlene Makley, "Gendered Boundaries in Motion: Space and Identity on the Sino-Tibetan Frontier," *American Ethnologist* 30:4 (2003): 597–619 (in Labrang, "the vigorous cycles of monastic life contrasted sharply with the stillness of state work units . . .").

256. "Monks, Chinese Police Coexist Uneasily at Tibetan Buddhist Monastery," AP, Dec. 3, 2001.

257. "Living Buddha: Tibetans Enjoy Religious Freedom," *People's Daily*, March 13, 2000: 2, http://english.peopledaily.com.cn/200003/13/eng20000313n102.html .

258. "China Protecting Places of Worship in Tibet," Xinhua, March 25, 1998.

259. "Tibetan Scholar on Religious Freedom in China," Xinhua, Aug. 8, 1997.

260. "Jokhang Monastery to be Better Protected," Xinhua, July 28, 2002.

261. Watts 2005.

262. Bruce Matthews, "Religious Minorities in Myanmar—Hints of the Shadow," *Contemporary South Asia* 4:3 (1995): 287–308; *Civil and Political Rights, Including Religious Intolerance*, U.N. ESCOR, 57th Sess., Agenda Item 11(E): 8 U.N. Doc. E/CN.4/2001/63 (Feb. 13, 2001) (Bhutan bans Christian churches from conducting religious activities); U.S. State Department, "Bhutan: International Religious Freedom Report, 2004," www.state.gov/g/drl/rls/irf/2004/35515.htm; USSD, "Burma: International Religious Freedom Report, 2004," http://www.state.gov/g/drl/rls/irf/2004/35393.htm.

263. Human Rights Watch/Asia, *China: State Control of Religion* (1997): 43–45; Ronald Schwartz, *Circle of Protest: Political Ritual in the Tibetan Uprising* (1994).

264. "NPC Foreign Affairs Committee Issues Statement on Dalai Lama's Speech at EP General Assembly," Xinhua, Oct. 27, 2001; "Tibet Official Says Fight Against 'Dalai Clique' Must Continue," Xinhua, Feb. 16, 2001. Émigré leaders have held that Tibet has always been independent and that a PRC precondition for negotiations–that the Dalai Lama give up "splitist" activities—is not acceptable. "Chinese Offer 'Not Genuine,' " TNS, Feb. 4, 2002, in WTN, Feb. 5, 2002. A distinction is often made between the Dalai Lama's "normal" role as a religious leader and his political role. For example, a young Lhasa Tibetan woman has said "Some people may respect him as a spiritual leader, but we don't want any political trouble

from him." Thepchai Yong, "Lhasa Turns into a China Boom Town," *Nation* (Thailand), June 16, 1999. Conversations with Tibetan cadres and intellectuals indicate many want to see him return as spiritual primate, but not as a political leader.

265. TIN, *Cutting off the Serpent's Head: Tightening Control in Tibet, 1994–1995*, Pt I, § 4 (1996). There is no evidence it is illegal to merely have a picture of the Dalai Lama, but émigré leaders represent that monks are even murdered for that reason. "Tibetans in Indian Town Protest against Execution of Monks," DPA, June 13, 1997.

266. TIN, *A Sea of Bitterness: Patriotic Education in Qinghai Monasteries* (1999) [Hereinafter A Sea of Bitterness]; "Education Improves Lamaseries Administration," Xinhua, June 18, 2001.

267. Melvyn Goldstein, "The Revival of Monastic Life in Drepung Monastery," in Melvyn Goldstein and Matthew Kapstein (eds.), *Buddhism in Contemporary Tibet: Religious Revival and Cultural Identity* (Berkeley: University of California Press, 1998): 49.

268. Miller 1998: 85 (quoting Robert Thurman).

269. "*Dalai Lama is 'Hooligan,'*" Xinhua, July 10, 2000, In BBC/M, July 10, 2000.

270. "Tibetan Eminent Monks Doubt Dalai Lama's Status as a Religious Leader," Xinhua, May 15, 2001.

271. "Reports from Hong Kong Journalists' Tibet Trip," Zhongguo Tongxunshe, BBC/SWB, July 16, 1991.

272. "Rinpoche Seeks Full-fledged Autonomy for Tibet," *The Tribune* [Chandigarh], Sept. 3, 2005 (Samdhong Rinpoche observes that in marking the 40th anniversary of the TAR, "the Chinese government did not accuse the Dalai Lama of anything"); Lodi Gyari, "The Sino-Tibetan Dialogue Process," *TB* 10:2 (Mar.-Apr. 2006):19–24.

273. "Tibetan says Buddhism could help China," UPI, July 18, 2005.

274. TIN, *Relative Freedom? Tibetan Buddhism and Religious Policy in Kandze, Sichuan, 1987–1999* (1999): 98 (local and diachronic differences on display of Dalai Lama photos and sympathy toward religion of Party and State organs).

275. Miller 1998: 84; Laura Newby and Zhang Lijia, "Little Tibet: Even Better than the Real Thing?" *China Review* No. 27 (2003): 27; Patrick Baert, "Tibetans Hold Traditional New Year Celebration in Xiahe," AFP, Feb. 9, 2001 [Baert, *New Year Celebration in Xiahe*]; P.Baert, "Strong Ties to Dalai Lama in Chinese-Dominated 'Greater Tibet,' " AFP, July 29, 1999; "Tibetans Aim to Reclaim Lives," AP, July 11, 1998; "Beijing Easing Up Slightly on Tibet's Buddhist Monasteries," AFP, June 28, 1997.

276. Miller 1998: 84. The author observed large portraits of the Dalai Lama at the Kumbum monastery in Qinghai in 2002. See also Newby and Zhang 2003:27 (photos of Dalai Lama now more common in Labrang monastery monks' rooms than five years ago); Melinda Liu, "Searching for Shangri-La,"

Newsweek, March 26, 2001 (many Dalai Lama photos on public display in Tibetan areas outside TAR). Such photos could be purchased in the TAR until 1994. TIN, "Anti-Dalai Lama Campaign: Sale of Dalai Lama Photos Banned," Oct. 16, 1994.

277. Henry Chu, "In Tibet, Dalai Lama Remains People's Choice," *LAT*, Aug. 28, 1999: A1.

278. James A. Beverley, "Buddhism's Guru," *Christianity Today*, June 11, 2001: 64–72.

279. Yoon 1999.

280. Ethnic minority Buddhist monks outside Tibet have been significantly less constrained than Tibetan monks. Tai Lue monks in southwest Yunnan province, for example, are free to go abroad to study the dharma, to invite senior monks from abroad to their monasteries, and to ordain large number of boy novices. Sara Davis, "China's Contested Ethnic Borders," *FEER* 168:10 (Nov., 2005): 48–52.

281. John Pomfret, "Invitation by Chinese Seen as Sign of 'Thaw' with Tibetan Exiles," *WP*, Sept. 12, 2002 (journalist asserts that since 1993, Beijing's strategy has been to await Dalai Lama's death); Mike Blanchfield, "Hu Defends Human Rights Record," *Ottawa Citizen*, Sept. 10, 2005: A3 (émigré "skeptics" believe PRC leaders "just stalling for time and waiting for the Dalai Lama to die.")

282. Some Tibetan émigré leaders apparently no longer make that assumption. "Tibet Settlement Hopeful in Dalai Lama's Lifetime: Exile Prime Minister," AFP, July 5, 2005 (Samdhong Rinpoche states China now considers the Dalai Lama part of the solution, not part of the problem,) "Dalai Lama's Special Envoy to Speak on China-Tibet Dialogue at National Press Club," WTN, Oct. 29, 2005 (Lodi Gyari states "there is an increasing interest among some Chinese officials and policy-makers in dialogue with the Dalai Lama"); Tashi Ragbey and Tseten Wanchuk Sharlo, *Sino-Tibetan Dialogue in the Post-Mao Era: Lessons and Prospects* (Washington: East-West Center, 2004): 28–29 and fn. 50 (senior Tibetan Communists and military officers in Tibet favor negotiations with Dalai Lama). A Hong Kong newspaper has reported "the decision-making hierarchy of Beijing has begun to accept the following viewpoint: The Dalai Lama is a 'troublemaker' as well as the key to the resolution of the Tibet question," Chi Hsiao-hua, "General Secretary Hu Jintao Wants to Make a Breakthrough on Tibet," *Sing Tao Jih Pao*, Aug. 27, 2003 in World News Connection, Aug. 27, 2003.

283. Patrick Tyler, "Tibet Crisis Centers on 6-Year-Old Living Buddha," *NYT*, Oct. 1, 1995: 10 (Western experts believe Dalai Lama's strategy is to build negotiating position for compromise after Deng's death); Catherine Field, "God-King Sees Hope Amid Tibet's Despair," *Observer*, June 5, 1994: 21 (Dalai Lama states that after Deng's death, "hardline" policy on Tibet "may not last for long.")

284. See Amitabh Pal, "My Visit to the Dalai Lama's Town," *The Progressive* (India), Oct. 26, 2005, in WTN, Oct. 27, 2005 (General Secretary of TYC, speaking of influence of Dalai Lama on thinking of émigré community on violence, states "After him, our thinking may change.")

285. Brent Fulton, "Freedom of Religion in China: The Emerging Civic Discourse," in *Civic Discourse, Civil Society and Chinese Communities* (1999): 53–66; Michael Dillon, *Religious Minorities and China* (London: Minority Rights Group International, 2001): 12–14; Robert Thomson, "Politics and Prayer Meet in Tibet," *Financial Times* [FT], March 3, 1988: 4.

286. "Religious Affairs Official Reviews 'Patriotism Education' to Restore Order in Lamaseries," *XZRB*, Nov. 11, 1997: 2 in BBC/SWB, Dec. 20, 1997.

287. "Changing Life of Lamas in Tibet," Xinhua, March 20, 1979; Solomon Karmel, "Ethnic Tension and the Struggle for Order: China's Policies in Tibet," *Pacific Affairs* 68 (1995): 504. According to a TGIE-affiliated NGO, some DMCs are "relatively independent and relatively democratic." TCHRD, *Annual Report 2000: Enforcing Loyalty* Ch. 2, http://www.tchrd.org/pubs/2000/chapter2.shtml.

288. Steven T. McFarland, Testimony to U.S. Commission on International Religious Freedom before the Committee on International Relations of the United States House of Representatives (May 10, 2001).

289. *Religious Affairs* 1997; "Education Improves Lamaseries' Administration," Xinhua, June 18, 2001; *"Question of the Violation of Human Rights and Fundamental Freedoms: Report of the Sub-Commission under Commission on Human Rights Resolution" 8 (XXIII)*, U.N. ESCOR, 51st Sess., U.N. Doc. E/CN.4/Sub.2/1999/NGO/13 [*Question*].

290. David Germano, "Remembering The Dismembered Body of Tibet: Contemporary Tibetan Visionary Movements in the People's Republic of China," in Goldstein and Kapstein 1998: 56.

291. For a discussion on expulsions and arrests, See *Question* 1999.

292. Erik Eckholm, "Dalai Lama's Envoy Hopeful for China Talks," *NYT*, Sep. 30, 2002: A6.

293. "Chinese President, Premiere Address Tibet Work Meeting in Beijing," Xinhua, June 29, 2001, in, [BBC/M], Aug. 2, 2001.

294. Erik Eckholm, "China's Upbeat Governor in Tibet Promises Investment," *NYT*, Nov. 7, 2001: A3.

295. Jasper Becker, "Kicking Karl Marx out of the Party," *SCMP*, Jan. 26, 2002: 16.

296. Ching Cheong, "Is China Facing New Era of Religious Freedom?" *Straits Times* (Singapore)(*ST*), Jan. 10, 2002; "National Conference Held on Management of Religious Affairs" and "Religious Affairs in China Entering 'New Phase,' Agency Says," Xinhua, Dec. 1, 2001, BBC/M, Dec. 13, 2001.

297. Frank Ching, "Atheist Party Starting to See Light on Believers," *SCMP*, Feb. 17, 2001: 9.

298. Charles Hutzler, "Beijing Rethinks Religious Policies," *Asian Wall Street Journal*, Feb. 6, 2002:1. Ye Xiaowen's analog in the TAR, Director of the

Ethnic & Religious Affairs Commission Tarqen [Ch: Tareqing], is Tibetan. The head of the Commission's Religious Affairs Department Thubden [Ch: Tu Deng] is also Tibetan. "Reincarnation of Living Buddhas in Tibet," *Xinhua*, May 24, 2001; J. Gittings "Cultural Clash in Land on Roof of the World," *Guardian*, Feb. 8, 2002: 17. Tibetans have directed the Patriotic Education Campaign on the regional level. "Tibet Official Says Monks Complaining of 'Chaos,' Rotten Religious Practice," *XZRB*, Nov. 11, 1997: 1, in BBC/SWB, Dec. 3, 1997.

299. Goldstein 1998: 22.

300. Mehru Jaffer, "Tibetan Monks Dream of Returning Home," *Jakarta Post*, Sept. 23, 2001.

301. C.K. Yang, *Religion in Chinese Society* (1961): 183; Kim-Kwong Chan, "A Chinese Perspective on the Interpretation of the Chinese Government's Religious Policy," in Alan Hunter (ed.), *All Under Heaven: Chinese Tradition and Christian Life in the People's Republic of China* (1992): 38.

302. Tanya Storch, "Law and Religious Freedom in Medieval China: State Regulation of Buddhist Communities," in Joel Thierstein and Yahya Kamalipour (eds.), *Religion, Law and Freedom: A Global Perspective* (2000): 34–44. Almost all the 44,600 Buddhist monasteries in China were closed by order of the emperor in 845 AD and the 260,500 monks and nuns ordered to take up secular life. Sun Shuyun 2003: 21.

303. "Wrong Line of Work," *Progressive* (US), Oct. 2004: 11.

304. Chu 1999. The same cannot be said for China proper, where rapid development, the urban one-child policy, and a strong Buddhist revival have resulted in an acute shortage of monks. Sun Shuyun 2003: 21.

305. The reported 25,000 monks and nun "refugees" from Tibet who came to India from 1986–1996 are an indication there are tens of thousands of "clergy" in Tibet. *Situation in Tibet: Hearing on Humanitarian Aid to Tibet before the Senate Foreign Relations Committee*, 104th Cong. (1997). Half the monks and nunas who came from Tibet to India during this decade emigrated to N. America, Europe or Australasia to staff dharma centers. The absence of many *geshe* degree holders from South Asian Tibetan communities has resulted in a shortage of senior gurus to instruct monks. Frechette 2002: 111–113.

306. Chu (1999) gives this figure, while Gittings (2002) gives 110,000. Xu Mingxu states that there were 112,605. Xu Mingxu, *Yinmo Yu Qiancheng: Xizang Saoluan De Lailong Qumai* [Intrigues And Devoutness: The Origin and Development of the Tibet Riots] (1999): 174. On the internet, where "Tibet Supporters" enjoy free rein to exaggerate, it is claimed that "Compared to pre-1959 levels, only 1/20 Monks are still allowed to practice." Miguel Llora, "Introduction to the Economic Displacement, Gradual Cultural Genocide and Population Transfer in Tibet," Canada Tibet Committee, at http://ctcvan.ca/docs/freedomcultural1.html.

307. Sautman and Eng 2001: 63–64. Ireland's lone remaining seminary produced just seven priests in 2004. "Crisis Looms as Priesthood fails to draw Irish Catholics," *SCMP*, June 16, 2004: A12.

308. Dan Boylan, "Last Rites Loom for Dwindling Priesthood," *SCMP*, July 17, 2001: 12. In 2003, the US reportedly had one priest for every 4,723 Catholics. Ian Fisher, "Uninvited Guest Turns Up at Catholic Synod: Issue of Married Priests," *NYT*, Oct. 7, 2005: 10. The earlier figure may include retired priests.

309. U.S. Department of State, *International Religious Freedom Report 2003: China*, http://hongkong. usconsulate.gov/uscn/hr/2003/121801.htm.

310. Martin Slobodnik, "Destruction and Revival: the Fate of the Tibetan Buddhist Monastery Labrang in the People's Republic of China," *Religion, State and Society* 32:1 (2004): 7–19.

311. "Buddhism Wins Over a New Generation of Converts in Russia," AFP, Feb. 16, 2002.

312. *Tibet: Proving Truth from Facts* (Dharamsala: T61E, 1993): 79.

313. State Council Information Office, "New Progress in Human Rights in the Tibet Autonomous Region," Feb. 24, 1998, at http://www.fmprc.gov.cn/eng/ 32270.html.

314. Seth Faison, "Icy Wind from Beijing Chills the Monks of Tibet," *NYT*, Nov. 18, 1998: A3 (debates at Drepung monastery); Patrick Smithers, "High Road to Lhasa," *The Age*, Feb. 28, 1998: 11 (debates at Sera monastery); Michael Dempsey, "Re-Educated but not Suppressed," *Independent*, Oct. 2, (Dharamsala: T61E, 1993) (Sera debates).

315. Before 1959 " only ten percent of monks were really studying Buddhist texts, the others were meeting their own needs." Fabienne Jagou, "La Politique Religieuse De La Chine Au Tibet" [*China's Religious Policy in Tibet,*] *Revue d'Etudes Comparatives Est-Ouest* 32:1 (2001): 41, fn. 6. See also Axel Strom, "Between Tibet and the West: on Traditionality, Modernity and the Development of Monastic Institutions in the Tibetan Diaspora," in Frank Korom (ed.), *Tibetan Studies: Tibetan Culture in the Diaspora* (Vienna: Verlag Der Osterreichischen Akademie Der Wissenschaften, 1997), Vol. IV: 33–50.

316. Goldstein 1998: 33–34, 161 fn. 36.

317. Jagou 2001: 36.

318. Hongyi H. Lai, "The Religious Revival in China," *Copenhagen Journal of Asian Studies* 18 (2003): 40–64.

319. U.S. State Department 2003.

320. Many younger, highly educated Han in Beijing and other large cities are attracted to Tibetan culture and spirituality. Philip Pan, "China's Hippies Find Their Berkeley," *WP*, Sept. 22, 2003: A17; ICT, "Chinese Journal Analyzes Spread of Tibetan Buddhism in Chinese Community," Oct. 1, 2003 in Phayul, www.phayul.com/news/article.aspx?id=252&t=4. Some former top Chinese leaders and their families are said to be interested in or even practice Buddhism. Mainland Chinese now visit Dharamsala to meet the Dalai Lama and a senior émigré official has said that in Dharamsala "Monks say they get greater offerings from Mainland Chinese than exiled

Tibetans." "Dalai Lama's Spiritualism Softening Chinese Hearts," *Hindustan Times*, May 12, 2005 in WTN, May 15, 2005.

321. Jasper Becker, "Past a Matter of Faith for 'Atheist' " City, *SCMP*, Feb. 15, 2002: 12.

322. Sun Shuyun 2003: 20.

323. "Up to 1,200 Temples Destroyed or Closed in Chinese Crackdown," AFP, Dec. 13, 2000. No one conceives of such measures as "auto-genocide," however.

324. Melvyn Goldstein, "Religious Conflict in the Traditional Tibetan State," in Lawrence Epstein and Richard Sherburne (eds.), *Reflections on Tibetan Culture* (Lewiston: Edward Mellen, 1990): 231–47. Traditionally, each Tibetan family was obligated to send a boy to become a monk, but today in ethnic Tibetan Bhutan many rural families do not want to force sons to be celibate. This is the case even though Buddhism is officially promoted. In Nepal, Sherpa families reportedly no longer want to send their children to become novices. Kunda Dixit, "Nepal-Culture: Winds of Change Sweep Sherpaland," Inter Press Service [IPS], Sept. 21, 1995. In some PRC Tibetan areas, the main problem for monasteries is not that authorities limit the number of monks, but that there are ever fewer young men willing to take vows. See Makley 2003: 614; interview with a high Tibetan official, Lhasa, July 14, 2000.

325. David Holley, "Hope, Fear, Defiance Permeate Lhasa Monasteries: Tibet's Monks Battle China's Hold," *LAT*, Feb. 19, 1989:12 (influx of boy monks to Tashilunpo monastery); "Reports from Hong Kong Journalists' Tibet Trip," *Zhongguo Tongxunshe*, July 10, 1991, BBC/SWB, July 16, 1991 (200 boy monks among 650 monks at Drepung monastery). The proportion of child novitiates at Drepung in Lhasa was higher than at the exiled Drepung in south India, which in the late 1990s had over 3,500 monks, of whom 260 were between the ages of 8 and 14. Keya Acharya, "Tibet: Dalai Lama says Tibetan Culture Safer in India," IPS Jan. 15, 1999.

326. Catriona Bass. *Education in Tibet: Policy and Practice Since 1950* (London: TIN and Zed Books, 1998) p.104.

327. Ben Hillman, "Monastic Politics and the Local State in China: Authority and Autonomy in an Ethnic Prefecture," *China Journal*, no. 54 (2005): 29–51. The same disturbances led to the suspension of examinations for the highest monastic degree (*geshe*). "Tibet Lamas Enjoy their New Freedom," Xinhua, Sept. 13, 2005.

328. *Implementation of the Declaration on the Elimination of all forms of Intolerance and of Discrimination based on Religion or Belief*, U.N. ESCOR, 49th Sess., U.N. Doc. E/CN.4/1995/91 (1994): 3.

329. Jagou 2001: 35; Walter Glaser, "Where the Soft Chants Echo Again," *FT*, Feb. 17, 2001: 20.

330. Gittings 2002; "China: Monastery's Legacy Well Preserved," *CD*, July 16, 1999: 8.

331. Goldstein 1998: 50 n.33, 161; see also Erik Eckholm, "From a Chinese Cell, a Lama's Influence Remains Undimmed," *NYT*, Feb. 23, 2003: 6 (dozens of young monks at Lithang monastery); Qun Zeng, "Laodongzhe Sushi Di Shi Fazhan Xizang Jingji De Zhuygo Zhiyue Yinsu" [The Chief Constraining Factor on Tibet's Economic Development is the Low Quality of its Workers], *Chinese Education* and Society 30: 32 (1997) (most monks and nuns in Chamdo are school-age children).

332. U.S. State Department 2003. At Labrang too, there are underage, unofficial monks. Slobodnik 2004: 13.

333. Baert 2001 ["New Year Celebration in Xiahe"].

334. *A Sea of Bitterness* 2001:98; Janet Upton, "Home on the Grasslands? Tradition, Modernity, and the Negotiation of Identity by Tibetan Intellectuals in the PRC," in Melissa Brown (ed.), *Negotiating Ethnicities in China and Taiwan* (Berkeley: Center for Chinese Studies, 1996): 188; Goldstein 1998: 44 (400 boys in Drepung's school in 1995). Some child monks or nuns leave when secular education becomes available. "Tibetan Girls Back to School," Xinhua, Oct. 3, 2000.

335. *Declaration on the Elimination of all Forms of Intolerance and of Discrimination Based on Religion or Belief*, G.A. Res. 36/55, U.N. GAOR, 36th Sess., Supp. No. 51, At 3, U.N. Doc. A/RES/36/55 (1981). Empirical studies in the United States have found significant academic deficiencies in religious education compared to secular schooling. James Dwyer, *Religious Schools Versus Children's Rights* (1998). Beatings of young monks by t eachers in Tibet's monasteries are reportedly common. Richard S. Ehrlich, "Tibet: Obsessed with Money," *Laissez Faire City Times* 3: 25 (June 21, 1999).

336. David Bradley, "Language Policy for the Yi," in Stevan Harrell (ed.), *Perspectives on the Yi of Southwest China* (Berkeley: University of California, 2001): 195–213.

337. Zhou Minglang, "Language Attitudes of two Contrasting Ethnic Minority Nationalities in China: The 'Model' Koreans and the 'Rebellious' Tibetans," *International Journal of the Sociology of Language* no. 146 (2000): 1–2.

338. Brian Walker, "Plural Cultures, Contested Territories: A Critique of Kymlicka," *Canadian. Journal of Political Science* 30 (1997): 220–221.

339. Sautman and Eng 2001.

340. Roland J.-L. Breton and Ranka Bejeljac-Babic, "Too many Languages or too Few?" *Media Asia* 27 (2000): 150–151.

341. "Autonomy is Best Solution for Tibet, says Dalai Lama," AFP, Sept. 11, 1997.

342. Devinder Sharma, "I Pray for a Change of the Guard in China," *Jerusalem Post*, September 16, 1992: 1.

343. *Hearing of the House International Relations Committee on Religious Persecution*, 105th Cong. (1999) (statement of Rep. Frank Wolf (R-VA)), FNS, Sept. 9, 1997.

344. "Policy Favors Minorities to Foster Education," Xinhua, Dec. 10, 1994.

345. "Putonghua Taken as Key Factor to Booming China's Western Economy," Xinhua, Sept. 18, 2002.

346. Zhou Minglang, "The Politics of Bilingual Education in the People's Republic of China Since 1949," *Bilingual Research Journal* 25 (2001): 15–160; Tian Jiadong, "Xizang De Shuangyu Jiaoxue" [Bilingual Education in Tibet], in Zhu Chongxian & Wang Yuanxin (eds.), *Shuangyu Jiaoxue Yu Yanjiu* [Bilingual Education and Research] (Beijing: Zhongyang minzu daxue chubanshe, 1998): 131–137.

347. Bonnie Johnson, "The Politics, Policies, and Practices in Linguistic Minority Education in the People's Republic of China: The Case of Tibet," *International Journal of Educational. Research.* 33 (2000): 594; "Explanation of Minority Nationalities Law," *Renmin Ribao* (Beijing) June 4, 1984, BBC/SWB, June 19, 1984.

348. "Circular Concerning the Use of and Examination on Han Language Teaching Materials by Minority Nationality Middle and Primary School Students in the Tibetan Region," Oct. 28, 1994, in *Chinese Education & Society* 30 (1997): 38–40.

349. Jing Lin, "Policies and Practices of Bilingual Education for the Minorities in China," *Journal of Multilingual & Multicultural Development* 18 (1997): 197.

350. John Gittings, "Claims of Forced Abortions in Tibet are Untrue, says Report," *Guardian*, Feb. 25, 2002a: 13.

351. Lobsang Sangay, "Education Rights for Tibetans in Tibet and India," in John Montgomery (ed.), *Human Rights: Positive Policies in Asia and the Pacific Rim* (Hollis NH: Hollis Publishing, 1998): 285–307.

352. Bass 1998: 233; "China Denies Education Clampdown in Tibet," AFP, May 7, 1997; "Senior Tibetan Official Meets U.S. Ambassador to China," Xinhua, Apr. 7, 1997.

353. "Tibetan Language Dominates Local Life," *Xinhua*, Sept. 2, 1997.

354. John Gittings, "A Railroad to Progress or Just Another Chain to China?," *Guardian*, Feb. 9, 2002: 15.

355. Miller 1998: 85. TAR officials insist "parents always have the possibility of choosing between a class of Tibetan and Chinese mixed or a class only in Tibetan." Gilles Campion, "Schools," AFP, June 9, 1997.

356. Bass 1998: 95–96.

357. Ibid.: 233–234; "Education for Tibetans Boosted in Qinghai," Xinhua, Nov. 30, 1991; Wu Bangfu "The Tibetan Language School of Sichuan Province" (1999), http://www.khamaid.org/programs/education/tibschool.htm; Ashild Kolas and Monika Thowsen, *On the Margins of Tibet: Cultural Survival on the Sino-Tibetan Frontier* (Seattle: University of Washington Press, 2005): 95–99.

358. "Tibetan Language in Wide Use," Xinhua, Aug. 2, 2000.

359. Mary Kwang, "Tibet Today," *ST*, Nov. 5, 1999: 26. Émigré leaders have condemned the school for its supposed "slighting of the Tibetan language"

and its integration of Tibetan and Han students. Kevin Platt, "Culture Clash Over Teaching Tibet," *CSM*, Sept. 24, 1999: 8 [Platt, *Culture Clash*].

360. Bonnie Johnson and Nalini Chhetri, "Exclusionary Policies and Practices in Chinese Minority Education: The Case of Tibetan Education," *Current Issues in Comparative Education*. 2 (2000), http://www.tc.columbia.edu/cice/articles/bjnc122.htm; Gittings 2002a "Claims of Forced Abortions"; "Legislation Boosts Position of Tibetan Language," Xinhua, March 17, 1989.

361. Campion 1997 "Schools."

362. Education Commission of the Tibet Autonomous Region and the Leading Group for Tibetan-Language Instruction of the Regional Education Commission, "Summary of Pilot Project Work in Middle-School Tibetan-Language Instruction," *Chinese Education & Society* 30 (1997): 41–48.

363. "New Tibetan Language Textbooks to be Used," *CD*, June 28, 1999: 3. In 1991, only 39 percent of high school teachers in the TAR were Tibetans and other minorities. Zhou Runnian, "Xizang Jiaoyu Sishi Nian De Zhuyao Chenyjou Ji Jingyan" [*The Major Achievements and Experiences in Education in the Past Forty Years of Education in Tibet]*, *Minzu Yanjiu* 6 (1991): 28.

364. "*First Set of Tibetan Textbooks Published*," WTN, Jan. 21, 2001.

365. "Tibetan Parents Worried by Spread of Chinese Language," Reuters, Nov. 29, 2001. Many Tibetan parents want their children to study at a middle school in China proper. David Hsieh, "Beijing Glorifies Tibet's Progress," *ST*, Nov. 13, 2001: A3. Visits to Lhasa in July, when thousands of Tibetans take inland school entrance exams, confirm competition is fierce. By regulation, 70 percent of Tibetan students at these schools must be from peasant or herder families. They receive instruction in Tibetan and visits by monks. In 1985–2001, 23,560 Tibetan primary school graduates studied in Tibetan classes or Tibetan schools in China proper. Zhu Zhiyong, *State Schooling and Ethnic Identity: Aa Study of an Inland Tibet Middle School in the People's Republic of China* (Unpublished PhD dissertation, University of Hong Kong, 2004): 46. More than 10,000 became university graduates. "China's Top Universities to Enrol Tibetan Post Graduates," Xinhua, Nov. 7, 2002. Some 13,000 Tibetan students enrolled in inland secondary schools in 2002, including Tibetan-only secondary schools in Beijing, Shanghai, Chengdu, and Tianjin. "Inland Schools Help Educate Tibetan Students," Xinhua, Oct. 20, 2002. Émigré leaders view the schools as "taking the brightest Tibetan students to special schools in China and indoctrinating them in communist ideology and political worldview [a]s part of a series of mechanisms to assimilate Tibetans into the Chinese mainstream and blur the distinctiveness of Tibetan language, culture and history." TCHRD, *Education in Tibet: a Briefing Paper for the Special Rapporteur* (Dharamsala: TCHRD, 2003).

366. Bass 1998: 260. The preferred MOI for Tibetans in India is still English, now seen as the medium of élites and social mobility in India. Santosh

Kumar Khare, "Truth about Language in India," *Economic & Political Weekly* 37:50 (Dec. 14, 2002): 4993–4994; Siddharth Srivastava, "English as a Ticket to the Good Life," *IHT*, Sept. 3, 2003: 9. The preference of many Tibetan parents in Tibet for Chinese as the secondary school MOI also mirrors the preference for English of Hong Kong Chinese parents. David Li, "Hong Kong Parents' Preference for English-Medium Education: Passive Victims of Imperialism or Active Agents of Pragmatism?" in Andy Kirkpatrick, *Englishes in Asia: Communication, Identity, Power and Education* (Sydney: Languages Australia, 2002): 29–61; Stephen Evans, "The Medium of Instruction in Hong Kong: Policy and Practices in the new English and Chinese Streams," *Research Papers in Education* 17:1(2002): 97–120. Similar parents' demands that their children be taught in a major language are found throughout the world, e.g., among black parents in South Africa. R.W. Johnson, "Goodbye isiXhosa," *Prospect Magazine* No. 122 (May, 2006).

367. Samuel Huntington, "The Hispanic Challenge," *Foreign Policy* (March/Apr. 2004): 30–45.

368. Tom Templeton, "The Man who would be King," *Observer*, Oct. 10, 2004.

369. Robert Kaplan, "Where Europe Vanishes," *Atlantic Monthly* 286:5 (2002): 67–79.

370. Bass 1998: 188; Sangay 1998: 297; Edward J. Kormondy, "Observations on Minority Education, Cultural Preservation and Economic Development in China," *Compare* 25 (1998): 161–178.

371. "Increase in Chinese Medium Teaching in Tibetan Schools," *TIN*, Nov. 27, 2001.

372. AFP, May 7, 1997.

373. Gittings 2002 ["Claims of Forced Abortions"].

374. Bass 1998: 260. The MOI in grades 6–12 remains English. i.e. from age eleven. The curriculum at all levels, except in social studies, is the one pre-scribed by the Indian Government. B. Tsering Yeshi, *Tibetanisation Project: Teachers' Meanings and Perspectives* (unpublished PhD dissertation, University of Virginia, 2001): 65–66. The official in charge of education in the TGIE has said that Tibetan schools in India have failed in providing a grounding in Tibetan language and culture." "The Wrong Side of the Mountains," *The Economist*, Dec. 20, 2005.

375. Dahlstrom 2005: 176.

376. Jonathan Glancey, "Sweet Valley High, *Guardian*, Jan. 28, 2002, at 10.

377. J. Stapleton Roy, "Human Rights Situation of the Tibetan People," *Department of St ate Bulletin*, Dec. 1987: 49; Platt, "Culture Clash . . .".

378. Janet Upton, "The Development of Modern School-Based Tibetan Language Education in the PRC," in Gerard Postiglione (ed.), *China's National Minority Education: Culture, Schooling, and Development* (New York: Falmer Press, 1999): 307, 311. An Indian journalist also found that in Tibet "School textbooks might remain silent on the 14th (present) Dalai Lama but

they don't belittle the earlier Dalai Lamas or Tibetan heroes." Uday Mahurkar, "The New Tibet," *India Today*, Oct. 17, 2005. A British specialist of Tibetan education found that lessons with an apolitical moral purpose found in primary school textbooks of the 1990s incorporated Tibetan and Buddhist moral tales, while those designed to teach "socialist morality" interpreted "Tibet's Buddhist heritage as a non-religious cultural/architectural heritage that is part of a common Chinese cultural heritage." Catriona Bass, "Learning to Love the Motherland: Educating Tibetans in China," *Journal of Moral Education* 34–4 (2005):433–449.

379. Gerard Postiglione, Ben Jiao, and Sonam Gyatso, "Education in Rural Tibet: Development, Problems and Adaptions," *China: an International Journal* 3:1 (2005): 1–23.

380. Ibid. TIN, *News Review No. 29: Reports* from Tibet, 2000 (2001):55.

381. "Tibet: Ngapoi and Bainquen Stress use of Tibetan Language" (Lhasa Radio, Lhasa, July 4, 1987), in BBC/SWB, July 8, 1987; "Decision on use and Development of Tibetan Language" (Lhasa Radio, Lhasa, July 11, 1987), BBC/SWB, July 15, 1987; "Commission for Guiding Use of Tibetan Language" (Lhasa Radio, Feb. 10, 1988), BBC/SWB, Feb. 17, 1988.

382. "First Meeting o f Tibetan Language Commission on Problems Caused by Leftism" (Lhasa Radio, Lhasa, March 13, 1988), in BBC/SWB, March 16, 1988.

383. "Tibetans Pass First Law to Protect Mother Tongue," Xinhua, May 22, 2002. The full text of the law is at TIN, http://www.tibetinfo.net/publications/docs/languagelaw.htm.

384. "Tibetan Language Assumes Larger Role," *CD*, Aug. 5, 2000: 4.

385. Ibid.: "Tibetan People Embracing Change, Retaining Culture," *CD*, June 28, 1999.

386. "Use of Tibetan Advocated," *CD*, Aug. 3, 2000.

387. "Tibetan Government in Exile Refutes Chinese White Paper," AFP, Feb. 26, 1998.

388. "Modern Media Brings Tibetans Closer to Outside," *CD*, Dec. 20, 2001; China Tibet information Center, "Media," http:// www.tibetinfor.com.cn/english/reports/soc_tech/media/media_01_Zl.jtm; "China Launches TV Channel for Tibetan Dialect Speakers," Xinhua, Feb. 28, 2006.

389. "Language and Tibetan Identity" 2001: 57–58; "Full Text of White Paper on Tibetan Culture," Xinhua, June 22, 2000; "Tibetan Language Widely Used in Tibet," Xinhua, Aug. 9, 2000; PRC Embassy in the United States, "Tibet's March Toward Modernization," Nov. 8, 2001, http://www.china-embassy.org/eng/20484.html; "China's Media Drive Goes West," *FT*, Feb. 7, 2002, in BBC/M.

390. ABC 2002.

391. Miller 1998: 86.

392. Zhou Wei, *Xizang de yuyan yu shehui* [Tibetan language and society] (Beijing: Zhongguo Xangxue chubanse, 2003): 124 (100% of sample of

over 400 TAR urban Tibetan population speak Tibetan; 7% of male heads of household and 18% of their wives cannot at all read Tibetan); "China Opens Tibetan Access Road to Information Superhighway," AFP, Oct. 13, 1997 (95% of total TAR population speaks Tibetan); Zhou Minglang 2000: 4, 14.

393. Zhongguo Shehui Kexue Yuan Minzu Yanjiu Suo, *Zhongguo Shaoshu Minzu Yuyan Shiyong Qingkuang* [The Situation of Chinese Ethnic Minority Language Use] (1994): 750–753. Tibetans who do not speak Tibetan may nevertheless retain other aspects of Tibetan culture. The Dalai Lama was born into a family which, living at the edge of the Tibet Plateau, spoke Chinese as its first language.

394. Zhou Wei, "Xizang Xiandai Taocheng Zhong Yuyan Shiyong Moshi De Fenxi Yu Taolun" [Analysis and Discussion of Language Use Models in the Process of Tibet's Modernization,] *Zhongguo Xangxue* 4 (2001): 29. According to the PRC Government, "[I]n Tibet, the Tibetan Language is the only everyday oral and written means of the 2.4 million ethnic Tibetans." "Law Guards Tibetan Language," Xinhua, May 24, 2002.

395. Zhou Wei, 2001. See also Regie Stites, "Writing Cultural Boundaries: National Minority Language Policy, Literacy Planning, and Bilingual Education," in Postiglione 1999: 115 ("Tibetans with anything beyond a rudimentary grasp of *putonghua* comprise a very small portion of the total population").

396. Cees Flinterman, et al., "Tibet Mission Report," in UNPO, *1997 Annual Report* (1998): 208–209.

397. Steven Venturino, "Signifying on China's Dialogue with Minority Criticism: African-American Literary Theory and Tibetan Discourse," in Eric Huyot, et al. (eds.), *Sinographies: Writing China* (Minneapolis: University of Minnesota Press, forthcoming 2006). On the misconstruction of the China/Tibet relationship as "colonialism," see Barry Sautman, "Colonialism, Genocide and Tibet," forthcoming in *Asian Ethnicity* 7:3 (October, 2006).

398. "TV Chief Accuses France of 'Cultural Genocide' in Brittany," AFP, Sept. 1, 2005; Jaime Castillo, "Scare Tactics on Immigration are Hooey—in any Language," *San Antonio Express*, Dec. 11, 2004; "Native Canadians Reveal Legacy of Abuse," *NYT*, March 7, 2004: 11; "Maori Deserve an Apology: Sharples," *Nelson Mail* (N.Z.), June 7, 2002: 2.

399. Daniel Nettle and Suzanne Romaine, *Vanishing Voices: The Extinction of the World's Languages* (Oxford University Press, 2000); David Crystal, *Language Death* (Cambridge: Cambridge University Press, 2000); Lenore Grenoble and Lindsay Whaley, *Endangered Languages: Language Loss and Community Response* (Cambridge: Cambridge University Press, 1998); Tove Skutnabb-Kangas, *Language Genocide in Education, or Worldwide Diversity and Human Rights* (Mahwah: Erlbaum, 2000). Tibetan may become imperiled however. Linguists hold there are "killers" of languages—English, Spanish,

Portugese, Russian, Arabic, Swahili, Chinese, and Indonesian/Malay—that will wipe out hundreds of "small" languages in the next generation and may ultimately destroy all other languages. Margit Waas, "Taking Note of Language Extinction," *Applied Linguistics Forum* 18:2 (2003): 1–5.

400. Nicholas Tournadre, "The Dynamics of Tibetan-Chinese Bilingualism," *China Perspectives* no. 45 (2003): 30–36.

401. See TIN, www.Tibetinfo.net/publications/docs/languagelaw.htm for an English text.

402. Guy Lanoue, "Language Loss, Language Gain: Cultural Camouflage and Social Change among the Sekani of Northern British Columbia," *Language & Society* 20 (1991): 87–92 (arguing that English is preferred despite it being at odds with the Sekani's pan-Indian sentiments); Tove Bull, "Language Maintenance and Loss in an Originally Trilingual Area in North Norway," *International Journal of the Sociology of Language.* 115 (1994): 125–127 (explaining shift from bi- or trilingualism to monolingualism among children in coastal Norway).

403. Leanne Hinton, "Language Loss and Revitalization in California: Overview," *International Journal of the Sociology of Language* 132 (1998): 83–87.

404. "Lakota Language Teaching Anchors Indian Culture Revival in Denver," DPA, Feb. 6, 2004.

405. Rodrigue Landry, et al., "French in South Louisiana: Towards Language Loss," *Journal of Multilingual and Multicultural Development* 17 (1996): 464–465.

406. Ana Celia Zentella, "The Hispanophobia of the Official English Movement in the US," *International Journal of the Sociology of Language* 127 (1997): 74–77; Colin Baker, *Foundations of Bilingual Education and Bilingualism* (1996): 170.

407. Alejandro Portes and Lingxin Hao, "E Pluribus Unum: Bilingualism and Loss of Language in the Second Generation," *Sociology of Education* 71 (1998): 269–294.

408. Richard Alba, "Only English by the Third Generation? Loss and Preservation of the Mother Tongue among the Grandchildren of Contemporary Immigrants," *Immigrants Demography* 39 (2002): 480. English not only supplants ancestral languages among migrants, but also displaces languages where few people are of British origin. In Singapore, where 77% of the population is of Chinese descent and most of the rest of Malay or Indian ancestry, the 2000 Census showed 35.8% of families of children aged 5–14 speak English at home. Kao Chen, "Will Chinese become a Dumpling House Language?" *ST*, March 31, 2001: H16. In 2003, the number of primary one students from English-speaking households exceeded those from Chinese-speaking homes for the first time. Sonia Kolesnikov-Jessop, "Tongue-Tied," *SCMP*, Jan. 26, 2004: A11.

409. Rachel Swarns, "Children of Hispanic Immigrants Continue to Favor English, Study of Census Finds," *NYT*, Dec. 8, 2004: 26. The figure is 71 percent for third-generation Mexican-American children.

410. Jorge A. Vélez, "Understanding Spanish-Language Maintenance in Puerto Rico: Political Will Meets the Demographic Imperative," *International Journal of the Sociology of Language* 142 (2000): 16–18.

411. "Taiwan Students Caught in a Clash of Words," AFP, March 14, 2004.

412. Lauren Alderfer, *Project Demonstrating Excellence: Educators and Students as Leaders in Language Preservation* (unpublished Phd Dissertation, Union Institute, 2001) (study of language preservation in Dharamsala).

413. Ranjit Devraj, "Materialism Drowns Out Young Cries for a Free Tibet," IPS, Dec. 14, 2004: Conger Beasley, "The Spiritual Exiles of Tibet," *National Catholic Reporter*, July 30, 2004 (language loss among Tibetans in Darjeeling).

414. "Tibetan Youths' Taste for Western Lifestyle Unnerves Older Generation," AFP, July 6, 2005. See also Randeep Ramesh, "Indian Dream Seduces Tibet's Exiled Young," Guardian, Feb. 5, 2005 ("The new generation [are] either leaving to make a new life abroad or being consumed by the culture of their adopted homeland").

415. "New Year Interviews with Samdhong Rinpoche," WTN, Feb. 21, 2004; Sonam Topgyal, "Jetsun Pema La Speaks To Small Group of Tibetans at Tibet House in NYC," WTN, Dec. 18, 2003; Serin Houston and Richard Wright, "Making and Remaking Tibetan Diasporic Identies," *Social & Cultural Geography* 4:2 (2003): 217–232.

416. Ross Marowits, "Religious Beliefs Unite Tibetans," *TS*, March 9, 1990: C4.

417. Gyaltsen Gyaltag, "Exiled Tibetans in Europe and North America," in Bernstorff and von Welck, 2004::244–265.

418. *Language and Tibetan Indentity* 2001: 58.

419. Amy Lavine, *The Politics of Nostalgia: Social Memory and National Identity among Diaspora Tibetans in New York City* (unpublished PhD dissertation, University of Chicago, 2001).

420. John Hughes, "The Farewell Poignancy of the Dalai Lama's Tour," *CSM*, May 16, 2001: 9.

421. "Tibetan Language in Wide Use: Article," Xinhua, Aug. 3, 2000. Newspapers in Tibet are said to all have Tibetan editions. In 1987–1995, 3.8 million books were published in Tibetan by the main TAR publishing house. Zhou Wei, "Policy Changes with Regard to the Tibetan Language," *China's Tibet* No. 4 (2003): 16.

422. In 2000, total adult literacy among TAR Tibetans was 47.3 percent. Guowuyuan renkou pucha bangongshi, *2000 renkou pucha fenxian ziliao* (Beijing: Zhongguo tongji chubanshe, 2001): 540; Attane, s.d.:15. A literacy drive has since aimed at reducing the number of illiterates by 100,000 annually. "Tibet to Sharply Slash Illiteracy Rate," Xinhua, Nov. 22, 2003. Illiteracy among young and middle age Tibetans (15–49 years of age), which was 90 percent in 1965, is said to have declined to 22 percent by 2004. "Facts and Figures: Changes in Tibet," Xinhua, Sept. 1, 2005; "Tibet to Basically Wipe out Illiteracy in Three Years," Xinhua, June 15, 2004.

423. Lauri Malksoo, "Language Rights in International Law: Why the Phoenix is still in the Ashes," *Florida Journal of International Law* 12 (2000): 432–434, 448–454.

424. European Charter for Regional or Minority Languages, Nov. 5, 1992, Art. 8, Europe. T.S. No. 148, http://conventions.coe.int/treaty/eN/treaties/html/148.htm. See also Wang Shuping, "The People's Republic of China's Policy on Minorities and International Approaches to Ethnic Groups: a Comparative Study," *International Journal on Minority and Group Rights* 11 (2004): 15–185 (limited range of rights protected by European approach to minority rights makes it far from effective model for China).

425. "Beijing Struggles to Make Polyglot Nation Conform," AP, Dec. 3, 1004.

426. David Graddol, "The Future of Language," *Science* 303 (Feb. 27, 2004): 1329–1331.

427. Margie Berns, "English in Europe: Whose language, which Culture?" *International Journal of Applied Linguistics* 5:1 (1995) 21–32.

428. "Tibet's March toward Modernization" 2001.

429. For an overview, see Danzhu Angben, *Zangzu Wenhua Fazhan Shi* [History of the Development of Tibetan Culture] 2 (2001): 1181–1222.

430. Geoffrey Samuel, "The Gesar Epic of East Tibet," in Jose Cabezon and Roger Jackson (eds.), *Tibetan Literature: Studies in a Genre* (Ithaca: Snow Lion, 1996): 358.

431. TIN, "Writing in Today's Tibet," *TIN Testimonies*, Apr. 19, 2005.

432. Lauran Hartley, *Contextually Speaking: Tibetan Literary Discourse and Social Change in the People's Republic of China (1980–2000)* (unpublished PhD dissertation, Indiana University, 2003).

433. Tsering Shakya, "The Waterfall and Fragrant Flowers: The Development of Tibetan Literature Since 1950," *TB* 28 (July–Aug. 2001): 39–40.

434. Bhuchung Tsering, "When Sera Means Two Different Places," *TR* (July 2001): 28.

435. "China's Propaganda War on Tibet Gets Cultural," AFP, June 29, 1999 [*China's Propoganda War*].

436. K . Platt, "Tibetan Music Sings Out Amid the Mishmash," *CSM*, Dec. 31, 1999: 18 [Platt, *Tibetan Music*].

437. "China's Propaganda War" 1999.

438. Colin Mackerras, "Tradition and Modernity in the Performing Arts of the Tibetans," *Int'l J. Of Soc. Econ.* 26:1–3 (1999): 1–25.

439. Charlene Makley, "Performing Autheticity: Tibetan Song and Dance Ensemble Makes Its Argument," *Journal of the International Institute* 4:2 (s.d.), www.umich.edu/~iinet/journal/vol4no2/tibet.html.

440. Frechette, 2002: 106. This TGIE school "promote[s] the idea that all Tibetans must work to get the Chinese out of Tibet." There, "Tibetan children learn to hate the Chinese. Young boys at the Atisha School, in discussing the Chinese, would routinely stand up and, making the motion of driving a knife into someone, say that they just want to kill all Chinese."

Ibid.: 162. Tibet independence activist Tenzin Tsundue, 2004, notes that an "unreformed stereotype" of Chinese as brutal "is still being put up in the exile stage."

441. Elke Hessel, "Modern Artists of Lhasa," *Tibet Journal* [*TJ*] 27: 1–2 (2001): 217–236.

442. "Avant-garde Artists Strive to Express Rage and Aspirations of Modern Tibet," *AFP*, Aug. 22, 2005.

443. Rob Liarothe, "Creativity, Freedom, and Control in the Contemporary Renaissance of *Reb Gong* Paintings,"*TJ* 26 (2001): 5–90.

444. Mark Stevenson, "The Politics of Identity and Cultural Production in Amdo *Reb Gong,*" *TJ* 24 (1999): 45.

445. "The Art and Politics of Tibet: Lecture by Kasur Tenzin N. Tethong at the Asian Art Museum," June 2, 2005, in WTN, June 20, 2005.

446. Clare Harris, *In the Image of Tibet: Tibetan Painting Since 1959* (1999): 192–196.

447. Antonio Atlasani, "Tibetan Secular Theatre: The Sacred and the Profane," *PAJ: A Journal Of Performance And Art* 21(1999): 1–2.

448. Minister Tashi Wangdi, Message from the Kalon [Department of Religion and Culture, Dharamsala], http://www.tibet.net/eng/religion/message; Jean Bartlett, "Chaksampa, Tibetan Dance and Opera Company, Offers Thrilling Cultural Insight," *Pacifica Tribune*, Aug. 15, 2001, WTN, Aug. 20, 2001.

449. Most traditional Tibetan performances, for example, do not feature Tibetan characters and are not set in Tibet. Mackerras 1999: 20.

450. Bhuchung Tsering, "Making Sense of the Music Scene in Tibet," *TR*, Feb. 2002, at 27. (quoting Chopathar Wayemache, *Musical Artist in Tibet: Selected Essays by Tibetan Musician and Composer Chopathar Wayemache* (Bloomington: Department of Central Eurasian Studies, Indiana University, 1998). Platt 1999, "Tibetan Music."

451. Platt 1999, "Tibetan Music."

452. Janet Upton, "The Politics and Poetics of Sister Drum: 'Tibetan' Music in the Global Marketplace," in Timothy Craig and Richard King (eds.), *Global Goes Local: Popular Culture in Asia* (Honolulu: University of Hawaii Press, 2002): 101.

453. Wangpo Tethnong 2004: 414.

454. Athrin Schaer, "Tibetan Enchantress Brings a Tear to her Audiences," *Sunday Star-Times* (Auckland), Feb. 14, 1999: F3.

455. Dorsh Marie de Voe, "Tibetans in India," in *Encyclopedia of Diasporas: Immigrant and Refugee Cultures Around the World* (Dordrecht: Kluwer Academic, 2004): 1119–1130. Other émigré musicians incorporate non-Tibetan musical forms in their music. See, e.g., Beth Pearson, "Hail to the Spiritual Leader," *Herald*, May 28, 2004 ("In the west, some Tibetan musicians incorporated electric guitars and digeridoos into their compositions"); "Tibetan Beauty Goes from Tending Cattle to Winning Pagents,"

IANS, Dec. 25, 2003 (Dolma Tsering, first "Miss Tibet" and her band Music Tibet "sings Tibetan songs and dances to English and Bollywood numbers").

456. Julian Gearing, "Struggle for Tibet's Soul," *Asiaweek*, Oct. 20, 2000: 62.

457. Knud Larsen and Amund Sinding-Larsen, *The Lhasa Atlas: Traditional Tibetan Architecture and Townscape* (2001).

458. Andrew Anders, "Tibet Carries Scars of 'Cultural Genocide,' " *Guardian*, June 17, 1993: 9.

459. "Beijing Makeover Revives Debate About Megacities," IPS, Feb. 27, 2004.

460. See "Now is the Best Time in History: Shanba Pucog Interviewed by Foreign Reporters," *China's Tibet* No. 6 (2003): 3–7 (governor of Tibet discusses his role in placing "modern" street lamps in traditional Barkhor area).

461. "Central Lhasa Gets Facelift with 'Tibetan Characteristics,' " TIN News Update, Dec. 30, 2004, in WTN, Dec. 31, 2004.

462. Miloš R. Perović and Žoran Zegarac, "The Destruction of an Architectural Culture: The 1999 Bombing of Belgrade," *Cities* 17 (2000): 396; Robert Bevan, *The Destruction of Memory: Architecture at War* (London: Reaktion 2006).

463. William Semple, "Tibetan Architecture: Exploring A Cultural Continuum," in *Cultures in Transition:Representations of Change* (1996): 98. See also Singer, 2003: 247–252 on the de-emphasis of Tibetan architectural traditions in Dharamsala. The office of the Dalai Lama is described as "like the institutional Government of India buildings."

464. Martin Cohn, " 'Little Lhasa' Belies Tibetan Ideal," *TS*, Dec. 8, 2003: A10; Lynne O'Donnell, "Little Lhasa's Growing Pains," *Australian*, June 16, 2001.

465. "China's Tibet Policy Reminiscent of Cultural Revolution: Dalai Lama," AFP, March 10, 2000; John Grey, "Modernise, or Else!: Building the New Lhasa," *Himal* (Jan.–Feb. 1995): 10, 13; *Social Evils: Prostitution and Pornography in Lhasa* (London: TIN, 1998).

466. Kevin Platt, "Chinese Migrants Change Face of Tibet," *CSM*, Sept. 10, 1999: 8.

467. Yong 1999.

468. Teresa Poole, "Paying the Price of Progress," *Independent*, Aug. 20, 1995: 10; "Raids on Entertainment Spots in Tibet," Tibet People's Broadcasting Station, Lhasa, Sept. 19, 1996, in BBC/SWB, Oct. 22, 1996.

469. J. West, "Tibetans Accuse Dalai Lama of Spiritual Betrayal," *Sunday Telegraph*, Apr. 26, 1998; Ajay Singh, "Tibet: Fires of Frustration," *Asiaweek*, Sept. 11, 1998: 52 ("not a few" Dharamsala Tibetans gravitate to drugs); Isabel Hilton, "Children of a Lhasa God," *Guardian*, March 6, 1999: 24 (Dharamsala Tibetan youth says "A lot of people my age turn to drugs and alcohol"); Keila Diehl, *Echoes from Dharamsala: Music in the Life of a Tibetan Refugee Community* (Berkeley: University of California Press, 2002): 48 (young Tibetan men sell hashish in Dharamsala); Audrey Prost, "The

Problem with 'Rich Refugees': Sponsorship, Capital, and the Informal Economy of Tibetan Refugees," Modern Asian Studies 40: 1 (2006): 233–253 (Dharamsala Tibetan youths' use of drugs with foreigners); S. Vasudeu, "New Buddhism: The Buddha Bar," *India Today*, July 22, 2002: 50 (widespread drug use in Dharamsala and monks' involvement in heterosexual sex); Dilip Ganguly, "Dalai Lama's Return to Tibet Enmeshed in Negotiations," AP, Jan. 5, 1987 (TYC says youth in Dharamsala like discos); Abhik Chanda, "Tibetan Youth Increasingly Frustrated with Credo of Non-Violence," AFP, Feb. 20, 2000 (well-known émigré teacher on "flashy lifestyles" and "degeneration of moral standards" of some monks) . High rates of alcoholism and drug use may be related to high youth joblessness among Tibetan émigrés, with "unemployment amongst the youths who are educated in general studies . . . as high as 75%." Dawa Norbu, "The Settlements: Participation and Integration," in Bernstorff and von Welck, 2004:186–212.

470. Tibetan migrants have reportedly organized into criminal gangs that have divided certain districts in some major PRC cities among themselves. Thomas Heberer, "Some Considerations on China's Minorities in the 21st Century: Conflict or Conciliation?" in Yokoyam Hiroko (ed.), *The Dynamics of Cultures and Society Among Ethnic Minorities in East Asia* (Osaka: National Museum of Ethnology, 2004): 1–31.

471. "Basement Blues to Rock Dharamsala," *Phayul*, Oct. 20, 2005 in WTN, Oct. 20, 2005.

472. "Dirty Dancing in Kathmandu," *SCMP*, July 9, 2000: 1.

473. "Thailand to Host World Buddhism Summit Without Dalai Lama," AFP, Nov. 2, 2000. Southathip Sundara, "Do Drinking and Devotion Belong in the Same Place?" *Vientiane Times*, Dec. 19, 2003: 9 (monks' exposure to "vices" in Laos); Eric Unmacht, "Monks Behaving Badly," *FEER*, Dec. 5, 2002 (paedophilia, drug-taking, violence among Cambodian monks).

474. Scott Berry, Monks, *Spies and a Soldier of Fortune: the Japanese in Tibet* (New York: St. Martin's Press, 1995): 145; Christopher Hale, *Himmler's Crusade: The Nazi Expedition to find the Origins of the Aryan Race* (Hoboken: John Wiley & Sons, 2003): 259.

475. Jagdish Bhatt, "Tensions Between Locals, Tibetans Rise in Manoli," *TI*, July 7, 1999 (local Indians state Tibetan youth "drink homemade brew and engage in brawls"); Sandra Penny-Dimri, "Conflict amongst the Tibetans and Indians of North India: Communal Violence and Welfare Dollars," *Australian Journal of Anthropology* 5:3 (1994): 280–293 (local Indians resent sexual mores, violence of Tibetans).

476. Local Indian resentment of poverty relative to Tibetan settlers, attributed to less education, skills, and political privilege, as well as Tibetan ethnic disparagement, resulted in anti-Tibetan riots in Dharamsala in 1994. Penny-Dimri 1994. In Arunachal Pradesh, there has been communal violence between the locals and Tibetans and in Himchal Pradesh, in the late 1990s, "there were continuous conflicts between the Tibetans and the local Indian

communities, as local people harbour feelings of social isolation within their own territory due to the presence of foreigners [Tibetans]." Kharat 2003: 301. Tibetans are said to regard Indians as lazy and cheats and themselves as hardworking and honest. Dahlstrom 2005: 181. An Indian teashop owner, for example, "complained about their having land and owning shops. And we work for them. They have the wherewithal to run establishments. Not an eyebrow is raised if they encroach [on forests]." B. Pankaj, "'A dharmsala' (About the recent conflicts in Dharamsala," *Dharamsala Tribune*, May 22, 1994, in WTN, June 7, 1994. See also Gyatso, 2004: 233 (local Indians resent Tibetan monasteries' affluence); T.C. Palakshappa, *Tibetans in India: A Case Study of Mundgod Tibetans* (New Delhi, 1978): 99 (local Indians resent that their land is given to Tibetans); A.V. Arakeri, *Tibetans in India: the Uprooted People and their Cultural Transplantation* (New Delhi: Reliance Publishing): 299–300 ("In general the local population was very much jealous of the Tibetans for taking so much benefit from their government and they thought it is at their cost"); Jayanti Alam, *Tibetan Society in Exile* (Delhi: Raj Publications, 2000): 189 (local Indians view Tibetans as "allowed to grab their land and eat up the 'scarce' resources of 'poor' India); "A Tibetan Enclave in Srinagar," *IE*, June 21, 2004 (local Indians resent Tibetan self-segregation); Ramtanu Maitra, "Nepal Bows to China's Demands," *Asia Times*, June 17, 2003 (local Indians resent Tibetan illegal settlement in Arunachal Pradesh and illegal securing of Scheduled Tribes status); "BJP wants Immigrants' Deportation," *S(I)*, Dec. 21, 2004 (BJP in Darjeeling complains that Tibetans and other ethnic groups illegally procure citizenship and take jobs from locals); "Making Locals Homeless for Tibetans," TNS, Sept. 20, 2004, in WTN, Sept. 20, 2004 (local Indians complain they are evicted from forest areas, but Tibetan settlers are not).

477. Amy Mountcastle, *Tibetans in Exile: The Construction of Global Identities* (unpublished PhD dissertation, Rutgers University, 1997): 190.

478. Lafitte 1999: 165.

479. *Language and Tibetan Identity* 2001:60; See Diehl 2002, Ch. 3 for a discussion of the deep influence of Indian speech, films, music, and culture on Tibetans in Dharamsala.

480. [1]Lafitte 1999: 165.

481. Pico Ayer, "Experiment in Exile," *Time Asia*, Aug. 7, 2005, in WTN, Aug. 12, 2005.

482. "Dalai Lama in Slovakia Says Tibetans Facing Cultural Genocide," *Slovak International Telegraph Agency* [SITA], Oct. 16, 2000, BBC/SWB, Oct. 18, 2000.

483. Claire Macdonald, "Inside Lhasa: Tibet's Tale of Two Cities," *Asiaweek*, May 28, 1999: 68.

484. D. Filkins, "Land of Thunder Dragon Opts for Democracy Without Dissent," *LAT*, Feb. 13, 1999: A8.

485. Ranjit Hoskote, "Lamas Cope with Change in Tropical Shangri La," *TI*, Aug. 1, 1999.

486. Uttera Choudhury, "Tibetan Boy Lama Sets Off on First Pilgramage Around India," AFP, Feb. 21, 2001.

487. Meenakshi Ganguly, "Generation Exile: Big Trouble in Little Tibet," *Transitions* (Kampala) 10:3 (2001): 4.

488. Aditi Kapoor, "More Indian Than Tibetan," *The Hindu*, July 30, 2000.

489. Ramananda Sengupta, "Don't Fight Terror with Terror: Dalai Lama," WTN, Feb. 7, 2002.

490. Kalpana Sharma, 2000; "Dalai Lama Breaks the Ice with Broken English, Spreads Laughter," Express News Service, March 13, 2000, http://www.friendsoftibet.org/130300i.html.

491. Phuntsog Wangyal, "Tibet and Development," WTN, March 29, 2004.

492. Rob Linrothe, *Paradise and Plumage: Chinese Connection in Tibetan Arhat Paintings* (New York: Rubin Museum of Art 2004).

493. Poole 1995.

494. Pico Iyer, "Tibetan Reflections: Lhasa Today is a Worn Tibetan Amulet Inside a Gaudy Chinese Box," Nepali Times, Oct. 29, 2004, in WTN, Nov. 19, 2004. A Tibetan painter in Lhasa has said that "Many people simplify Tibet. They ask, 'How can Tibet have things like Christmas trees or fast food or Nikes? But young Tibetans have already accepted these things.' " Craig Simons, "At a Gallery in Lhasa, Tibet Joints Art World," *NYT*, Nov. 22, 2004. Note that none of "these things" are of Chinese provenance.

495. A.C. Sinha, "Bhutan in 1994: Will the Ethnic Conflict be Resolved?" *Asian Survey* 35 (1995): 167–168; Ben Saul, "Cultural Nationalism, Self-Determination and Human Rights in Bhutan," *International Journal of Refugee Law* 12 (2000): 326–335; Michael Hutt, *Unbecoming Citizens: Culture, Nationhood, and the Flight of Refugees from Bhutan* (Delhi: Oxford University Press, 2003).

496. Pascal Bruckner, *La Tentation De l'Innocence* [The temptation of innocence]: 123 (2000).

497. See the essay by the well-known Chinese intellectual, Wang Xiaodong, a self-proclaimed nationalist and democrat, "The West in the Eyes of a Chinese Nationalist," *Heartland: Eurasian Rev. of Geopolitics*. 1 (2000): 19 (as to the Tibet Question "it appears that Westerners are full of a sense of justice, but they are completely under the influence of an ill-natured propaganda by the hegemonic media").

498. "WB Loan to Benefit the Poor," *CD*, July 2, 1999: 4.

499. "World Bank Loans to Promote Qinghai Aid-The-Poor Project," Xinhua, March 23, 1999; Pieter Bottelier, "Was World Bank Support for the Qinghai Anti-Poverty Project in China Ill-Considered?" *Harvard Asia Quarterly* (Winter 2001).

500. Susette Cooke, "The Politics of Population Transfer," TIN, Oct. 28, 1999.

501. 2000 census figures showed a lower percentage of Han and higher percentage of Tibetans in Haixi. Of the prefecture's 332,094 persons, Han were 215,706 (64.9%), Tibetans 40,371 (12.2%), Hui 39,644 (11.9%), Mongolians 24,020 (7.2%), Tu 5,792 (1.7%), Salar 3,569 (1.1%), Others 2,992 (1%). 2000NRKPCZGMZRKZ 20003. The figures supplied to the World Bank may have been from the 1990 Census or 1995 Mini-Census.

502. World Bank, *China: Western Poverty Reduction Project*, Annex: Social Aspects Report, Project Information Document No. 6960, June 1, 1999, http://www-wds.worldbank.org/servlet/wdscontents erver/wdsp/ib/1999/06/12/000178830_98111703525331/rendered/indexmultiopage.txt [hereinafter World Bank, Poverty Reduction Project Report].

503. "China's Poor See Hope in Resettlement," Reuters, Aug. 11, 1999, 1999/8/11_5.html; W. Kazer, "Controversy Dogs China Relief Project," Reuters, Aug. 10, 1999, http://www.tibet.ca/wtnarchive/1999/8/ 11_4.html [W. Kazer, *Controversy*].

504. "Qinghai: Developing Status," *China Econ. Rev.*, March 13, 2001; *Development and Population Transfer in Qinghai—The Qaidam Basin Project*, TIN, Apr. 27, 1999 [Development and Population Transfer].

505. Renee Schoof, "Helping Some of China's Poorest People—But at what cost?" AP, Sept. 5, 1999.

506. W. Kazer 1999, *Controversy*.

507. World Bank, Poverty Reduction Project Report, 1999.

508. Isabel Hilton, "Climate of Fear: Clare Short Tries to Dismiss Complaints about the Brutal Plans of Chinese Leaders as 'Hollywood Fantasy,' " *Guardian* , June 28, 2000.

509. World Bank 1999 Poverty Reduction Project Report.

510. Ibid. "World Bank still Reviewing Controversial Loan to China," DPA, July 24, 1999. The figures for Dulan County, like those for Haixi, were out of date. The 2000 Census showed a population of 57,670. Han were 30,320 (52.6%), Tibetans 13,503 (23.4%), Mongols 7,423 (12.9%), Hui 5,033 (8.7%), Tu 670 (1.2%), Salar 490 (0.8%), Others 231 (0.4%). 2000 NRKPCZGMZRKZL 2003.

511. Paul Lewis, "U.S. may Try to Stop Loan Seen as Bad for Tibetans," *NYT*, May 30, 1999: A4.

512. World Bank 1999, Poverty Reduction Project Report; Bottelier 2001; Charles Hutzler, "World Bank Draws Fire Over Plan to Put Poor Chinese in Tibetan Lands," AP, June 18, 1999.

513. "World Bank Under Renewed Pressure Over Divisive Project," AFP, June 17, 1999.

514. Even those generally skeptical of Western news sources in turn readily adopted the ICT's "information" on the resettlement program. See, e.g., Waldo Bello and Shalmali Guttal, "Programmed to Fail: the World Bank Clings to a Bankrupt Development Model," *Multinational Monitor* 26:7–8 (2005)(claiming pressure from "NGOs" forced World Bank withdrawal from "project that involved resettlement of 58,000 ethnic Chinese").

515. Joseph Kahn, "World Bank Rejects China's Proposal to Resettle Farmers," *NYT*, July 8, 2000: A3.

516. Susette Cooke, 1999.

517. Felix Cohen, *Handbook of Federal Indian Law* (1982): 247–252.

518. Bottelier 2001.

519. W. Kazer 1999, *Controversy*; TIN 2001, Development and Population Transfer.

520. "WB Loan to Benefit the Poor" 1999.

521. Bottelier 2001; William Kazer, "World Bank Walks Away and Poor Pick Up the Party Bill in Qinghai," *SCMP*, July 14, 2000.

522. "World Bank Loan to Help Alleviate Poverty in Western China," Xinhua, July 14, 1999.

523. "Relocation Project will Assist Farmers," *CD*, Aug. 9, 1999: 8.

524. Press Release, "Urgent Action Appeal: Stop Population Transfer in Tibet," TCHRD (May 20, 1999), http://www.tchrd.org/press/1999/Pr19990520.shtml. Migration is a flow of population to a place to live temporarily or permanently. Displacement is when incoming migrants drive out the pre-existing population.

525. "World Bank Approves China Loan but Sidesteps Tibetan Issue," AFP June 25, 1999.

526. Florence Chong, "The Dalai Lama Ensures Bucks Stop at the World Bank," *Australian*, July 12, 2000.

527. TCHRD, *Annual Report, 1999—Tibet: Tightening of Control*, http://www.tchrd.org/pubs/1999/08_population.shtml.

528. Maris Gillette, *Between Mecca and Beijing: Modernization and Consumption among Urban Chinese Muslims* (Stanford: Stanford University Press, 2000); Dru Gladney, *Muslim Chinese: Ethnic Nationalism in the People's Republic* (Cambridge MA: Harvard University Press, 1996); Rafael Israeli, "Muslim Plight Under Chinese Rule," in R. Israeli (ed.), *The Crescent in the East: Islam in Asia Major* (London: Curzon Press 1989).

529. Li Shujiang and Karl Luckert, *Mythology and Folklore of the Hui: A Muslim Chinese People* (New York: State University of New York Press, 1994); Dru Gladney, "Clashed Civilizations?: Muslim and Chinese Identities in the PRC," in D. Gladney (ed.), *Making Majorities: Constituting the Nation in Japan, Korea, China, Malaysia, Fiji, Turkey, and the United States* (Stanford: Stanford University Press, 1998): 106–131.

530. Jonathan Lipman, *Familiar Strangers: A History of the Muslims in Northwest China* (1997). Michael Black, et al., "A Genome-Based Study of the Muslim Hui Community and the Han Population of Liaoning Province, PR China," *Human Biology* 72 (2001): 811 (genetic basis for separate historical origins of Hui and Han paternal ancestries).

531. "The Current Population Transfer Policy in Tibet," WTN, March 30, 1995.

532. "Clash between Tibetans and Chinese Mulims Injures Hundreds," AP, Feb. 23, 2003 (large number of Muslim-owned shops and restaurants ransacked by Tibetans).

533. *Annual Report, 1999—Tibet: Tightening of Control* 1999.

534. Abid Aslam, "Fears for Tibet Over World Bank Project," WTN, June 8, 1999.

535. The Ngulra are famed warriors. See Li An-Che, *Labrang: A Study in the Field* (Tokyo: Institute of Oriental Culture, 1982 [1957]): 11.

536. "Nomads Killed in Pasture Fights," TIN, June 21, 1999.

537. Editorial, "Bank should Retract China Loan," *LAT*, June 27, 2000:B8.

538. "Urgent Action Appeal: Stop Population Transfer in Tibet" 1999.

539. Ma Wei, Ma Jianzhong and Kevin Stuart, *The Folklore of China's Islamic Salar Nationality* (Lewiston: Mellon, 2001): 2–3.

540. Arienne Dwyer, "Ethnogenesis in Amdo Qinghai: Historical Questions on the Development of Salar Identity," Paper Presented to the Annual Conference of the Association of Asian Studies (1999).

541. Beth Ranson, "The Salar of Northwest China," Women's Missionary Union, http://www.wmu.com/wmu/organizations/aom/people/salar.html; Zhongguo shehui kexue yuan minzu yanjiu suo 1994: 887.

542. Arienne Dweyer, "The Text of Tongues: Languages and Power in China," in William Safran (ed.), *Nationalism and Ethnoregional Identities in China* (London: Frank Cass, 1998): 78; Ma Yin, *China's Minority Nationalities* (Beijing: Foreign Language Press, 1989): 121.

543. World Bank, *Poverty Reduction Project Report* 2000: 108.

544. Gao Bingzhong, "Qinghai Huzhu Xian He Minhe Xian Tuzu Diqu Diaocha" [Local Investigation of the Qinghai Huzhu County and Minhe Counties], in Ma Rong et al., *Zhonguo Minzu Shequ Fazhan Yanjiu* [Studies in the Development of Chinese Minority Communities] (Beijing: Beijing daxue chubanshe, 2001): 216–291.

545. Sathnam Sanghera, "Tibet Report Dispute Throws World Bank into Disarray: Directors' Ruling on Publication has Fuelled Anger Over Loan," *FT* (London), June 26, 2000:10; "World Bank Oks Loan to China Despite U.S. Objection, *JEN*, June 24, 1999 (Benjamin Gilman, Chair of House International Relief Committee: "For Tibetans, it is not development or poverty alleviation, it is cultural genocide.") It was reported "The Dalai Lama sees the proposed resettlement—which would affect the area where he was born—as 'cultural genocide.' " "Bank Should Retract China Loan" 2000:B8. The Dalai Lama also stated that "Under the present circumstances this [project] would be a source of more problems. Therefore it is not the right time." "World Bank Internal Review Criticizes Loan to Relocate Chinese Farmers," AP, June 23, 2000.

546. Lewis 1999: A4.

547. "World Bank Plays Down 'Tibet Issue' in Mass Relocation Project," AFP, June 17, 1999.

548. "Tibetans Oppose World Bank Project," TIN, June 15, 1999.

549. Abid Aslam, "World Bank Nears Vote on Tibetan 'Death Sentence,' " IPS, June 21, 1999.

550. Ibid.

551. Schoof 1999.

552. *Height of Darkness* 2001: 17. See also ICT, *The Myth of Tibetan Autonomy: A Legal Analysis of* the *Status of Tibet* (1994).

553. Dawa Norbu, "Han Hegemony and Tibetan Ethnicity," *International Studies* 32 (1995): 304 (stating TAR has "puppet government"); James Seymour, "Toward an East Asian Confederation of Independent States?," *Bulletin of Concerned Asian Scholars* (July–Sept. 1993): 44–48 (autonomy for minorities in PRC "fake"); Warren Smith, "The Nationalities Policy of the Chinese Communist Party and the Socialist Transformation of Tibet," in *Resistance and Reform in Tibet* 1994: 5–75 (Tibetans only have autonomy in theory); Davis 2005 (Tibetans have "no autonomy at all"). But see Guo Xiaolin, *Rice Ears and Cattle Tails: A Comparative Study of Rural Economy and Society in Yunnan, Southwest China* (unpublished PhD dissertation, University of British Columbia, 1996) (comparing two counties in northern Yunnan province, one autonomous and the other not, and finding autonomy provides substantial advantages). Scholars not directly affiliated with the émigré administration also generally conclude that autonomy provides some power to Tibetans. See *Tibetan Autonomy and Self-Government: Myth or Reality? Report of the Proceedings of the Workshop held in Nov. 1999* (Tibetan Parliamentary and Policy Research Centre, 2000); Theodore Sorenson and David Phillips (eds.), *Legal Standards and Autonomy Options for Minorities in China: the Tibetan Case* (Cambridge: Harvard University, Belfer Center, 2004).

554. "WB Loan to Benefit Poor," 1999.

555. Interviews with State Ethnic Affairs Commission Officials (*Guojia Minwei*), Beijing (June 2001).

556. Zhang Guanghua, *Zhongguo Ge Sheng Qu Shaoshu Minzu Renkou* (1998): 576, 582–583; 2000NRKPCZGMZRKZL 2003: 638.

557. "Haixi Appeals for World Bank Funds Poverty Relief Project Beneficial," *CD*, Oct. 1, 1999: 2.

558. "No Longer Poor, Beijing Barred from Low-Cost Loan Window," IPS, June 29, 1999.

559. David Sanger, "Karma and Helms; A Stick for China, A Carrot for Tibet's Lobby," *NYT*, July 11, 1999: 4:18.

560. David Sanger, "World Bank and Treasury Nominee at Odds Over Loan to China," *NYT*, June 23, 1999: A3.

561. Hilton, June 28, 2000.

562. "World Bank Inspection Panel Report on the China Western Poverty Reduction" (June 26, 2000), http://www.mail-archive.com/ smongol-l@taklamakan.org/msg00130.html.

563. A consultant for the Inspection Panel, a London School of Economics political economist, observed, "[A]ll the heat and fury of the current debate has obscured the fact that the Qinghai project represents a historic

breakthrough . . . [T]he Chinese government has agreed to have the environmental and social assessments carried out by 'internationally recognized experts' whose work will be disclosed locally and in Washington. More important, a panel of experts will be assembled to provide independent technical advice to the bank and the Chinese government. Their regular reports to the bank and the government will be made public without being censored by either side." Robert Wade, "A Move for the Good in China: The World Bank has been Unfairly Criticised Over the Qinghai Resettlement Project," *FT*, July 4, 2000: 15.

564. Christopher Bodeen, "China Pushing Ahead with Controversial Resettlement of Farmers to Tibetan Lands," AP, Jan. 22, 2002; "China Revives Controversial Tibetan Migration Project," AFP, Jan. 23, 2002.

565. "Resettlement and Urban Reconstruction in Former World Bank Project County," TIN, Feb. 17, 2002.

566. "China's Poor See Hope In Resettlement" 2001. The same might be said of the likely effect of increased income levels of Tibetans. As one Tibetan in Lhasa observed when asked about the effect of the controversial Qinghai–Tibet Railway, "When transportation is developed, local people's lives will become better, and there will be more alms giving to temples." "Tibetan NPC Deputies Hail Construction of Qinghai–Tibet Railway," Xinhua, March 7, 2001. Samdhong Rinpoche has said that "Tibetan culture is 'too deep rooted in Tibet and well preserved in the Tibetan diaspora' to be unsettled" by the railway, which he does not oppose because "it would open up huge possibilities for growth of trade in Tibet." "China's Attitude Toward Tibet Changing: PM in Exile," *India Express*, May 2, 2006, in WTN, May 3, 2006.

567. "Lives will be Lost but so will Tibet, if we don't Resist," DPA, Nov. 2, 1994.

568. Elliot Sperling, "Exile and Dissent: The Historical and Cultural Context," in Melissa Harris and Sydney Jones (eds.), *Tibet Since 1950: Silence, Prison or Exile* (New York: Aperture, 2000): 31–36; Henry Zhuo, "Forms on the Roof of the World," *New Left Review* 13 (2001): 146–151. See also remarks of Elliot Sperling in "Roundtable Before the Congressional-Executive Commission . . ." 2002: 13 ("China publishes a tremendous amount of material in Tibetan . . . They publish old classical Tibetan books, they have magazines; they have newspapers. There is a lot going on in terms of Tibetan publishing.") The promotion of Tibetan culture is appreciated by Tibetan elites. Lin Yi observed that in his native Huangnan Tibetan Autonomous Prefecture in Qinghai, "[P]ositive policies and measures towards Tibetan people and culture, coupled with the resurgence and popularization of Tibetan Buddhism among both Tibetans and Han, fostered pride in Tibetan ethnic culture and a celebration of Tibetan ethnic identity among Tibetans. For example, among my informants, some Tibetan elites were particularly keen to adopt the word bodjingshen (extensive knowledge

and profound scholarship) to describe their culture." "Choosing Between Ethnic and Chinese Citizenship: the Educational Trajectories of Tibetan minority Children in Northwest China," in Vanessa Fong and Rachel Murphy (eds.), *Chinese Citizenship: Views from the Margin* (New York: Routledge, 2006): 41–67.

569. Ed Douglas, "The Rape of Tibet," *Guardian*, Sept. 29, 1997: T2; Georg Blume, "Antje Vollmer's Secret Diplomacy Between Peking and the Dalai Lama," WTN, Aug. 20, 1998. Many Western specialists of China's minorities also reject such claims. See, e.g., Heberer 2004: 3 (no ethnocide exists in China).

570. Phuntsog Wangyal 2004, "Tibet and Development." See also Phuntsog Wangyal, "Revisiting My Native Land," WTN, March 28, 2006, www.tibet.ca/en/wtnarchive/2006/3/28_1.html.

571. Eckholm 2001, "China Wins."

572. Alex Alvarez, *Governments, Citizens and Genocide: a Comparative Approach* (Bloomington: Indiana University, 2001), p. 33.

573. Helen Fein, "Genocide, Terror, Life Integrity and War Crimes: The Case for Discrimination," in Andreopolous 1994: 95; Walter Ezell, "Investigating Genocide: A Catalog of Known and Suspected Causes and Some Categories for Comparing Them," in Yehuda Bauer (ed.), *Remembering the Future: The Impact of the Holocaust on Jews and Christians* (Oxford: Pergamon Press, 1989), v. 3: 2881.

574. Susan Rolef, "Battling the Demagogy of 'Genocide,' " *JP*, Oct. 21, 1991; Johann Hari, "Don't Let the Livingstone Row Blind Us to the Growing Threat of Anti-Semitism," *Independent*, Feb. 23, 2005: 31.

575. Jack N. Porter, "Introduction: What is Genocide? Notes toward a Definition," In J.N. Porter (ed.), *Genocide and Human Rights: A Global Anthology* (Lanham: University Press of America, 1982): 9–10.

576. Michael Ignatieff, "The Danger of a World without Enemies: Lemkin's World," *New Republic*, Feb. 26, 2001: 27.

577. "Dalai Lama Brands Chinese Rail link 'Cultural Genocide,' " AP, Sept. 12, 2005.

578. Laurence Brahm, "Conciliatory Dalai Lama Expounds on Winds of Change," *SCMP*, March 14, 2005: 4. The accuracy of recording of the Dalai Lama's statements in this interview has not been challenged by the TGIE or ICT. See "Tibet Stance Unchanged," *SCMP*, Apr. 2, 2005:14 (TGIE); "Tibet Autonomy Stance," *SCMP*, March 19, 2005: 14 (ICT). The Dalai Lama made this statement despite the concern of his host, the Indian government, that any suggestion that Tibetan culture is part of Chinese culture may have implications for India's ethnic Tibetan minority in Ladakh and elsewhere. Philip Bowring, "New Delhi's Nightmare Scenario," *SCMP*, Dec. 13, 2004: 13. His statements accord with the view of Tibetans who oppose separatism. "China International Tibet Seminar Opens," Xinhua, Aug. 20, 1997 (Doje Cedain, head of the China Tibetology Research

Center, says "Tibetans are an organic component of Chinese civilization and have contributed greatly to world civilization"). The Dalai Lama had earlier acknowledged the PRC government wants to preserve Tibetan culture. See, e.g., "Press Conference at Sheraton Wall Centre, Apr. 17, 2004," www.swimwithme.com/ dlvisit/ dlvisit1_17.html (stating he "understands that China wants to build one unified country and also to preserve Tibetan culture").

579. "Dalai Lama In Slovakia says Tibetans Facing Cultural Genocide," SITA, Oct. 16, 2000, in BBC/SWB, Oct. 18, 2000.

580. Eetta Prince-Gibson, "The Chosen Ones," *JP*, Aug. 25, 2000: 18.

581. Barbara Crossette, "Dalai Lama sees a Culture Endangered," *NYT*, March 22, 1989: A3; "Cultural Looting," *IHT*, Sept. 18, 1995.

582. DIIR, "A Tale of Cultural Genocide," *TB* (July–Aug. 2000).

583. DIIR, "Potala Palace Desecrated," *TB* (March–June 2001).

584. Rinbhur Tulku, "The Odyssey of Jowo Mikyo Dorjee: A Search for Tibet's Holiest Buddhist Statue," 1987, http://www.tibet.com/buddhism/ jowo-mikyo-dorjee.html.

585. Unidroit Convention on Stolen or Illegally Exported Cultural Objects of 1995, 32 1.L.M. 1332, www. unidroit.org/english/conventions/ c-cult.htm . Only twenty-six states had ratified the treaty as of late 2005. China did so in 1997. Neither the United States nor European states with large antiquities collections garnered abroad have ratified it. International Institute for the Unification of Private Law, http://2ww.Unidroit.org/ English/implement/I-95.htm.

586. "Demand for 'Lost' Tibetan Art Soars," UPI, June 27, 2001; Jasper Becker, "Last of Tibet's Religious Art Falls Prey to Rich Collectors," *SCMP*, Aug. 29, 2000: 18.

587. "Tibetan Art Dealer Arrested in Attempt to Stop Relics Theft," TIN, July 20, 1999, WTN, July 28, 1999.

588. Radio Free Asia, "The Plunder of Tibet's Treasures," Aug. 2, 2005 in WTN, Aug. 2, 2005.

589. Geraldine Norman, "Tibetan Survivors," *Independent*, May 28, 1995: 94.

590. Lynne O'Donnell, "Raiders of the Lost Art," *Weekend Australian*, Aug. 12, 2000: R2.

591. Isabel Hilton, "A Culture in Urgent Need of Repair," *FT*, Aug. 12, 2000: 1.

592. Ibid.; S. Melikian, "Dealers and Scholars in Uneasy Dilemma" *IHT.*, Apr. 24, 1999: 9.

593. James MacDonald, "US to Investigate Chinese Looting of Tibet," *Art Newspaper*, Nov. 2, 2005, www.theartnewspaper.com/article01.asp?id-57.

594. Robert Wistrich, *Hitler and the Holocaust* (2001): 22, 34, 42.

595. Zuo Wenxing, "Tibet Today," *G & M*, March 12, 2004.

596. Liu Weitao, "Culture Exhibition Exposes Dalai's Lies," *CD*, Nov. 30, 2001; Xin 2001.

INDEX